Introduction to Political Philosophy

Introduction to Political Philosophy

GEOFFREY THOMAS

Duckworth

First published in 2000 by
Gerald Duckworth & Co. Ltd.
61 Frith Street, London W1V 5TA
Tel: 0171 434 4242
Fax: 0171 434 4420
Email: enquiries@duckworth-publishers.co.uk

A catalogue record for this book is available
from the British Library

ISBN 0 7156 2644 2

Typeset by Ray Davies
Printed in Great Britain by
Redwood Books Ltd, Trowbridge

Contents

2. Power, authority, sovereignty, law, and the state

3. Justice, equality, rights, and property

6. Endnote

Preface

My principal thanks are due to my students at Birkbeck College, London University, with whom many of the topics in this book have been discussed since 1984.

Three of these students – Jim Batty, Jan Brown, and Stephen Mather – have read earlier versions of chapter 1. I thank them for criticisms and suggestions.

Garo Avakian earns special mention, from my 'Rise of the Modern State' lectures, February-April 1997, for his ability to pose unexpected and wholly fascinating questions. Armenian philosophy is alive and well, and articulating itself through Garo. Peter Davidson, from the same lecture course, raised deep questions about the proper approach to the classic texts.

My discussion of utopian political thought in chapter 1 has been most helpfully informed by discussions with Patrick Hemmer. Patrick's parallelism, conjectural but fascinating and not explored in the present text, between Kuhnian 'paradigm shifts' in natural science and utopian political projections bears the imprint of the truly creative research student.

My friend Colin Donne deserves his own paragraph. When a large chunk of the book was at risk from the perversities of a faulty computer, Colin stepped in with the loan of his own PC, on which the text was completed. This was an act of signal generosity which, done for no reward, earns my heartiest thanks. I am also grateful to Colin for creating all the Figures in the text.

Scott David, first student then friend, gets his own slot. It has been fascinating to share ideas with this luminous, intrepid philosophical spirit. In particular, Scott's unpublished dissertation, 'What status does reflective equilibrium have in Rawls' doctrine of justice as fairness?', has been an invaluable aid.

Only once or twice in a generation does a student such as George Walker come along. George's 'occasional' work in political philosophy, a subject in which he has only a marginal interest, illuminated every topic he discussed *en route* to his inevitable First. I am privileged to have taught him – and to have learnt so much from him.

Adam Tebble, my teaching assistant in 1996-7, has often jolted my thinking when I have been resting on preconceptions. 'Now *Hayek* says' – the insistence of that enthusiastic voice has been a welcome goad.

I have discussed many matters with three friends, Gabriel Apata, Don Pincham, and David Rodway. Conversations over the years have left a distinct mark on my political thinking.

I am also grateful to the London University Political Philosophy Group, chaired by Jo Wolff. The group's learned and lively exchanges at our informal seminars have been a constant source of stimulation. So here are thanks to Jo, to Alan Carter, John Charvet, Andrew Chitty, Sebastian Gardner, David Lloyd Thomas, and Michael Saward. Special thanks go to Roger Scruton who introduced me to the group in 1988.

Older and more general debts are also a pleasure to acknowledge. My days *in statu pupillari* are long over but I recall making first acquaintance with political philosophy when the late F.W.G. Benemy, Head of the Department of Social Science, William Ellis School, London, introduced his sixth formers to Hobbes, Locke and something bafflingly called 'the state of nature'. I also call to mind 'Uncle Ben's' animadversions on Plato as an enemy of democracy. Deeper was the influence of the late H.J.C. Oram, who taught me most of the economic history I know. Oram's rule, 'Play it down and put it back' ('The Industrial Revolution, whatever Arnold Toynbee might say, did not begin in 1760; its antecedents lie much earlier. Nor did anything dramatic happen in 1760. 1760 was a perfectly ordinary year'), has been as good a guide to economics as any I know. Oram's expert teaching has also informed my whole understanding of the relation of economics to politics.

One of my most memorable privileges is to have been taught by the late Michael Oakeshott when I was an undergraduate at the London School of Economics in the mid-1960s. My debt to Oakeshott is not of the past but one constantly renewed. Oakeshott is 'the master': I learn from him every time I open his books. My thanks go also to seven talented teachers: Professor Maurice Cranston, Professor Morris Ginsberg ('What can you recommend on socialism and property, Professor Ginsberg?': his tired old eyes surveyed me, perhaps sensing my bottomless ignorance, and he mildly answered, 'It's what socialism is all about'), Dr John Morrall, Dr David Nicholls ('That's not my reading of Aquinas, but of course if you say so ...'), Dr Robert Orr ('Political theory is all fashion. Nothing lasts. Everything goes in the end'), Leslie Wolf-Phillips, and Professor K.B. Smellie ('Don't waste time reading Laski that you could spend reading Plato': 'What have you chosen as your Special Text? ... Mill's *On Liberty*? That's fine, I'll put you down for Plato's *Republic*': 'Now Mr Thomas, I want you to read chapter 1 of Bosanquet's *Philosophical Theory of the State* but you are in no circumstances to read more – the result could be disastrous'; naturally in face of the forbidden I read more and the result is the present book. The reader must decide whether it is disastrous). Cranston, Ginsberg, Nicholls and Smellie are no longer with us, but all these scholars in their different ways set a lasting imprint on my approach to political philosophy. David Thurston, a fellow student, earns his place too. David's deep knowledge of nineteenth-century Continental thought, and the fine edge of his political intelligence, were the background to all our conversations.

John Morrall has read most of the book in manuscript. His comments have illuminated every topic they have touched. Time and again, a draft has provoked within days of John's perusal a long disquisition – learned, lucid, and exactly apt – transforming my crudities into a reasonable level of understanding.

Still the debts run. At Oxford in the late 1960s I was supervised by Professor John Plamenatz. I have come to see the value and distinction of Plamenatz's work. One of my regrets is that I failed to override some superficial barriers (mainly Plamenatz's tendency to expound without quotation) which concealed from me his painstakingly scrupulous and really acute reading of 'the great, dead philosophers'.

Some good came of this failed relationship: for I quickly adopted an unofficial supervisor. Philosophy cast its spell on me. That marvel of philosophical erudition, Dr David Rees, of Jesus College Oxford, threw open for me the philosophical heartland of epistemology and metaphysics, mind, and language. David's deep and exact scholarship stands in a long Oxford tradition – the tradition of J.A. Smith, Harold Joachim, C.C.J. Webb, and Sir David Ross. 'I am in no way to be compared with the scholars you list,' David protests. 'I would ask you to tone down your references to me.' But not the least thing David has taught me is to exercise my judgement. I well remember that frequent and provocative, 'What do *you* think?'

The Birkbeck philosophy department is a Platonic Academy in miniature. Constantly in the course of writing this book I have thought, 'What would Scott say to this?', 'How would Dorothy object to that?', and also wondered cautiously whether some claim or other would attract David Wiggins' gracious refutation ('Well, it isn't *quite* like that'). Here is the count: Professor John Dupré, Professor Dorothy Edgington, Dr Miranda Fricker, Dr Anthony Grayling, Dr Sebastian Gardner, Dr Samuel Guttenplan, Professor Jennifer Hornsby, Dr Christopher Janaway, Dr Sarah Patterson, Anthony Price, Dr Barry Smith, Dr Scott Sturgeon, and Professor David Wiggins.

Finally, there is Leslie Marsh, who read the whole text and helped at every stage in every way.

Highgate
13 April 1999
g.thomas@philosophy.bbk.ac.uk

Geoffrey Thomas

Abbreviations

ASU = Nozick, R., *Anarchy, State and Utopia*, Oxford: Blackwell, 1974.

CG = St Augustine, *Of the City of God* [*De Civitate Dei*], tr. H. Bettenson, Harmondsworth: Penguin, 1984. Original text: 413-26 AD.

DI = Rousseau, J.-J., *The Discourses and Other Early Political Writings*, ed. & tr. V. Gourevitch, Cambridge: Cambridge University Press, 1997. Original text of the *Second Discourse*: 1755.

F = Hamilton, A., Madison, J., & Jay, J., *The Federalist*, ed. M. Beloff, Oxford: Blackwell, 1948. Original text: 1777-8.

FT = Locke, J., *First Treatise of Government* [*The False Principles and Foundation of Sir Robert Filmer ...Detected and Overthrown*], in P. Laslett, ed. *Two Treatises of Government*, Cambridge: Cambridge University Press, 1991. Original text: published 1690, mainly written 1680-1.

L = Hobbes, T., *Leviathan*, ed. R. Tuck, Cambridge: Cambridge University Press, 1991. Original text: 1651.

NE = Aristotle, *Nicomachean Ethics*, tr. Sir David Ross, London: Oxford University Press, 1969. Original text: circa 330 BC.

OL = Mill, J.S., *On Liberty* in *On Liberty and Other Writings*, ed. S. Collini, Cambridge: Cambridge University Press, 1989. Original text: 1859.

P = Aristotle, *Politics*, tr. J. Barnes, ed. S. Everson, Cambridge: Cambridge University Press, 1988. Original text: circa 325 BC.

PCE = Machiavelli, N., *The Prince*, tr. & ed. P. Bondanella & M. Musa, Oxford: Oxford University Press, 1998. Original text: 1513.

PKM = *The Portable Karl Marx*, ed. E. Kamenka, Harmondsworth: Penguin. Original texts: 1841-82.

PPS 1 *Philosophy, Politics and Society*, 1st Series, ed. P. Laslett, Oxford: Blackwell, 1956.

PPS 2 = *Philosophy, Politics and Society*, 2nd Series, ed. P. Laslett & W.G. Runciman, Oxford: Blackwell, 1962.

PPS 3 = *Philosophy, Politics and Society*, 3rd Series, ed. P. Laslett & W.G. Runciman, Oxford: Blackwell, 1967.

PPS 4 = *Philosophy, Politics and Society*, 4th Series, ed. P. Laslett, W.G. Runciman & Q. Skinner, Oxford: Blackwell, 1972.

PPS 5 = *Philosophy, Politics and Society*, 4th Series, ed. P. Laslett & J. Fishkin, Oxford: Blackwell, 1979.

PR = Hegel, G.W.F., *The Philosophy of Right,* ed. A.W. Wood, tr. H.B. Nisbet, Cambridge: Cambridge University Press, 1991. Original text: 1821.

R = Plato, *The Republic*, tr. H.D.P. Lee, 2nd ed., Harmondsworth: Penguin, 1974. Original text: circa 375 BC.

SC = Rousseau, J.-J., *The Social Contract and Other Later Political Writings*, ed. & tr.

V. Gourevitch, Cambridge: Cambridge University Press, 1997. Original text of the *Social Contract*: 1762.

SL   =   Mill, J.S., *A System of Logic Ratiocinative and Inductive*, London: Longmans, 1970.

SPL   =   Montesquieu, *The Spirit of the Laws*, ed. A.M. Cohler et al., Cambridge: Cambridge University Press, 1989. Original text: 1748.

ST   =   Locke, J., *Second Treatise of Government [An Essay Concerning the True Original, Extent, and End of Civil Government]*, in P. Laslett, ed. *Two Treatises of Government*, Cambridge: Cambridge University Press, 1991. Original text: published 1690, mainly written 1681-2.

TJ   =   Rawls, J., *A Theory of Justice*, Oxford: Oxford University Press, 1972.

The normal style of citation is via the internal organisation of the text, where the author or editor has divided the work in numbered paragraphs, chapters or books, and to follow this with the pagination of the preceding editions. Thus ST, §27: 287 refers to paragraph 27 of Locke's *Second Treatise of Civil Government*, Laslett's Cambridge edition, page 287. P III.8: 62 refers to Book III, ch. 8 of Aristotle's *Politics*, page 62 of Barnes' translation. Occasionally line references are also given for Plato and Aristotle, using the notation employed by all editors and translators: thus 'R I 352D' and 'P II.8 1269a20'. Bibliographical items are cited by author's name, date of publication, and page number. Lawrence, 1989: 49, for example, refers to page 49 of P.K. Lawrence, *Democracy and the Liberal State*, Aldershot: Dartmouth Publishing Company.

A decision has had to be made about the manner of citation for historical texts. With some misgivings I have followed the now common practice of citing the date of the edition used. So Hume, 1978 refers to P.H. Nidditch's edition of David Hume's *A Treatise of Human Nature*, though Hume wrote in the eighteenth century. I have in all such cases put the date of original publication in the bibliography.

FOR

Garo Avakian

Peter Davidson and Patrick Hemmer

AND TO THE MEMORY OF

Alexei Nikolayevich

1. Introduction

1. ABOUT THE BOOK

'Introduction' is meant seriously in the title of this book. If you are unsure about the nature of philosophy in general or of political philosophy in particular, this is no problem. Things will slide rapidly into place as we check out the nature of philosophy, see how political philosophy as a branch of philosophy shares in that nature, and scan political philosophy's central concepts, theories, and puzzles. The book is introductory in a further way. If one aim is to give a reliable first view of the subject, another is to make sure that, having finished the book, you do not stop. References and signposts abound on the frontiers of every topic. This is a book for beginners who will continue their journey beyond it.

Political philosophy is an inquiry. There are four questions to ask about any inquiry. (1) What is its domain, subject matter, or problem field? (2) What is its approach to that domain? (3) What is the structure of the inquiry, its organisation and sub-divisions? (4) What value does the inquiry have?

So the key words are:

- domain
- approach
- structure
- value

2. THE DOMAIN OF POLITICAL PHILOSOPHY

Etymology might prompt us to start a discussion of the scope and limits of politics, the domain of political philosophy, with a discussion of the Greek word from which 'politics' and 'political' derive.

'Politics' and 'political' indeed come from the Greek, *politike*, 'having to do with the affairs of the *polis*'. *Polis* is usually translated as 'city-state'. There are problems with this rendering since, as we will see (§14.5), it is by no means clear that the *polis*, as it flourished in Greece in the fourth and fifth centuries BC, was specifically a state. But then, if the nature of the *polis* is unclear, so is the sense of *politike*, and etymology throws only problematic light on the nature of politics. Matters are the wrong way round, if we have to use political analysis to determine the nature of the *polis* when the nature of the *polis* was meant to clarify the nature of politics. We need to start elsewhere.

2.1 The nature of politics

We already have – how could we avoid it? – some impression of politics and the political. If the United States Senate, the British Parliament, and the Russian Duma, are said to be political institutions we register no surprise. The surprise comes if anyone tells us they are not. Equally, if we hear about 'office politics', 'church politics' or 'family politics', we may be uncertain whether marginal or metaphorical uses of the term 'politics' are in play. But we are at no loss to know how they might have some application. Finally, if Newton's law of gravity is described as political, we are genuinely nonplussed. If the description has any meaning, we have no idea what it is. So we have intuitive reactions, initial reflective judgements, that loosely map out the idea of the political.

There is nothing privileged about these reactions. They are not immune from error; perhaps we will have to revise them. Still, they are a starting-point. We can edge forwards if we bring them to bear on some formal statements about politics and the political. Here is a first experiment. Consider the following definition of politics from Bernard Crick (b. 1929), a British political writer:

> Politics, then, can be simply defined as the activity by which differing interests within a given unit of rule are conciliated by giving them a share in power in proportion to their importance to the welfare and survival of the whole community (Crick, 1964: 21).

One might have two reactions to this definition. The first is that it is packed with terms and phrases – 'interests', 'welfare', 'a share of power', 'importance' – vitally in need of clarification. The other is that the definition is persuasive or stipulative. It recommends or confines attention not to politics as such but to a particular style of politics. On Crick's definition Nazi Germany was not a political system since it lacked the features Crick describes.

We are testing a definition of politics against our pre-theoretical impressions, and finding that Crick's definition is – first bit of jargon – 'extensionally' inadequate. That is, it does not cover enough of the domain of the political. Four other approaches to the nature of politics are next in line:

- teleological
- presuppositional
- forum
- process

2.2 The teleological approach

Telos is the Greek word for end, object, aim or purpose. Some activities and human relationships are definable in terms of aims or purposes. Medicine, for example, is an activity internally related, conceptually tied, to the promotion of health and the reduction of disease. Is medicine the right, purpose-bound model for understanding politics? Roger Scruton thinks not:

> Some human relations presuppose a common purpose, and fall apart when that purpose is fulfilled or discontinued. (Consider, for example, a business partnership.) But not all relations are of that nature. The pursuit of a certain mechanical analogy has led to the belief (widely held but seldom stated) that an activity without an aim is merely aimless. So that if we are to consider political activity as a form of rational conduct, we should ally it to certain aims – to a social ideal that translates immediately into policy. ... Such a view is in fact confused. Most human activities, and most relations that are worthwhile, have no purpose. No purpose, that is, external to themselves. There is no 'end in view', and to attempt to provide one is to do violence to the arrangement (Scruton, 1984: 22-3).

Scruton is right: some activities are purposive by definition, others are not. It is an open question into which category politics falls. Consider the case of economic activity. An influential account of economic activity, that of Lionel Robbins, defines it as any activity involving 'ends and scarce means which have alternative uses' (Robbins, 1984: 16). This expands the economic realm to cover virtually the whole area of rational choice, but the key point is that Robbins' definition does not assign any aim or purpose as inbuilt in economic activity.

What of another activity, namely morality? Does morality have an inbuilt object or purpose? That it has, and that this object is the maximisation of utility, however precisely understood (e.g. as happiness or the satisfaction of preferences), is the view of utilitarians. But there are rival traditions of moral thought for which certain actions are wrong and never to be done (e.g. the taking of an innocent human life) however much utility may be at stake.

From these two examples, of economic and moral activity, it is plain that the assigning of inbuilt goals or pre-set purposes to activities is risky. But if we *were* able to fix such an object or purpose for politics, there would still be a catch. Even when an activity has a pre-set purpose, that purpose does not automatically fix the rational intentions of those pursuing the activity. Connecting the *telos* of an activity with the practical reasoning of an agent is always indirect and hazardous.

Medicine as an activity may have the inbuilt purpose of promoting health. But a particular doctor might have the personal goal of making $10 million, while another might with equal rationality devote his or her services to the poor with little financial recompense. This distinction is examined in Nozick, ASU: 233-5; J. Wolff, 1991: 123-4 (see also §18.3). Politics is (for many) a career, a profession. Tadpole and Taper, political jobbers in Disraeli's novel *Coningsby* (1844), and the worlds of H.G. Wells' *The New Machiavelli* (1911) and C.P. Snow's *Corridors of Power* (1964) are never far away.

A variant of the teleological approach to politics is worth noting. In the view of Aristotle (384-321 BC) there is a double political teleology. The first works from polis to citizen: the goal of the *polis* is the well-being or flourishing of its citizens, their *eudaimonia*. This is the inbuilt *telos* of political activity. The second teleology works from the citizen to the polis: 'man is by nature a political animal' (P, I.4: 3). This means, first, that human beings have a natural tendency to adapt to a life of active citizenship in the *polis*. Secondly it means that the inseparable conditions of *eudaimonia* – the only terms on which it can be had – are the possession and exercise of specific excellences of mind and character outlined in the *Nicomachean Ethics*. If we have and exercise these excellences, we flourish; otherwise we do not. Only in the polis – this is the key point – can these virtues be fully acquired and practised.

The problem from our point of view is Aristotle's certainty that he knows the conditions for human flourishing. He is here speaking on behalf of an objective, substantive theory of the human good: objective, because (roughly) it is a theory that claims to be true or otherwise rationally binding. And substantive because (roughly again) it spells out specifics about living rightly and living well. Assurance about his or any such theory is no longer available in a consensual way that might ground a political teleology.

For some of the finer questions about Aristotle's political teleology, see Keyt, 1987; Roberts, 1989. Substantive theories of the good are specified more closely in §13.3.2.

A final point worth making is that, if (conceptually) politics as such does not have an inbuilt object or purpose, it is perfectly possible (practically) to follow a goal-seeking, purposeful style of politics. Call this 'secondary teleology'. An example of such a style would be an 'enterprise association' approach to politics (§24.2).

2.3 The presuppositional approach

'Let's find out what children need in order to equip them for life, and take the politics out of education'. This remark, a commonplace of media debate, can be read as follows. If we can agree on the proper aims or objectives of education, we can leave the rest to experts. In fact we can agree on these aims or objectives. So let us move educational affairs out of the realm of politics.

But not so fast: we might agree on the relevant aims or objectives yet still disagree over the relative importance to be given to education among the possible aims of public policy and so find ourselves, even on this line of thinking, back in the political realm. The background assumption is clear that politics rests on disagreement(s) of some kind. End the disagreement, and politics loses its rationale. We find this idea in Jean Blondel. For a situation to be political, writes Blondel, 'there must be some problem, a conflict; if everybody agrees, there is no scope for political action. Politics implies disagreement because it is about ways of resolving it' (Blondel, 1966: 123).

Can we be more specific about the nature of the disagreement? Consider the following remarks from the late political philosopher and historian of ideas, Sir Isaiah Berlin (1909-97), on the subject of political studies:

> [T]hese studies spring from, and thrive on, discord. Someone may question this on the ground that even in a society of saintly anarchists, where no conflicts about ultimate purpose can take place, political problems, for example constitutional or legislative issues, might still arise. But this objection rests on a mistake. Where ends are agreed, the only questions left are those of means, and these are not political but technical, that is to say, capable of being settled by experts or machines like arguments between engineers or doctors ... That is the meaning of Saint-Simon's famous phrase about 'replacing the government of persons by the administration of things', and the Marxist prophecies about the withering away of the state and the beginning of the true history of humanity (Berlin, 1969: 118).

The French socialist, Claude-Henri de Rouvroy, comte de Saint-Simon (1760-1825), actually has no such phrase as Berlin cites. It is a gloss by Marx's collaborator, Friedrich Engels (1820-95), on a position that Saint-Simon held (Engels, 1969: III.1, 292). But our main concern is analytical, not historical. Berlin claims that politics presupposes disagreement about ends. In other words, he holds that such disagreement is a necessary condition of politics. Reflection shows that it is neither necessary nor, to consider another possibility, sufficient. We can have politics without this kind of disagreement. Even with this kind of disagreement we still might not have politics.

Intuitively, disagreement about ends is not necessary for politics. We can disagree politically without disagreeing on ends as formulated in general terms. For one thing we might agree about ends but disagree about their relative priority in general or in a particular situation for action. For example, we might accept freedom and equality as ends while being unable to agree on which value is more stringent when they clash. Berlin could counter that agreement about ends has to cover prioritisation as well. But this will not carry the conclusion he wants. Within a realm of agreed and prioritised ends we can disagree over the application of rules to cases.

How? As follows: we might agree that justice is the central value in terms of which our society should be organised. Suppose we agree on justice as an end; we accept a rule of justice. But is positive discrimination or affirmative action a proper application of justice? Suppose that in the distribution of some advantage or resource (income, property or whatever) a particular social group has been systematically discriminated against on the basis of an irrelevant difference (race, say, or gender). Is it now right, a requirement of justice, to discriminate in favour of that group on the basis of that very characteristic?

This is a rather blunt formulation of the issue; more refinement is needed (§17.5). But the fact that there can be an issue at all, and one over which sharp political divisions arise, shows that political disagreement of the rule/ case kind can survive agreement about ends. To return to our starting point: we can still have politics even without disagreement over ends. Such disagreement is not a necessary condition of politics.

But now, Berlin might reply: suppose we include agreement over rule/ case issues as well as agreement over priorities between ends. What scope would remain for politics? One point in reply is that Berlin is rather quick in his treatment of 'means' and the merely 'technical'. Human cognitive capacities, even those of experts, can never eliminate the need to make decisions under conditions of risk and uncertainty. Consider the current disagreements among scientists over the safety of genetically modified foods; political decisions have to be made while the experts are divided. How we ought to proceed under such conditions is not itself a purely technical matter, nor is it resoluble by agreement over ends however widely construed.

If disagreement over ends is not necessary for politics, I suggest also that it is not sufficient. For politics is only one way of handling such disagreements. A society divided over ends may adopt any of a number of strategies for handling the situation. Two come readily to mind: it may partition itself and pre-empt any shared politics. Or it may exclude the relevant ends from the political sphere, relegating their pursuit to the market or to voluntary associations.

A different presuppositional approach from Berlin's is taken by the German political and legal theorist, Carl Schmitt (1888-1985). *The Concept of the Political* (1927) contains Schmitt's main contribution to the definition of the political. Here he argues that integral to politics is the friend/enemy relationship. This relationship holds not between individuals but groups. It need not be a matter of disagreement over ends in Berlin's sense. Enmity arises wherever another group is intensely or provocatively strange to one's own in the sense that it 'constitutes the negation of one's own kind of existence, and must therefore be repulsed or fought, in order to preserve one's own way of life' (Schmitt, quoted in E.M. Burns, 1963: 224). One might, on Schmitt's behalf, draw a distinction between conflict and combat. Enmity may only require conflict, though where groups think in the terms just quoted the outlook for avoiding combat is unpromising.

Schmitt's definition has the merit of stressing the fact of conflict. A dispute occurs in sociology between equilibrium and conflict theories of society. Any adequate social theory must recognise both equilibrium and conflict. Certainly, conflict over power, status and wealth is a fact of political life. As a corrective to equilibrium theorists who exclusively stress the harmony of interests in society or the ready adjustment of imbalance when interests conflict, Schmitt serves well enough.

There are many objections to Schmitt's definition of the political. My inclination is to reject the idea that we cannot have politics without seeing other groups as representing 'the negation of one's own existence'. The desire to eliminate, literally or metaphorically, is implicit in Schmitt's description, but surely we can recognise politics in conditions of group conflict less dire than this. Moreover, in Schmitt's presentation there is a tendency to celebrate conflict and not merely to embed it conceptually in the nature of politics.

See Schmitt, 1976; for commentary Gottfried, 1990; P.Q. Hirst, 1987; Levy, 1993: 121-2; Lilla, 1997; Neocleous, 1996; R. Wolin, 1992. Wolin's article carries many further references. There are shades of Schmitt's position in Georges Sorel's *Reflections on Violence*, with its stress on confrontation, not conciliation, as the heart of politics (Sorel, 1950; Scruton, 1983: 440).

2.4 Politics as forum, politics as process

Neither the teleological nor the presuppositional approach has taken us much forward. Let us change tack. We can identify institutions which are widely accounted political. I mentioned earlier the US Senate, the British Parliament, and the Russian Duma. We might add the civil service, the police and armed forces of all three countries. We think of these as central institutions by which decisions that bind the whole society are made, implemented, and enforced. This is the forum or arena view of politics. By contrast there is a process view. This sees politics wherever there are relationships of power; it also sees such relationships as omnipresent in society. The process view is strongly linked with the work of the French historian and philosopher, Michel Foucault (1926-84) though it is also present in the ideas of Georges Sorel (1847-1922) who saw 'violence', in the broad sense of conflict and opposition, and hence politics, as ubiquitous in social relationships (Sorel, 1950). For more light on the forum and process views, see Leftwich in Leftwich, 1984: 10-11; Eder, 1993; Blaug, 1996b: 56; Duverger, 1966: ix.

These contrasting views do not present us with an 'either/or'. We can accept the Foucaultian omnipresence of politics and also recognise that the central institutions embody a concentration of power that makes them genuinely special. We will return to Foucault when we examine theories of power. But political philosophy, both historically and at present, typically takes the forum or arena view. To go down a level of detail with this view, consider the following model of the political.

2.5 A five-part model of the political

If a society has a political system, we can typically identify:

- a public
- a public realm
- policy choices for that realm
- forms of collective decision-making for policy choices
- an apparatus of administration and coercive power

The word 'typically' is important here. These are not necessary and sufficient conditions. Berlin's society of saintly anarchists would lack the fourth feature but would not for that reason, Berlin's reservations aside, lack a political system.

A public
At its minimum a 'public' is the group of people, a society, affected by collective decisions and, it may be, taking part in making them. The further characteristics of this group, or society, are endlessly various. It may constitute a civil or an enterprise association (§24.2). It may, in Ferdinand Tönnies' terminology, exhibit *Gemeinschaft* (community) or *Gesellschaft* (mere reciprocal self-interest). It may be a 'nation' in any of the shades of meaning of that term.

A public realm
The public realm is the range of matters about which collective decisions (decisions by which all must abide) are made. These matters are general in the sense that they either affect everyone in the society or affect groups or corporate bodies under descriptions. The impact may be categorical or conditional. This sounds complex but examples will carry us briskly along.

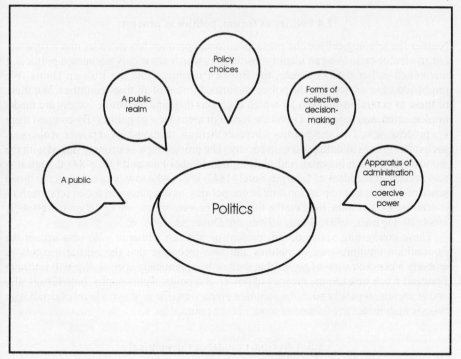

Figure 1. Five-part model of the political

Matters that affect everyone are, for example, the condition of the environment and personal safety. There are also matters that affect groups and corporate bodies under various descriptions. Take the descriptions, 'aged over 65', 'currently pregnant', 'school leaver', 'unemployed teenager', 'carrier of a contagious disease'. These descriptions identify groups for which we may and do want to make provisions and exemptions. Matters affecting them belong to the public realm.

Further, matters in the public realm may affect groups and corporate bodies categorically or conditionally. In 1916, when conscription was introduced into the UK, liability to military service was a matter that affected all able-bodied, unmarried men between the ages of 18 and 41. The men who comprised this group could nothing about the liability; a description applied to them ineluctably – categorically – and the law took its course. By contrast, the conduct of a UK union planning a strike is a doubly conditional matter. The law requires the union to hold a ballot: but (1) the description 'union' applies to people only on condition that they voluntarily associate in certain ways and (2) the requirement under UK law to hold a ballot applies only on condition that the union opts for this way of pursuing its dispute.

Beyond the public realm lies the private realm, the range of matters exempt from collective decision making, though it is in some sense a collective decision to exempt them. John Stuart Mill's liberty principle, which aims to define a domain of properly self-regarding action, is concerned with the public/private divide (§22.8; cf. §32.1.2). To recognise no private realm – no sphere in which I can do what I want because I want – is to endorse totalitarianism, the ultimate expansion of the public realm.

The history of politics is the history of dilations and contractions of the public realm. In the United Kingdom in the mid-nineteenth century, policies of *laissez-faire* were influential. *Laissez-faire* meant that, beyond the barest minimum, the government did not intervene in the economy and did not provide welfare (see §30.1 for a fuller account). *Laissez-faire* excluded from the public realm matters such as unemployment insurance, health care, pensions and so forth which welfare-state policies later drew into it.

Policy choices

Politics is about the making of policy choices for matters in the public realm – the formulation and adoption of public policies. The American political scientist Harold Lasswell famously said that these policies fix 'who gets what, when, how'. Typically, policy choices (1) mobilise resources (from individuals, corporations and so on); and (2) distribute benefits and burdens. But, more widely than Lasswell suggests, they also (3) apply behavioural controls to regulate individual and inter-personal conduct through the law.

The mobilisation of resources means, most notably, the getting of money through taxation, but it can also include the expropriation of property, conquest, draft labour, recruitment of a cadre of public employees, etc. The range of options is wide and not all are used in all political systems. The essential point is that there can be no policy choices without the resources to select and carry them out. How resources are mobilised is itself a policy choice of higher order.

With resources mobilised there are benefits or services, burdens or costs, to allocate. Some of the benefits will be so-called 'private goods', of which the provision to some people reduces the quantity available to others. Others will be 'public goods'. These are items of use or consumption which are characterised by non-rivalry in consumption and non-exclusion of supply. The first feature means that the good can be consumed or used by one person or group without reducing its usefulness or availability to others. The second means that if it is supplied to one person or group, others cannot in practice be excluded from consuming or using it. Defence and clean air are stock examples of public goods. The supply of such goods has traditionally fallen within the remit of the political system, not least because non-exclusion of supply looks generally unattractive to private business. Various views about the proper ends and due limits of collective decision-making will prevail or compete.

Behavioural controls abound in all societies. The specific actions that are mandatory, permissible or proscribed vary from one society to another and across time. The mechanisms of control are also highly flexible. There are laws, moral rules, customs, folkways, cultural ideals and so forth. Laws are (roughly) rules that impose requirements of action supported by coercive sanctions. They are among the policy choices of all typical political systems.

Forms of collective decision-making

Forms of collective decision-making are the organs by and through which policy choices are made, public policies are formulated and adopted. In modern Western societies such organs include (1) a legally constituted electorate, comprising the main body of the adult population, who select through regular elections (2) a legislature (Congress in the USA, Parliament in the UK) who in turn decide what policies shall be enacted on the electorate's behalf. The main activity here is that of making and changing laws. 'Who should rule?' and 'Who does rule?' are major questions to ask about these organs.

An apparatus of administration and coercive power

To formulate and adopt public policies is one thing; to implement them, another. There is a need, in the first place, for an executive, comprising in the US and the UK respectively the President or Prime Minister with his or her most senior advisers, responsible for mapping out, in a high-level way, the implementation of the policies adopted and the laws made by the legislature. This is top-level planning and it is normally identified as the role of the executive. The reality, to some degree in the USA and overwhelmingly in the UK, of the executive's controlling the legislature's agenda and thus having virtual law-making power, is a separate question.

Next, policies have to be routinely applied to particular situations and cases by the administration or bureaucracy. But equally in the application of policies to particular cases, disputes may arise which cannot be settled by agreement. Violations of laws may require corrective action. These matters define the sphere of the judiciary.

Finally, the legislative, executive, administrative, and judicial functions need to be enforced against resistance. Public policies themselves and even the forms of collective decision-making that produce them, encounter opposition, non-compliance, dissidence, and rebellion. The political system itself may be subject to external attack. To provide against these multifarious mishaps is the traditional task of the police and the armed forces. Call this the apparatus of coercive power. Designed to quell all opposition and ensure compliance, it involves, not only and not least, intentional acts or threats of violent physical harm.

To a first approximation, 'government' refers *en bloc* to the legislative, executive, administrative, and judicial functions. And roughly, the 'state' appears when we add the apparatus of coercive power. An anarchist society might well have a government but could not accommodate a state. This rough sketch of the state is elaborated and refined in §13.1.

Two comments before we move on. The first is that this is a structural model of politics, static in the sense that it does not explain why things happen politically – why the range of the public realm is shortened or widened, why particular policies are chosen, and so on. To make these things clear is a task, on the one hand, for political science (§3.2) and, on the other, for the type of speculative philosophy of history to be found in marxism (§31.4.1). We will return to the point from a different angle in §2.6.2 when we consider the causal autonomy of the political.

The other comment is that a political system is self-reflexive in the sense that the correct extent of the public realm, the proper ends, and due limits of collective decision-making, questions about who should rule, and the appropriate apparatus of coercive power are themselves matters that can (and typically do) enter the public realm.

2.6 The autonomy of politics

A society could not have a political system and nothing else. The political system is a sub-system within the wider social system; it stands in a relationship of part to whole. The nature of this relationship is what we have to examine.

2.6.1 Conceptual autonomy

We have an entire vocabulary of politics, a set of terms that we use to identify political systems, their institutions and practices. We refer to 'the British Parliament', 'the US Senate', 'the Israeli Knesset', 'constitutional monarchy', 'representative democracy' and so on. A question arises of whether this vocabulary is merely a convenient shorthand that might in principle be replaced. Could all statements about political (and other) institutions be reduced to statements referring purely to individuals and their interactions?

'Methodological individualism' is the label for the view that such replacement is possible. It stands opposed to 'social holism'.

Even a precise statement of the issue is hard to come by. All responses to it are controversial. One problem for methodological individualism concerns certain of the properties that we ascribe to political institutions; we claim, for example, that the British Parliament has existed for more than five hundred years. This property cannot be ascribed to any of the individuals who are or have been members of this institution. If we make the obvious move and say that the five hundred years' duration of this 'institution' relates merely to the existence of a group of people which has persisted over time, its membership being gradually replaced and renewed, we have hardly kept to the challenge of talking only of individuals and their interactions. For we have referred to a 'group', which seems like another institution, and the members of this group have not interacted across five hundred years. Interactions have occurred only within sub-sets of the group at particular times.

For more on methodological individualism first read the discussion in Lukes, 1973b, which is brief but excellent; G. Macdonald, 1985-86; Nozick, 1977; Pettit, 1985-86; Tiles, 1984 (with a reply by Pettit in the same volume). Methodological individualism is often linked to 'abstract individualism', the idea that human drives or behavioural characteristics are socially and historically invariant. Holists argue that such drives and characteristics are socially contextual.

2.6.2 Causal autonomy

I earlier referred to our five-part model of the political as static. It identifies certain structural features of a political system but does not explain why things happen politically. It omits the dynamics of politics.

A standard view of the political system under representative democracy is that it operates causally as an instrument of the popular will. Voters express their preferences, with the result that policy choices are made – usually on behalf of the majority. We will later examine some difficulties in this account (§23.3).

A different, and somewhat harsher view, also sees the political system in general as serving an instrumental purpose. It is roughly correct to say that Marxism sees the political system as subject to economic determination. Marxism will come under review in §31.

There is a kind of inverse economic determinism in the work of liberal writers such as L. von Mises and F.A. Hayek, who argue that freedom depends on a regime of private property. That public ownership of the means of production, combined with central planning, opens in Hayek's phrase 'the road to serfdom'. These issues will resurface in §31.4.

2.6.3 Axiological autonomy

Politics resists one form of axiological reduction, that of having an inbuilt *telos*, goal or purpose (§2.2). Political agents may assign politics a goal or purpose adventitiously in the light of their values. This takes us into the domain of ideology, which will be examined in chapter 5. On the one hand we encounter the typical liberal view that the state should be neutral in respect of theories of the good life (which are matters of reasonable disagreement) and that it should be both inclusive of, and fair towards, all ways of life practised by people who themselves are willing to abide by the terms of fairness (Neal, 1995: 206; but cf. Raz in §30.5). On the other hand, we find conservatism, socialism, and a variety of other 'isms' stressing the political relevance of particular values.

Values enter politics as ideals and principles. Roughly, a principle is procedural. It is a rule of conduct which primarily addresses *how* we act rather than the end-state that our action produces. In the conventional jargon, principles are deontological. They are about what it is right or obligatory to do, irrespective of outcomes. Ideals, in contrast, are teleological. They look to certain end-states as goals of action. If we aim to create a society in which wealth is distributed according to a certain pattern, say 'to each according to their needs', then we are promoting an ideal. We have fixed on a certain end-state which provides a goal of political action. If, on the other hand, we rule out retrospective legislation, or require that all laws are to be general and conditional in form, then we are signing up to a principle. Cf. §24.2 on the enterprise versus the civil association views of politics.

We might tease out connections between principles and ideals. It is not to be expected that political discourse exactly matches the distinction outlined above. But some such distinction can be broadly drawn, and the language of 'principle' and 'ideal' is roughly suitable for it. The point for our purposes is that if, unlike the practice of medicine, politics does not have an inbuilt end, object, aim or purpose, values can be inserted into it through the principles and ideals of different societies and practitioners. See further §§10.1, 29.2, 30.5.

A final point turns on the question whether political agents are subject to the same moral code as private individuals. This is the issue of 'dirty hands' (§24.3).

3. POLITICAL PHILOSOPHY'S APPROACH TO POLITICS

There are a variety of approaches to the study of politics. Political philosophy's distinctive angle can be explored as follows.

3.1 Approaches to the study of politics

The political realm falls within the purview of at least three academic disciples. The first is history; the second is political science; the third is philosophy. In the following section the contribution of these three disciplines will be examined, and the distinctiveness of the philosophical approach marked out.

3.2 History, political science, and philosophy

1.1 'History' has at least three senses. It refers to:

- the things that have happened, the sum total of past events, activities, processes or states of affairs, attributable to human agency
- the activity of inquiry by which we arrive at knowledge of, or rational belief about, past events and the rest
- the narration or statement of what we have come to know through that activity of inquiry

The activity of inquiry and the styles of narration have changed over time. We no longer conduct the activity as Herodotus ('the father of history') did, nor do we write in his way. The study of these multifarious changes belongs to 'historiography' in one sense of that richly indefinite word.

Historical inquiry is distinctively concerned with the past. While 'speculative' philosophy of history seeks to predict the future from the past, projecting trends, laws or rhythmical recurrences from past to future, it is always about the past that the historian inquires. Political history fixes on past political phenomena.

In this way it differs from political science which is concerned to describe and explain current political phenomena. Political science takes note of the past only insofar as historical data aid that process of description and explanation. Another point of difference, though this is more controversial, is that political science aims to generalise. It seeks to establish empirical correlations between (say) income and voting behaviour; to check also how changes in political institutions are regularly linked to changes in other institutions. This urge to generalise makes it 'nomothetic'. In contrast, historical inquiry has been standardly taken to be 'idiographic', concerned with unique events. A historian tries to explain, for example, the March 1917 revolution in Russia – this specific occurrence in all its circumstantiality. The political scientist looks (as Aristotle did in his *Politics*) at the types of social and economic conditions that regularly produce revolutions.

The German sociologist and economic historian, Max Weber (1864 -1920), projected the goal of a 'value-free' (*Wertfrei*) social science, including political science and history. There are real doubts about the feasibility of this project. Weber himself acknowledged that values are reflected in one's selection of subject-matter. More than that, the language of historical and political description and explanation are value-laden. When we explain why a historical agent acted as he or she did, we make a value judgement (e.g.) in deciding that, faced by a (perceived) threat or attack, that person was 'forced' or 'compelled' to do the action. And value-neutrality in face of the Holocaust seems to me indecent and misplaced.

It remains true, however, that history and political science aim on the whole to provide descriptions and explanations which do not presuppose particular ideals or principles (§2.6.3). Political philosophy makes no attempt to eschew the normative; it readily invokes, or attempts to establish, ideals and principles.

On political science, see Collini, Winch & Burrow, 1983; W.J.M. Mackenzie, 1967 & 1970; Mackridis, 1955. On history, see E.H. Carr, 1962 (reviewed in Trevor-Roper, 1962); Clark, 1985; Collingwood, 1993; Gardiner, 1961; L. Hunt, 1986; R. Martin, 1977; Oakeshott, 1933, ch. 3 and 1983 (with Franco, 1990: 31-43 and Greenleaf, 1966: 24-9 as good first guides); Walsh, 1967. Lessnoff, 1974: ch. 6 has a good discussion of value-freedom. On the relation of history to political science, see Oakeshott, 1936; Poulantzas, 1978: 37-43.

3.3 Political philosophy as philosophy

If political philosophy is distinct from both political science and history, it is not an isolated or unconnected subject but belongs to philosophy, and shares the nature of philosophical inquiry.

3.4 The nature of philosophy

What is philosophy? Philosophers are famous, perhaps notorious, for asking this question and the point is often made that the question is itself a philosophical enquiry while the corresponding questions, e.g. 'what is mathematics?' or 'what is history?' are not respectively mathematical or historical. Just why this contrast holds is a matter to which I will return.

In face of our question, etymology (not for the first time) is of little help. The ancient Greek term, *philosophia*, from which our word 'philosophy' derives, means 'the love of wisdom, the quest for truth'. This is uninformative in the sense that the love of wisdom and the quest for truth do not distinguish philosophical inquiry from a host of others, though there is actually more in the old Greek meaning than meets the eye. Human beings, intermediate between the gods and the rest of nature, do not possess wisdom but they can have the right attitude towards it. They can still 'love' and aspire to what they cannot fully have (Burnet, 1930: 197). This ancient sub-text conveys the risky character of philosophy, the provisional nature of philosophical 'results'.

From etymology we might turn to a simple list of what 'philosophy' has covered and included in its long history. But this is of slight help, too. Philosophy has 'hosted' a number of disciples which in the course of time have crystallised and disengaged themselves as separate inquiries (J.L. Austin, 1961: 180). Natural science was once 'natural philosophy': Newton's great work of 1687 was entitled *Philosophiae Naturalis Principia Mathematica* ('The Mathematical Principles of Natural Philosophy'). But nobody now includes natural science within philosophy.

The process of detachment has not been all one-way. Philosophy has, at different times in its long history, had to disengage itself from extraneous controls. In ancient Greece, the Platonic dialogues were an attempt to free philosophy from the trammels of poetry and myth (Havelock, 1963). In the Age of Faith the regulation of philosophy by theology was itself an article of faith. St Thomas Aquinas (1225-74) was quite clear, first and negatively, that while philosophy need not submit its premises to theology, it must submit its conclusions. He also believed, secondly and positively, in his view of *philosophia ancilla theologiae* (philosophy as the servant of theology), that theology may properly direct philosophy to the investigation of particular problems (Maritain, 1947: 95). The political control of philosophy has been a greater problem in recent times. Russian philosophy under Soviet rule is a byword for intellectual robotry (§26).

Pertinent as these thoughts are, they take us straight back, yet more urgently, to the task in hand. If history and etymology are such limited guides, and if philosophy has this capacity for permanent renewal and a need for autonomy, just what is philosophical inquiry as currently understood?

Even as currently understood there is no 'essence' of philosophy, no single kind of inquiry that must go on wherever philosophy is done. Nonetheless there are three typical philosophical activities:

• conceptual analysis
• high-level theorising
• the investigation of aporias

These activities, one or more of them, are found in all present-day work credited as philosophical. They also provide an element of historical continuity. Socrates, Plato, Aristotle, Aquinas, Hobbes, Locke, Hume, Kant, and Hegel, 'the great, dead philosophers', were all recognisably engaged in these activities whatever else they may have been doing.

3.5 Philosophy as conceptual analysis

This is an opaque phrase which is likely to convey little at the moment. The questions come rushing in:

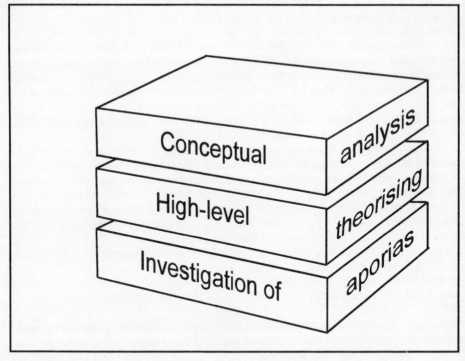

Figure 2. Structure of philosophy

1. What is a concept?
2. What is it to analyse a concept?
3. With what concepts is philosophy concerned?

As we work through these questions, the nature of philosophy as conceptual analysis will become clear.

3.5.1 The nature of concepts

Sales executives have taken to using 'concepts' to denote marketable ideas. The philosophical usage is older and wider. A concept is a classificatory tag. Suppose I say, 'This chair is red', 'That geometrical figure is a square', 'That work of art is so ugly', or the truly exciting 'I am too warm in this pullover'. These statements all involve terms – classificatory pigeon holes – that we use in many different situations – 'chair', 'red', 'geometrical figure', 'square', 'work of art', 'ugly' and so on.

When we have mastered the intelligent use of these words or when we can make the right recalls or perceptual discriminations, we have the relevant concepts. It is important to say 'we'. Concepts are public. You and I both have the concept of a chair: we can recognise chairs when we see them, distinguish them from elephants and table lamps, think about them in their absence and so on.

3.5.2 The nature of analysis

What, then, is it to analyse a concept? The quick answer is that to analyse a concept is to pick out the conditions for its application. Sometimes, not always, these will be necessary and sufficient conditions. Take the geometrical concept of a rectangle. This concept has the following conditions for its application:

S is a rectangle if and only if S is a plane, rectilinear, four-sided figure with four right angles.

Being a plane, rectilinear, four-sided figure with four right angles is a necessary condition for being a rectangle. Unless S has this full set of properties, then (whatever else it may be) it is not a rectangle. These properties are also sufficient. If S has this set of properties, then nothing else is needed. S is a rectangle – period, no discussion.

Not all concepts admit of the tidy tying-down that we practised on the concept of a rectangle. Some are too complex to yield to any brief formulation of conditions; others are too unsystematic in their behaviour to 'close' under necessary and sufficient conditions at all. We will need to look later at some of the extra tangles we have on our hands (§4.1). But at least some concepts can have the conditions for their application pinned down in this way. In establishing this, in the example of the rectangle, we have made a first pass at conceptual analysis.

3.5.3 Philosophy's concern with concepts

Philosophers are not concerned, however, with just all and any concepts. There is selective attention; so we need now to be clear about the principles of selection. The best quick formula is that philosophers are interested in basic concepts. But basic to what, and in what way?
   Philosophy is concerned with two kinds of concept:

- concepts of wide application across whole ranges of inquiry and activity
- framework concepts for particular inquiries or activities

Some concepts apply to everything that exists. Here are two such: existence itself and, on Bishop Butler's cue that 'Everything is what it is, and not another thing', identity. Beyond these, there are concepts that are pervasive in our experience. Perhaps not all, but a vast spectrum of inquiries and activities use the concepts of space, time, object, event, action, process, causation, quality, and relation. These are general concepts.
   Framework concepts are different. To see how, consider aesthetic activity – the activity of making works of art. In this area of experience we should be hard pressed to describe or respond to anything unless we had at command the concepts of beauty, elegance, gracefulness, plainness, originality, harmony, and so forth.
   Again, it would be an odd experience to try making moral judgements without talking and thinking in terms of 'ought', 'right', 'good', 'duty', 'obligation', 'virtue'. Or imagine the impossible: scientific inquiry going on without use of the concepts of experiment, falsification and verification, hypothesis, and theory.
   In these three cases, which are mere illustrations, we are presented with framework concepts: concepts that are deeply entrenched in, and perhaps even definitory of, certain kinds of activity and inquiry.

3.5.4 Analytical variations: connective, functional, and dialectical

Conceptual analysis is a flexible activity. Fixing conditions for the application of a concept, as illustrated briefly above, is just one option. It is a form of reductionism in which a concept is 'reduced' to the conditions for its application – in this sense resolved into its elements. Another possibility is connective analysis, in which we probe concepts, not down into their elements, but across to their alignments; we connect them with other concepts by way of tension, contrast, and reinforcement. If the law can enforce morality, this connects the concepts of morality and law (§15.5.2); if freedom undermines equality as Nozick insists in his slogan 'liberty upsets patterns' (i.e. patterns of equality (§17.4)), this is another connection. Connective analysis usually occurs at the level of high-level theorising (§10). Aside from reductionist and connective analysis, the main further options are functional analysis and the dialectical method.

Functional analysis looks to consider why we need a certain concept, in other words what the concept is functional to (Craig, 1986-87). We will take a further look at functional analysis in §4.4.

'Dialectic' is a term with a long history. In one of its Greek senses it refers to a method of conversational confutation. Someone makes a claim. The implications of this claim are then deduced by question and answer. The upshot is that the claim-maker is brought up sharp against an unwelcome implication, often that the claim contradicts some other claim to which he or she is just as firmly committed. This conversational method is famously associated with the Socrates of Plato's early and middle dialogues. The notion of dialectic is modified as it moves through the work of later philosophers, mainly Aristotle, Kant, Hegel, and Marx. Hegel (1770-1831) is the main figure for present purposes, for he applies the notion specifically to conceptual analysis.

Hegel is concerned to show how concepts are mutually implicatory and dependent in ways that mean we cannot isolate a concept in its uniqueness. Take the concept of being or existence. If we applied purely this concept to something, X, the result would be self-defeatingly bizarre. How could X have literally nothing but being or existence? It would have no shape, extension, quantity, solidity, motion or whatever. What is it that exists in this case? As Hegel says, being and nothingness come to the same thing here. So in the dialectical play of concepts, being and nothingness merge. To distinguish them, we need (Hegel says) the concept of becoming. This involves the idea of something existing with determinate qualities, which then change.

But the idea of quality, Hegel argues, is unsustainable without the idea of quantity, which in turn generates the concept of measure: and so the dialectic wings on its way generating triads (being-nothingness-becoming, quality-quantity-measure and so on in a great sweep that eventually embraces every basic concept). These triads are dialectically related to one another in just the way in which their member-concepts are. Moreover, as the triads inform different areas of human activity and inquiry, so these areas in turn are dialectically related. Philosophy turns out to occupy the summit. This is just as it should be on Hegel's account, since only philosophy has a view of the full dialectical progression and knows the truth about all other areas and levels of experience.

The Hegelian dialectic is apt to produce a double impression. Most readers have a sense that, as concepts collapse and triads emerge, the dialectic zigzags tortuously along the path to the Absolute – the only fully consistent concept. Many of the transitions seem artificial and contrived. The other impression is a sense of brilliant illumination in some of the transitions as Hegel dialectically relates morality and religion, art, science, and philosophy. The kind of conceptual analysis followed in this book will not be Hegelian, though Hegel will crop up in different connections at various times. I defer to the prevailing modes of conceptual analysis, and these are not Hegelian.

On Hegel, see Findlay, 1958: 58-82; Joad, 1936: 402-7; Singer, 1983; Stace, 1955: 121-53.

3.6 Philosophy as high-level theorising

There are no straight divisions in intellectual inquiry; conceptual analysis is a form of theorising. To spell out a set of necessary and sufficient conditions for justice – that justice is a matter of treating like cases equally, of treating different cases differently, and of treating different cases differently to the extent of their differences (§17.2) – is to propound a theory of justice. But this is not the high-level theorising to which I refer. A high-level theory of justice would be, for example, the kind of theory that John Rawls (b. 1921) offers when he argues that justice requires social arrangements in which any economic inequalities are to the maximum benefit of the least advantaged (§17.3). This is, we might say, a conception of justice – a controversial account of what, under certain conditions that Rawls describes, we are committed to if we accept that justice is a matter of treating like cases equally.

'Theory' is a term of many meanings. It has a tolerably precise sense in science, where it contrasts with 'law' on the one hand and 'hypothesis' on the other. A hypothesis is a tentative claim that two or more variables are functionally or causally interrelated (for example, the pressure, volume and temperature of a gas). When such an interrelation has been significantly tested and remains tenable, then we have a theory; if the interrelation holds good invariably to the best of our knowledge, we talk of a law. Beyond this fairly specific usage, 'theory' can refer, at its laxest, in everyday conversation, to any unproved assumption or general statement.

A philosophical theory is typically (1) a general claim involving (2) one or more basic concepts, with (3) some pattern of argument supporting the claim. The pattern may be one of 'proof', where the arguments have a tight deductive structure with conclusions derived from premises under formal rules of logic. On the model of Euclid, Spinoza's *Ethics* (posthumous, 1677) is wholly given over to attempted proofs of this kind. At the opposite extreme, Wittgenstein's *Philosophical Investigations* (1953), which claims to eschew argument, assembles considerations, 'reminders', thought-experiments, actually in a thoroughly argumentative way but with no outward show of deriving conclusions rigorously from premises.

In the matter of argument, it is not my view (though the claim is contentious) that philosophy uses any distinctive forms of argument. Philosophers employ *modus ponens* ('If p then q; p; therefore q'), *modus ponendo tollens* ('A is either B or C; A is B; therefore A is not C'), and so forth. The content may be specific to philosophy but the forms of argument can be heard in any office, bus queue or television interview. A form of argument called 'transcendental', due to the German philosopher, Kant (1724-1804), is often thought to be distinctive of philosophy. Such an argument works backwards from the fact that X exists or occurs to the necessary and universal conditions of its possibility (Scruton, 1982: 23, 33-5, 55-7). 'How is X [knowledge, morality, aesthetic judgement] possible?' This is just an inquiry into what X presupposes. There is nothing peculiarly philosophical about such an inquiry and nothing special about the sorts of argument that are used to answer it. See further Bednarowski & Tucker, 1965; Passmore, 1970: ch. 1.

There are three main styles of philosophical theorising:

• classical
• second-order
• non-autonomous

3.6.1 Classical theorising

Classical theorising is foundational in the sense that it attempts to ground other activities and inquiries. This grounding takes a variety of forms. Three typical forms are the following. In the first place, a philosophical theory, as we glimpsed just now in Kant, may try to spell out the conditions on which something – knowledge, morality, aesthetic judgement or whatever – is possible. Kant takes this task in hand with regard to knowledge (mathematical, scientific, and metaphysical) in the *Critique of Pure Reason* (1781).

Secondly, a philosophical theory may seek to specify the ultimate nature of reality. Thus Berkeley argues in *The Principles of Human Knowledge* (1710) that all that exist are minds and their ideas.

Thirdly, the aim may be to establish the validity, point, rationale or value of some inquiry or activity. In this way Plato (*c.* 429-347 BC) sets out in the *Republic* to vindicate the moral life as inherently preferable to the life of injustice.

Classical philosophical theories also aspire to proof. I referred to Spinoza's Euclideanly-formatted *Ethics*, but even where this kind of explicitly deductive structure is missing, the aim is still to demonstrate. Descartes in his *Meditations* (1641) wants to render the existence of God beyond the reach of rational doubt, for all the easy readability of his style.

3.6.2 Second-order theorising

A different, recently more prominent style of philosophical theorising is the exploration of the logical structures or categorial frameworks of other inquiries and activities. Here we have philosophy as a 'second-order' discipline. Another label, 'metaphilosophy', carries the same meaning, with the aid of Greek – philosophy as proceeding in the wake of, and shadowing, other disciplines. Peter Davidson has dubbed this activity 'philosophy as conceptual watch-dog'. One might, for instance, look at the logical form of historical inquiry and an issue we glimpsed in §3.2: is historical inquiry essentially concerned with the description and explanation of unique events (the French Revolution, the Bolshevik Revolution, the First World War and so on)? If so, it differs from scientific inquiry, which focuses on classes or types of event. Our earlier probings into the teleological character, or otherwise, of political, economic, and moral activity also fall under this heading.

3.6.3 Non-autonomous theorising

The label for this third style of philosophical theorising is daunting but if we peel it off, what is underneath is not hard to make out. This is a view of philosophy as continuous with other activities and inquiries rather than as an independent source of validation (as on the classical view) or of scrutiny (as on the second-order view). On the non-autonomous approach, philosophical theorising and philosophy in general:

> is part of a larger matrix of inquiry; it is roughly the conceptual side of scientific inquiry and philosophy on such a conception is usually the philosophy of something or other: the philosophy of biology, economics, morals, politics, mathematics, and the like. A philosopher here is a scientist, albeit *sometimes* a scientist more in the way that a mathematician is a scientist, who throws out hypotheses, analytical or otherwise, or draws out the logical implications of other hypotheses, clusters of hypotheses, theories or conceptions, and makes hypotheses on this basis. And these hypotheses, like all others, require, to be genuine

hypotheses, an empirical check, though sometimes the check will be indirect. The philosopher is not, no more than is the theoretical physicist or theoretical biologist, interested (at least *qua* philosopher) in doing the checking herself. But she does, or at least should, realize that it is essential to have a genuine hypothesis at all, that the hypothesis be empirically testable. Typical hypotheses set afloat by such philosophers ... would be 'Knowledge is justified true belief ', 'To act rationally is to so act as to maximize your net expected utility' (Nielsen, 1991: 267-8).

3.7 Philosophy as the investigation of aporias

Aporia is a Greek word usually translated as 'problem', 'puzzle' or 'difficulty'; *aporiai* is the plural (anglicised to 'aporias' from now on). There is no need to be fazed by the Greek. In his *Metaphysics* and *Topics*, Aristotle was much concerned with aporias, by which he usually meant specific, stubborn difficulties or paradoxes (Aubenque, 1961). 'Brain jammers' would be a good term instead.

Aporias are of two main kinds. A typical case of an Aristotelian aporia is that of finding oneself divided between two opposite opinions, equally compelling, on the same question (*Metaphysics* B, 995a24-995b4). Kant dwelt on this sort of division in discussing the so-called antinomies in the *Critique of Pure Reason* (A405-567/ B432-595); one of the antinomies is that we are drawn both to accept and deny that the world has a beginning and end in space and time.

The other kind of aporia occurs when one is baffled how to proceed with a question, problem or issue. If a pile of sand is a heap, it cannot cease to be a heap by having one grain removed from it. If n grains of sand are a heap, then so are n-1. By this logic, however, if 1000 grains constitute a heap, then by successive subtraction so must 1 grain. This is the Sorites Paradox; in its initial grip one does not know quite how to respond. Again, there is Zeno's paradox that motion is impossible; for to cover a distance one has first to cover half of that distance and, before that, half of that half-distance. Since any distance to be covered is infinitely divisible in this way and an infinite series cannot be completed, no distance can ever be covered and so motion is impossible. QED and, in Garo Avakian's phrase, 'seamlessly baffling'.

This completes our sketch of the nature of philosophy. There is no shortage of material with which to follow up. Useful items include: Berlin, 1978; Danto, 1968; Grayling, 1995; Hollis, 1985; Lacey, 1982; Maritain, 1947; O'Hear, 1985.

3.8 The branches of philosophy

Philosophers, then, do conceptual analysis, produce high-level theories, and probe aporias. But there is a degree of further organisation. The three activities tend to group or cluster, partitioning the subject into branches.

Certain concepts inform human experience generally – the notions of substance and object, matter and form, event, process, space, time, change and causation, possibility and necessity, existence, reality, truth, identity and so on. These concepts fall within metaphysics. The name 'metaphysics', formidable-sounding or just opaque, has a simple origin. Aristotle wrote on such concepts; his principal editor, Andronicus of Rhodes (1st century AD), not knowing what to call the twelve books that Aristotle had entitled 'First Philosophy' or 'Wisdom', inserted them after Aristotle's *Physics* – *ta meta ta phusika* ('the [books] next after his work on natural science'). The name stuck. Metaphysicians conduct conceptual analysis, produce (and destroy) high-level theories, and investigate aporias within this circle of notions. Within metaphysics, the specific inquiry 'what is there? what exists?', falls within ontology (from the Greek word for being or existence, *on*).

Another block of concepts, theories and aporias, those concerning knowledge, yield epistemology (from one of the Greek words for knowledge, *episteme*). Knowledge, belief, certainty and the challenge of scepticism, evidence, the possibility of knowledge underived from sense experience (so-called 'a priori' knowledge), all these matters come within the ambit of epistemology. Cross-connections readily form. Your metaphysics will inform your epistemology; what is real determines what can be known.

Two other highly general branches of the subject are the philosophy of mind and the philosophy of language. Mind and language are extensive human phenomena, if not precisely so co-extensive as might be wished. The philosophy of mind fixes on the concepts and associated theories and aporias of mind and brain, intention and motive, emotion, etc., along with more rarefied concepts such as consciousness. The philosophy of language sets itself likewise on the concepts of meaning, metaphor, the logical form of different types of sentence, the idea of grammar, the nature of translation and much besides.

Next in line are those branches of philosophy that centre on particular types of inquiry or activity. Here, for example, we meet with ethics or moral philosophy, aesthetics or the philosophy of art, the philosophy of religion, the philosophy of history, the philosophies of science and mathematics – and political philosophy.

There is general agreement among philosophers that metaphysics, epistemology, the philosophy of mind and the philosophy of language are the philosophical heartland. This is because all other branches of philosophy make assumptions that fall squarely within these areas. In ethics we ask, for instance, whether moral judgements can be true or false and whether some can be known to be true. The notions of truth and knowledge take us straight back to metaphysics and epistemology respectively. We also ask whether someone can know a moral truth but fail to act on it, and this prompts questions about *akrasia*, or weakness of will, which are firmly down to the philosophy of mind.

On the relation of political philosophy to the central areas, see the references in §34.4.

3.9 The schools of philosophy

In epistemology and metaphysics certain theories are so fundamental, and have such significant implications for other branches of philosophy, that they have time-honoured labels now virtually impossible to remove. Empiricism is one such theory with its distinctive claim that all knowledge derives from sense experience. It is opposed by Rationalism, the doctrine that reason is a source of knowledge independent of sense experience. Idealism stakes out different ground; it holds that reality consists wholly of minds and their ideas. At the limit Idealism becomes Subjective Idealism or Solipsism, the theory that only I exist, the solo mind. (An admirer once wrote to Bertrand Russell: 'I am so glad you have become a solipsist. I have always wondered that there were not more of us'.) Materialism or physicalism, with its doctrine that everything which exists is matter or an attribute of matter, is a denial of Idealism.

'Scholastic' philosophy, represented below by St Thomas Aquinas (1226-74) on natural law (§15.5.1) and on property (§20.2.4), is so-called because it was meant for the medieval school or university. It was philosophy for an organised body of scholars set on systematic study and instruction. Because of this, it put the accent on brevity, precision and a rigidly logical method of discussion. Questions were divided and sub-divided; general issues passed into particular problems. The Scholastics regarded faith as superior

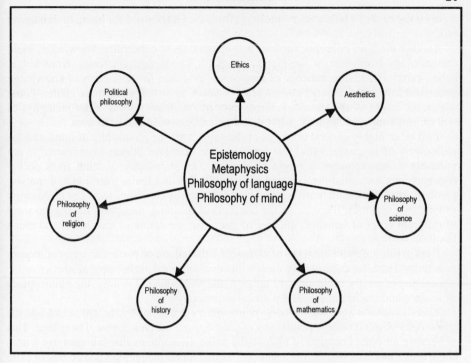

Figure 3. Philosophy and some of its main branches

to philosophy but also regarded philosophy as free to establish rationally whatever did not conflict with faith.

Finally, in this brief survey, there is 'analytical philosophy', a label that will rapidly become familiar if you take your philosophical studies any distance. Analytical philosophy is marked by a strong emphasis on conceptual analysis. Its theorising tends to be of the second-order, non-autonomous kind (§§3.6.2-3.6.3). It is also generally opposed to any idea of the distinctiveness of philosophical argument (§3.6). Philosophy has to establish, or at least to defend, its claims by whatever means any other discipline might. And past philosophy has current interest not in its own right but only on condition that it contributes to present-day problems (§9.2.1).

The present book falls largely within the analytical tradition, though as mentioned earlier it takes political philosophy to involve a modified form of classical, rather than non-autonomous, theorising.

The relations of the schools of philosophy to political philosophy is a tricky issue (§34.4 indicates how to make a start on empiricism).

4. CONCEPTUAL ANALYSIS: TESTS FOR ADEQUACY

We have seen briefly what conceptual analysis, high-level theorising, and the investigation of aporias amount to as activities. What remains, before we look at how they drive political philosophy, is to consider some tests of adequacy for these activities: first, conceptual analysis.

Concepts are a logically diverse bunch; we need to look at four varieties. Next we have to note three tests of adequacy for their analysis: (1) logical independence, (2) extensional and intensional equivalence, and (3) functionality.

4.1 The logical diversity of concepts

Any attempt at a complete taxonomy of concepts is beyond our limits. But particularly in doing reductionist analysis (§3.5.4), you need to be clear about the differences between at least four kinds of concept. Political theorists often refer to them, not always discriminatingly:

- closed
- essentialist
- family resemblance
- essentially contested

The pitfalls are to run together, on the one hand, closed and essentialist concepts and, on the other, family resemblance and essentially contested concepts.

4.1.1 Closed concepts

Time to tick off the list. A closed concept is one that is definable in terms of necessary and sufficient conditions:

(1) X is S if and only if P

That is, a necessary and sufficient condition for X's being S is P. So, for example, it is a necessary and sufficient condition for a work of art's being an antique that it is more than a hundred years old. The conditions can run into more complexity than that:

(2) X is S if and only if $[P_1$ and P_2 and P_3 and ... $P_n]$

In this case a conjunction of conditions zips across the page: X is S if and only if X is P_1 and P_2 and P_3, and so on through to P_n. S has to satisfy the whole of that item-upon-item array of conditions if S is to be X.

4.1.2 Essentialist concepts

Both (1) and (2) are also examples of essentialist concepts. In (1) a single property, P, and in (2) a conjunction of properties, P_1 and P_2 and P_3 and ... P_n, is common and distinctive to all instances of S. There is an 'essence' of S, i.e. those precise properties. Typically, essentialism goes along with scientific theories of 'natural kinds' which group objects by their 'essential' properties, i.e. those properties which an item cannot lack while remaining the kind of thing it is. A lump of gold may acquire and lose all sorts of properties – being painted, varnished, legally owned and so on. It is still a lump of gold with or without them; but there is one property is cannot lose if it is to remain gold, and that is its atomic structure of weight 79. See Kripke, 1980: 134-9 and Wilkerson, 1993.

But, to shuffle the possibilities, if all essentialist concepts are analysable in terms of necessary and sufficient conditions and hence are closed, it does not follow (nor is it the case) that all concepts analysable in terms of necessary and sufficient conditions are essentialist. Here is an example of a closed concept which is not essentialist:

(3) X is S if and only if [P₁ or P₂ or P₃ or ... Pₙ]

None of the conditions is necessary (it is not necessary, for example, for X to be P₂) but any one is sufficient and the whole set, the combined disjunction, is both necessary and sufficient. But there is no property common and distinctive to all cases of X. One case may show up P₁, another P₂: and there is little sense in holding that the disjunction is itself a property that all cases of X possess. A disjunction of properties is not a property any more than a choice of dinners is itself a dinner.

Still, as long as you realise the potential difference, you should not generally need to hold closed and essentialist concepts firmly apart. Overlap is the rule rather than the exception.

4.1.3 Family resemblance concepts

With the closed/ essentialist distinction now in place we can switch to our second pair of types: family resemblance and essentially contested. The label, 'family resemblance', is applied to concepts by Wittgenstein in *Philosophical Investigations* (1953). Wittgenstein is chiefly gunning for essentialism run amok. He does not deny that there are essentialist concepts, concepts properly analysable in terms of common and distinctive properties possessed by all items to which the concept applies. But he suggests that we should be flexible in our expectations. We should look and see, not assume in advance of investigation that a concept is open to an essentialist analysis. There are, in Wittgenstein's famous example, no properties common and distinctive to games. Instead 'we see a complicated network of similarities overlapping and criss-crossing: sometimes overall similarities, sometimes similarities of detail' (Wittgenstein, 1953: I.66). The concept of a game is non-essentialist.

To help formalise the idea, we can update an example of Renford Bambrough's. We can talk of the Kennedy Face. This a family resemblance concept (Bambrough, 1968: 190-1: Bambrough referred to the Churchill Face). There is a range of typical features. For simplicity, A, B, C, D, and E. One person with the Kennedy Face may have typical features A, B, and E (P₁); another, B, D, and E (P₂); a third, A, C, and D (P₃). There is no feature which they all have in common. But from the range they each have enough features to count as possessing the Kennedy Face.

The best discussion of relationships between closed, essentialist, and family resemblance concepts – one to which this account is indebted – is Beal, 1974. Ideologies will feature as family resemblance concepts in chapter 5 when we pick out typical features of conservative, socialist, liberal and other styles of political thinking.

4.1.4 Essentially contested concepts

Finally we come to essentially contested concepts. This terminology dates from Gallie, 1955-6, a revised version of which is printed in Gallie, 1964: ch. 8. Essential contestation is a process that occurs on two main conditions.

In the first place, there is a paradigm case (or star example) for the application of a concept. As regards democracy, one of Gallie's examples, this would be 5th century BC Athens. Everyone accepts that in some sense Athens in the 5th century BC was a democracy (§23.2). Secondly, the concept even in its paradigmatic application is internally complex. For instance, one feature of Athenian democracy was that each citizen had (at least constitutionally) an equal opportunity to participate in collective decision-making. Another feature was that there was a broadly reliable correspondence between acts of governance and the wishes with respect to those acts of the citizens who were affected by them. The conceptual complexity of democracy in ancient Athens is well brought out in Pericles' Funeral Oration, where a whole host of features of the democratic political order are celebrated (Thucydides, 1954, II.4: 115-23).

The vital step towards essential contestability occurs when, out of the original complexity, different strands or elements are stressed as the concept is employed (in this instance) by different theorists and political agents in a diversity of situations.

For example, if we stress the correspondence between acts of governance and citizens' wishes, there is room (on certain assumptions) to downplay the need for equal participation. If the Party knows the citizens' wishes in the sense either of their 'criticised' wants and preferences or of their 'real' interests (§§ 12.2, 18.1, 24.1) better than the citizens themselves, those wishes can perhaps best be served with a minimum of citizenly participation. In a society run by the party, everyone exercises their human powers and realises their humanity. This is the idea; it opened the door directly to the 'people's democracies', the *strany narodnoi demokratii*, of Eastern Europe's yester-year.

On the other hand, if we underline citizenly participation, then (on certain other assumptions) the single party view seems positively undemocratic. A common thought is that citizens cannot run politics directly in a complex modern society, but they can choose who does: and since political credentials are disputable and even élites can decline, this calls for competition between political parties. Hence (in a compressed nutshell) the Cold War disputes about 'true' democracy between East and West.

The typical fate of an essentially contested concept is that rival theorists attempt to 'close' the concept under necessary and sufficient, even essentialist, conditions when there is apparently no objective way of choosing between them on grounds of conceptual correctness.

Further discussion can be found in Connolly, 1983: ch. 1; Emmet, 1979: 12-13; Lee, 1985: 17-24.

The main result so far is that, given the logical diversity of concepts, we cannot fix a universal requirement on conceptual analysis to come up with the philosophers' favourite, namely necessary and sufficient conditions. 'Look and see' is the only safe rule. But two requirements, of independence and equivalence, are of general importance.

4.2 First test: logical independence

One of those requirements rules out analysis by synonymy, as in 'rectangle = oblong', 'freedom = liberty'. It also puts a block on analysing a concept in terms which presuppose that very concept. Suppose, for instance, that I analysed the concept of knowledge in terms of information: 'S knows that P if and only if S has the information that P'. 'Knowledge' and 'information' are not synonyms, but one could make little progress on the concept of information without invoking the concept of knowledge. To analyse the concept of knowledge through that of information is to analyse knowledge in terms that presuppose the very concept of knowledge. Logical independence is preserved in, for example, the putative analysis of knowledge as justified true belief. The concepts of evidential justification, belief, and truth in no way assume the concept of knowledge. There are problems with this particular conceptual analysis of knowledge, but these do not harm the illustrative point.

4.3 Second test: extensional and intensional adequacy

When an analysis is on offer, we want the analysis to be extensionally adequate. The 'extension' of a concept is the set of things to which the concept applies. So the requirement of extensional adequacy is just that the analysis apply to – enable us to identify or pick out – all and only the things to which the concept itself applies. Also we want the analysis to be intensionally adequate. Roughly, this means that it should capture the meaning of the relevant word(s). An analysis of the concept of justice should match the meaning of the word 'justice'.

The readiest way to test the extensional and intensional adequacy of an analysis is to check it against our intuitive reaction to real or imaginary cases of (say) knowledge, justice, or whatever the relevant concept. When an analysis fails the test, it is usually said to have been defeated by counter-example. (Be wary of philosophers who, convinced that a particular analysis is right, are immune to the art of counter-example.) If I analyse the concept of justice in terms of harm, and say that an injustice occurs only when a person is harmed, it is an easy counter-example that somebody may be unfairly passed over for a minor honour which in fact they do not want. The injustice is patent; the harm is not evident. My analysis of justice fails the test of extensional adequacy.

This, with a glance over past ground, is the method used in the first chapter to flush out a first impression of the political. Let me strike a cautionary note, however. The test of intuitive reaction really needs to be deepened by inclusion in something like the Rawlsian method of reflective equilibrium (§5.5). This is mainly a device for testing moral and political theories, but even intuitive reactions are theoretical (if in a pretty minimal way). For example, the intuitive reaction, shared by many people, that positive discrimination is no proper part of justice does involve a view of the nature of justice: and this view contains revisable assumptions (§17.5). Revision may take place *en route* to reflective equilibrium. (Be reassured, the idea of reflective equilibrium is no dark philosophical secret to be painfully unlocked; we will soon have it in clear view.)

Intuitive reactions about extensional and intensional equivalence can also be modified when we look to the functionality of a concept.

4.4 Third test: functionality

Functional analysis scans and probes the logical space that a concept might occupy. Take the concept of belief, mentioned in this regard in §3.6.3. The concept of belief is in full working order. So why do we need the concept of knowledge? First move: a belief can be false and we want a concept that enables us to identify being right about something, accepting as true what is true. Then why not simply rely on the concept of true belief? Because a true belief can be true by guesswork or fluke, therefore we need to be able to identify being non-accidentally right. The person who knows is a non-accidentally reliable informant in a way in which the mere true believer is not. Along these lines we can work towards a concept of knowledge that fills the logical space left vacant by the concept of true belief.

Note that in shaping the concept to what we need it for, we do not have to respect the full range of intuitive reactions about extensional and intensional equivalence. However, to diverge widely from those reactions is to risk misunderstanding, as has perhaps happened with the recent adoption and revision within biology of the concept of selfishness ('the selfish gene').

For a general defence of the functional approach to conceptual analysis, see Craig,

1986-8. Functional analysis will surface at a number of points in this book, e.g. in our examination of sovereignty (§14.6.1) and in the discussion of negative freedom (§22.3).

5. HIGH-LEVEL THEORY: TESTS FOR ADEQUACY

Some contemporary philosophers peer askance at theorising. Saul Kripke (b. 1940), a leading American philosopher, dismisses a particular thesis in the philosophy of language with the remark:

> It really is a nice theory. The only defect I think it has is probably common to all philosophical theories. It's wrong. You may suspect me of proposing another theory in its place; but I hope not, because I'm sure it's wrong too if it is a theory (Kripke, 1972: 280).

Next on stage is David Hamlyn (b. 1924), who offers a different account of what may be wrong with philosophical theories:

> the use of the term 'theory' in philosophy may suggest little more than that the philosopher who puts forward the theory is putting forward a point of view which, however much it may be argued for, does not admit of proof. It is vitally important, therefore, when discussing a philosophical theory to be quite clear what the issues are, what questions are being asked, what problems raised. For only insight into these can save a theory from being pretentious and uninformative (Hamlyn, 1970: 4).

For Kripke the danger (virtually unavoidable) is that philosophical theories are false. For Hamlyn the danger (avoidable with care) is that philosophical theories are too vacuous even to be capable of being false. Let us take Kripke first.

Kripke offers no explicit grounds for his anti-theoretic stance, which in a sense itself involves a philosophical theory, and so seems in danger of self-refutation. But we can probably infer its motivation from elsewhere in his article. Theories are unrestricted generalisations within a domain. The pressure of a gas (P) times its volume (V) is equal to the temperature of the gas (T) times a constant (R). This is a theoretical statement because it applies to every sample of gas. Kripke's view is that only within science can theories hope to hold good, because only within science is there any likelihood of our being able to employ precise enough terms to group things, kind for kind by their intrinsic or essential properties. There is nothing wrong with theories as such, so long as they are scientific theories.

Once we move outside science (which answers a narrow set of demands centring on prediction, manipulation and control), our groupings reflect the diverse and inconsistent demands of social practice. These demands defeat the hope of arriving at unrestricted generalisations. Philosophical theories, which run on non-scientific language and categories, are too 'neat' in offering unrestricted generalisations where in fact only broad and approximate conclusions can be had.

This is almost certainly true. But we should note Aristotle's advice not to seek more precision (*akribeia*) in any inquiry than its subject-matter allows. It would be foolish, a simple misunderstanding, says Aristotle, to expect the same degree of precision from a mathematician and an orator (NE I.3, 1094b23-7: 3; cf. I.7, 1098a29-32: 14). This is undoubtedly right, though it gives us no measure of the degree of precision right for different fields. Nor does it provide any 'reason why' for the different degrees. The 'reason why' in Aristotle's view connects with the relative amounts of necessity and contingency in the subject-matter.

The point for us is that, if we are unlikely to reach (sound) unrestricted generalisations in our political philosophical inquiries, we can at least look to systematise our general attitudes and specific reactions. Theories in political philosophy may be seen as attempts to introduce greater systematicity, so that our specific reactions are not simply *ad hoc*, a disconnected heap, but can be supported by general attitudes – general attitudes which themselves exhibit a degree of order through entailment or at least consistency. There is no assignable limit to our potential success, and all the theories coming up for consideration are endeavours to tighten our thinking in those respects.

So much, then, for Kripke and the falsity of philosophical theories. We can deal more briefly with Hamlyn's point. It is unfortunate that Hamlyn calls on the idea of proof, which requires not just good reasons (considerations that properly weigh in favour) but conclusive reasons (reasons that outweigh or invalidate all others). The theories with which political philosophy is concerned are usually theories of the type called 'classical' in §3.6.1. They are foundational, telling us the bases on which the social order should be organised, but they need not (unlike the standard classical theories) claim to be *a priori* and they also need not aspire to proof. Good reasons are normally presumed to be good enough. For developments of this general idea in philosophy, see Nozick, 1981: 1-24; Reid, 1962: 9-13; Waismann, 1956.

In specifying criteria of adequacy for political theories, one part of the task is easy. We have only to bring forward the standard tests for 'good' theory everywhere. These are: internal consistency (the theory contains no logically incompatible claims or implications); simplicity (the theory delivers its results on the smallest number of assumptions); smoothness (when aporias arise, the theory needs few qualifications in order to meet its difficulties); metaphysical and scientific compatibility (the theory fits well with our general world-view and with the 'best' science); inter-theoretic support (the theory meshes well with other political theories that pass the previous tests). Dunbar, 1995: 80 has more details.

These tests are in roughly descending order of importance. Internal consistency is vital; inter-theoretic support merely desirable: lack of inter-theoretic support is never enough to overturn a theory. The tests are also of descending definiteness; internal consistency is 'either/ or', either the theory is consistent or it is not. But inter-theoretic support admits of degrees.

Beyond such routine requirements the criteria are problematic. The following may be mentioned:

- moral theory
- truth
- rationality
- discourse theory
- reflective equilibrium

Postmodernism gives its own subversive spin to the justification of political theories, as Steve Fuller will show in §33.2.

5.1 Moral theory

A not uncommon view of political philosophy is that it is simply the application of moral philosophy to public affairs. On this approach, the test for political theory is whether it squares with the deliverances of the best available moral theory. Two main problems arise.

In the first place, moral philosophy is in no position to offer more than claimants to the title of best moral theory. Utilitarianism vies with Kantianism; contractarianism competes with moral realism; Aristotelian eudaimonism enjoys renewed support. The Age of Chivalry may be dead but the jousting of moral theories continues unchecked.

Secondly, this view of the relation of moral to political theory relies typically on some such idea as Sidgwick's that 'Ethics' – moral philosophy – 'aims at determining what ought to be done by individuals, while Politics' – political philosophy – 'aims at determining what the government of a state or political society ought to do and how it ought to be constituted' (Sidgwick, 1967: 15).

The trouble here is that issues about the conceptual autonomy of politics and of abstract individualism return to haunt us. In particular, if human drives and behavioural characteristics are socially and politically contextual (§2.6.1), then the moral life (concerned with the individual) is already implicated with the political. Any simple foundational role for moral theory in relation to political theory is a non-starter.

5.2 Truth

At least since Parmenides contrasted 'the way of truth' with 'the way of seeming', when even Socrates was young, truth has been an explicit goal of philosophical activity. The quest for truth has included the truth about the nature of truth. Correspondence, coherence, pragmatist, semantic, minimal, and redundancy theories contend. One of them may well be true.

The quest for truth in political theory, no less than in moral and aesthetic theory, has received two serious challenges relating respectively to:

- the extent of political disagreement
- the inti .tability of political disagreement

On the one hand, we face the sheer extent of political disagreement. No political theory attracts the consensual support which (say) relativity theory and quantum theory enjoy in natural science.

On the other hand, while scientific disagreements also occur, political disagreements are more intractable. In science the assumption is that, where there is truth, we can either appeal to a decision procedure by which rival truth-claims can be adjudicated (e.g. properly controlled experiments) or we can identify a real convergence of judgement and provide an explanation for whatever disagreements persist. Thus we can identify a convergence of judgement that a cloudless sky looks blue to normal observers in sunlight, and also explain why to a colour-blind person it does not. By fairly sharp contrast, there is no agreed decision procedure for adjudicating rival political theories. The present discussion would be unnecessary if there were. To compound the problem, in politics the explanation of why convergences and divergences occur is itself contentious; the marxist offers one account, the liberal another, the feminist a different account again.

Truth has been claimed for some political theories but other sources of support are more commonly invoked. We will look at those sources next. A loop-back before we move on: the general lack of closed or essentialist concepts in political discourse is a definite extra complication for truth-claims. If, for instance, democracy is an essentially contested concept, the claim (say) that democracy produces the tyranny of the majority will be controversially true or controversially false no matter how much empirical investigation or critical reflection we do.

5.3 Rationality

The appeal to rationality has three dimensions in political theory:

- right reason
- instrumental rationality
- consistency

Right reason is the power of attaining truth, particularly necessary truth; this power has been thought to operate in the moral and political spheres no less than in the logical and mathematical ones. The idea of right reason in ethics and politics is of long standing; the Greeks had the corresponding term *orthos logos* and the Romans *recta ratio*. It suggests intuitive knowledge – *noesis* – rather than discursive knowledge – *dianoia*. Discursive knowledge proceeds from premises to conclusions; intuitive knowledge perceives directly, it grasps an essential truth without any process of inference. The idea of intuitive knowledge was probably at its most influential in the Western tradition in the Middle Ages, though it is also to be found in the 1641 *Meditations* of Descartes, far into the modern era; it is clearly present in the greatest work of medieval theology, St Thomas Aquinas' *Summa Theologiae*. The problem about it is that it runs on the notion of truth. All the elusiveness of truth in moral and political theory comes back into play from the last section.

Instrumental rationality involves calculation of the most efficient means to one's ends (normally taken to be self-interested). Much political theory in the present century has invoked the support of instrumental rationality. Where theories are defended on utilitarian grounds, the appeal to instrumental rationality is generally direct. But we find the appeal also in a non-utilitarian writer such as Rawls, who argues in TJ that under conditions of impartiality, rational people will choose his two principles of justice. The appeal to instrumental rationality is a plausible strategy and we will pick up on it as we go along.

Finally there is the appeal to consistency. This found its earliest elaboration in the moral philosophy of Kant. Kant regards reason as the faculty of principles. In the theoretical sphere these principles include the laws of logic: 'If p then q; p; therefore q' and the rest. These are principles for all rational minds in all their quest for knowledge. Kant looks for an analogue to these principles in the practical sphere; he finds it in certain principles of decision-making. Roughly, in deciding whether to do something we must ask ourselves if it would be possible for everyone to act as we are proposing to do. Kant sees it as a requirement of practical reason that we act on principles that anyone might follow, even when we are on the receiving end, and do not make exceptions in our own favour. This idea of practical reason has direct implications for political theory (§22.6).

Rationality appears in slightly different guise in discourse theory and in Rawls' idea of reflective equilibrium. I will therefore consider them separately.

5.4 Discourse theory

Discourse theory is particularly associated with the name of Jürgen Habermas (b. 1929). Habermas calls up the idea of an ideal speech situation. In this situation there is free and rational debate, without domination of one person or group by others; the proper test of any political theory, and indeed of any political proposal, is its acceptance by all participants in such a dialogue. The idea connects with Rousseau's account of ascertaining the general will (SC, II.3). This is its direct philosophical provenance. 'The ethics of discourse' is a familiar label for Habermas' views (cf. §23.2).

The assumption is clear that there will be convergence on the acceptability or otherwise of theories and proposals in these conditions. It is not equally clear on what grounds the assumption can be vindicated. But a more practical problem from our point of view is that the ideal speech situation does not obtain between the reader and the writer of this book. We cannot submit the theories that we examine to the kind of dialogic test that Habermas requires.

On Habermas, see Avio, 1997; Benhabib, 1992 passim; Bernstein, 1979: Pt IV; Heath, 1995; D. Held, 1989: ch. 3; O'Sullivan, 1997: 742-4; Vetlesen, 1995. To tackle Habermas direct, try Habermas 1984, 1987 & 1993.

5.5 Reflective equilibrium

The final test for political theories takes us into John Rawls' decision procedure for normative theorising. The keystone of this procedure is the idea of 'reflective equilibrium'. As we pursue reflective equilibrium, so we systematise our moral and political thinking. The pursuit proceeds in the following way.

In the first stage we have a number of intuitive normative reactions to matters of public concern, issues in our private lives, historical events we have read about, and so forth. These reactions, intuitions, or particular judgements, are capable of being critically examined. I may come to realise that my reaction to this issue or that concern rests on irrelevant or unreliable information or that it is distorted by favouritism, prejudice or self-interest. In fact this happens to me all the time. Reactions that survive critical scrutiny are, while I retain them at least until the next bout of self-examination, my considered judgements.

In the next stage, we generalise from these considered judgements, trying to formulate the rules and principles implicit in them. Principles have implications, not all of which are immediately obvious. A tension can occur between our principles (or moral theory) and our considered judgements. Sometimes a considered judgement is so entrenched in our normative sensibility that we block the implication and amend the principle; sometimes the principle connects so firmly with the general structure of our principles and other judgements that we surrender the particular considered judgement. There is interplay between principles and judgements with the aim of arriving at a coherent set of considered judgements. Whatever we accept, if only provisionally, at this level is our state of 'narrow' reflective equilibrium.

In the final stage, our considered judgements and our principles (or moral and political theory) are brought into critical alignment with our background beliefs, empirical and philosophical, about human beings and society, the scope and limits of human knowledge, and even the nature of reality. Nothing is too deep, broad or vague to figure in this exercise. 'Wide' reflective equilibrium is the point at which our considered judgements, or principles or moral and political theory, and our background beliefs form a coherent whole.

Aside from problems about the exact details of the method, the idea of reflective equilibrium has been subject to two interpretations, one conservative and the other radical (these are just the normal labels, and 'conservative' should not be directed linked to conservatism as an ideology (§29)). On the conservative interpretation, there is a privileged class of initial normative reactions. These foundational reactions are not subject to revision but will on occasion necessitate amendments in our principles or moral and political theory and even in our background beliefs.

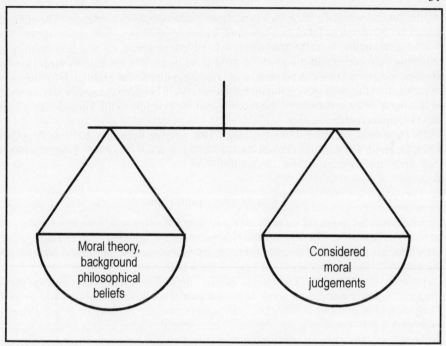

Figure 4. Wide reflective equilibrium

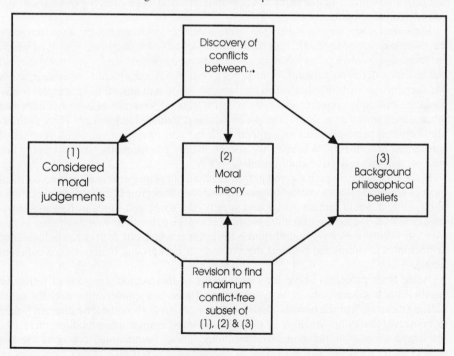

Figure 5. Reflective equilibrium - conservative interpretation

On the radical interpretation, by contrast, everything is revisable. Any or all of our initial normative reactions, principles, or background beliefs may be surrendered or amended in the interests of wide reflective equilibrium.

While Rawls is thought by some to waver between the two interpretations (see A. Brown, 1986: 75), nothing in his account commits him to the conservative view. The opposite impression rests on a mistake about the role of reflective equilibrium in Rawls' *A Theory of Justice*. Rawls unfolds a thought experiment of which the initial postulates are not revised; from this experiment emerge two principles of justice on which the rest of the book is based. But the thought experiment is not meant to illustrate any process of reaching reflective equilibrium. On the contrary, it is we, the readers, who are meant to carry out that process: and Rawls' claim is that his two principles will survive in our condition of wide reflective equilibrium.

The method of reflective equilibrium cannot be followed in this book. It is not something the author can enact for the reader; it is by its nature a slow, iterative process which has to be carried out by each person for himself or herself, though not necessarily in isolation and not necessarily without convergence of result between different people. Rawls in fact relies on such convergence, as we will see in §17.3; he has been criticised

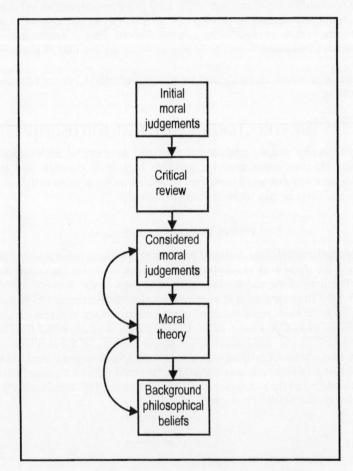

Figure 6. Reflective equilibrium - radical interpretation

accordingly for attempting 'the displacement of politics'. Broadly, the critics' thought is, first, that there will be no substantive normative disagreements relevant to politics if the reflective equilibria of all (rational) inquirers converge on Rawls' principles of justice; secondly, that there is no likelihood of such convergence. Not all inquirers are rational; rationality does not necessarily yield Rawls' principles. Political life is a domain of irreducible normative disagreement (Honig, 1993; O'Sullivan, 1997: 744-5). In fairness, other tests of adequacy for political theories, most notably that involving the idea of truth, also incline to the displacement of politics.

To go deeper into the idea of reflective equilibrium, see Rawls, 1974-75; A. Brown, 1986: 74-8; N. Barry, 1981: 130; Daniels, 1979 & 1980; Delaney in Nielsen & Shiner, 1977: 153-61; DePaul, 1987 & 1988; R. Dworkin, 1978: 159-68; Holmgren, 1989; W. Norman, 1998; Sandel, 1982: 43-4, 47-8.

6. APORIAS: TESTS FOR RESOLUTION

Aporias sometimes yield to conceptual analysis, as an appearance of paradox disappears on fuller investigation of key terms. Perhaps more commonly the puzzles they involve have to be resolved by belief revision of the kind that Rawls describes in his account of reflective equilibrium. It may be that only the adoption of an ideology will enable us to avoid or escape certain aporias, as for example liberals have generally avoided Rousseau's paradox about being forced to be free by shunning the idea of positive freedom (§22.4.1).

But there is no single, fixed method for puncturing aporias, as our later discussions will make clear.

7. THE STRUCTURE OF POLITICAL PHILOSOPHY

Political philosophy exactly replicates the general structure of philosophy. Political philosophers do conceptual analysis, produce high-level theories, and investigate aporias. We have just examined some tests for the adequacy of these activities. It is time to trace the activities as they occur in political philosophy.

7.1 Analysis of political concepts

Take conceptual analysis first. Political philosophy's angle is normative or valuational. It locks on to the framework concepts of political appraisal. One such concept is that of the state. The days of the nation state, at least in parts of the Western world, may be passing. But the state apparatus, at a regional level in the European Union and still at a national level in the USA, remains central to political argument. What the state must, may or must not do is as live a topic as ever. Along with the state come the concepts of sovereignty, law, power, and authority. The state's policies, or the condition of society, are said by many to be inegalitarian, unjust, to deny groups or individuals their rights – not least in respect of property ownership. The favoured form of the state is democratic, to ensure freedom and the promotion of the public interest. This rapid survey produces a list of twelve central political concepts:

- power
- authority
- state
- sovereignty

- law
- justice
- equality
- rights
- property
- freedom
- democracy
- the public interest

These concepts are central to normative or valuational political discourse in the sense that all such discourse, in its full variety of levels, either explicitly invokes or tacitly presupposes them. Just beyond this central ring of concepts are others which are equally open to analysis but which lack their pervasiveness in political appraisal and argument: war, colonialism, empire, federalism, left/right, party, revolution and *coup d'état*, totalitarianism, national character, and many besides. I do not totally relegate them. The left/right distinction will surface for scrutiny in §27.1; federalism comes up in §14. But I largely sideline them for the purposes of this book.

It is worth noting that all twelve concepts map readily on to the five-part model of the political outlined in §2.5. The *state* embodies the third and fourth elements of the model. *Sovereignty* is widely taken to be an essential attribute of the state. Policy choices, the second element of the model, become *laws* – made and changed by the legislature. On due conditions, *authority* attaches to the forms of collective decision-making. A political system displays *power* in its fifth feature, as an apparatus of administration and coercive power. Policy choices may aim at the establishment of *justice* or *equality*, the preservation of *rights*, the protection of *property*, or the promotion of *freedom*. Such choices may involve contestation or consensus about the proper extent of the public realm. Forms of collective decision-making can be, perhaps should be, *democratic*. A standard view is that policy choices should address the *public interest*.

7.1.1 The historical diversity of political concepts

Political concepts are not fixed points of reference, invariable across time and culture. A number of points need to be noted. Concepts are logically complex. They have constituents; it is probably true that, for any major normative political concept, its constituents are available elsewhere (historically or culturally). What is not true is that different times and cultures group the same constituents under the same concepts.

To illustrate: we can draw out the constituents of the Greek concept of *dike* or *to dikaion*. We can talk of compensation or legal proceedings, of rendering to each their due, of the whole sum of morality, and of what is congruent with nature. We can thus identify the constituents of this Greek concept, which are present (in some form or other, scattered across different words and phrases) in our own ways of thinking. But no single modern concept groups these constituents exactly as the Greeks grouped them *en bloc* under *dike* or *to dikaion*, though 'justice' comes closest.

This point still applies even when etymology suggests otherwise. One has to examine the relation of Roman *libertas* to modern 'liberty', not assume conceptual equivalence from linguistic derivation.

Add another point yet. Even within a tradition of political discourse, concepts undergo development. Constituents are added, deleted, refined, downplayed or accentuated as practical circumstances alter and contexts of argument vary. *Dike* in Homer or Hesiod is not *dike* in Plato or Aristotle. Nor is freedom in Hobbes in the seventeenth century the same as freedom in Rousseau in the eighteenth or T.H. Green in the nineteenth. Again, the term 'state' has undergone a development which we will briefly trace later (§14.1). This process of development can both deepen and destabilise a concept. Deepening typically occurs when constituents are added, deleted or refined under analysis. Destabilisation comes normally when different constituents are downplayed or emphasised by different theorists; 'essential contestability' lies at the end of this route.

For our twelve central concepts, the following table sets out the closest conceptual equivalencies between the three main Western traditions of political discourse. At least two equivalencies on the Greek side are at best highly approximate – *to sumpheron* for public interest and *moira* for rights. *Moira* is often translated as 'due proportion'; it is within calling distance of 'rights', though it also carries connotations of one's individual fate or destiny, of what has been allotted to one (an allotment graphically rendered in Plato's Myth of Er in R, X), which is totally absent from 'rights'. One is verging on saying that 'rights' has not the correct sense for a translation of *moira*. *Dikaion, dikaia* (plural), in the sense of 'what is due', has some of the right associations. Even on the Roman side 'rights' pose a problem; Roman *iura* are primarily legal while modern 'rights' are moral as much as legal. The identification of the Greek *polis* with the modern state is a favourite crux (§14.5). *Auctoritas* only imperfectly matches 'authority' (Friedrich, 1972: 47-8).

Greek, Roman and modern political concepts

Modern	Greek	Roman
Power	Kratos (the most directly political), Bia (force, violence), Dynamis (power or ability in general)	Potestas
Authority	Arche	Auctoritas, principium
State	Polis	Res publica
Sovereignty	To kurion	Imperium, maior potestas
Law	Nomos	Lex
Justice	Dike, to dikaion	Ius, iustitia
Equality	Isonomia	Equabilitas
Rights	Moira, dikaia	Iura
Property	Ktesis	Res, proprietas
Freedom	Eleutheria	Libertas
Democracy	Demokratia	Democratia, civitas popularis
Public interest	To sumpheron, koinon agathon	Utilitas communis, bonum publicum

There is a good, detailed discussion of many Greek political concepts in Havelock, 1978, which is full of insights, as are all Havelock's books. An older work, Myres, 1927, retains a good deal of value. Nothing quite like Havelock is available for Roman political thought, though Adcock, 1964; Hammond, 1951; Jones & Sidwell, 1997: ch. 1-4, are well worth checking along with the standard texts on Roman law (e.g. Gaius, 1925). For the Greeks you might usefully supplement Havelock with Glotz, 1929, an old book which retains a good deal of value.

7.2. High-level theorising

High-level normative theories involving these concepts are legion. Some of the most influential and important will be examined in the chapters that follow. Cases in point are theories about the basis of authority, the conditions on which one person or a group is entitled to issue commands to others; theories about the nature of freedom, whether (for instance) freedom is a matter of being able to do what one wants irrespective of the origin and character of those wants; theories of rights, and particularly the status of certain rights as 'natural' or 'human'. I suggest in §10 that the theories with which we are typically concerned in political philosophy have modified characteristics of classical theorising.

The ideologies examined in chapter 5 are in effect extra-high-level theories which impose their own shape on the concepts, theories, and *aporias* examined earlier. There are further remarks about them before we leave this chapter in §7.

The branch of political philosophy concerned with high-level normative theories – their formulation or critique – is generally called simply 'political theory'.

7.3 The investigation of aporias

Aporias abound no less. Can I be forced to be free, as Rousseau held (§22.4.1)? Can justice require affirmative action, positive discrimination, or are the two notions incompatible (§17.5)? Are different moral standards applicable in politics from those of ordinary life (§24.3)?

Political philosophy thus draws us into philosophy's three standard activities. A complication, an extra level of theorising, should be noted. Ideologies – socialism, liberalism, conservatism, feminism, anarchism among them – stress particular concepts, inter-relate them in specific fashions, reject certain ways of theorising about them, handle aporias distinctively. Ideologies are the ultra-high-level political theories. They are political philosophy's equivalent to comprehensive standpoints such as empiricism and idealism in epistemology and metaphysics. In fact the relationship is more complex than this. Some ideologies, such as marxist socialism, offer reasons why particular philosophies like empiricism prevail; these philosophies in turn offer a vantage-point from which ideological claims can be assessed.

7.4 Political philosophy and the philosophy of social science

The philosophy of social science is a reflective, second-order activity directed on to the aims and methods of the social sciences (§7.4), including political science.

Since the nineteenth century, the proper methods of the social sciences have been a matter of intense debate. Two main approaches can be identified, with variations of interpretation and emphasis within each. They are, first, the 'naturalist' view that the methods of the natural sciences (observation, hypothesis, experiment, derivation of universal laws) can be applied to the study of society with the same results (of prediction, control, and explanation). The greater complexity of social phenomena and the practical difficulties of controlled experimentation lessen the precision of the social sciences (it is usually conceded), but they drive no logical wedge between the social and the natural sciences.

The second approach is the 'antinaturalistic' one, which argues that the social world is endowed with 'meaning' or 'significance' in ways that render the methods of the natural sciences largely irrelevant to its proper study. Two quotations from Max Weber give the flavour of this approach:

[W]e are cultural beings, endowed with the capacity and the will to take a definite attitude toward the world and to lend it significance (M. Weber, 1959: 81)

Action is social in so far as, by virtue of the subjective meaning attached to it by the acting individual (or individuals), it takes account of the behaviour of others and is thereby oriented in its course (M. Weber, 1964: 88).

In the background here are the views of the nineteenth-century German philosophers, H. Rickert and W. Windelband, and the highly distinguished and deeply learned philosopher and historian, Wilhelm Dilthey (1833-1911). The problem is, however, that at this level of generality (on which Weber hardly improved elsewhere), it is difficult to see how 'meaning' and 'significance' make much methodological difference. The world has meaning and significance for rats in a jungle, yet the study of their behaviour falls firmly with the biological sciences.

But the antinaturalist has a reply. The behaviour of rats in a maze is context-independent. Rats as species have characteristic (law-bound or law-like – 'nomological') ways of behaving, and these ways continue to be realised whatever the rats and whatever the maze. Human beings are not like this, it is claimed. The explanation of human action, no less than that of animal behaviour, is via states of mind – attitudinal states of belief, desire, aversion, attachment and so on. But in the case of human beings and with regard to their specific objects, these states of mind are products of unique social configurations; they are relative to historically specific societies, informed by distinct conceptual frameworks. There may well be law-like behaviour within a society. But between societies, particularly historically distant ones, attitudinal states of mind are not continuous because conceptual frameworks are discrepant. A Neanderthal woman cannot have wanted to write a cheque. This antinaturalist position links directly back to the viewpoint of social holism outlined in §2.6.1.

One small point of language. Antinaturalism is often connected with the term, 'hermeneutics' (from the Greek verb *hermeneuo*, 'to interpret'), which came into use at first in connection with the interpretation of theological and legal texts in the late eighteenth and early nineteenth centuries, and registered the need for scholarly sensitivity to the different times and conditions in which these texts had been written (Føllesdal in Martin & McIntyre, 1994: 233 and Mueller-Vollmer, 1986: 1-5).

Not all antinaturalists would base their case on the discrepancy of conceptual frameworks. Sometimes the antinaturalistic objection is rather to the 'impossibility' of prediction in the social sciences, or to the 'involvement' of the social scientist with his or her subject-matter.

On the score of prediction an argument deriving from Sir Karl Popper (1902-94) goes roughly as follows. Future human actions will be strongly influenced by presently unavailable knowledge (discoveries and inventions). Since we cannot predict what this knowledge will be, because in order to do so we should need to have it already, we cannot predict future human actions. For Popper's own statement, see Popper, 1957: v-vii; for critical commentary, Gibson, 1968: 370-3; Gilbert & Berger, 1975: 108-10.

The 'involvement' argument is that as social scientists we interact with the objects of our study, not least because those objects include ourselves, in ways from which the natural sciences are free. One development of this argument concerns the possibility of 'value-free' social science. Antinaturalists sometimes claim that the avoidance of subjectivity, idiosyncrasy, and prejudice is peculiarly difficult (if not impossible) in the social sciences. Weber first marked out this territory in his idea of a *wertfrei* – value-free, ethically neutral – social science (§3.2). See M. Weber, 1959; E. Nagel in Martin & McIntyre, 1994: ch. 36; Overend, 1983: 14-18.

The best single guide to the philosophy of social science is currently Martin & McIntyre, 1994. But see also Cowling, 1963b; Fay, 1975; Lessnoff, 1974; Mill, 1970: 545-622, reprinted in Mill, 1987b; Ryan, 1970, 1973 & 1984a; Shaw, 1975; Voegelin, 1952; Winch, 1958; Wolf-Phillips, 1964. On Diltheyan hermeneutics, see Dilthey, 1961; Hodges, 1944; Makkreel, 1975; Rickman, 1979. On the direct relation of political philosophy to the social sciences themselves, see Runciman in PPS 2: ch. 2.

No simple distinction holds between political philosophy and the philosophy of social science, though we see readily enough the broad contrast. Political philosophy is crucially concerned with how politics ought to be organised, the proper ends and limits of political action; the philosophy of social science is about the methods of studying politics and social phenomena generally. But, on the one hand, there is some overlap of conceptual analysis through 'shared' notions of power and law, for instance; on the other, those who deny the possibility of a value-free social science are apt to see implicit assumptions about the proper ends and limits of political action in all forms of social inquiry, including the philosophy of social science.

7.5 Political philosophy and the history of ideas

Systematic study of the history of political ideas began in the mid-nineteenth century and became a flourishing academic industry with the work of A.O. Lovejoy in the 1920s. Later practitioners include Hardin Craig, Edwin Greenlaw, R.F. Jones, E.M.W. Tillyard, Sir Isaiah Berlin, Leo Strauss, W.H. Greenleaf, Quentin Skinner, Reinhart Koselleck, and Melvin Richter. See Levi, 1974: ch. 1 for a helpful run-over of perspectives on the history of ideas; follow up with Freeden, 1997.

'Ideas' refers mainly to two things – individual concepts and particular ideologies. We can take a concept, such as freedom, and anatomise its development. We can chart its early meanings, trace its diverse senses in legal documents, philosophical texts, political pamphlets, and *belles lettres*, for a given period and across different periods; we can also ascertain its role in practical politics. Equally with an ideology such as socialism, we can date the emergence of socialist language, identify the first full-fledged socialist theorists, unthread the different strands of socialist thinking, and see which strands predominate in different writers or periods; we can examine the influence of socialist thinking on domestic legislation and foreign policy. (It is said of one Oxford philosopher, drafted into the British Foreign Office during World War II, that he addressed his new colleagues with the remark, 'The first thing to do is to find out if our foreign policy is socialistic'. In the Foreign Office of Anthony Eden, the investigation must have taken little time.)

This way of studying the history of ideas, or conceptual history, is sometimes called by its German name – *Begriffsgeschichte*. It is not the only approach to the subject. The present-day historian of ideas, J.G.A. Pocock (b. 1924), explores rather the 'languages' in which political debate is conducted. Thus in the sixteenth century, questions of law, authority, freedom, and power were discussed in a variety of discourses – baronial, civic, ecclesiastical, and parliamentary. For a good overview of Pocock, see Hampsher-Monk, 1996. Pocock speaks for himself in Pocock, 1971 & 1993.

Whatever the approach, one thing strikes the philosopher. Missing from the history of ideas is the kind of critical, appraisive exercise that we find in political philosophy. Historians can and do apply standards of intellectual excellence to the history of ideas. That is not the point. The historian who finds two opposed concepts of liberty in John Stuart Mill's *On Liberty* (1859) will be chiefly interested in questions such as: 'How do the two concepts come to be present in Mill's work, from what sources did he derive them?', 'Is the conflation common in other contemporary writers?' and so on. The political philosopher's questions are more likely to be: 'In this argument does Mill use the same word "liberty" in a different sense in different parts of the argument, thus invalidating his conclusion?' and 'Could the argument be reformulated so as to preserve consistency?'

7.6 Political philosophy as inquiry and activity

Political philosophy is not only an inquiry. It is also an activity or practice, and increasingly an institutionalised one. It is pursued mainly in university philosophy and politics departments; these institutional settings create minor differences in the activity or practice itself. For instance, in philosophy departments political philosophers are likely to be more urgently sensitive to developments in epistemology and in the philosophy of mind and language – matters in which their colleagues are involved and with which they have themselves some familiarity through their basic philosophical studies. In politics departments political philosophers are likely to be in closer touch with sociological evidence bearing critically on the assumptions that political theorists make.

Differences even carry across to the study of the classic texts. In a politics department greater stress will usually be laid on the social and political context of (say) Locke's *Second Treatise of Civil Government* – on the nascent capitalism which informed his discussion, making private property a central political concern. In a philosophy department, by contrast, we might puzzle rather more about how Locke's account of persons as possessing natural rights (including the right to acquire property) fits with his view of personal identity in the *Essay Concerning Human Understanding* (1690); or about how to square Locke's assumption in the *Second Treatise* that reason is a source of moral knowledge, discovering the requirements of natural law, with his empiricism in the *Essay*, whose official line is that all knowledge derives ultimately from sense experience.

Another inter-departmental divergence, notable though less pervasive, is the tendency within politics departments for attention to spread beyond the classic texts to the *scripta minora* of tracts, pamphlets and even plays, poetry, and novels. Richard Ashcraft has particularly championed this approach to the history of political thought, which can fit well with the purposes of history and political science (Ashcraft, 1986: Introduction). After all, the classic texts are only one part of a huge literature, and of an immense set of artefacts, in which political consciousness is expressed. If our aim is to understand, say, the condition of political culture in which the English revolution of 1688 occurred, then the high philosophical politics of Locke's *Two Treatises of Government* marks only one direction and level of pertinent political reflection. Historical explanation must include but also go beyond it.

In the philosophy department, matters look different. In concentrating on the classic texts and marking them off from the bulk of a vast political literature, philosophers are not denying that (for other purposes, those of history and political science) the classic text/minor literature distinction can properly be downplayed. But the philosophical perception is that the classic texts represent a level of self-conscious political reflection (conceptual, theoretical, and aporetic) that sets them in clear relief (cf. Oakeshott, 1991: 223-4).

8. THE VALUE OF POLITICAL PHILOSOPHY

There are views of the nature of philosophy which rule out any practical application that political philosophy might have. The main such view may be represented by Michael Oakeshott (1901-90) and F.H. Bradley (1846-1924). Oakeshott stresses that philosophy aims solely at understanding. Any desire for action is extraneous (Oakeshott, 1933: 1). Earlier, Bradley had written:

> Philosophy in general has not to anticipate the discoveries of the particular sciences nor the evolution of history; the philosophy of religion has not to make a new religion or teach an old one, but simply to understand the religious consciousness; and aesthetic has not to produce works of fine art, but to theorize the beautiful which it finds; political philosophy has not to play tricks with the state, but to understand it; and ethics has not to make the world moral, but to reduce to theory the morality current in the world (Bradley, 1927: 193).

This anti-practical idea is also present in David Hume (1711-76) in the famous passage where the prince of sceptics draws no practical implications from all the intellectual devastation he has wrought: 'I dine, I play a game of back-gammon, I converse, and am merry with my friends'; also in Hegel, PR, Preface: 23; and in Wittgenstein ('Philosophy ... leaves everything as it is': Wittgenstein, 1953, I: §124). Its polar opposite appears in Marx's Eleventh Thesis on Feuerbach (1845): 'Philosophers have only *interpreted* the world the world in various ways; the point is to *change* it' (PKM: 158).

My reservations about the anti-practical idea are twofold. In the first place, it is unclear whether the quest for understanding is not, as pragmatists claim, itself ultimately guided by practice. Secondly, the philosophical tradition does not support reticence in the face of practice. Our inquiry, says Socrates in the first book of Plato's *Republic*, 'is not a trivial one; it is our whole way of life that is at issue' (R I.352D: 98). Aristotle draws a distinction, in *de Anima* III.7 and NE VI-VII, between reason as aiming at action (practical reason) and reason as aiming at truth (theoretical reason). But he places ethics and political philosophy firmly within the sphere of practical reason. Even in the relatively austere domain of epistemology, Descartes wants us to revise drastically our whole understanding of how to acquire knowledge and to alter our practice as mathematicians and scientists accordingly. The prescriptive, practical impulse is as deeply rooted as any other in the philosophical tradition.

There is, however, a distinction to be drawn and also a real limitation to be recognised. The distinction is between the practical application of political philosophy and what one might term, more loosely, its political relevance. The practical application of political philosophy is a matter of methods or results being directly translated across to the realm of practical politics. Political relevance is a more oblique and circumspect matter. Rousseau's defence of direct, participatory democracy, for instance, under the highly special conditions of the *Social Contract*, in which all citizens contribute personally to collective decision-making without the use of representatives, might provide a stimulating model against which to measure the shortcomings of present-day mass politics. It is not that one need try or want to reproduce the political system that Rousseau recommends. But he enlarges one's horizon. The practical value of political philosophy may helpfully, then, be discussed under these two heads of application and relevance.

The limitation concerns the practical application of political philosophy, and it may be developed as follows.

8.1 The practical application of political philosophy

If we look to apply the methods and results of political philosophy directly to the realm of practical politics, a number of breaks and disanalogies present themselves.

First we may note two disanalogies of method (Galston, 1980: 43-4). The first is that a philosophical discussion – a dispute in political philosophy in our case – can be taken up, extended, put down, resumed, at will. (I have never quite been able to work out how long the discussion in Plato's *Republic* would actually take or whether anyone's philosophical stamina would sustain the uninterrupted play of argument.) If a conclusion eludes one in philosophy, that is all there is to be said for the time being – 'I must think more about it' is always an appropriate reply. Practical politics is quite different. Conclusions must be reached, not in the philosophical sense of satisfying one's mind on some point or other, but in the practical sense of making a binding decision on a public issue.

The second disanalogy is that a philosophical discussion is possible only on restricted conditions. Ideally one needs something like the situations of discourse set out in Plato's dialogues, where small groups analyse and argue (now haltingly, now flowingly) over some problem or range of topics. The university tutorial or seminar replicates this kind of discourse, with the interactive lecture as a diluted version of it. (Even this book creates a dialogue of sorts: I talk, you think and respond. It is just that I cannot hear your comments.) Such conditions, highly relevant to democratic discussion, are rare in practical politics. Even the Athenian Assembly with its active audience of hundreds, a paradigm example of face-to-face democracy, was much too large a forum for philosophically informed political discussion. Socrates, 'whose concern' (as David Rees reminds me) 'was above all with the individual respondent', stood outside, and discussed philosophy in the *agora*: and naturally the Athenians took their revenge.

Beyond these disanalogies of method, two crucial breaks occur between political philosophy and practical politics. The first concerns the 'results' of political philosophy, the practical application of such theories as a political philosopher might deliver. Though a philosophical theory will almost inevitably employ empirical assumptions, the translation of a political theory into prescriptions for practice will always involve empirical assumptions and practical insight beyond the professional competence of a philosopher. There are skills and circumstantialities of time and place, vital to the practical implementation of any policy (philosophically-inspired or otherwise), of which the philosopher has no knowledge. Could T.H. Green (1836-82), the Oxford philosopher who inspired many of the British welfare reforms of 1906-14, have drafted legislation, managed the parliamentary timetable, and so on?

The second break centres on the fact that different criteria are apt to be applied to the acceptance of philosophical theories and the adoption of public policies. Broadly one can say that philosophical theories are answerable to requirements of moral theory, truth, rationality, discourse theory, or reflective equilibrium (§§5.1-5.5). Even when, as regrettably happens, a theory is widely neglected because it runs counter to prevailing orthodoxies in philosophy, it generally receives impartial attention in some quarter or other of the philosophical community. Plans and proposals in practical politics, even those informed by philosophical theories, face obstacles and objections of a cruder order – hasty attention, prejudice, vested interests, and all the other intellectually sub-standard factors with which all politicians have to contend and to which some politicians contribute.

A deeper thought is due to Hegel. Just this: that in ethical and political matters, it is only when a way of life or form of culture has passed its peak that any lucidity of philosophical reflection on it is possible. Adequate philosophical reflection needs its object to have attained a state of full development. To be available for such reflection, it will either be on the point of decline or have already deteriorated. Hegel has a famous if gnomic remark: 'When philosophy paints its grey in grey, a shape of life has grown old, and it cannot be rejuvenated, but only recognized, by the grey in grey of philosophy; the owl of Minerva begins its flight only with the onset of the dusk' (PR, Preface: 23). The colour-language here means that theory and theorising, as second-order reflection, are 'grey' relative to the vitality and vividness of a thriving form of life. Only when vitality has begun to ebb in a declining form of life does philosophy (alias Minerva, goddess of wisdom) come into its own; the greyness of theory matches the greyness of an old and passing form of life. There is some truth in this. The most brilliant analysis of the *polis* came from Aristotle, who wrote in the *polis'* declining years. A whole theory of knowledge is involved in this Hegelian claim, and we cannot pursue it here. See further Findlay, 1958 passim. Nicholson, 1973 is of sharp general relevance.

8.2 The strange and the familiar

Part of the value of political philosophy comes from its historical range. The classic texts, which feature in any education in political philosophy, display a rich variety of political landscapes (§9.2). The late G.C. Field saw political philosophy's historical dimension as liberating:

> There is always a temptation to think of our own ideas at the present moment as repre-
> senting, so to speak, the natural order of events and the final culmination of the historical
> process, instead of being, as they are, merely a fleeting and transient stage in a continuous
> development. Some knowledge of history is a valuable corrective to this. On the one hand,
> by presenting us with a state of things in which ideas are taken for granted which seem
> strange and startling to us to-day, it helps us by contrast to become aware of what we are
> taking for granted ourselves and to realise that they are not self-evident truths but can be
> doubted and criticised. On the other, by showing us some ideas very similar to our own,
> appearing under very different historical conditions, it helps us to analyse our own ideas and
> to see which elements in them are purely the product of temporary conditions of the
> present-day and which are of more universal application (Field, 1963: 1).

8.3 The relevance of the impossible

Even when a political theory is utopian in the sense either that it could not be put into practice or that it is too far removed from mainstream politics to be adopted (for a more specialised sense of 'utopian' as, in Patrick Hemmer's apt phrase from an unpublished dissertation, 'depicting an imaginary society in order to project the ideal society', see §9.2), it can still be politically fruitful. For one thing, it can bring to light neglected problems or neglected aspects of problems. An example is Robert Nozick's defence of the minimal state in *Anarchy, State and Utopia* (1974). It is unlikely, leastwise for the foreseeable future, that any Western regime will slim itself down to the dimensions of the Nozickian state. But Nozick's stress on the 'historical' dimension of justice in property holdings, by which the justice of a distribution of wealth depends on how it has come about and not on whether it answers to some social ideal (§17.4), brought the ethics of redistribution into sharp focus.

Again, a political theory may open the door on conceptions that later enter practical politics, however idealistic or absurd they appear at the time. Two examples readily present themselves. The first is William Godwin's anarchism; the second is early French socialism. Godwin will come in for attention when we consider anarchism in its own right (§28). Horsburgh, 1958, and Macpherson, 1962: ch. 3 will repay study.

8.4 The vocabulary of politics

Political philosophy's contribution can also be more humdrum. There is a remark of Lord Keynes' that:

the ideas of economists and political philosophers, both when they are right and when they are wrong, are more powerful than is commonly understood. Indeed the world is ruled by little else. Practical men, who believe themselves to be quite exempt from any intellectual influences, are usually the slaves of some defunct economist. Madmen in authority, who hear voices in the air, are distilling their frenzy from some academic scribbler of a few years back (Keynes, 1964: 383).

Cases in point: every so often a cry arises about the need for 'a new social contract'. Or appeal is made to 'the rule of law'. Or proposals are castigated as 'liberal' by three-quarters of the British tabloid press. Whole theories, often misunderstood or misrepresented, lie behind such claims and phrases. These theories fall within the domain of political philosophy, where we attempt to deal accurately with them.

8.5 Political philosophy and personal praxis

We noted above some of the difficulties that beset and embarrass the direct practical application of political theories. One point concerned the empirical knowledge and practical insight which the philosopher, purely as such, may lack. But a different path to political relevance is open. This takes us into the Marxist notion of *praxis*, the unity of theory and practice. On this approach political philosophy is not a distinct discipline producing 'results' which are then available to inform practical politics. Instead of this external relationship between philosophy as inquiry and politics as activity, there is an internal relationship in the life of the politically active individual.

Praxis is a Greek word which Marx reintroduced and used in various senses (Lefebvre, 1965: 12-13). The sense relevant here is that of the interplay between knowing and acting. Marx rejected the possibility of purely theoretical knowledge. He saw praxis as a radical, indeed revolutionary, activity in which one has projects and commitments, tries to carry them out, hits empirical snags and conceptual confusions in the subsequent process of dealing with them and reworks one's projects and commitments, and so on, in an evolving cycle of theory-cum-practice. Political theory and practical politics are continuously interlocked in the life of the individual, as was clearly the case with Marx himself.

For some, political philosophy tumbles into a gap of disillusionment between political values and political practice. We all have our political heroes – Abraham Lincoln, Woodrow Wilson, Mahatma Gandhi and others. But these are unusual figures, and no particularly jaundiced view of politics is required to see careerism, the pressure of self-seeking lobbyists and special interest groups, sleaze and graft, even plain and simple evil, among the ingrained characteristics of political life. Yet the implications for political philosophy should be cautiously drawn. Cf. Nicholson, 1973.

In the first place, political philosophy is concerned with the conceptual no less than the normative. Political concepts stand in need of analysis, whatever our values. Political arguments about sovereignty, for instance, often need straightening out conceptually; political philosophy has its part to play in that process.

Secondly, the world of professional politics aside, there is no reason why we cannot as individuals get the right relation of values to practice at least in our own lives. We can form our own political views, views (say) about the proper scope and limits of state action, backed by general beliefs about the nature of human beings and society. These views can inform political practice, if only at the ballot box, on the protest march, or at the neighbourhood meeting. The shortcomings of professional politicians should not set the normative limits of politics.

Thirdly, normative considerations can have real negative force in many political situations. A policy or state of affairs, set up or kept going for whatever murky reasons of prejudice or self-interest, can be highly vulnerable to normative critique. This is the sphere of Habermas' 'ethics of discourse'. For instance, in the United States and Western Europe, under pressure of public debate – with the filtering out of considerations that cannot be openly appealed to in such debate and the necessary inclusion of considerations such as fairness – a policy that blatantly discriminates against some group or other will always have to be abandoned or modified in the end.

In fact the position is sociologically more complicated than this. A political culture (on which any political system runs) is a network of institutions and practices, beliefs and attitudes, from which the normative is never wholly absent and which ineluctably informs the motivation of politicians even at their most self-serving and cynical. The gap between values and practice is never a total chasm (T.H. Green, 1986: 89-106).

9. THE WAY IN TO POLITICAL PHILOSOPHY

A number of approaches – the analytic, the 'great books', the deconstructionist, and the topical issues approach – vie for our favour. Let us see what they have to offer and what their comparative merits might be.

9.1 The analytical approach

The analytical approach is the one developed so far in this chapter and in the rest of this book. Its main outlines should be clear by now. Instead of further exposition at this point, some contrasting approaches should set it usefully in sharper relief. We also need to consider the merits of the following three approaches:

- the 'great books' approach
- the deconstructionist challenge
- the topical issues approach

9.2 The classic texts – 'great books' – approach

There is a standard view that the best introduction to political philosophy is provided by its classic texts.

Full agreement is lacking on which texts have classic status. This only means that if we took a poll among teachers of political philosophy, not everyone's list would contain all the same texts. Still, some texts would appear on everyone's list. These are, in order of antiquity:

Plato (*c.* 429-347 BC) *Republic* (*c.* 375 BC)
Aristotle (384-322 BC) *Politics* (*c.* 325 BC) *Nicomachean Ethics*, Bk V (*c.* 330 BC)
Niccolò Machiavelli (1469-1527) *The Prince* (1513)
Thomas Hobbes (1588-1679) *Leviathan* (1651)
John Locke (1632-1704) *Second Treatise of Civil Government* (1690)
J.-J. Rousseau (1712-1778) *The Social Contract* (1762)
G.W.F. Hegel (1770-1831) *The Philosophy of Right* (1821)
John Stuart Mill (1806-1873) *On Liberty* (1859)

The list, modest enough to scan easily, is neither timeless nor immune from criticism. I once read a nineteenth-century critic who referred to an obscure writer, one Thomas Hobbes of Malmesbury, whose *Leviathan* was now lost to sight, 'like a whale disappearing from a Shetland "voe" [little bay] into the deep, with all the hooks and harpoons of his enemies along with him'. Writing much later A.E. Taylor, one of the finest philosophical scholars of the twentieth century, dismissed *Leviathan* in short order: 'a rhetorical and, in many ways, a popular *Schreitschrift* [polemic, journalistic rant]' (Taylor, 1965: 35). No political theorist has stepped so decisively from nineteenth-century obscurity into late twentieth-century prominence as Hobbes.

A poll conducted before the First World War would almost certainly have included in most lists Bernard Bosanquet's *The Philosophical Theory of the State* (1st ed., 1899); one before the Second World War, Harold Laski's *A Grammar of Politics* (1925). The Shetland fate has overtaken both.

Everyone has extra items. Some would add St Augustine's *The City of God* (*De Civitate Dei*, 413-426 AD), perhaps the deepest work of political theology ever written. But the relations of religion to politics are matters of past, no longer of present, concern to many in the West. There is no dust on my copy, but *The City of God* is no part of the working capital of most political philosophers.

John Rawls' *A Theory of Justice* (1972) and Robert Nozick's *Anarchy, State and Utopia* are modern classics; whether they will be longer-term classics remains to be seen.

Currently *The Federalist* (1787-1788) falls just outside the master class. It is a powerful plea, by Alexander Hamilton, James Madison and John Jay, for constitutional government under a separation of powers. It is important rather in its subtle and perceptive application of existing ideas, many deriving from Locke, to the novel circumstances of the emerging American republic, than for radical originality. But this claim is open to dispute. *The Federalist* would appear on many teachers' lists, as would Edmund Burke's *Reflections on the Revolution in France* (1790).

Disputes beyond the central range raise one point about the central texts. Another point is the fact that some political philosophers, whose work is vital for anyone in the subject to understand, produced no single text containing a full statement of their central or most characteristic views. Marx is probably the clearest case here: *The Communist Manifesto* (1848), a brisk, exhilarating pamphlet written with Friedrich Engels, offers only a polemical summary of some of Marx's main ideas at a certain stage of his thinking. To gain anything like the full measure of Marx we have to read much else besides (§31.1). Marx presents us not with a 'big book' but with a group of writings.

Jeremy Bentham (1748-1832) is a related but different case. Here again the material is dispersed but there is also the tantalising 'might have been' of treatises which have seen the light of day only in recent years – treatises which, with earlier publication, might have won classic status (see F. Rosen, 1996).

A further point to note about the classic texts is that, though some of them describe supposedly ideal forms of government and society – this is true, for instance, of Plato's *Republic*, Aristotle's *Politics*, and Rousseau's *Social Contract* – they are not, as literary productions, in one sense 'utopias'. The term 'utopia' was devised by Sir Thomas More (1478-1535), better known as the man who stood firm against Henry VIII on the issue of divorce and paid for it with his life. 'Utopia' means 'noplace' – and not, be it noted, 'ideal place', which would be more fittingly rendered '*eutopia*'. Admittedly, More's 1516 *Utopia* depicts the affairs of an imaginary people who are *supposedly* perfectly wise, secure, and happy, by virtue of the ideal institutions under which they live. But More adds some ironic touches to keep us guessing about just what he approves and what, in utopia, he ascribes to human folly.

Whatever More's intentions, however, and minus his irony, a utopia is now a projection, under the guise of some narrative description, of ideal politics and society. A utopia depicts 'an imaginary society in order to project the ideal society' as we noted earlier from Patrick Hemmer (§8.3). But, unlike (say) Plato's *Republic*, Aristotle's *Politics*, or Rousseau's *Social Contract*, it does so without any depth of argued connection with general beliefs about human beings, society, and the state. In Logan and Adams' phrase, a utopia is a 'fictional travelogue', not an argumentative construction (More, 1989: xviii). It is an image conjured to persuade or influence, perhaps even 'to picture the awful distance between the possible and the probable' (Shklar, 1966: 26), not a system of ideas meant rationally to convince by weight of argument.

To keep the scholarly record straight, however, there is a further sense of 'utopian' in which would-be practical publicists such as Gerrard Winstanley (1609-?1676), the Diggers' leader, and Charles Fourier (1772-1837) put forward detailed proposals for achieving an ideal society 'here and now'. None of these writers was engaged in spinning fictional travelogues. Though clearly over-optimistic, they all put forward systems of ideas meant rationally to convince by weight of argument. So far from evincing a sharp sense of Shklar's 'awful distance between the possible and the probable', they thought it a simple matter to transform society, once they could interest the right person or group with the right proportion of political or financial power.

Thus we note Winstanley's attempt to interest Cromwell in turning Commonwealth England into Winstanley's ideal society and Fourier's daily vigil for his expected philanthropic millionaire. 'No doubt they were wildly unrealistic,' as John Morrall has reminded me, 'but they did not see themselves as writers of imaginative fiction, rather as advocates of proposals of a starkly practical and topical nature, ripe for immediate implementation'. Marx was the first to use 'utopian' in this sense of the unrealistic. In his view 'utopian' socialism contrasted abruptly with his own 'scientific' socialism. Marx was sure he knew what was desirable (the removal of exploitation and alienation), and could track the path to its realistic achievement. For their part, the utopians could only fantasise and dream (see Marx & Engels, 1950: 86-142; Goodin & Pettit, 1995: 334-5, 337, 342, 345, 352).

At the least, utopias in either sense are clear guides to political discontents, indicating (as J.S. Mackenzie notes) 'the main defects that were felt to be present in the existing social order at particular times' (J.S. Mackenzie, 1918: 185). For instance, More's *Utopia* upbraids (diversely) the over-use of capital punishment and the practice of enclosure.

The master class of utopias as imaginary travelogues includes, besides More's *Utopia*, Tommaso Campanella's *City of the Sun* (1623), Francis Bacon's *New Atlantis* (1626), Samuel Gott's *New Jerusalem* (1648), Edward Bellamy's *Looking Backward* (1887), and William Morris' *News from Nowhere* (1890). A variant of the utopia is the dystopia, the depiction of the vividly undesirable, as for instance in George Orwell's *Nineteen Eighty-Four* (Orwell, 1949). On More, see the introductions to More, 1965 and 1989; also J. Coleman, 1990: ch. 4. More generally on utopian thought, follow up with Dahrendorff in PPS 2: 107 ff.; Galston, 1980: ch. 2; Goodin & Pettit, 1995: 46, 215, 245, 248, 251, 255, 323); Goodwin, 1982 (a spirited defence of the utopian tradition); Jowett, 1925: cccxvii-ccxxix; Manuel, 1973; Mosse, 1970: ch. 6; O'Sullivan, 1998. On Orwell see Symons, Ash, and Simecka in Mount, 1992; MacRae, 1961: 212.

Classic texts have cross-relationships. They form in fact, if not a continuous dialogue, at least a complex scheme of echoes and reflections. Aristotle answers Plato (among many differences note §20.4 on property); Hobbes denounces the entire Greek tradition ('there was never any thing so deerly bought, as these Western parts have bought the learning of the Greek and Latine tongues' (L ch. 21: 150)). A specific disputes centres on sovereignty and law (§14.6). Rousseau answers Hobbes slammingly on authority and power (§13.1). Hegel answers the whole political tradition before him, not least Plato on property (§20.4), while giving special praise to Rousseau for putting forward 'the will as the principle of the state' (PR §258: 277). Marx subverts Locke on property (§20.2.2) and claims to have turned the Hegelian dialectic rightside-up (§31.4.1). The cross-commentary is not always discerning or penetrating. If Rousseau scores palpable hits against Hobbes, Aristotle often misses Plato's drift in the *Republic* and never more so than in the case of Plato's irony, of which he seems supremely unaware.

The case for studying the classic texts is fourfold. In the first place, they remain vital presences in the subject. Current discussions of justice still use the Aristotelian distinction between distributive, corrective, and commutative justice (§17.2). Present-day theories of property still respond to Locke's account of the entitlement to acquire private property (§20.2). Few discussions of sovereignty omit to mention Hobbes. T.A. Sinclair explains why in his view this relevance continues:

> Broadly speaking the reasons are first, that the problems posed by ethical and political philosophy are not of a kind that can be solved once and for all and handed on to posterity as so much accomplished; and second, that the problems are still the same problems at bottom, however much appearances and circumstances may have altered in twenty-three centuries. How can men live together? ... How in particular can top-dog and under-dog be made to live together? ... How perennial are the problems of government and how little they have changed are indeed all too clear (Sinclair in Aristotle, 1981: 18; cf. §14.5 contra Collingwood).

Secondly, and contrastively, 'the dead open the eyes of the living'. The classic texts bring us face to face with assumptions, ideas, and arguments markedly different from our own. This liberates us from the mind-set of what we have never questioned. That democracy might be a rather poor option for government is hardly a viewpoint readily available in late twentieth-century political thought. But if we turn to Plato, we find this icon of the present age dismissed as only one rung above the worst possible form of government. Only outright one-person tyranny has a lower score (R VIII-IX; cf. Hegel, PR Preface: 20; Haddock in Forsyth et al., 1993: 117). Plato's *Republic* breaks explosively on the modern reader, like thunder on a clear summer afternoon.

Thirdly, the hallmark of a classic text is that it presents new facets to successive generations. The classic texts have a teeming, inexhaustible suggestiveness; there are always 'fresh lights from the ancient monuments', with one idea or argument emerging after another as if they had stepped into existence of themselves to address new concerns.

Fourthly, the classic texts are impossible to read in an easy, unpuzzled frame of mind. Their coherence is always incomplete. They have their fair share of ideas that are hard to make out precisely. There are problems about how far the author realises the implications of particular arguments. Sometimes a text represents a particular stage in the development of a thinker's politics, or the political facet of the thinker's much wider philosophical system, where the relation to other stages or to the wider system is not fully clear. Grappling with such difficulties is widely seen as bracing intellectual exercise for students and teachers alike.

My view is that an education in political philosophy cannot dispense with the classic texts, but should not be led by them. I have two grounds for this view.

First, though the classic texts are genuinely philosophical, they are generally much besides. We find, not just conceptual analysis, high level theorising and the investigation of aporias, but also judgements of empirical fact (psychological, sociological, economic, scientific) and estimates of probability together with personal valuations and predilections below the level of philosophy. W.J.M. Mackenzie once dryly remarked, in the light of this indiscriminate mingling of diverse material, that the classic texts would not satisfy the examiners in the work of a Ph.D. student (W.J.M. Mackenzie, 1967: 53). Whatever the case, the classic texts (cover to cover) are not now paradigmatic philosophy. This is an important, in fact a disabling, consideration if they are to be made anyone's entry-point into political philosophy.

Secondly, the classic texts are presentationally daunting to the beginning student in philosophy. A reader who expects the classic texts to queue up their points neatly in precise lines of argument, might as well expect the return of the Dodo. Argument is the lifeblood of philosophy (Hamlyn, 1984: 271), but the structure of argument is often perplexingly obscure in the classic texts, for all their frequent strikingness of literary style. David Keyt's remarks on Aristotle's *Politics* can be generalised:

> It is not always clear where in the text a particular argument begins or ends. Nor is it always clear what a particular argument is meant to establish. Important premises are presupposed. Those that are furnished are at crucial spots loosely expressed. The order of steps is often unclear (Keyt, 1987: 65).

This exactly states my experience as student and teacher. It is also the view of an expert in the analysis of philosophical argument, Alec Fisher (see Fisher, 1993).

This obscurity of argumentative structure has perhaps two main sources. One is that the classic texts all use informal arguments. The other is that they have an 'element of particularity', not least the need to persuade a contemporary readership (Oakeshott, 1991: 227). The most effective manner of persuasion for a contemporary readership is not always the most perspicuous order of logic for a later generation. In my view, the first experience in understanding and analysing arguments is better gained from less vexing models.

To move the classic texts from centre-stage in the introduction to political philosophy is (to repeat) not to section them off altogether beyond some *cordon sanitaire*. On many topics we will turn to the classic texts. It is not a question of whether we should use them, but of how best to do so.

Aside from this matter of giving the classic texts a secondary rather than a central role in the introduction to political philosophy, there is a different though related question about the manner in which they should be studied. Three approaches to the interpretation of texts in the history of philosophy may be distinguished:

- rational reconstruction
- historical reconstruction
- deconstruction

9.2.1 Rational reconstruction

The idea of rational reconstruction is essentially that of 'revising' a text, rejecting or amending some of its premises, adding assumptions, deducing implications, exposing presuppositions. and so on, beyond anything that we find in the original. All this is done in the interests of rendering the text a contribution to current philosophical debate.

Here is how it might go. A rational reconstructionist, scanning Hobbes' *Leviathan*, will see the essential logical form of the main political argument: given certain fixed features of human nature, Hobbes tells us, the social situation will inherently tend, in the absence of a supreme coercive power, towards a 'state of nature', a condition of violence, distrust and general lack of co-operation. A supreme coercive power (a political unit with the ability to quell all opposition and ensure compliance) is overridingly to be recommended to regulate interpersonal behaviour as a safeguard against this appalling condition.

The rational reconstructionist will wonder: no matter what Hobbes thought, does his argument need total selfishness or will it go through on an assumption merely of predominent self-interest? Can Hobbes' argument be released from its political frame to suggest a general, game-theoretic problem of rational choice? A 'game' is any situation in which rational decisions are interpersonally interdependent. The problem is that even if great mutual gains would come from regular co-operation, those gains will not result if players cannot trust one another to co-operate consistently. It is rational to seek the benefits of co-operation, but not rational to co-operate consistently when others cannot be relied upon to reciprocate. Hobbes' sovereign is only one device – a shared morality might be another – by which to secure the benefits of reliable co-operation. See Hollis, 1985: ch. 8; Kavka, 1985 passim.

There is no good reason for it, but some suppose a constraint on rational reconstruction to be whether Hobbes, or whoever, could have been brought to accept this reworking of his ideas. Richard Rorty talks of rational reconstructions as 'conversations with the great re-educated dead' (Rorty, 1984: 51; cf. Janaway, 1988).

9.2.2 Historical reconstruction

Historical reconstruction is particularly, though not exclusively, associated with the methodology of Quentin Skinner (b. 1940), the Cambridge intellectual historian. It involves a two-stage process:

- to discover the questions which a text is trying to answer within a tradition (or confluence of traditions) of discourse
- to identify the answers it provides

As a control on both stages of the process, Skinner recognises a need to keep within 'the range of descriptions which the agent [the author] himself could at least in principle have applied to describe and classify what he was doing' (Skinner, 1969: 28).

To take up again the example of Hobbes: Hobbes' questions in *Leviathan* would be (e.g.) how to deal with 'the disorders of the present time' (L: 491) – how to avoid a repeat of the breakdown of social peace that occurred in the seventeenth-century English civil war and, also relevant, the sixteenth-century French wars of religion. And he was writing within a variety of traditions, not least the Galilean scientific tradition. How, he wanted ot know, can we apply Galilean science to the analysis of society? And how – Hobbes discovered geometry late in life – can we bring the rigour of Euclidean geometry to political argument?

There are plainly problems about Skinner's qualification, 'at least in principle'. Does it confine us to using only descriptions, in discovering Hobbes' questions and answers, that Hobbes himself was actually familiar with? But if we go beyond this range, how far can we exceed it? What limitation does 'in principle' impose?

On Skinner, see Parekh & Berki, 1973; Minogue, 1981. With Skinner on question and answer, compare Collingwood, 1939: ch. 5. For a related methodology to Skinner's, see references to Pocock in §4.5. See also Ayers, 1978.

9.2.3 Deconstruction

The 'great books' approach is open to another style of critique, and one about which we need to be cautious. I refer to deconstruction.

Deconstruction, mainly associated with the name of Jacques Derrida (b. 1930), is a body of ideas and an activity. The activity of deconstruction is applied to the classic texts and in fact to all forms of writing, not only in political philosophy. As a body of ideas, deconstruction has exerted more influence in language and literature than in philosophy departments in the UK and USA.

This philosophical disregard is perhaps to be explained in two ways. First, deconstruction is a doctrine in the philosophy of language, but it is so remote in its terminology from the standard analytical approaches to language, in the work of Quine, Davidson, Dummett and Chomsky, that it seems alienly intrusive, rather as an out-of-doors heckler might sound to the members of a closed meeting in an inner room. Secondly, Derrida appears to be making, exaggeratedly, points about meaning that we already have in more plausible forms. His standing among Anglo-American philosophers is also not helped by the fey, allusive quality of his responses to criticisms.

Derrida constructs an elaborate framework of new terminology – the metaphysics of presence, logocentrism, *différance*, and a whole variety of others terms with which any reader of his work rapidly becomes (usually rather bemusedly) familiar. Perhaps the key notion, the guide to the labyrinth, is that of the metaphysics of presence.

This is the idea that we confront a world of separate objects and events, all of which have determinate essential natures about which we can have clear and distinct concepts, which in turn confer firm, determinate meanings on the corresponding words. 'Logocentrism' is Derrida's term for the matching faith in truth and reasoning and in the possibility of an ideal language free from the truth-deflecting shortcomings of ordinary language – shortcomings of ambiguity, metaphor and the rest. Thought and language can represent the world transparently; in this sense the world can be 'present' in thought and language.

The repeated 'can's' are important here. Few, if any, philosophers in the Western tradition have supposed themselves or anyone else to be in actual possession of any such language. But, Derrida would reply, the ideal persists and is delusive; moreover the practice of philosophical commentary on classic texts is typically the search for firm, determinate – indeed, single objective – meanings.

What account of thought and language is to replace logocentrism? Here we encounter Derrida's idea of *différance*.

For Derrida, the words of a language form an endlessly complicated system of mutual relationships. Each word takes its meaning from its contrast with every other word; for every other word is rejected when we use the particular word that we do. Every word has, therefore, a contrastive meaning conferred by the entire remainder of the language. Its individual meaning is 'deferred', not ascertainable, until the whole set of contrasts is in hand.

When we add that the language is constantly changing and that (mind-spinningly) the meaning of the particular word in question is itself a part of the contrastive meanings of the other words whose meanings define its own, any notion of fixing the determinate meaning of a word is a lost cause.

Applied to the classic texts, this line of argument is seen by deconstructionists as having an important implication. Scholars and commentators are taken to assume that the sentences of a text have determinate, ascertainable meanings or (at the minimum) limited ambiguities, and that there is a single, coherent, and correct interpretation of the text as a whole in the light of these meanings. 'A deconstruction, then, shows the text resolutely refusing to offer any privileged reading. [D]econstructive criticism clearly transgresses the limits established by traditional criticism' (Leitch, 1979: 24-5; cited in Ellis, 1989: 69). Even the author has no authority. Owing to *différance* (a Derridean neologism to convey indefinite contrastiveness and the consequent endless deferral of meaning (C. Norris, 1987: 15)) the author has no more insight into the limitless network of contrastive meanings than has his or her reader. Any main argument that we might think we have identified can be shown to be contradicted, in the ceaseless instability and incompleteness of meanings, by other elements in the text. (Note carefully that if Derrida rejects the idea of a single, coherent, and correct reading of the text, this does not commit him to the idea that simply any reading is as good as any other.)

In illustration we can return to Hobbes. The political portion of *Leviathan* recommends that on grounds of self-interest we set up or support a supreme coercive power, autocratic and irremovable, the mere existence of which, provided it ensures the conditions for civil peace, creates (for reasons that Hobbes gives) a moral obligation of obedience. The Derridean response to this interpretative claim might be that elements of the text of *Leviathan* subvert the consistency of this recommendation. Hobbes' autocratic politics is overlaid by concessions to a different, more liberal style of political thinking. There is his stress on consent, for instance, which draws consent even from extreme situations of 'your obedience or your life' engineered by a conqueror (L: 485); it is worth noting also Hobbes' allowance that there is no obligation to obey a law which threatens one's life (L ch. 27: 208).

I offer two comments. To begin, there is every plausibility in Derrida's claim that texts are imperfectly consistent and host recalcitrant elements that mar the coherence of the whole. It is another matter whether the reason for this is the one that Derrida offers, namely indefinite contrastiveness and the endless deferral of meaning. It might equally be that politics – to keep just to political texts – is a realm of incommensurable values (§30.5) which any morally sensitive thinker will try to accommodate.

Secondly, if meanings were subject to *différance* and endless deferral in the radical way Derrida suggests, however, language as a means of even approximate communication would be unlearnable. Reference to Wittgenstein's anti-private language argument is germane. Wittgenstein stresses how the idea of a purely private language runs into insuperable difficulties. Rules, (that is) some kinds of lawlike regularities, are essential to language. But rules are impossible unless we have in principle some means of determining whether the rule has really been followed – whether, for instance, a word really is being used in the same way on two occasions. A private language-user could have no means in principle of determining whether she really has used the same word in the same way on two occasions as opposed to merely seeming to herself to have done so (Wittgenstein, 1953, I: §§1.243-315, 348-412; O'Hear, 1985: 31).

An inseparably public dimension of language thus emerges. Without a large measure of interpersonal agreement on what counts as the same use of a word by different speakers or writers, e.g. to refer to the same object or event, the requisite lawlike regularities are missing. But there precisely is such agreement in any language-community; we do communicate through words that have enough commonality of meaning between different language-users for this to be possible. Derrida's sceptical onslaught invokes a spectre of endless deferral that is wholly unreal.

For a further look at the anti-private language argument, see Wittgenstein, 1953: I. §§256-79. On Derrida's distinctive ideas, try (contra) Ellis, 1989, Murdoch, 1992: ch. 7; Nuyen, 1993, Teichman, 1993 and Verges, 1992; (broadly, discriminatingly or totally pro) Dews, 1987: ch. 1 & 3, Leitch, 1979 and C. Norris, 1985 & 1987. Rowe, 1992, on the intellectual validity of textual commentary, is important. Derrida speaks perhaps most cogently for himself in Derrida, 1976.

My attitude to the other two approaches is that, while the historian can dispense with rational reconstruction as irrelevant to his or her inquiries, the rational reconstructionist cannot sensibly avoid historical reconstruction. This is for the simple reason, urged by Skinner, that if we are looking for contributions to current debate, we can underrate or misconstrue those contributions if we fail to look closely – contextually – at the precise questions a text is trying to answer; we can look closely only through the lens of history. A practical example will emerge in chapter 4. Many commentators too easily tie John Stuart Mill up in knots over his account of harm in connection with the 'liberty principle' (§22.8.1). Because they do not take this account contextually, they miss his full contribution to current debate.

9.3 The topical issues approach

Reviewing *Life's Dominion*, by Ronald Dworkin, Richard Norman praises a particular way of doing moral and political philosophy:

> Dworkin describes it as an example of 'philosophy from the inside out'. Rather than formulating a general philosophical theory and then 'applying' it to specific practical issues, the book proceeds in the opposite direction, starting with the concrete problems, trying to make sense of them and working out the theoretical positions which enable us to do so (R. Norman, 1996: 43).

This direction of inquiry is not special to Dworkin. Nearly all the classic authors have taken the same route. Hobbes (see §9.2.2) wrote against the background of the English Civil War and the French Wars of Religion – 'the disorders of the present time' (L: 491). The failure of civil peace was his 'specific practical issue' or 'concrete problem'. He evolved a political theory that, in his view, shows the inescapable precondition for such peace – namely, the installation of a sovereign, blending supreme power and supreme authority. Again, Burke (1729-97) was alarmed by the French Revolution and the contagion of its example in England. The revolutionaries seemed to him to misunderstand totally the nature of political society and his 'concrete problem' was to check their influence. *Reflections on the Revolution in France* contains the theoretical position he worked out as a counter-measure. And so the examples could go on.

Norman recommends the 'from the outside in' approach as a way of doing philosophy, not necessarily as a way of introducing newcomers to the subject. But this last idea is worth considering. In my view there are three main points against it.

In the first place, there is a false contrast between 'theory' and 'problem'. The very definition of a problem always assumes a level of theory. Put another way: there is only a problem on the basis of certain assumptions. Assumptions are theoretical.

Secondly, concrete problems and specific practical issues are packed round with factual, often technical, considerations. If our problem or issue were, say, the United Kingdom's continued membership of the European Union (and anyone can see how I am making assumptions in the very act of defining it as a 'problem'), then indeed the full probing of this issue could well produce an elaborate political theory. But the relevant military, economic, and legal considerations would entangle the inquiry at an early stage. 'So be it', may be the response. But the slowness and difficulty of introducing political philosophy in this way are obvious.

Thirdly, the topical issue, or 'from the inside out', approach is right for someone confronting an issue of serious personal interest, to which they have to work out a theoretical response. This does happen to students, and it should be encouraged. No one who has taught political philosophy needs to be told how particular problems, unpredictably variable from one person to another, capture the imagination and exercise the ingenuity of students. But this could not be the whole of one's engagement with a subject as a beginner. Finding one's way into political philosophy means discovering the state of the subject – the concepts that are analysed, the theories that are going the rounds, and the quandaries that are matters of active debate.

A variation on the topical issues approach takes the line that such issues are only contemporary versions and specific applications of perennial or at any rate highly general problems of politics and hence of 'the' basic problems of political philosophy. Should there be a state? If so, what should the ends and limits of state action be? If so, again, what should be the proper form of the state? That there are such problems, and that introductions to the subject should be organised around them, is the standard assumption of legions of books on political philosophy. We have already glanced at the 'perennial problems' idea in T.A. Sinclair (§9.2).

I do not claim that the problems approach, pursued by many writers, is wrong. This book, no less than any other, discusses the highly general problems just mentioned. The main question is how the book should be organised with regard to them. My approach is to red-circle a number of concepts which have been central to normative political discourse since the seventeenth century and in some, many or all cases earlier (depending on one's response to the table on p. 35). These twelve concepts are the conceptual pack of cards which we endlessly cut and re-deal in the course of political disputes; they are our basic 'vocabulary of politics' (Weldon, 1953). Around these concepts, to vary the metaphor, an intricate web of analyses, theories, and aporias, has been woven. Only within this web can 'the problems of political philosophy' be identified. Part of the web will be lifted out and presented in the chapters that follow.

10. PLAN OF THE BOOK

In 7.1 we identified the twelve central political concepts just mentioned:

- power
- authority
- state
- sovereignty
- law
- justice
- equality
- rights
- property
- freedom
- democracy
- the public interest

The whole book could be devoted to unravelling the complicated webs of relationship between these concepts. The central political concepts are all inter-connected. Just to tug on a part of the thread, take property: if I own property then I have a right to a particular kind of freedom, the freedom (within limits) to use or consume certain objects as I wish. But if property has been improperly acquired, may not a substantial redistribution of property be a requirement of justice? Property is protected by law: and law is answerable to the public interest or common good. And so we could go on. (All sound teachers of political philosophy should be able to permute any central political concept, taken at random, with five others.)

As the book is organised, the twelve concepts are put in groups, with one chapter for each group:

- power, authority, state, sovereignty, law
- justice, equality, rights, property
- freedom, democracy, and the public interest

Concepts can be grouped together on a variety of bases. The simplest is that of definitional overlap. For instance, in epistemology one might group the concepts of knowledge, belief, and truth on the assumption that belief and truth enter into the definition of knowledge. I cannot know something unless I believe it; I cannot know something unless my belief is true. On our political list this kind of internal relationship holds together power, authority, state, sovereignty, and law.

Another basis for clustering is external; it applies where concepts are connected through a high-level theory. For instance, Nozick argues that the pursuit of equality is incompatible with freedom. An equal distribution of goods is a 'patterned' distribution, one in which society show up a pattern of equality, and 'liberty upsets patterns' (ASU: 160). Clustering is a form of connective analysis (§3.5.4).

My groupings respect and reflect both bases for clustering. Beyond that brief indication, it would be long-winded and not particularly helpful at this stage to explain in detail why the concepts are clustered in the way they are. The rationale will emerge *en route*. If at the end you decide that the concepts would better have been grouped differently, or not at all (in an unordered list), this will be a fine self-educative step in political philosophy.

Each of the chapters 2-4 goes through conceptual analysis, high-level theorising, and the probing of aporias, with the focus falling on particular concepts and some cross-connections between them.

Chapter 5, which represents a shift of gear, is concerned with ideologies, extremely high-level theories which prioritise or downgrade particular political concepts, analyse and theorise them in particular ways, and negotiate aporias accordingly.

It would not be plausible to suggest that the book strikes no ideological notes before the final chapter. For instance, John Stuart Mill's liberty principle (§22.8) is a product of liberal political theory; the enforcement of morality (§15.5.2) is more typical of conservative political theory than of liberal or socialist. At least the final chapter will alert you to how innocent-seeming discussions, interesting in their own right, carry ideological echoes.

An Endnote looks back over the ground covered and suggests some directions for future study.

One consequence of splitting the discussion across the twelve concepts is that issues tied to other, less focal concepts are dealt with piecemeal. Take the concept of the market, which impinges on political philosophy at five points. The first is the issue between state socialists and economists such as F.A. Hayek over the relative efficiency of centrally planned and market economies (§31.4). The second concerns the likely extent of market failure in the case of so-called 'public goods' and the consequent need for state provision (§13.2). The third is the relation of the market to economic justice, a problematic connection because the market responds to effective demand, not needs: 'If you can't afford it, you can't have it' (§31.4). The fourth is the increasing sway of the market as a model for all social relationships and institutions; this has been an area of worry to communitarians, who stress the need for the market to be 'embedded' in a network of non-market relationships (§29.5). The fifth is the application of the market model to the institution of free speech, interpreting free speech in terms of a free market for ideas (§22.8). Strictly, this last point is a particular application of the fourth.

It would have been neat to handle all five issues in a single stretch of text, but a degree of dispersal has proved necessary.

2. Power, Authority, Sovereignty, Law, and the State

11. INTRODUCTION

This chapter centres on five concepts – those of power, authority, sovereignty, law, and the state. Power is a plausible starting-point for any discussion of politics. This is not to say that power is the only thing that politics is about. Nor is it to equate power with military might, as in Stalin's exclusion of the Pope from the peace negotiations in 1945 with the question: 'How many divisions has Pius XII?' 'Signor Stalin will meet my legions in the other world', commented Papa Pacelli (1876-1958; *Pontifex Maximus*, 1939-58) when the story reached him.

But power is ineliminable from politics; between power and this chapter's other concepts the links quickly multiply. There may be in a political system an ultimate decision-maker, a supreme coercive power. Yet this power might be exercised without authority, without any entitlement to command. When the ideas of power and authority are put together then, to a first approximation, we have the concept of sovereignty. But then, sovereignty is widely seen as an essential attribute of the state, though the logical relationship between the two concepts is by no means simple. Law is often joined to the idea of sovereignty; on one theory law is the command of the sovereign; the law is a major medium of state action.

In examining these concepts and ideas we will engage in, and see others conduct, the three typical philosophical activities of conceptual analysis, high level theorising, and aporia-tackling.

12. POWER

Power readily appears a vividly glamorous or a sinister concept. 'Power', said Henry Kissinger, 'is the great aphrodisiac.' 'I find a priest more powerful than I', observed Napoleon, 'for he reigns over minds, while I rule over matter.' We hear of 'power politics' and the disregard of all morality, perhaps with Nietzsche's idea of 'the will to power' (*der Wille zur Macht*) in the background. 'I have twice been given the power', said Papa Doc (Dr François Duvalier, dictator of Haiti, 1957-71). 'I have taken it, and, damn it, I will keep it forever.' 'Who whom?' asked Lenin (1870-1924): who has power over whom? This, for him, was the central question of politics. Its sanguinary edge was felt by those who willingly exchanged the Tsar for Alexander Kerensky (1881-1970), and lived unwillingly to exchange Kerensky for Lenin. Many know, if few quote correctly, Lord Acton's 1887 dictum: 'Power tends to corrupt and absolute power corrupts absolutely.' Plato is aware of the danger – see especially R IX.576B: 397-8 – but believes it will be overcome if the rulers are philosophers who are guided by their knowledge of the Good, and are saved from the corruptions of power by their preference for the life of contemplation. Last word to George Bernard Shaw: 'Power does not corrupt men. Fools, however, if they get in a position of power, corrupt power' (Safire, 1972: 520). Power – an aura, fascinating or repelling, envelopes the subject.

The plan of the discussion is as follows. We will check out some basic conceptual analysis, first with Robert Dahl, then with Bertrand Russell. Next we will take in some conventional theories of power, looking initially at Dahl's theory as criticised by Bacharach and Baratz, then at that of Steven Lukes. Finally the doctrine of the separation of powers will supply our aporia.

12.1 Basic distinctions

The first analytical move is easy enough. Power is a relational concept. At least two terms are citable in a power relationship: 'A has power over B.' 'A' might be a person and 'B' an inanimate object but, in the understanding of power central to politics, 'A' and 'B' are persons, classes, societies, nations, states and the like. Power relationships are inter-personal, and human power over the non-human world (all too real and disturbing in many ways) is not the prime focus of conceptual analysis.

We can quickly move on to the parameters of power. The American political scientist Robert Dahl has identified five of these – five constituents of the power relationship (Dahl, 1965: 375-6; Harsanyi, 1965: 379):

- the *base* of power (the type of resources available in the form of economic assets, constitutional prerogatives, public esteem, military forces and so on)
- the *means* of power (the instrumentalities through which these resources can be exerted – force and coercion, promises, threats, public appeals and the rest)
- the *scope* of power (the set of actions that a person with power can get others to do)
- the *amount* of power (in respect of action X, the net increase in the probability of B's doing x resulting from A's using his/her means of power against B)
- the *extension* of power (the range of individuals or groups over whom A has power

But what is the power relationship itself in general terms? In this section I first consider Bertrand Russell's analysis, then (recognising that the line between concept analysis and high-level theorising is particularly thin in the case of power) I treat the main conventional analyses under the heading of theory – those of Robert Dahl and Steven Lukes. Foucault's theory of power is considered separately in §14.6.2 as implicating the ideas of authority and sovereignty.

First, then, I take Russell whose analysis of power is expressed in the formula: 'power is the production of intended effects' (Russell, 1938: 35; Lukes, ed., 1986: 18). This is a wide definition, one that brings within the ambit of power all our dealings with the external world. It has no special reference to inter-personal relationships. We can create that reference for ourselves by glossing the definition just slightly. In inter-personal relationships, Russell's definition means something like the following: 'A has power over B when A produces certain intentional effects in B's behaviour'. The reference to 'behaviour' renders the definition politically more apt. Russellian power could be the production of effects in somebody's personality, character, imaginative capacity, and so forth. But the stress on behaviour is a politically useful focus.

Three comments immediately press. In the first place, surely we should stretch the modality of Russell's definition. 'Modality' is a philosophers' term for talking about what is actually, possibly or necessarily the case. A has power over B if A can, regardless of whether A actually does, produce intentional effects in B's behaviour. There is no reason for Russell to reject this amendment and we can regard it from now on as part of the definition. Secondly, what is the operative notion of 'intentional'? Suppose we try the following:

A produced an intentional effect E in B's behaviour if (sufficient condition):

1. A produced effect E
2. A was aware that he or she was producing (or was likely to produce) this effect
3. A wanted to produce this effect
4. A produced effect E because he or she wanted to.

Philosophers of mind would have much more to say about the nature of intentional action, but conditions 1-4 will fix the concept to a first approximation (see further Beardsley, 1978). What now of 'effects'? Are 'effects' the same as 'consequences' and 'results'? In an act of crass buffoonery, and wearing a mask of terrifying aspect, I lunge out of the shadows at someone, C, at a party. C starts to shake, tremble, and faint. These occurrences are effects produced by my action. The result of my action is that C is badly frightened: results are not effects. The consequence of my action is that C, annoyed by the turn of events, decides on an early night, leaves the party at 21.00 hours and confides appalling thoughts about me to her diary. I directly produced the effects I did; I did not and could not directly produce the consequences, which were mediated by C's decision-making.

There is no likelihood that the ordinary use of 'effect', 'result', and 'consequence' exactly matches these distinctions, which is bad news for Vendler, 1967. But the distinctions themselves are significant; Russell's definition of power can readily be extended to include them. If, with regard to your behaviour, I can produce certain effects, bring about certain results, and render certain consequences likely, then I have Russellian power in these respects.

There remains a problem. Why should we accept a restriction to 'intended' effects, results, and consequences? Is intention necessary for power? When I produce these things, even if they are unintentionally brought about and are in fact quite unknown to me, I have some kind of power. I may bring about significant changes in other people's circumstances and behaviour. Intentionality hardly makes a difference to the fact of power.

12.2 Conventional theories of power

We have now tampered with Russell's analysis extensively. We have revised its modality. We have cut out the reference to intention. We have introduced a reference to behaviour. Let us make a fresh start with Dahl's account of the nature of power, which accommodates all these changes. In Dahl's view:

'A has power over B to the extent that he can get B to do something that B would not otherwise do' (Dahl, 1965: 374; Lukes, ed., 1986: 2).

Questions quickly arise. First, how are we to take the idea of doing something one would not otherwise do? Does it include reference not only to the action one does but also to the way in which one does it? If I can get you to run down the street rather than gently stroll, but I cannot alter the fact that you go down the street because you want to, is this a case of power? Lukes raises this point. It is a fair question but not a crucially disabling one. Dahl might simply say 'yes' without embarrassment to his analysis.

Secondly, if you are planning to go to Italy and, by the deftness of my practical reasoning, I persuade you to go to India instead, I alter your behaviour and get you to do something you otherwise would not do, but does this mean that I thereby exercise power over you? Lukes regards it as a defect of Dahl's definition that it 'lets in' examples of this sort (Lukes, ed., 1986: 2). It is but fair to add that Dahl sees conflicts of interests as typical of power relationships, and as the key to the practical relevance of the concept of power. (Dahl construes interests as the satisfaction of wants and preferences, which he takes as given. Lukes, as we will shortly see, is more interested in the origin of wants and preferences.) By this secondary criterion, the practical reasoning example does not count as an exercise of power if I am giving you good advice. Equally, however, as anyone knows who has read Nietzsche's critique of Socrates in *Twilight of the Idols*, a hectoring use of reasoning can be all too clear an exercise of power. So there will be times when we will want to let in precisely such examples, and Dahl is right not to exclude them.

So Dahl's definition is not false in the sense of having nothing to tell us about power, but it is widely regarded as inadequate. The main point, first made in Bachrach & Baratz, 1962 and 1970, is that it is too agent-centred and neglectful of the context of decision-making. In your decision-making, if I can get you to do X rather than Y when left to yourself you would have done Y, this is an exercise of power. Dahl focuses solely on (overt) decisions to do what you otherwise would not; for this reason his analysis has been called one-dimensional and decisionist.

Plausibly, however, power is also involved if I can remove Z from your agenda, so that Z never even enters into your deliberations. This is commonly called a two-dimensional approach to the analysis of power, because it includes non-decisions (matters that can be effectively kept from the political and social agenda) as well as decisions to do actions that one otherwise would not. This plainly has implications for the range of issues included in the public realm (§2.5). The Bachrach and Baratz position is more commonly and aptly known as 'non-decisionalism'.

Steven Lukes takes the contextual approach further in his three-dimensional analysis (Lukes, 1976). Power means not only getting people to do actions which, in the light of their wants and preferences, they otherwise would not; not only preventing certain wants and preferences from featuring in the collective decision-making process. There is a third dimension in the ability to condition and manipulate the processes by which wants and preferences are formed and consequently the way in which people understand their interests. Suppose you decide to do X rather than Y. Suppose further that your preference for X is something that I have managed to shape or influence? It is then not a question of my here and now intervening in the decision-making process and getting you to do what you otherwise would not, and choose X rather than Y. Nor is it a matter of my having kept certain potential choices (W and Z) from the agenda. Rather I can let things take their course, because I have already brought it about that you prefer X.

Lukes calls his analysis of power a 'radical view' because the full account of the determination and inducement of preferences takes us through a story about class structure and through a left-centre critique of social practices.

The main criticism which Lukes' analysis has attracted is the following. If actual preferences have behind them the manipulative or distortive origins that Lukes says they have, what should be put in place of, and override, such preferences? Lukes appeals to the idea of people's real interests. Identification of these interests depends on a substantive theory of the good (§13.3.2), a view of human flourishing specifying ways of living rightly and living well – a view itself dependent on some notion of a 'human essence', a common human nature by virtue of which human beings as a natural kind have shared and distinctive conditions of well-being. But huge difficulties attend any attempt to vindicate any particular such view (Hay, 1997: 47-8 with reply by Doyle, 1998; Benton,

1981). So any specific demonstration of the three-dimensional view remains 'not proven' (cf. §24.1 on real interests as informing the public interest).

See further Lukes, ed., 1986 and the excellent conspectus of ideas and issues in Hay, 1997.

12.3 The separation of powers

The 'powers' in question are the three central powers or functions of government highlighted in §2.5:

* legislative
* executive
* judicial

There is a rooted, normative idea in the history of political thought that the separation of powers, in the sense of the parcelling out of these functions between distinct organs and personnel, is a necessary safeguard against tyranny (the arbitrary engrossment of one such function, and of those who exercise it, over the others) and also against what the writers of *The Federalist* called the sway of 'faction' (the domination of a bare majority, lobby or special interest group, in some stampede of opinion or insidious exercise of pressure, over all three functions). But the notion proves more problematic than first appears.

One clarification: as normally understood, 'executive' covers not only the top-level planning function of §2.5 but also what we there picked out as the administrative function and the apparatus of coercive power. Essentially, the legislature makes laws which represent policy choices for the public realm; the executive carries them out; the judiciary pronounces on violations of them and disputes concerning them.

That a political system includes three such powers was recognised by Aristotle in P IV.14: 102. And the recommendation, the normative idea, of a separation of powers is present in Locke, ST, ch. 12-13: 364-74, who stresses the separation of the legislative and executive powers with a view to the protection of individual rights to life, liberty and property (ST, §§143-4: 364-5). But Locke includes the judicial in the executive power (ST, §153: 369-70); he artificially distinguishes as a separate function a 'federative' power, essentially the responsibility for foreign policy and war (ST, §146: 365), which is properly part-legislative and part-executive. Locke also exempts a chunk of executive activity from legislative control as 'prerogative': 'the good of the Society requires, that several things should be left to the discretion of him, that has the Executive Power' (ST, §159: 374).

Setting aside Locke's account, along with the dark and distantly anticipatory remarks of Polybius in book 6 of his *Histories of Greece and Rome* (Adcock, 1964: 44-7), we may note that Montesquieu (Charles-Louis de Secondat, Baron de Montesquieu, 1689-1755), gave the doctrine of the separation of powers its first recognisably modern expression in his *Spirit of the Laws* (1748). This book, beneath the urbane elegance of its impeccable French, and despite the author's barony, was a polemic against the despotism of the *Ancien Régime* and the arbitrary power of absolute monarchy. Montesquieu thought that the British constitution observed the separation of powers. 'All [freedom] would be lost if the same man or the same body of principal men, either of nobles, or of the people, exercised these three powers: that of making the laws, that of executing public resolutions, and that of judging the crimes or the disputes of individuals' (SPL, 11.6: 157).

No commentator on Montesquieu or the United Kingdom has ever agreed that the British constitution significantly embodies the separation of powers. In fact the nineteenth-century publicist, Walter Bagehot (1826-77) held that the combination, not the separation, of powers was the 'efficient secret' of the constitution (Bagehot, 1963: 65). In the British parliamentary system, the executive (mainly the Prime Minister and cabinet) are Members of Parliament, which is the legislature. And one branch of the legislature, the House of Lords, also constitutes the supreme court of appeal. Historically a better example, cited by Montesquieu, is the Roman Republic (SPL, 11.6: 164). Here the power of decision was distributed among the senate, the consuls, and the tribunes.

Montesquieu's ideas had a strong influence on the framers of the US constitution. In the political theory behind that constitution, as set forth in *The Federalist*, Madison said flat out that 'The accumulation of all powers, legislative, executive, and judiciary, in the same hands, whether of one, a few, or many ... may justly be pronounced the very definition of tyranny' (F, 47: 245-6). The Federalists added a refinement that the legislative power itself should be divided between an upper and lower house – a Senate and a House of Representatives. This in their view, expressed in *The Federalist*, No. 62, 'doubles the security to the people, by requiring the concurrence of two distinct bodies in schemes of usurpation or perfidy, where the ambition or corruption of one would otherwise be sufficient' (F: 318). There was also the idea that a longer-serving Senate would be less likely to yield to 'the impulse of sudden and violent passions, and to be seduced by factious leaders into intemperate and pernicious resolutions' (ibid.).

Even so, the US constitution does not embody a complete separation of powers. The President has a limited suspensive veto over Congressional bills. The Senate's approval is required for Presidential appointments both to the Cabinet and to federal judgeships. Congress, as all the world knows, can move to impeach the President for 'high Crimes and Misdemeanors'.

This dip into practical politics prompts a refinement of the doctrine. The strict and complete separation of powers entails an absolute division of personnel and responsibility between the legislature, executive, and judiciary. A limited or relative separation, involving a 'system of checks and balances', requires only (1) that none of the three powers can be controlled by either of the others in its central work and (2) that any power can be checked by the others if it exceeds its proper sphere, not (3) that there cannot be a partial overlap of personnel or responsibility.

Textual matters are not our main concern but there are signs that Montesquieu himself would have accepted this relaxation of the strict doctrine. A limited overlap of responsibility is implicit in his remarks at SPL, 11.6: 162 allowing executive regulation of the timing of legislative meetings (condition (3)) but this does not amount to control of the legislature in its central work (condition (1)). The aspect of 'checks and balances', condition (2), is captured and stressed in the prefatory declaration to the whole discussion of the separation of powers: 'So that one cannot abuse power, power must check power by the arrangement of things' (SPL, 11.4: 155).

Certainly it was the 'relaxed' reading which Madison took, ascribing to Montesquieu the view which he himself accepted that: 'where the *whole* power of one department is exercised by the same hands which possess the *whole* power of another department, the fundamental principles of a free constitution are subverted' (F, 49: 247 (emphasis in original)).

A final conceptual point is that the doctrine, strict or limited, does not assume the equality of the three powers. In Laski's phrase: 'the separation of powers does not mean the equal balance of powers' (Laski, 1925: 297). Locke makes the basic point here when he says that that, among the branches of government, law-making is 'the Supream Power' (ST, §151: 368). This may just mean that the legislature holds the purse-strings, but there is the further point that, as the central locus of collective decision-making – the body charged with the adoption of policy choices for the public realm – the legislature embodies the basic rationale of the political system. The executive and judiciary take their conceptual point of departure from this central fact. The executive carries out the legislature's policy choices. The judiciary sorts out disputes about their application to specific cases and rules on violations of them.

How are we to appraise the doctrine? Two points may safely be made. In the first place, the separation of powers is not, as a safeguard, either a sufficient or a necessary condition against tyranny or faction. It is not sufficient, because separate powers can always co-operate; distinct personnel can collude. It is not necessary, because tyranny and the sway of faction can be avoided in a tolerant and inclusive political culture even where there is a parliamentary system which links the legislature and the executive. Secondly, unless there is a degree of co-operation ('fraternal collaboration', as the nineteenth-century historian, Léon Duguit termed it (Duguit, 1893: 399)) effective government is stymied.

On the doctrine of the separation of powers and its various aspects, follow up with J. Austin, 1954: Part I, lecture 6; Dye & Zeigler, 1972: ch. 9; Forsyth in Forsyth et al., 1993: 29-34 (on Madison); Freedman, 1978: 260-1 (again on Madison); Hayek, 1978: 101-2; W.T. Jones, 1942: 245-7 (on Montesquieu); Pangle, 1989: ch. 5 (also on Montesquieu); Pasquino, 1998 (on Locke); Plamenatz, 1963, I: 282-94 (on Locke and Montesquieu); Scruton, 1983: 424-5; J. Wolff, 1996b: 107. John Stuart Mill's discussion in *Representative Government*, 14, repays study (Mill, 1958: 194-212; or Mill, 1991: 393-410). Among the classic texts, aside from Locke's ST, see Hegel, PR, §273: 308-12. Note a writer easily missed, Rousseau. When Rousseau observes at SC, III.4: 92 that a people of gods (*un peuple de dieux*) could be governed democratically but that so perfect a government is unsuited to human beings, he is making a point about the separation of powers. He is considering a situation where all, or most likely a majority, not only wield the legislative power, the locus of sovereignty, but apply the executive power as well.

In practice the doctrine of the separation of powers assumes representative government (§23.2) in which legislative, executive, and judicial powers are exercised on the citizens' behalf and not by the citizens themselves. Given the citizens' 'alienation' of those powers, what principally matters, because of the potential risk to the public interest, is to prevent the concentration of different powers in the same hands. It was only the reverse side of this assumption that led Marx, endorsing in *The Civil War in France* (1871) the example of the Paris Commune, in which the popular assembly allowed no such alienation, to see no scope for a concentration of powers potentially hostile to the public interest and hence no need for the separation of powers (§31.5.1; PKM: 513ff.).

For general reading on the concept of power, see N. Barry, 1981: ch. 4; Dowdling, 1996; Hay, 1997; Hindess, 1996; G.C. Lewis, 1898: ch. 17; W.J.M. Mackenzie, 1975; Minogue, 1959; Partridge, 1963.

13. AUTHORITY

'[Y]ou have that in your countenance which I would fain call master', observes Kent to King Lear in Shakespeare's play. 'What's that?' 'Authority.' Rome knew authority earlier than ancient Britain. 'For I am a man under authority, having soldiers under me: and I say to this man, Go, and he goeth': thus the centurion in the *New Testament*. But the centurion still had his problems. So do we, though ours are conceptual rather than spiritual.

We have four tasks in hand. They concern:

- the varieties of authority
- the logic of authority
- the rationale or ground of authority
- the basis of authority

Spelt out, the first task is to distinguish, among the varieties of authority, the kind which is most relevant to politics.

The second task is to probe the logic of political authority, specifying the logical form of ascriptions of authority. These first two tasks will occupy us under the heading of basic distinctions.

Thirdly, we need to consider the rationale of authority, the ground on which in general the existence of political authority is useful or desirable.

The fourth task is to explore the basis on which a political unit, and those who staff it, possess authority. Ground and basis are conceptually distinct; the reason why we need political authority, if we do, does not automatically carry over to bestow authority on a particular political unit, person or group. Divine right, knowledge, and consent-based theories of political authority will be our main focus.

Tasks one and two fall within conceptual analysis; tasks three and four come under high level theorising. The aporia on which we will concentrate is the tricky notion of tacit consent.

13.1 Basic distinctions

It is customary to distinguish three varieties of authority (Beran, 1983: 487; cf. Friedrich, 1972, ch. 4; Weldon, 1953: 53-6):

- authority-on
- authority-with
- authority-over

Thus I am an authority on Ricky Nelson (1940-85, 'the Hollywood Hillbilly'). My friends, who tend to prefer Mahler, endure this fact with what stoicism they can manage. But the truth is, I know the main dates and events of Ricky's life, I regularly listen to his music, and even spend time pondering the whys, wherefores and might-have-beens of his career. When people ask me questions about Ricky, I answer promptly and accurately from the full fund of my knowledge. The key to authority-on is **knowledge**. Whatever claim knowledge may have to be a basis of political authority (see §13.3.2), it is not quite what we want at this stage. To say that X has political authority is not just or precisely to say that X has knowledge of some sort.

Authority-with betokens matter-of-fact influence and is often known appropriately as *de facto* authority. If I regularly seek and take your advice, or often take your unsought advice, then you are someone I 'listen to'. I may take 'no notice' of anyone else or pay less attention to others. In this sense it is likely that Margaret Thatcher, the ex-British prime minister, and Ronald Reagan, the former US president, still have authority-with large number of voters. The key to this kind of authority is contingent **influence**, but such influence omits the element of entitlement which belongs to the intuitive idea of political authority.

In contrast, authority-over is precisely about **entitlement**. To a first approximation, where a person or group has authority-over then he, she or they have an entitlement to make decisions with which certain others have some reason to comply; an entitlement to command. This is the kind of authority with which political philosophy is most concerned; the relevant decisions involve the making of policy choices with respect to matters in the public realm. Such authority is commonly called *de jure* authority (or *de iure*, as strict classicists will prefer), authority as of right – an entitlement to command. The entitlement may be, in later language we shall encounter, a claim-right (§19.1).

To a second approximation, and trying to pinpoint the exact nature of the authority relationship, we may venture the following:

A has political authority over B only if the fact that A requires B to Φ (i) gives B a normative reason to Φ and (ii) excludes some of B's reasons for not-Φ-ing.

In these terms I shall refer to 'de jure authority', alternatively to authority as 'entitlement to command (or rule)' where the entitlement is taken to be moral.

Five quick comments on this definition of authority: first, the normative reason could in theory be legal, pragmatic or ethical. 'Why should I pay my taxes?' 'Because it is illegal not to do so', is certainly taken to supply a normative reason within the American and British legal systems. 'Because you will face severe penalties if you do not', provides a pragmatic reason. But in the tradition of political theory the normative reasons of prime concern are ethical: a normative reason is a moral reason. 'Morally, why ought I to pay my taxes?' In any event, without a normative element of some kind, all hint of entitlement is missing and we are dealing at best with power, not authority. I will return to this directly after the fifth point below.

Secondly, 'a' normative reason is 'some' reason, not necessarily a conclusive, overriding reason.

Thirdly, political authority relates to a particular public (§2.5, first element in the five-part model of the political). Call this the particularity thesis.

Fourthly, there is no reason, dogmatism aside, for uniformity of moral reason; that is to say, for '*some* reason' to be the *same* reason for all those to whom it applies. Typically the theories about the basis of authority that we will examine make this uniformity assumption, but one theory might bind one group of citizens and another theory, others. It is logically possible.

The fifth point is that in the definition the formal, content-neutral factor is high. If you have authority over me, then the mere fact that you require me to do something gives me some reason for doing it and rules out some of my reasons for not doing it. If I am to vet the content of everything you require of me, and to decide whether I will or will not comply with your wishes, then whatever the relationship between us it is not one of authority. In this case the fact that you require something of me counts for nothing; only I count as an independent decision-maker. Cf. L. Green, 1988: 41-2.

To return to the distinction between authority and power. We see this distinction in the following conditional: if A has the power to make a coercive threat to B to do Φ on pain of incurring a penalty, this certainly (i) gives B a reason to Φ and (ii) excludes some of B's reasons for not-Φ-ing. We can, however, describe this situation as one of power without invoking the notion of authority at all, as Rousseau forcibly reminds us, scoring a point against Hobbes, in SC, I.3: 43-4.

It does not follow that authority is unrelated to power. There are at least three points of contact. First, the recognition of a person or group as presenting one with normative reasons for action will typically increase the power of that person or group. Secondly, a body with entitlement but without any power of enforcement would be politically irrelevant, an 'authority' only in name. Thirdly, there is a structural symmetry between power and authority. Dahl's parameters of power carry across to authority (§12.1). We can distinguish:

- the *basis* of authority (that by virtue of which a particular person or group, or political unit, has authority)
- the *means* of authority (the instrumentalities through which authority can be exerted – e.g. law making)
- the *scope* of authority (the set of actions that a person with authority can require others to do)
- the *amount* of authority (in respect of action X, the strength of the reason, at the limit overriding, for complying)
- the *extension* of authority (the range of individuals or groups over whom A has authority)

But none of these connections reduce authority to power. Further discussion can be found in Benn & Peters, 1959: 20-1, 259-63, 297-8; Jouvenel, 1957: 32; Raphael, 1970: 69-76.

13.2 The ground of political authority

Why should authority be a functional necessity, or at least a desirable feature, of human social life? Aside from Tom Paine's famous reminder at the beginning of his *Common Sense* (1776), 'Society is produced by our wants, and government by our wickedness', five central considerations can be advanced.

The first is the humdrum one that, without a political unit charged with taking certain collective decisions for us, there would be high demands on citizens' time (Dahl, 1970: 8, 40-56).

The second relates to the so-called collective action problem with respect to public goods. These, you may recall (§2.5), are items of use or consumption which are characterised by non-rivalry in consumption and non-exclusion of supply. Such items readily attract 'free riders'. Suppose, for example, that the whole community will benefit from the provision of street lighting. In a market situation, this public good will be provided only if people contract to pay for it. All the free rider has to do is to let others pay; once the lighting has been provided, he or she will benefit from it anyway. But then, realising this strategy, others may be decline to enter into a contract from which all benefit but for which only they themselves pay or may themselves join the prospective ranks of free riders: and so the street lighting is not provided. Culyer, 1980: 31-4, 48-9; Laver, 1981: 35-99 will take you further. One justification of political authority is widely held to be that, by making and enforcing collective decisions, an authority can prevent this kind of individualistic calculation from blocking the provision of public goods and also stop the unfairness of free riding. But there are market options such as linking the provision of certain private goods with public goods production: see Culyer, 1980: 34. The possibilities run into considerable complexities.

The third consideration relates to game-theoretic matters of self-interest and co-operation. There is a special connection between rationality and self-interest. Morality aside, the pursuit of self-interest is pre-eminently rational. Such ideas are commonplace. There are circumstances, however, in which the unrestricted pursuit of individual self-interest produces outcomes that are worse for all concerned than schemes of co-operation in which self-interest is moderated. Typically such outcomes occur when the benefits of co-operation cannot be secured because of lack of trust. Game theory, the branch of decision theory in which such matters are explored, suggests the need for political authority to enforce co-operation or otherwise to make trust safe. On game theory, see Hollis, 1985: ch. 8; W.J.M. Mackenzie, 1967: 119-37; Scruton, 1983: 184-5. Hobbes' political theory has been seen as an anticipation of game theory (§§9.2). Game-theoretic situations are often pictured under the image of 'the prisoner's dilemma', from a particular example, famous in the literature, of the benefits and failure of trust (Runciman & Sen, 1965).

The fourth consideration centres on problems of social co-ordination. These are cases where there is a need for common arrangements – matters ranging from the rule of the road to the type of currency. Interactions between people can be facilitated by a political authority requiring conformity to rules and practices rather than having independent agents combining their actions in ways that seem individually best to them. See Kavka in E.F. Paul, 1995: 5-6.

The final consideration relies on the fact of Berlin-style disagreement over ends where unanimity is not to be had but some decision needs to be made (§2.3).

13.3 The basis of political authority: divine right, knowledge, and consent-based theories

As noted earlier, the rationale of political authority, the grounds on which we might sensibly desire to have authority as a feature of our social life, does not translate directly into a reason why a particular person or group, or political unit, should possess or exercise it. Such a reason provides a basis of authority. Three such bases have been urged influentially by political theorists at different times: divine right, knowledge, and consent.

Just a preliminary remark: contra Klosko, 1987 I see no reason, in face of the particularity thesis (§13.1), to accept a corresponding generality thesis by which a theory (or set of theories) about the basis of authority must be valid for, i.e. yield some reason for compliance to, all or most of the relevant public. In any case, reasons for compliance may rest on grounds of political obligation distinct from those of authority (§13.4).

13.3.1 Divine right

The doctrine of the divine right of kings is apt to receive short shrift. I include it here, not because it is a live option for most people – the last monarch claiming and widely acknowledged to rule by divine right was Nicholas II (1868-1918), Tsar of Russia (1894-1917) – but rather because it is a frequently-cited and commonly misunderstood account of political authority, a miscast pantomime character in political theory. Most political philosophy students 'know' only that, as expounded by Sir Robert Filmer, Locke subjected the doctrine to a devastating critique in the *First Treatise of Civil Government*.

Filmer, though the best known proponent of the theory, was not its sole or its most powerful advocate. We find the theory not only in Filmer's *Patriarcha* (c. 1636-39) but also, for example, in King James VI and I's *The Trew Law of Free Monarchies* (1598) and most cogently in Edward Forset's *A Comparative Discourse of the Bodies Natural and Politique* (1606) and *A Defence of the Right of Kings* (1624). Bodin, another important champion of the theory, will reappear when we discuss sovereignty (§14.6).

A good guide to the theory is Greenleaf, 1964a, especially chs 2-5; Greenleaf is usefully reviewed in Elder, 1966. See also Greenleaf, 1964b for a briefer treatment. You might additionally look at J.W. Allen, 1928; Jouvenel, 1962: 26-35; Laslett's Introduction to Filmer, 1949: 1-43; also Laslett's Introduction to Locke, ST: 94-5; Lippmann,

1937: 338-42 (for the relation of the doctrine to the separation of powers); Lord, 1921: 25-8; McPherson, 1967: 30-1. But the classic text is Figgis, 1896.

The theory carries four main claims (Figgis, 1896: 5-6):

- monarchy is a divinely ordained institution
- hereditary right is indefeasible (the right cannot be forfeited by individuals who have it)
- monarchs are accountable to no one but God
- non-resistance and passive obedience are enjoined by God

The non-accountability of monarchs came into conflict with the well-entrenched doctrine of the rule of law. To hold that the monarch should be under the law was, King James I affirmed, simple treason (Lippmann, 1937: 339). It also means that the normative reason for compliance is, on this model of political authority, a conclusive reason.

Roughly two sets of arguments were used in support of the doctrine: one biblical, the other based on analogies and correspondences between the natural world of the family and the political. I will keep mainly to Filmer as the theorist you are most likely to come across. The biblical arguments were largely to the effect that, as Filmer put it, all kings 'either are, or are to be reputed, as the next heirs of those progenitors who were at first the natural parents of the whole people, and in their right succeed to the exercise of supreme jurisdiction' (Filmer, 1949: 60-1). In a word, Adam was the first king, with supreme jurisdiction, and other kings are, or are to be presumed, his heirs.

But, as Rousseau pointed out, if we start from King Adam we may not get so far as present kings:

> I have said nothing about King Adam, or about emperor Noah ... I hope my moderation will be appreciated; for since I am a direct descendant from one of these Princes, and perhaps from the elder branch, for all I know, I might, upon verification of titles, find I am the legitimate king of humankind (SC, I.2: 43).

The second set of arguments rested on correspondences and analogies between the natural and the social worlds. By appeal to the order of nature, patriarchy within the family was used as a political model. Kings stand to their subjects as fathers stand to their children; the Russian Tsar was, in exact illustration *batyushka*, 'the Little Father'. But Aristotle had long since shown the limitations of the patriarchal family model as applied to politics (P I.12: 17ff.). And few would now accept the patriarchal family as an intrinsic part of the order of nature. In any event Locke felt he was able to show the incompleteness of the analogy. The 'superiority' of fathers to their children is temporary only, until the children reach years of discretion when they are sufficiently mature to run their own lives (ST, ch. 6: 303-18). It is worth mentioning that divine rights theorists were apt to jib at this very point; part of the rationale of kingship was that reason and adequate will were permanently lacking in the main citizen body, a deficiency to be supplied by their rulers. (Moral: there is always a reply in politics.)

It would be quite wrong to suppose, the point should be noted, that Christians have traditionally inclined to the doctrine of divine right. In particular in medieval political theology there was a strong tendency to measure the king's legitimacy by the test of justice (E. Lewis, 1954: 143). St Thomas Aquinas, arguably the greatest Christian theologian, gave no countenance to the doctrine: politics is ordained for the common good and a defaulting king has no authority. Locke, the most ardent critic of divine right, was himself a totally convinced (though perhaps not strictly orthodox) Christian.

13.3.2 Knowledge

The most ambitious attempt to found political authority on knowledge is that of Plato in the *Republic*. Plato invites us to accept that every systematic human activity admits of skill which can be developed and which is possessed in different degrees by different people. In *Republic* VI he produces the parable of the ship. If we were embarking on a sea voyage, he asks us to reflect, we would surely seek to enlist the skills of a trained navigator. He describes a voyage on which precisely the opposite happens. The captain is rather dim and is persuaded, or even forced, to pass the navigation over to people who deny that any special knowledge is needed. The result is a meandering round of pleasure in which the ship follows no determinate course and the trickster pseudo-navigators help themselves to whatever the ship provides. This, for Plato, is an exact image of democratic politics, the dim captain being the general run of citizens and the tricksters, the politicians who insinuate themselves into power (R VI.488A-489A: 282-3). We need knowledge in order to navigate: what is different between navigation and politics? This approach to authority explains Plato's implacable antipathy to democracy (§23.4.2.2).

The force of Plato's question cannot be denied. Most political systems, those at least with a representative element (§23.2), run on assumptions of knowledge as a basis for political authority. When we choose others to make choices for us – British Members of Parliament or American Members of Congress – we assume, rashly or wisely, that such persons will have a fuller grasp of the conditions of policy and of the consequences of collective decision-making than we have ourselves. At the least we let others specialise in political activity in order that we may save time, attention, and energy (Dahl, 1970: 8).

Even so, a crucial difference between navigation and politics may seem quite evident and we may wonder how Plato missed it. The navigator is given a goal or end, to conduct the ship skilfully to a destination which he or she does not appoint. The navigator is merely a technician, an expert who is (to adapt Laski's phrase) on tap and not on top. In politics the expert, the professional politician, is equally a kind of technician, somebody whose role is to accomplish the public will and not to appoint the ends of policy. Renford Bambrough made precisely this point in a classic paper (PPS 1: 105).

But Plato has a reply. The ends of policy are in broad terms uncontentious and agreed; they are to achieve *eudaimonia*, happiness or well-being, under the shared conditions of social life. Who is prepared to torpedo Plato's ship at the cost of denying that they would like to be happy and to flourish as a human being? And how can this goal be accomplished except within the confines of a common life? So the political expert does not need to prescribe a goal any more than the navigator needs to decide where the ship is going: political goals and seabound destinations are already fixed and given. In this line of argument Plato anticipates the teleological approach to politics which we noted in Aristotle (§2.2).

Yes but, we are apt to reply, this approach to politics only holds good (at most) at a level of generality. As the *Republic* unfolds it is clear that Plato is offering a comprehensive vision of the good life, 'a substantive theory of the good' in a phrase which John Rawls has made familiar in political theory.

A substantive theory of the good offers:

- a theory of human flourishing, based on a view of a common or shared human nature, specifying ways of living rightly and living well; in other words
- an account (the same for everybody) of the states of mind and character and also of the kinds of activity constitutive of a fully human life; along with
- a specification of the practical requirements and preconditions for human flourishing

To cross-connect: a substantive theory of the good might also be said to (seek to) identify people's real interests (§12.2). And there are links with another notion that has surfaced already. Substantive theories of the good assume a common human nature in terms of which real interests can be specified. Implicit here is the notion that human beings share this nature as members of a natural kind (§4.1.2). Three elucidatory comments:

First, the assumption is always that the good is jointly realisable ('compossible'), in principle or in fact, by all human beings. Secondly, this does not mean that it is realisable by all human beings to an equal degree. Plato excludes this possibility; only his philosophers are capable of complete realisation of the human good. Thirdly, there may be an assumption, beyond mere joint realisability, that the good is achievable only in common. This is clear in the view of Marx, another proponent of a substantive theory of the good (§31.2.1), that 'the free development of each is the condition for the free development of all' (PKM: 228).

A substantive theory of the good, while it may contain straightforward empirical information, is typically such that people with the same empirical information can reasonably disagree about it. Note that this characterisation does not assume that all substantive theories of the good must forever be matters of reasonable disagreement, only that such disagreement is, in fact and now, a regular predicament for their proponents.

Traditional religions and a whole stream of 'philosophies of life' besides the Platonic – Aristotelian, Stoic and Epicurean in ancient times, existentialist in the twentieth century, among many others – have presented and defended just such theories. Nor should the point be overlooked that a substantive theory of the good can accommodate plural and diverse realisations. When St Thomas Aquinas says that the ultimate end of human life is, by living virtuously, to enjoy God in eternal felicity, this is his Christian version of a substantive theory of the good. Yet as Kenneth Kirk wrote:

> There is only one ideal of the Christian life; but it will express itself in many different forms according as a man is called, by circumstance or endowment, to the cloister, the library, the workshop or the office (Kirk, 1920: 31; cf. J.S. Mill on 'diversity in … modes of life' (§22.8) and Raz on incommensurability (§30.5)).

Certain features of Plato's own substantive theory of the good, certainly as offered in the *Republic*, need to be isolated. Plato's theory of the good is presented as objective, i.e. as true or otherwise rationally binding. But Plato would not accept the common criteria for knowledge. Received wisdom is concentrated error; sense-based beliefs are incapable of truth. Only an austere path of philosophical study, on which Plato represents even himself as being merely on the lower slopes, can produce genuine knowledge. Moreover, at the topmost level of the path, attainable only by the few, intellectually most highly gifted (the future guardians or 'philosopher-kings' – and queens), there will be vouch-safed an intuitive, self-authenticating vision of the Form of the Good, the ultimate explanatory principle of reality and value (R VII.518C-D: 322). This vision, furthermore, will have a practical aspect; it will yield practical insight into the requirements of action in managing political affairs so as to achieve *eudaimonia* under the shared conditions of social life (R VI.497C-D: 293). (The future tense is important; Plato does not claim to have the knowledge which his philosopher-rulers will possess.)

Aristotle mounts a critique of Plato on the lines that the Form of the Good, which explains everything in general explains nothing in particular (NE I.6: 7-10); that theoretical vision and practical insight cannot be seamlessly joined in the way Plato supposes (NE VI.7: 144-7). Plato has a further problem which arises from the fact that the vision of the Form of the Good cannot be common property since it is open only to the few. If the guardians have experienced this self-authenticating vision, on which their substantive theory of the good relies, then how are they to present their political credentials to the rest of the citizenry? Since those citizens have not experienced the vision, they cannot tell whether the guardians' claim to knowledge of the good is valid or not. They would need themselves to have experienced the vision, in which case they would not require the guardians' knowledge since they would have it themselves.

Plato confronts the difficulty by manufacturing consent. Though consent is not the basis of the guardians' entitlement to rule, it is a political asset. Since the bulk of the citizenry can neither know what the guardians know nor even know that the guardians know it, they must be otherwise induced to accept the guardians' rule. This is to be accomplished by means of a myth, a convenient fiction' formally false but substantially true, that the children of gold are born to rule and the children of baser metals, silver, bronze and iron, are born to comply. This is the *gennaion pseudos* (what the older translators called the royal or noble lie) of R III.414B-415C: 181-2. Plato's *Republic* might fitly be called the politics of the gold standard.

Plato recognises the equal and opposite problem of getting his philosophers to agree to rule, the contemplation of ultimate truth being more congenial than the business of administration (R IV.419A-421C: 185-7; cf. 465D-466A: 251-2). The allegory of the cave suggests that their consent is to be secured through pressure of moral suasion; the polis has provided the leisure, personal security and material well-being without which their education would have been impossible (R VII.519C-520E: 523-5).

Plato's real challenge is independent of the specific features of his substantive theory of the good. If there were an objective theory of the good, and this were available only on the basis of expert knowledge, would we not be well-advised to bow before Platonic professionalism and defer to the guardians? What better foundation for authority-over the citizenry than Platonic authority-on the human good? It might prove (as John Stuart Mill supposed in *Representative Government*, ch. 3) that shared collective decision-making, and the intellectual and moral development that results from it, is one constituent of that good. It equally well might not. See Mill, 1991: 238-56; Lucas, 1976: ch. 5. The political knowledge possessed by Rousseau's Legislator is separated sharply from authority for reasons not dissimilar from Mill's (SC II.7: 68-72).

13.3.3 Consent

Moving on now to consent as the basis of political authority, one must distinguish between:

* consent as necessary for the existence of a stable political society
* consent as important as a political goal
* consent as necessary for the entitlement to command
* the nature of consent
* the criteria for consent

The first and second of these views about consent are to be found as early as Plato and Aristotle. Take the myth of the metals (§13.3.2) as registering the first view and NE, VIII.1 and IX.6 as marking the second. Plainly our concern in normative political theory is with the third view. This was plainly and vigorously expressed by the seventeenth-century Leveller, Colonel Thomas Rainborough, in the so-called Putney Debates:

Really I think that the poorest he that is in England has a life to live as the greatest he: and therefore truly, Sir, I think it's clear that every man that is to live under a government ought first by his own consent to put himself under the government: and I do think that the poorest man in England is not bound in a strict sense to that government that he hath not had a voice to put himself under (Clarke, 1891: 301).

But what is it to consent? To a first approximation, I consent to your doing some action, or to your occupying some role, X, if (sufficient condition):

1. I foresee certain consequences, Y, of your doing that action or of your occupying that role
2. I desire those consequences, or prefer them to alternatives, under some description
3. I indicate by some intentional action, Z, that
4. It is my choice that you do that action or occupy that role, or (if the decision is not wholly mine) I accept your doing the action or occupying the role

Consent so characterised does not require that I, the consenter, positively desire that you do the action or occupy the role; I may reluctantly accept this as the least of several evils. Moreover, an austere account of consent could run on conditions 1, 2 and 4 alone. This is logically possible but psychologically bizarre. I include condition 3 to make consent psychologically intelligible. Condition 3 is in my view an indispensable motivational element.

The above schema sets out the conditions for actual consent, which can be either express or tacit. In express consent I formally make a declaration, sign a document, utter a conventional form of words (e.g. 'I agree to your doing Y'); in tacit consent, my consent to Y can be reasonably inferrred on either of two conditions: (1) *ex silentio*, (2) where I expressly consent to X and by the strongest implication X involves Y. In the first case, I tacitly consent to your smoking if, in face of your statement, 'Unless anyone objects, I shall light a cigarette', I remain silent. In the second, I expressly consent to your translating my book into Italian and tacitly consent to your translating it into a European language. Both express and tacit consent are, to repeat, actual consent as distinct from hypothetical consent. Hypothetical consent relies on the idea of what people would agree to in certain circumstances – say, if they were fully or better informed or (more) rational (§§18.1, 24.1). I shall ignore hypothetical consent for present purposes; to talk of what people would agree to is not to talk of what they do agree to. Hypothetical consent is not consent. But see further Horton, 1992; Kavka, 1986: 398-407; and Bosanquet, 1923: ch. 7 on the 'real will'.

A further point concerns the 'moral magic of consent'. All else equal, when I consent to your doing the action or to your occupying the role, you now have rightful expectations. That is, you have a normative – a moral – reason to expect me to let you do the action or to occupy the role, with the foreseen consequences. When the role is the political role of decision-making, you now have political authority. When you require me to comply with a decision, I have a normative reason for doing so and this excludes some of my reasons for not complying (such as my simply preferring to do otherwise).

The magic of consent has been questioned. It has been argued that consent is neither necessary nor sufficient to justify compliance with acts of governance. For instance, if such an act is immoral then I ought not to comply with it even if I have consented to the relevant political authority. So consent is not sufficient. Moreover, if an act of governance is an enactment of justice (say) then, all else equal, I ought to comply with it even if I have not consented to the authority.

These points are well-taken on their own account; see further J. Paul, 1983; Simmons, 1979. But they miss the mark for our present discussion. They fix on the content of what is required of us, its justice or immorality. Political authority, we saw, is a more formal notion (§13.1). The problem of political authority is to puzzle out how, if at all, the mere fact that A requires B to Φ (i) gives B a normative reason to Φ and (ii) excludes some of B's reasons for not-Φ-ing. This is, let us face it, an extraordinary relationship between human beings. It really does seem difficult to see what could provide a basis for such a relationship short of consent. Harry Beran makes the key claim as follows:

> I assume that biologically normal adults satisfy certain minimal conditions of rationality in belief and action; that they, therefore, have the capacity to review their beliefs and goals in the light of reasons, to make decisions appropriate to these beliefs and goals and to act on them in order to influence the way the world goes. Such persons are responsible for what they make of themselves and for what they do to others. In short, I assume that they are capable of personal self-determination. This right of persons consists of a number of component rights, including those to determine their marital, work, and political relationships. To ascribe such rights to normal adults is, most importantly, also to claim that no one else has a right to determine a person's political relationships for them. But if no one else has a right to determine a person's political relationships for him, then the basis of political authority must be that person's actual personal consent (Beran, 1983: 491).

It is fair to point out that a distinctively modern view of the individual is at work here. Ewart Lewis does well to remind us that in medieval political thought 'the consent on which authority rested could not be construed as the free choice of self-determining wills – with an open alternative, perhaps of continuing in primitive anarchy; it was a choice conditioned by the principle that authority must exist' (E. Lewis, 1954: 160). But in our own time, Beran's view of the individual has high intuitive plausibility, certainly within the liberal tradition.

The ideas of consent, contract, and democracy are closely entwined in practice, but conceptually they need to be held apart. Contract and democracy are forms of the politics of consent, supposedly conferring or embodying authority. As citizens we might express or instantiate our consent through a contract. We may also exercise and have the readiest means of withdrawing our consent through democratic procedures. But there can be consent where there is neither contract nor democracy. The doctrine of the divine right of kings, accepted by the citizen body (as it once widely was), is an example of this. There can also be a contract without democracy. In Hobbes' political theory, a commonwealth by institution is described in *Leviathan* by which the citizens make a mutual contract to obey a supreme coercive power (a political unit with the ability to quell all opposition and ensure compliance (§9.2.1)) in order to escape the disadvantages of the state of nature. There is no guarantee of that power's being democratic and every likelihood of its not being so (Hobbes prompts us) in the interests of efficient government.

A long tradition of political thought has sought to secure consent through contract; this is the tradition of 'social contract' theory. The heyday of contract theory was the seventeenth and eigtheenth centuries. The central texts are Hobbes' *Leviathan* (1651), Locke's *Second Treatise of Civil Government* (1690), and Rousseau's *Social Contract* (1762). On Hobbes' account, the social contract creates not only political society and a ruler but, through that ruler's exercise of supreme power, the very possibility of organised social life. In Locke, organised social life precedes the contract, which simply creates the political machinery to make social life accord with principles of justice; the role of political authority is to protect our natural rights to life, liberty, and property, and to prevent the excesses that arise when people act on their own perceptions of threats to, and violations of, those rights. Again, Rousseau's social contract does not create organised social life, but ushers in the political conditions to enable independence within that life.

There is a widespread view that a version of the social contract theory is to be found in Plato's *Republic* (R II.358E-359B: 104). As far as concerns political authority, however, this view is not accurate to the text. In the relevant passage Glaucon presents a social contract theory, not of political authority but of moral rules, and in particular of the rule of justice (*dike*), a theory rejected by Plato himself. See further Cross & Woozley, 1964: 71-4. It is more appropriate to read this part of the *Republic* as a prototype of moral contractarianism, the idea that the rules of morality are those rules of conduct that would be chosen by rational contractors under conditions of predominant self-interest (cf. Milo, 1995).

Straight back to real politics: if we are to talk of a 'social contract', what is the basic idea of a contract? It contains, I suggest, three elements. I give contractual consent to your occupying a role, X, if (sufficient condition):

1. I foresee certain consequences, Y, of your occupying X;
2. I desire those consequences, or prefer them to alternatives, under some description;
3. I indicate by some intentional action, Z, which takes the form of an explicit statement, that
4. It is my choice that you occupy the role, or (if the decision is not wholly mine) I accept your occupying the role; further that
5. If I fail to comply with what you require of me in respect of that role I will be liable to penalties, detriments or losses – 'punishment' in a word.

In legal terms, condition 4 adds a 'formal' element to consent, through the explicitness of declaration; and 5 adds an element of 'consideration', the loss that I can incur for the benefit I hope to gain.

Three objections are common coin in the critique of social contract theory. The first rests on the ahistoricity of the contract; it never happened in the history of any contemporary state. This objection is hardly decisive. It is effective enough against claims that the actual basis of political authority is a social contract. But a radical theorist such as Rousseau need maintain only that, if there were to be a political order possessing de jure authority, a social contract would be its underpinning. Rousseau is uncommitted to the position that there is any current basis of political authority; no political order possessing de jure authority exists outside the pages of the *Social Contract*. He makes clear in SC I.1 that he is not writing history.

The second objection is that, even if a social contract were the basis of political authority, it would bind only the original contractors. It is intuitively clear that contracts cannot bind third parties, in this case succeeding generations. But this argument works only against contract theorists who suppose that a social contract does or would bind in this long-term way. Against a theorist such as Thomas Jefferson (1743-1826), who argued for a regular renewal of political authority, the objection misses the mark. Each generation would renew or reject the contract explicitly on their own account.

The third objection is an attempt to defeat what might be termed the moral logic of contract theory. It stems from Hume's 1748 essay, 'Of the Original Contract' (Hume, 1987: 465-87). This is often presented as the classic refutation of social contract theory. It actually has a more limited status, that of a devastating critique of social contract theory, *given Hume's own assumptions*. Stripped to basics, Hume's argument is that the moral institution of promising is a product of state-supported society. Therefore any attempt to deduce a moral reason for obeying the state from a contract or promise – to use this as a basis for political authority – is back-to-front. Simply said, the state creates, in the sense of enabling the possibility of, the moral institution of promising; the institution of promising cannot provide a prior moral ground for obeying the state.

This argument is plainly a deft manoeuvre, one that shows the intellectual facility for which Hume is justly famous. But there is a crucial sense in which Hume's argument is loaded against the view he is attacking. For the argument relies on premises drawn from Hume's *A Treatise of Human Nature*, and these premises are not uncontentious.

A modicum of background needs to be sketched. Hume draws a distinction between the natural and the artificial virtues (Hume, 1978: 477-84; D. Miller, 1981: 60-1). The natural virtues are tendencies to behaviour which are rooted in human nature. For example we simply do have, within limits and on conditions that Hume spells out, an inclination to look after our children and in Good Samaritan situations to help strangers. Such benevolence is a natural virtue and, where inclination fails, we see it as a norm that yields moral reasons for action. Moreover and vitally, the requirements of benevolence hold good independently of any network of social institutions.

We have no such 'natural' inclination to respect property or to keep our promises. The institutions of property and of promise-keeping are 'artificial'. Hume does not mean that they are spurious or otherwise undesirable (on the contrary) but merely that they are contingent contrivances of social life. They are a part of morality only where certain general conditions of social trust prevail (cf. Hobbes, L ch.17).

Then to return to Hume's argument. If we say that the existence of the state is a necessary condition for promising as a moral institution, since the state creates the general conditions of social trust on which the utility of promising-keeping rests (utility is the final moral criterion for Hume), indeed we cannot ground a moral reason to obey the state on an institution which the state itself creates. But this is very much Hume's contestable interpretation of the nature of promising. As a natural law theorist, Locke (to take only one prominent social contract theorist) would feel no pressure to accept Hume's view of the institution of promising. Locke would reply that, by the exercise of reason, we can recognise a moral reason, indeed obligation, to keep our promises. This reason is grounded in the moral nature of human beings and is in no sense the product of the kind of convention that Hume has in mind. The argument might go to and fro. My aim is not to vindicate Lockean natural law theory. Broadly speaking, I accept Hume's theory here and elsewhere. That is not the point, which is rather that no one could take the Humean account of promising as uncontroversial. Most moral philosophers have rejected it.

All in all a student of political philosophy should be wary of accepting Hume's 'refutation' of social contract theory without a clear-sighted understanding and acceptance of the kind of ethical theory on which it rests. Everything 'costs' in philosophy. That is the best slogan I can devise. Any view or argument is linked, like a stitch, backwards to presuppositions, forwards to implications and consequences, which are barely visible when one first tugs on the thread. The Humean account of promising is not an isolated bright idea that comes free of any commitment to a wider ethical theory.

On Hume see §17 on his view of justice as an artificial virtue; see further Brownsey, 1978; D. Miller, 1981: ch. 4; Smellie, 1939: 71-7. On the social contract theory generally, consult E. Barker, 1951a: ch. 4; Boucher & Kelly, 1994; Field, 1963: 33, 39-41; Gray, 1989: ch. 3; Mabbott, 1958: 12-18, 27; C. Pateman in Keane, 1988: 101-27; again C. Pateman in Goodin & Pettit, 1997: ch. 3; Raphael, 1970: 85-93; Weldon, 1953: 95-6; J. Wolff, 1996b: 42-6. Edmund Burke's celebrated and bitterly ironic passage, 'Society is indeed a contract', should also be consulted (E. Burke, 1900: 107-8; Hampsher-Monk,

1987: 193; see §29.5). On Hobbes see Berki, 1977: 132-41; Kavka, 1986: ch. 10; Plamenatz, 1963, I: 132-53. On Locke see Ashcraft, 1987: ch. 7; Berki, 1977: 142-50; Lloyd Thomas, 1995: ch. 2. Rousseau's ideas are well presented in Berki, 1977: 159-67; Hall, 1973: ch. 6; Noone, 1981; Wokler, 1995: ch. 3-4. Hegel's views are given in PR §§258 & 281: 277-8, 324. On consent and authority, see L. Green in P. Harris, 1990: ch. 4.

13.3.3.1 The problem of tacit consent

Contract theorists have often made appeal to the idea of tacit consent in face of trying to justify such moral reasons as we may have to obey existing governments. Perhaps the best-known such appeal is that of Locke in ST ch. 8:

> Every Man being ... naturally free, and nothing being able to put him into subjection to any Earthly Power, but only his own Consent; it is to be considered, what shall be understood to be a sufficient Declaration of a Man's Consent, to make him subject to the Laws of any Government. There is a common distinction of an express and a tacit consent, which will concern our present Case. No body doubts but an express Consent, of any Man, entering into any Society, makes him a perfect Member of that Society, a subject of that Government. The difficulty is, what ought to be look'd upon as a tacit Consent, and how far it binds, i.e. how far any one shall be looked on to have consented, and thereby submitted to any Government, where he has made no Expression of it at all. And to this I say, that every Man, that hath any Possession, or Enjoyment, of any part of the Dominions of any Government, doth thereby give his tacit Consent, and is as far forth obliged to Obedience to the Laws of that Government, during such Enjoyment, as any one under it; whether this his Possession be of Land, to him and his Heirs for ever, or a Lodging only for a Week; or whether it be barely travelling freely on the Highway; and in Effect, it reaches as far as the very being of any one within the Territories of that Government (ST §119: 347-8).

When Locke talks of our being 'naturally free', he has in mind our condition in 'the state of nature'. This expression has three main references in his political theory (Winfrey, 1981: 425):

- the post-paradisaical condition of humankind immediately after the Fall of Adam and Eve
- the condition of humankind in the (for Locke) contemporary seventeenth-century Americas and other pre-state societies
- an abstract, ahistorical model of the condition of humankind prior to the advent of political authority

The first and third references map on to each other. Nothing that holds good of the one fails to hold good of the other. That made clear, Locke appears to be making a vital but questionable assumption in this passage. The assumption is that, having invoked express consent as the only mechanism, through the social contract, for the initial establishment (in the state of nature) of de jure authority among moral equals, with no natural political authority one over another, he must make an appeal *again* to consent in grounding the moral reason for obeying an existing government. In the second case the consent need only be tacit.

Suppose, though, that an existing government requires me to act in a way consistent with *justice*; it does not follow that the requirement binds me only if I have in some way consented to the government. It has independent normative force. See Beran, 1976;

Pitkin, 1965: 991; Plamenatz, 1963, I: 224; Rawls, who (to glance ahead) would argue for a moral reason, in fact an obligation, of justice to support the basic structure that emerges from the original position (§17.3). A person may also have moral reasons for compliance through benefits received, but we have equally no need in this case to talk specifically of *consent*; we can simply talk of the moral reasons. Of course, not just any receipt of benefit will create a moral reason for political compliance; the benefits may, for example, be trivial. Klosko has argued for a number of conditions including crucially (contra Nozick's public address system example, ASU: 93-5) that the benefits are 'necessary for an acceptable life for all members of the community' (Klosko, 1987: 246-59). Either way, consent is not necessary to create moral reasons for political compliance.

Does Locke in any case describe examples of tacit consent? There are two clear conditions on which tacit consent occurs: (1) the ex silentio condition and (2) that of strong implication from express consent (§13.3.3). In these terms, Locke's examples do not fulfil either condition.

Finally, even if Locke succeeded in showing that his examples are genuine cases of tacit consent, special circumstances might rule out moral reasons for compliant action. One thinks of the problem of unjust laws. Consent is not morally sufficient for political compliance.

For further discussion of the puzzling nature of tacit consent, useful are Flathman, 1973: 205-43; Franklin, 1996; Kavka, 1986: 124-5, 391-8; Simmons, 1979: 93; Singer, 1973: 47-59. Indispensable is Lloyd Thomas, 1995: 34-42. Portions of Hume's 1748 essay, 'Of the Original Contract', are also relevant: see Hume, 1987: 475-8, esp. 475 with its simile of the vessel ('We may as well assert, that a man, by remaining in a vessel, freely consents to the dominion of the master; though he was carried on board while asleep, and must leap into the ocean, and perish, the moment he leaves her'). Aside from residence, proposed by Locke and critiqued by Hume, and the receipt of benefits (really irrelevant to consent), a third criterion of tacit consent has been proposed – that of participation in free elections: see e.g. Plamenatz, 1968: 170.

Before we move on to consider the relation of authority to sovereignty, it is as well to add that, besides 'divine', knowledge, and consent-based theories of authority, there is a tradition-based account which will briefly be mentioned when we examine conservatism (§29.4).

13.4 Authority, legitimacy, and obligation

It will also be as well to draw some conceptual discriminations. Political authority and political obligation are often taken to be counterparts. That is to say that on a common assumption X has a political obligation to Y, an obligation to obey, if and only if Y has political authority over X. Equally, if Y has political authority, then the state within which Y has that authority is legitimate. Authority, legitimacy, and obligation all neatly dovetail. Call this the correlativity thesis. It is not absurd but it seems to me false.

What makes a state legitimate is whether it has an adequate rationale; whether it pursues proper ends and observes due limits; cf. the *ground* of authority (§13.2). What gives a state de jure authority is a matter of whether it has, in knowledge, consent, divine right or whatever, the basis of entitlement to command. We may settle the state's rationale, its proper ends and due limits without thereby deciding who is entitled to command. Again, I may still have an obligation to obey my state, in general or in some particular matter, even if that state lacks both legitimacy and de jure authority. Dilemmas are imaginable in which, to avert a worse evil, I ought to do what such a state requires of me. Moreover, where there is de jure authority there is 'some' reason to comply (§13.1), not necessarily the overriding reason that would create an obligation.

See further L. Green, 1988: 235-40.

14. STATE AND SOVEREIGNTY

Dramatic things have been said about the state. For Hegel the state is 'the march of God in the world' (PR § 258 Addition: 279). The Sun King, Louis XIV of France, had a more personal and practical approach: 'L'état c'est moi' ('I am the state').

We will first conduct a basic conceptual analysis of the state, then consider some views about the ends and limits of state action. Discussions of the state and politics, state and society, and state and polis cover the aporetic aspect. As to sovereignty, I will suggest an analysis in terms of power and authority. Theories of sovereignty will emerge *en route*. Our aporia about sovereignty will turn on the claim (which I shall offer reasons for rejecting) that sovereignty is an essential attribute of the state.

14.1 Basic distinctions

There is an ambiguity to uncover in discussing the state. 'State' can and does refer both (1) to a territorially demarcated area ('Its neighbours lay claim to large areas of the State of Israel') and (2) to a set of institutions within that area ('Anarchists seek to overturn the state'). Accordingly we can refer to the state in 'sense 1' and 'sense 2'.

We can elaborate on the institutions. On a common conception, where there is a state, there is:

- a distinct set of institutions and personnel
- comprising legislative, executive, administrative, and judicial functions
- operating centrally in the sense that decision-making radiates outwards from the institutions (the forum or arena of §2.4) across
- a territorially demarcated area, with respect to which these institutions employ not only an apparatus of coercive power, but
- supreme coercive power (i.e. the ability to quell all opposition and ensure compliance), and moreover
- de jure authority
- legitimacy

The two penultimate features, those of supreme power and de jure authority, define briefly the idea of sovereignty – of which, more later. The 'outward radiation' condition is not defeated by federalism; under federalism, power radiates from the centre but not solely from the centre. (Federalism is a system in which authority and power are so divided that the central and regional governments are each, 'within a sphere, coordinate and independent' (Wheare, 1963: 10).)

When we refer to the state in sense 2, a further ambiguity surfaces as we prise apart institutions and personnel. Anarchists seek to abolish the institutions as such (§28). Seen from this angle, which we can call (2a), the state is a persisting, 'impersonal' set of institutions that can be occupied by different personnel. Run of the mill revolutionaries, by contrast, and ordinary 'opposition' politicians, wish to replace the current personnel, not to abolish (though possibly to amend) the institutions. Taken from this second angle, call it (2b), the state is purely the current personnel occupying the institutions.

It is on the state in the (2a) sense that political philosophy has mainly focused. This is not to deny statehood to a set of institutions meeting all the above conditions save for the final two, normative elements. But political philosophers have been keenly concerned to see on what conditions those elements can be added. I will return to this point in the next section.

The meaning of the word 'state' has undergone development. Our first topic is just briefly to chart this linguistic evolution. The second, more important one is that of analysing the concept as it currently stands – showing its constituent elements and fixing its precise 'intension'.

On the linguistic question, help is to hand. As a short, scholarly guide to the historical evolution of the word 'state', Skinner, 1989 (reprinted in Goodin & Pettit, 1997: 3-26) can hardly be bettered. Skinner traces three main stages in the word's history.

In the fourteenth century, with variations across the Western European languages, *estat, stato* or 'state' referred to the repute or dignity of the rulers, 'the state and standing of rulers themselves' (Skinner, 1989: 91). This is the first stage, which survives residually in our word 'stateliness'. Its origins lie in the medieval canonists' language, as early as the twelfth century, in their talk of the *status ecclesiae* – the standing of the church.

The second stage involved a shift or extension of reference from the ruler to the realm, city or country – 'the state of the realm' (Skinner, 1989: 92). A city might have the *status civitatum*, a condition of political independence; with luck it would also be 'in a good and peaceful *stato*', a condition of peace and prosperity.

In the third and still dominant stage of its history, which seems to have originated primarily in the Italian city-republics of the fifteenth and sixteenth centuries but which crystallised sharply after the 1648 Peace of Westphalia that ended the Thirty Years War, 'state' refers neither to the condition of the rulers nor to that of the rulers; again, not to that of the realm. Rather it refers to 'an apparatus of power whose existence remains independent of those who may happen to have control of it at any given time' (Skinner, 1989: 102; cf. Mann, 1988: 4). This connects directly with the state in our sense (2a) above.

14.2 Theories of the state

Theories of the state answer three main questions:

1. Why have a state, do we need one?
2. What are the proper ends and limits of state action?
3. Who should rule?

(1) and (2) are questions of legitimacy. (3) is the question of de jure authority.

The high-level theories presented in this book all, in one way or another, answer one or more of these questions. Take the first question, that of rationale: anarchism tells us emphatically that we do not need a state (§28); Hobbes is equally positive that the state is indispensably necessary (§13.3.3). John Stuart Mill's liberty principle (§22.8) imposes one limit on state action; Rawls sets the state the end of ensuring that society's basic structure embodies justice (§17.3). Theorists about the basis of authority (§13.3) return answers to the question of who should rule; democratic theorists can be seen as developing the consent-based approach to authority in a particular way (§23.4).

The analytical intelligence naturally probes the relationship between the three questions. Are they independent or do answers to one question entail or presuppose answers to one or both of the others? It depends, the banal answer must come, on just how one answers them. It is possible to define the rationale of the state and carry it straight across to define the end of state action. There must, after all, be a fairly close fit between the reason why we want a state and what we want the state to do.

Yet there is logical space between the questions at a level of specificity. For instance, why do we need a state? Suppose we answer:

1. There are some desirable things that can only be done by the state
2. There are some desirable things which can be best (most efficiently, most reliably) done by the state

Thus it might be argued that the state provides 'public goods' (§§2.5, 13.2) more efficiently than either the market or the voluntary efforts of groups and individuals, or that it provides goods which the market and voluntary effort will not produce at all. Clean air, defence, and civil peace are commonly accepted examples.

Beyond such examples, there may be widespread disagreement and uncertainty about the proper range of state-delivered public goods. Is equality of opportunity such a good (§18.2)? Or distributive justice (§17.2)? We can be hesitant about such answers to the second question while being confident, as many are, about the 'public goods' answer to the first.

We can answer questions of legitimacy without automatically answering the question of authority: when we have decided on the rationale, ends and limits of state action it is a separate question, or may be, who should run the state.

Time to move on. The discussion of the state in the following three sections is taken up with a number of aporias. The relation of the state to politics, to society, and to the ancient Greek *polis*, come under review.

14.3 State and politics

We can be brief in our discussion of this matter; the main points are implicit in the earlier discussion of the nature of politics (§2.5). Politics and the state are often regarded as correlative notions: 'cause and effect', 'subject and object', 'politics and the state'. But this is too limited and limiting.

One point is that pre-state formations were clearly political; all the features of our five-part model of the political were exhibited by the Greek *polis*, yet there are real difficulties, set out in §14.5, in seeing the *polis* as a state. Secondly as we saw in §2.5, there can be government without the state. There can be collective decision-making without the mechanism of enforcement. This is a conceptual possibility whatever its practical likelihood. Thirdly, we should recall the process view of politics, with its stress on the existence of politics wherever there are (as there are pervasively) relationships of power.

See further D. Held, 1989: 1-2; W.J.M. Mackenzie, 1967: 155-298; Mason, 1990; Skillen, 1972, 1977 & 1985; A. Vincent, 1987: 4-6.

14.4 State and society

Philosophically important ideas about the state and society – that is, about the actual or correct relation between the two – are contained in the idea of 'civil society'. This idea has passed through three major phases.

In the first phase, which runs from ancient Greece and Rome down to mid-eighteenth-century Europe, the state or *polis* on the one hand and civil society on the other, were coterminous. A civil society – the Aristotelian *koinonia politike*, the Roman *societas civile*, Locke's seventeenth-century 'political or civil society' (ST, ch. 7: 318-30) – was simply the internal accusative of the *polis* or state. Where there is a state, there is a society: this is a civil society.

The second phase is launched in the writings of the economist Adam Ferguson (1723-1816) and the publicist Tom Paine (1737-1809). It finds its fullest expression in Hegel's account of *bürgerliche Gesellschaft*, PR §§182-255: 220-73.

Hegel defines an economic sphere, the system of needs, intermediate between the family and the state. This is the domain of the market, employment, trade associations and the rest. Also in civil society he situates the administration of justice, essentially the police and the courts, along with welfare and regulatory agencies. A standard comment is that Hegel cuts a line between the state and civil society at the wrong place. We are more inclined to see the administration of justice and welfare provision as part of the state apparatus, though trends in the USA and UK to privatise the prison service, pension provision and other matters give Hegel's account an eerie air of prescience. Another comment on Hegel's distinction is that it is not clear-cut, since there is an economic dimension to the employment of state officials; for these persons, the state is part of their 'system of needs', since it provides them with their livelihood. See further Berki, 1977: 172-9 esp. 176-7; Pelczynski, 1971: 10-13, also Pelczynski, 1984; Smellie, 1939: 118-21. Hegel's state/civil society distinction re-appears, transformed, in Marx. Marx takes the distinction, more or less, but gives it a notable twist. Civil society, as the economic base, selects a superstructure, including the state, which is functional to it (§31.4.1).

In the third phase, strongly marked in twentieth-century liberal thinking, 'civil society' refers to intermediary institutions between the individual and the state – Pangle's 'web of free or uncoercive private associations' (§14.5 below). These are trade unions, trade associations, firms, churches, peer groups, special interest groups, political parties, and so forth. Their key features are (1) voluntariness and (2) 'associational autonomy' (Dahl, 1989: 221) or exemption from direct state control: they owe neither their existence nor their legitimacy to endorsement by the state. Stress on the fact and importance of such institutions was a distinct feature of so-called guild socialism in the early years of the twentieth century. The main names are J.N. Figgis (1866-1919), G.D.H. Cole (1889-1959), and H.J. Laski (1893-1950). The guild socialists wanted to disperse the supreme power of the state across a wide variety of voluntary institutions. See Hsiao, 1927 and Nicholls, 1994. A recent counterpart to this style of political thinking is to be found in P.Q. Hirst, 1994; cf. C. Barker, 1997: 40-8.

Beyond the ambit of guild socialism the idea has been found important that freedom depends significantly on there being institutions intermediate between the individual and the state which do not owe their existence or legitimacy to the state's initiative or endorsement. See Etzioni, 1996 (reviewed in Sennett, 1997); Keane, 1988. For some thought-provoking reservations, see C. Barker, 1997: 40-8; and cf. Rousseau SC II.3: 60. One problem is that, while the institutions of civil society may be voluntary vis-à-vis the state, they may still exhibit exploitation and alienation: see the Marxist viewpoint in §31.3.1 and the feminist critique of the public/private distinction in §32.1.2. A further problem concerns the clarity of the state/society distinction in face of corporatism, the *de facto* integration of organised special interest groups into governmental decision-making and the *quid pro quo* influence of government over those groups.

On civil society, see further Honneth, 1993. On state and society in general, see Bosanquet, 1923: passim; Dunleavy & O'Leary, 1987: 320-2; Field, 1961: 186-207; Held, 1989: 56-7, 79-80; Mabbott, 1958: 79-86; Sweet, 1997: ch. 4 (for commentary on Bosanquet); A. Vincent, 1987: 22-4. The state/society distinction will recur in our discussion of the Greek *polis*, the next topic in hand. On corporatism, see Williamson,

1989. Associational autonomy is often labelled 'pluralism', though this term has also come to be used to refer, more specifically, to the recognition and respect for a diversity of ethnic cultures within a political unit.

14.5 State and *polis*

The *polis* was not purely a phenomenon of classical Greece. *Poleis* (pl.) continued to exist, with a fair degree of autonomy, under the Hellenistic and Roman empires. But was the *polis* a city-*state*? The polis was a wholly self-governing municipality small enough in population and area for citizens to take part directly in collective decision-making. (Aristotle refused to accept that Babylon, seat of the Assyrian super-power, could be a *polis*: it was too large for its citizens even to meet together (P III.3: 54).) Moreover, any such distinction as we might draw between state and society looks problematic. The institutions for collective decision-making, primarily the Assembly, were no 'impersonal' organisations staffed by personnel (like members of parliament or congress) distinct from the main body of the citizens; the citizens themselves occupied and ran them. Morality and politics were closely entwined; the moral virtues were seen as having their deepest and fullest expression in the responsibilities of citizenship. Religion and politics were equally linked. Religion was civil religion, the gods were the gods of the polis, and private devotion was not at all what Greek religion was about. The American political theorist, Thomas Pangle, has some pertinent remarks:

> The *polis* is not a city in our sense, for it is a self-sufficient and independent political community, but it is even less a state or a 'city-state.' The word 'state' cannot be used in translating Greek, for in modern usage it presupposes a distinction between 'state' and 'society,' as well as 'country,' distinctions which are wholly alien to ... Greek thought in general. Our word state' refers to the government, to the political authority which holds a monopoly on the use of legitimate violence. The state is opposed both to the web of free or uncoercive private associations which constitute 'society' and to the traditions and the land we think of when we speak of 'our country.' 'State' is therefore a cold word (Nietzsche said it was the name for the coldest of all cold monsters). *Polis* has none of these connotations, for in Greek life ... politics is not thus separated from, and subordinated in value to, the rest of social life. A good equivalent for *polis* might be 'country' if this term did not obscure the emphatically urban character of the *polis* (Pangle, 1988: 512).

Pangle's unexplicated claim that, in the Greek *polis*, 'politics is not ... separated from, and subordinated in value to, the rest of social life' requires elucidation. This is provided by Lowes Dickinson when he explains that:

> in the Greek view, to be a citizen of a [*polis*] did not merely imply the payment of taxes, and the possession of a vote; it implied a direct and active co-operation in all the functions of civil and military life. A citizen was normally a solder, a judge, and a member of the governing assembly; and all his public duties he performed not by deputy. but in person. He must be able frequently to attend the centre of government ... He must be able to speak and vote in person in the assembly ... The idea of representative government never occurred to the Greeks; but if it had occurred to them, and they had adopted it, it would have involved a revolution in their whole conception of the citizen (Dickinson, 1962: 49).

See also, along much the same lines. E. Barker, 1951b: 5-7; P. Burke, 1986; T.H. Green, 1986: 231, 306-7, 325; Hegel, PR § 356; Inwood in Pelczynski, 1984; Strauss, 1964: 30-5; Zimmern, 1915: 82.

My own view is twofold. One point is that we should not fail to note that the citizens were only a small proportion of the population; women, slaves, and resident aliens all suffered political exclusion. For such people the institutions of collective decision-making may well have been impersonal organisations standing, state-like, over against them. Nothing like universal suffrage was known.

The second point is that, in distinguishing the *polis* from the state, as in some respects we plainly must, we need to be careful in reading off the implications for political philosophy. It does not follow, because the *polis* was a different political entity from the state, that the citizen's attitude and relationship to the *polis* did not provoke much the same (I should personally say, just the same) ethical problems as do the citizen's attitude and relationship to the state. Socrates' imaginary Dialogue, in the *Crito*, with the Laws of Athens on why, having received the benefits of Athenian civilisation, he should comply with a judicial verdict with which he disagrees (*Crito*, 50A-54D; Plato, 1960: 174-91), is on all fours with Locke's account of the moral reasons for political compliance generated by tacit consent in ST §§119-22: 347-9. In more general terms, R.G. Collingwood's claim that because the *polis* is different from the state, therefore political philosophy cannot have a continuous *problematik* from ancient Greek to modern times (Collingwood, 1939: 61-2), is an overstatement. Other factors may challenge the continuity of political philosophy. One thinks, for instance, of the long period from St Augustine when political philosophy was largely concerned with the relationship of religion and politics, down to the secularisation of political philosophy from Machiavelli and (more rigorously) Hobbes. But the shift from polis to state is not the climacteric Collingwood claims it to be. So far T.A. Sinclair's view remains intact from §6.2.

On the state/ polis relationship, see further Kedourie, 1984: 210-12.

14.6 Sovereignty

'Sovereignty' derives from Old French *soverain*, which just means 'supreme'. The dictionary comes to the aid of philosophy. What could be simpler? In fact nothing is simple: the concept of sovereignty is notoriously tricky to analyse.

A useful first step in the analysis of sovereignty will be to flag a range of senses in which the term is used. These terms are not of equal philosophical significance but they need to be noted in order to keep the discussion clear:

- titular sovereignty
- state sovereignty
- popular sovereignty
- legal sovereignty
- political sovereignty

Titular sovereignty
This is a notion without philosophical depth. The titular or nominal sovereign is a king, queen, emperor, etc., occupying the role of head of state. The Anglican *Book of Common Prayer* used to refer to 'our most gracious Sovereign Lady, Queen Victoria'. Long did she reign, but she never ruled. We can side-step this usage, captured in Bagehot's distinction between the dignified and the efficient part of the constitution (Bagehot, 1963).

State sovereignty
State sovereignty applies when a political system is not subject, in its definition of the public realm, in its forms of collective decision-making or in its adoption and implemen-

tation of policy choices, to another political system. This is sometimes called 'external', 'territorial' or 'national' sovereignty.

Popular sovereignty

The root idea of popular sovereignty is that the basis of political authority is popular consent, i.e. the consent of the people or populace. This is essentially the idea we encountered in the quotation from Beran (§13.3.3).

Legal sovereignty

Legal sovereignty belongs to any unit within the political system whose actions and decisions are not open to legal challenge within the system itself. In the British political system this unit has traditionally been held to be the Queen-in-Parliament. But a corresponding body is difficult, if not impossible, to find in the US political system; the Supreme Court is the closest approximation to it. The legal sovereignty of the Queen-in-Parliament is little more than a myth in the British system, given the realities of European federalism.

Political sovereignty

Political sovereignty involves, in my view, two elements – de jure authority and supreme power.

There are two foundational philosophers of political sovereignty, Jean Bodin (1530-96) and Thomas Hobbes (1588-1679). On a strict reckoning Bodin, in *Les Six Livres de la République* (1576), is the first theoretician of political sovereignty, though there are prefigurations of the notion long before then: in Aristotle's reference to the 'supreme power' (*to kurion* – P III.10: 65) in the *polis*; in the Roman idea of *maior potestas*, the Emperor's predominant power; in the medieval notion of the *plenitudino potestatis* of the Papacy. All these concepts would suggest, if we looked further into them, the cross-over of power and entitlement.

Since it is mainly on political sovereignty that theorists have focused, from now on I shall omit the 'political' and refer just to 'sovereignty'.

As a theorist of sovereignty, Hobbes is modern in a way in which Bodin is not. Two points of contrast are especially clear. One is that Bodin looks back to the divine right of kings (§13.3.1). Sovereignty is an attribute of God's anointed; it is what kings have by divine right. Hobbes prefers monarchy to other forms of government, but only because one-person rule reduces the risk of division in the management of the state (L ch. 19: 131-3; Apperley, 1999).

The other point of contrast is that Hobbes develops the idea of sovereignty uncompromisingly. From the basic idea of a supreme power to make law and to enforce the law with overwhelming force, Hobbes moves forward ruthlessly. He has no truck with legal limitations on sovereignty. The sovereign, as the source of law, is above all law. Aristotle was quite wrong in his view that 'in a wel ordered Common-wealth, not Men should govern, but the Laws' (L ch. 46: 471). The Aristotelian reference is, I guess, to NE V.6: 123 where it is said that 'we do not allow a *man* to rule, but *rational principle*, because a man behaves thus in his own interests and becomes a tyrant'; also perhaps to P III.16. Bodin, by contrast to Hobbes, recognises certain fundamental rules which the sovereign cannot lawfully abrogate. Among such rules is the Salic Law, by which only males can inherit the throne. There is also a contrast with Rousseau, who argues that the sovereign cannot be above the law because nothing can be binding on a group other than a law which, as collective sovereign, they themselves have passed as expressive of the general will (SC II.6 & III passim; for commentary see MacAdam in R. Fitzgerald, 1980: 141-63).

So far Hobbes has captured one element in the idea of political sovereignty, that of the omnicompetent unit, a unit above the law and with complete ability to carry out its decisions and to block the decisions of others if necessary. The sovereign is a supreme coercive power in the sense that it has sufficient one– and two-dimensional power (§12.2) to quell all opposition and ensure compliance. (I omit Lukes' three-dimensional power as too laden with difficulties, not to be used at all but to inform the present discussion.)

Hobbes' argument for such a unit is that, given certain assumptions which he makes about the essential nature of human beings (in terms of §2.6.2 Hobbes gives explanatory priority to certain socially and historically invariant psychological qualities of human beings), there is no durable middle way between 'the state of nature', a chaotic condition of violence and distrust, and a politics of sovereignty (L 17: 117-21; Hampsher-Monk, 1992: 36-49; Kavka, 1986: 33-4; Mabbott, 1958: ch. 2; Sorell, 1986: ch. 9; Wolff, 1996b: 8-18). Only a politics of sovereignty can yield civil peace. For the state of nature, the sovereign is the sovereign remedy.

If Hobbes underlines sovereignty as supreme coercive power, he also stresses de jure authority; the sovereign has an entitlement to command (cf. Raphael, 1970: 61-2). This is the second element in the idea of political sovereignty. Hobbes himself has odd notions about the criteria for entitlement. Agreed, a de jure authority is one whose decisions have normative force. But Hobbes takes the view that something can have normative force only if there is an element of consent – 'there being no Obligation on any man, which ariseth not from some Act of his own' (L ch. 21: 150).

Such consent-based obligation can arise, Hobbes argues, even when one's life is spared by a conqueror on condition of future obedience. One chooses to comply; and that choice creates obligation. So he grounds the morality of commonwealths by acquisition and, by parity of reasoning, of commonwealths by succession. Hobbes' claim is not merely, with dubious plausibility, that consent is necessary for obligation, but further, with definite implausibility, that consent, secured no matter how, is also sufficient. Rousseau classically criticises this idea in SC I.3: 43-4. It is also attacked in Kavka, 1986: 395-7.

On authority in general see further Arendt, 1961: ch. 3; N. Barry, 1981: ch. 4; Flathman, 1980; G.C. Lewis, 1898: ch. 17; Nisbet, 1981; Raz, 1990; Shklar, 1972; Stankiewicz, 1976: ch. 3; Winch and Peters in Quinton, 1967.

14.6.1 Sovereignty and the state: critique of de jure authority

If the concept of sovereignty is to have any specific point, it must do work not accomplished by the mere concept of power. In this regard, its point is to join power with de jure authority, thus enabling us to talk of power supporting an entitlement to command, and to seek the conditions for such power. The concept of sovereignty must also do work not accomplished by the concept of de jure authority. In this regard, its point is the converse one of joining authority with power, thus enabling us to talk of de jure authority backed by supreme coercive power – of authority with not merely a moral but a politically effective dimension.

From our analysis, there is no plausibility in the claim that sovereignty is an essential attribute of the state. An essential attribute of X is a property or quality without which X cannot exist. Unless we are willing to say that X is not a state unless its supreme coercive power supports de jure authority, we have to allow that King Bomba's Two Sicilies ('the negation of God erected into a system of Government' (Gladstone)) and Papa Doc's Haiti

('Roman in its cruelty' (Graham Greene)) were states; that Hitler's Germany was a state; that innumerable past and present tyrannies are states.

To the extent to which you think that particular states lack an adequate rationale, do not pursue proper ends or observe due limits, or do not embody the correct forms of rule (§14.2), you will not consider de jure authority, to be among even their contingent attributes.

Supreme coercive power, minus the idea of de jure authority, remains a possibility as an essential attribute of the state. Here the ideas of Foucault are relevant.

14.6.2 Sovereignty and the state: critique of supreme coercive power

Foucault runs three main theses on power. The first is that power relationships are pervasive throughout society; the second, that power is 'productive'; the third, that modern power is characteristically what Foucault calls 'bio-power'. I shall expound Foucault on his own account, then try to assess the plausibility of his critique of sovereignty.

Foucault holds a process view of politics on which power and hence political relationships are pervasive throughout society. Power, he says, is 'co-extensive with the social body' (Foucault, 1980: 142; Wickham in Gane, 1986: 152). Foucault talks of 'micro-pouvoirs', and of the 'microphysics' of power, to emphasise this ubiquity reaching right down to the most trivial and least dramatic relationships and encounters.

As we move up through the larger social institutions, however, there is a particular feature to be noted about power. Power is not merely or even mainly repressive; it is productive. Foucault talks of 'pouvoir-savoir', or 'power-knowledge', to indicate this dimension of power. What it produces is, at the limit, through 'discursive formations', the subject himself or herself – a person's self-understanding, self-image, and perception of others.

Take Beran's characterisation of the individual as freely-choosing, self-determining, claiming and respecting rights and so forth. Foucault is not suggesting that this kind of view of oneself and others is in any way the intentional product of some determinate body of individuals or set of institutions. But he is saying that it is through a network of institutions and social practices – legal, educational, cultural and the rest – that this view of the person emerges. Ewart Lewis' warning that Beran-style views of the nature of the person would not have been possible in medieval Christendom, can be read as an anticipation of the point Foucault is making. ('The disappearance of the subject', i.e. the rejection of the subject as some pre-social atom of the kind favoured by individualism (§29.5), is a familiar label for this part of Foucault's thought; see Dews, 1989.)

Foucault's third thesis, that modern power is typically bio-power, involves the claim that individuals in their physical aspect are the characteristic targets of modern, large-scale power. Two quotations from the first volume of Foucault's *History of Sexuality* may provide a first understanding of this idea. Bio-power is bi-polar:

> One of these poles ... centred on the body as a machine: its disciplining, the optimization of its capabilities, the extortion of its forces, the parallel increase of its usefulness and its docility, its integration into systems of efficient and economic controls, all this was ensured by the procedures of power that characterised the disciplines: Anatomico-politics of the human body (Foucault, 1978: 139; Donnelly in Armstrong, 1992: 199).

The other pole:

formed somewhat later, focused on the species-body, the body imbued with the mechanics of life and serving as the basis of the biological processes: propagation, births and mortality, the level of health, life expectancy and longevity, with all the conditions that can cause these to vary. Their supervision was effected through an entire series of interventions and regulatory controls: a bio-politics of the population (ibid.).

How does this connect with our discussion of the state and sovereignty? The connection is threefold. In the first place, Foucault holds that the idea of sovereignty fixes largely if not exclusively on power as repressive, thus ignoring its socially most salient aspect. Secondly, he rejects the idea of the omnicompetent unit as falsely assuming a unique concentration of power. On these lines, the exercise of supreme coercive power is not even a contingent, let alone a necessary, attribute of the state. Thirdly, he argues that the 'juridico-discursive' conception of power – his label for these two defective notions – raises a false *problematik* for political theory. Given the repressive, omnicompetent unit, the prime question is how it might have de jure authority. But no 'problem' so misconceived in its basic assumptions can be illuminatingly addressed.

How are we to respond to this? A number of points present themselves. One is that the idea of sovereignty does not involve so restricted a notion of power as Foucault claims. Our own account of sovereignty took both the one-dimensional and the two-dimensional angles on power. Even the one-dimensional view, that of Dahl, does not restrict power to mere repression.

A further point is that Foucault's dismissal of the omnicompetent unit is defensible on other grounds than that of his own specific historical and social theory. One has only to consider the so-called pluralists' claim, at the beginning of the twentieth century, that no political society really exhibits such a unit. Not only do federal political systems, and those all those involving a separation of powers, block its possibility but also it involves an unreal separation of the political forum or arena from the rest of society. See Laski, 1917; Lamb, 1997; Nicholls, 1994; cf. §15.4.

Equally, from another angle, there is the fact of globalisation – the process by which the growth of world markets and information systems is reducing governments' power to control their own economies and societies. This sets further limits to the plausibility of supreme power within a territorial area: see further Hirst & Thompson, 1996. All this notwithstanding, there does seem to be a peculiar salience about certain political institutions that gives them a kind of quasi-sovereignty. The American presidency, for instance, is a locus of enormous power even if it is nothing like the omnicompetent unit of classical sovereignty theory. Its de jure authority is no small question; if so, the problem of authority is still a live issue in political theory.

Further on Foucault reading would best include Foucault, 1980; Coole, 1993a: 88; B. Allen, 1991; Dews, 1987: ch. 5-7; Merquior, 1985. On sovereignty in general, check out: John Austin, 1954: 194; Benn & Peters, 1959: ch. 11; Field, 1963: 58-80; T.H. Green, 1986: 102-4; Hinsley, 1966; Hoffman, 1997; Jouvenel, 1957; Jouvenel, 1962: ch. 2; G.C. Lewis, 1898, ch. 5: 41-57; Lindsay, 1923-4; Lindsay, 1943: ch. 9; Mabbott, 1958: 12-18; Raphael, 1970: 12-1651-3, 88-90, 157-61; W.J. Rees in PPS 1: ch. 4; A. Vincent, 1987: 45-60, 65-9. Among the classic texts the main references are: Hobbes, L, ch. 18-20: 121-45; Hegel, PR, §§275-86, 321-9: 312-28, 359-66; Rousseau, SC, I.7, II.1-4, III.12-14: 51-3, 57-64, 110-12.

Before we quit the discussion of the state and sovereignty, the following table summarises our results. The left hand column lists concepts, the right hand column spells out what they involve.

Sovereignty and the state: conceptual dependencies	
Power	One-dimensional power
	Two-dimensional power
Supreme coercive power	Sufficient one- and two-dimensional power to quell all opposition and ensure compliance
Authority	De jure authority: moral entitlement to command
Sovereignty	Combination of supreme coercive power with de jure authority
State	Set of institutions:
	• possessing de jure authority (contingently)
	• possessing supreme coercive power (problematically)

15. LAW

The Utopians, Thomas More tells us, have few laws because, with their social system, few laws are needed. 'The chief fault they find with other nations is that, even with infinite volumes of laws and interpretations, they cannot manage their affairs properly' (More, 1989: 84-5). In *Walden*, Thoreau (1817-62) even dreamed of a society without law.

Law has been thought to be dispensable on two quite different conditions: (1) when the social situation is so simple that there are few conflicts of interests to settle and control; and (2) when political wisdom is available to determine the exact requirements of each situation for action or resolution. Plato's ideal society depicted in the *Republic* meets the second condition.

Plato is quite clear, as anyone might be, that laws cannot, by their inherent generality, deal adequately with all situations. He sees a similar problem with moral rules. We could never pad out laws or moral rules with sufficient circumstantiality to match the fine grain of every quandary, predicament, unexpected development or special case. The ideal rulers depicted in the *Republic* have metaphysical insight into the Good and are able to translate this into prescriptions for particular situations; these rulers do not need laws.

In later works, Plato lowers his sights. The *Statesman*, also known as the *Politicus*, sees laws as a second-best alternative to the ideal ruler (*Statesman*, 293A-296A: Plato, 1961: 194-200). In the *Laws*, avowedly concerned with the second-best state, Plato turns full-circle and enmeshes all aspects of life with detailed regulations (Plato, 1970; Stalley, 1983: 17-19, 31-2). If even Plato failed to banish laws, we had better come to terms with them. Certainly, laws are among the most familiar items in the political world; a rich body of legal theorising awaits us.

The plan is as follows. First, after drawing some basic distinctions we will examine two theories of the nature of law, those of John Austin and Herbert Hart. Then we will consider the concept of the rule of law. Finally, we will take in two ideas that link law closely with morality – the ideas of natural law and of the legal enforcement of morality. There will be no need to take an aporia separately; aporias abound in this area. Keep your eyes open for them!

15.1 Basic distinctions

Laws are social rules. But not all social rules are laws; rules of etiquette are not, nor are all moral rules. What provides the differentia of laws, then, among social rules? We cannot answer this question without trenching on particular theories of law. However, a law is typically the following:

- a general rule
- concerned wholly or primarily with external action
- enforced by a determinate human authority

None of the theories we consider below rejects these three elements in the idea of law. They do, however, add to them in distinctive and controversial ways. Before we delve into them, it is informative to note an objection. The obvious element missing from this bullet-list, it may be urged, is the idea of enactment or promulgation. We tend to think of laws as enactments of Parliament, Congress, or of whatever may be the relevant legislative body. But in fact for much of its history law has been a matter of customary usage, having binding force, without being the enactment of any specialised body within the political system. Much of medieval law had distinctly this character.

There are basically three approaches to the theoretical study of law. The first, which coincides closely with 'jurisprudence', takes its start from within the legal system and looks at the kinds of law – civil, criminal, constitutional, international. It observes sub-classifications, as the civil law branches out into the law of tort, contract, and property, for example. It probes the notions of evidence and responsibility and so forth. These inquiries, emphatically the last two, open up genuinely philosophical matters in epistemology and the philosophy of mind.

The second approach aims to relate the concept of law in a connective or reductionist way (§3.5.4) to other concepts in terms of which is can be analysed – power, sovereignty, state, and authority.

The third approach is historical or sociological. It looks to the changing content and shifting functions of law. There is a regular link between the functions of law and the ground of authority (§13.2). Since authority typically expresses itself through law, the functions of the latter interlock with the ground of the former. That specific bond aside, law is generally taken to fulfil three main roles. The first relates to order. Laws require certain regularities and uniformities of conduct on which a secure and predictable social life depends. This is not to say that such social order as we find is wholly the product of law but only that the law helps towards it. The second role of law, which clearly sits in some tension with the first, is to induce social change (drastic, piecemeal, marginal or occasional) when policy choices are made in order to alter current arrangements. We will later encounter theorists such as F.A. Hayek who argue that projects of large-scale social change unavoidably mean a departure from law (§24.2). Law's final role is to protect the interests of individuals, groups or institutions through a network of legal rights and duties. This role has two aspects: (1) the safeguarding of the interests of one party against another in cases of clear violation of rights or neglect of duties and (2) the adjudication of disputes when there is situational uncertainty about balances, conflicts or applications of rights or duties.

This statement of the three roles needs a double qualification. In the first place, the extent to which the law of any society at any time actually accomplishes these roles is an open question; secondly, the roles can be given a less benign gloss that that provided here. In particular, marxists and feminists will have their own views of the kind of order which the law helps to maintain.

15.2 Austin and the command theory

Our representative of the command theory will be John Austin (1790-1859). Austin's main work is a slim volume first published in 1832, *The Province of Jurisprudence*

Determined. The book presents the text of six lectures which he delivered as University College London's first professor of jurisprudence.

Historical nicety prompts the comment that all the elements of the command theory of law can be found, with greater refinement and sophistication, in the work of Jeremy Bentham (1748-1832). See Bentham, 1970; F. Rosen, 1996: 127. Bentham was more original than Austin and had a wider range of his interests; mention should specially be made of Bentham's important work in ethics. But the command theory is indelibly associated with John Austin, not least because he stated the theory in compact, uncompromising form and because Bentham's legal writings have largely had to wait until the present century for publication.

On Austin's account all laws are commands. The concept of command is explained as follows:

> The ideas or notions comprehended by the term *command* are the following. (1) A wish or desire conceived by a rational being, that another rational being shall do or forbear. (2) An evil to proceed from the former, and to be incurred by the latter, in case the latter comply not with the wish. (3) An expression or intimation of the wish by words or other signs (J. John Austin, 1954: 17).

If all laws are commands, however, not all commands are laws. Only rules, with their element of generality, are laws. Austin explains:

> Every *law* or *rule* (taken with the largest signification which can be given to the term *properly*) is a *command*. Or, rather, laws or rules, properly so called, are a *species* of commands ... Now where it obliges *generally* to acts or forbearances of a *class*, a command is a law or rule. But where it obliges to a *specific* act or forbearance, or to acts or forbearances which it determines *specifically* or *individually*, a command is occasional or particular (John Austin, 1954: 13, 19).

Further, if all laws are rule-bound commands, not all rule-bound commands are laws for the purposes of jurisprudence and political philosophy. Only such commands issuing from the sovereign are relevant. These are 'positive laws'; from the scope of positive law Austin thus excludes alike the laws of God and private regulations of the kind that an employer or landlord might lay down. Private regulations are laws improperly so called; Austin designates them as 'positive morality' instead. The same ban of impropriety is extended to scientific laws, or laws of nature, which are laws only in a metaphorical sense.

Austin's theory might be taken in one of two ways. On the one hand, we can treat it as highlighting a class of phenomena – general, rule-based commands of the sovereign – which can be illuminatingly grouped together relative to some purpose (political, sociological or whatever). From this angle the question is largely irrelevant whether the theory squares with the ways in which we habitually talk and think about law. On the other hand, we can see Austin as a descriptive theorist who is trying to capture the common and distinctive features of law as we recognise it. Criticism has mainly taken this second direction, and our discussion will follow suit. There are two major points.

In the first place, there is a problem whether laws significantly embody the 'wish' of the sovereign, or let us just say of the legislator. It is hard to see how, in any psychological sense of 'wish', the entire corpus of English or American law is 'wished', item by item, by any individual or group. In full detail, probably it is not even within the cognisance of any legislative body. The reply to this criticism on Austin's behalf usually appeals to the idea of 'circuitous commanding'. The phrase is Austin's own, and the idea is that the legislature 'wishes' the entire body of the law in the sense that past laws have not been repealed and that, with the legislature's backing, subordinate bodies punish breaches of the law. We are dealing here with a form of behavioural or tacit commanding. My main reservation is that the power relationships that explain which laws are enforced, how and with what degree of vigour, extend beyond any such discrete group as the legislature.

Secondly, criticism attaches to the idea of sanction. Is it necessarily the case that where there is a law, there is a sanction? The standard objection to Austinian sanctions as an inseparable element of law is that many laws have the character of permissions rather than of commands backed by sanctions. The law often tells me what I may, not what I must, do. I may enter into a contract of a certain kind, to sell my car (say) or to form some private association. Hart brings this point strongly to bear against Austin (Hart, 1961: 33-5). But sanctions and commands are not quite out of the picture even here. It is not completely implausible to hold that, when the law grants me a permission in this way, there is an implicit sanction-backed command to others not to interfere.

See further N. Barry, 1981: 27-34; Hearnshaw, 1937.

15.3 Hart and law as a system of rules

The term 'positivism' was originally associated with the sociological-cum-philosophical scheme of August Comte (1798-1857). Philosophically it is now used more widely and loosely. Roughly, 'positivism' is the view that knowledge is confined to logical truths and matters of empirical fact, where a fact is empirical if it can be validated (preferably by scientific standards of rigour) through sense experience. There is also the 'non-cognitivist' implication that broad domains of human experience, especially those of morality, art, and religion, yield no knowledge whatever by these tests.

'Legal positivism' is not unrelated to this view but should not be simply identified with it. It is not just the application of positivism to legal matters. A useful, broad brush account of legal positivism in given in Hart, 1961: 253. Hart links legal positivism with the following views:

- laws are commands of human beings (not, e.g. of God)
- there is no necessary connection between law and morals
- the analysis of legal concepts is a distinct and valid inquiry in its own right, not hostile to sociology or history but also not dependent on them
- a legal system is a 'closed logical system' in which the validity of laws can be deduced logically from predetermined legal rules, and
- moral non-cognitivism, the exclusion of morality from the realms of truth and knowledge. See also Stankiewicz, 1976: ch. 5 & 6.

At first glance, laws are social rules for the regulation of conduct. Their logical form is three-way; they prescribe, permit or prohibit. That is they require us to act in certain ways, allow us to act in certain ways, or forbid us from acting in certain ways. Further, part of the ordinary understanding of law is that these prescriptions, permissions, and prohibitions are enforceable. Those social rules which are part of the legal system are backed by the coercive power of the state.

One of the most influential theories of law, that of H.L.A. Hart (1907-92), builds systematically on the simple insight or assumption that laws are social rules. The central text in which Hart sets forth his distinctive ideas is *The Concept of Law* (1961). Social rules are, on Hart's account, patterns of conduct and attitude. To say that there is a social rule is to say that there are regularities of behaviour within the relevant social group and, moreover, that such regularities are normatively charged. A 'critical reflective attitude' supports the relevant regularities and distinguishes them from mere habits.

Within the set of social rules Hart distinguishes rules such as those of chess, bridge, and etiquette which are no part of the legal system. This is because they impose no obligations – no requirements of action that apply whether those to whom they are directed like it or not. But if this marks off legal rules from other social rules such as those of chess, it does not serve to differentiate legal rules from moral rules. Morality is a realm of obligation too. On Hart's view, the type of sanction to be invoked provides the key to the distinction between moral and legal rules. Where the infraction of a social rule incurs merely general disapproval, the rule may be taken to belong simply to the group's morality; but where the ultimate sanction of physical force is applicable, there we have a kind of law. There are great differences between primitive legal systems, in which the employment of such force is intermittent and unorganised, and modern legal systems with their strictly regimented authorisation of the use of physical force. Those differences aside, 'law = social rule plus physical sanction' is a reasonable formula to capture this part of Hart's theory.

Hart's next step is to sub-divide the class of legal rules. So-called primary rules are the prescriptions, permissions, and prohibitions of which we spoke at the start. These are the citizen's prime point of contact with the law – the specific regulations to which his or her conduct is subject. But no legal system of any modern society could get by with just primary rules. The primary rules need alteration from time to time; infractions of them are often hard to determine and require adjudication; criteria are needed by which to determine the validity of primary rules. In other words we need secondary rules:

- rules of change
- rules of adjudication
- the rule of recognition

The rule of recognition is the final test for the validity of laws. In the United States, for instance, if a bill has been passed by both Houses of Congress, has been signed by the President, and is not regarded by the Supreme Court as unconstitutional, then it is a valid law. (Hart's reference to 'the' rule of recognition implies uniqueness but not necessarily simplicity; the American rule of recognition just cited has three distinct elements.) In the final part of his theory Hart stresses that, for there to be a legal system, there must also be general obedience to the primary rules among the population; consensual acceptance of the rules of change, adjudication, and recognition within the legislative and executive branches of government.

We should note that, on Hart's approach, something is a valid law just in case it satisfies the rule of recognition. This rule itself 'can neither be valid nor invalid but is simply accepted as appropriate for use in this way' (Hart, 1961: 105-6). The test, therefore, for the validity of a law is purely internal to the legal system in question. In this sense, legality and morality are wholly distinct. If you glance back up at Hart's account of legal positivism, it should be clear that his own theory is positivist quite definitely on counts (2), (3) and (4). He rejects (1), the command theory (Hart, 1961: 19-20).

It is also worth mentioning that Hart's theory has implications for the concept of authority. The state will normally express its requirements in the form of laws; in §§14.3.1-3 we examined the possible bases on which we might have normative, which effectively meant moral, reasons for complying with those requirements. These were bases of political authority. On Hart's theory, the validity of laws is unaffected by the availability of such bases. A law is valid if it fulfils the rule of recognition. This rule 'can neither be valid nor invalid but is simply accepted as appropriate for use in this way' (Hart, 1961: 105-6). Simply said, a law is a law regardless of whether the state has any of the bases of authority we considered.

The most fundamental and influential attack on Hart's theory has come from the American philosopher, Ronald Dworkin, who criticises Hart on two central points. In the first place, he denies the adequacy of the view of law as a system of rules; secondly, he argues that, when we trace the consequences of that inadequacy, we also lose the separation of law from morals.

What is essentially wrong with the 'system of rules' view, Dworkin contends, is that it is unable to deal with the problem of 'hard cases', i.e. of situations where no rule is relevant to the case or where a relevant rule is open to rivalrous interpretations (R. Dworkin, 1978: ch. 4). Note at once that Dworkin is not denying that the law is a system of rules. He is only denying it is wholly and nothing but a system of rules. In deciding hard cases, a judge must invoke standards which are not themselves rule-governed. These non-rule standards will include principles which are entrenched in social morality; so the pure separation between morality and valid law disappears.

More specifically Dworkin holds that the judge must be both a lawyer and a political and moral theorist. In a hard case, all the facts and the relevant body of law must be known, but in making a decision the judge must consider 'the great network of political structures and decisions of his community' (R. Dworkin, 1985: 245). The total body of law incorporates in effect a moral and political vision, a view of the conditions of human flourishing, of living rightly and living well, in other words a substantive or theory of the good. What the judge must do is to find the one right decision that best coheres with that vision. Principles, that are moral rules respecting individual or group rights, and policies, that advance or protect social goals, both of which are part of the network, will need to be called on and weighed (§19.3).

This process of weighing enables Dworkin to resist the assimilation of policies and principles to legal rules. Legal rules apply or do not apply; when they apply, they determine the outcome without more ado. Policies and principles need to have a level of importance assigned to them in particular cases. The further development of Dworkin's position involves the claim that 'rights are trumps', that in judicial decision-making principles are to be given general priority over policies. This idea, which is what Dworkin means by 'taking rights seriously', is discussed in §19.3.

Dworkin's views have been subject to numerous responses. There is throughout his work a certain ambiguity: is he doing descriptive sociology of law or offering normative views which may not be embodied in current American and British legal practice? Critics allege, not without plausibility, that while Hart tells us about the nature of law, that it is a system of rules, Dworkin offers a mixed bag of part-description of the nature of law, part-recommendation and prescription. He does appear to be correct in his claim that policies and principles are invoked in judicial decision-making, but the idea that 'rights are trumps' is a prescriptive position that may or may not reflect judicial practice and may or may not be defensible. Moreover, the way in which policies and principles often are actually invoked, i.e. via reference to legislators' intentions, does not quite square with Dworkin's account of the judge as independent thinker and discriminator within 'the great network'. Furthermore, the idea that there is a single right solution that best fits the moral and political vision embodied in a community's laws, seems at best a dogmatic assumption. Why should the vision be uniform and coherent and why should it best be served in one way?

On Hart and his critics, see further N. Barry, 1981: 36-41; Campbell in Goodin &

Pettit, 1995: 185-92; R. Martin, 1995; McCoubrey, 1987: 95-102. On sanctions as the key to the distinction between moral and legal rules, see Bentham, 1967: ch. 3; also chapter 3 of John Stuart Mill's *Utilitarianism* in Mill, 1991: 159-67; Locke, 1975: II.28.

15.4 The rule of law

The doctrine of the rule of law has long been celebrated in British and American jurisprudence, though its prominence in political theory dates largely from A.V. Dicey's *Introduction to the Study of the Law of the Constitution* (1885). Historically the key idea was that king and subjects alike were under God and 'the law' – first the divine or natural law and then, particularly from the sixteenth century onwards, the common law. '[T]he king', wrote Henry de Bracton (d. 1268) in his thirteenth-century text *De Legibus et Consuetudinibus Angliae* [Of English Laws and Customs], 'ought not to be under any man, but under God and under the law (*sub Deo et sub lege*), because the law makes the king' (Bracton in E. Lewis, 1954: 279). Note the contrast with Hobbes (§14.6).

Dicey (1835-1922) stressed three characteristics of the rule of law (Dicey, 1982: xxii):

- The law applies equally to all in society; nobody is above the law
- Nobody is subject to punishment except for a definite breach of the law as determined by the courts
- The courts are independent and not subject to political interference or control in making their decisions

Note that the rule of law, as thus characterised, requires the separation of powers (§12.3) to the extent that without some such separation there cannot be an independent judiciary. The accuracy of Dicey's account to nineteenth-century British practice, questionable enough, must be passed over here. More noteworthy is that the account has two backgrounds. The first is his desire to avoid a split in the law; he does not want a branch of legislation dealing with relations between citizens and a distinct branch concerned with relations between citizens and state. Just such a distinct branch he recognised as *droit administratif* in the French legal system, and it figures as an undesirable alien in his writings.

The other background is the common law tradition. This involves a view about the making of law that looks increasingly outdated in late twentieth-century Europe and America. It is the medieval idea that law evolves chiefly through customary usage and judicial decision; it is not primarily the product of a legislature, let alone 'the command of the sovereign'. Law is predominantly customary law (E. Lewis, 1954: 1-4).

Dicey's resistance to *droit administratif* might appear prejudiced and unduly suspicious. It is fair to say that the mere division between two branches of law was not what worried him; he feared *droit administratif* as a cloak for *raison d'état*, the use by the state of appeals to official secrecy and the public interest to prevent unwelcome intrusion into its activities. Such appeals are less likely to succeed, Dicey thought, when there is a single system of courts and one law for all. This is an empirical generalisation on which opinions are likely to differ.

What of the other background, the idea of law as primarily a product of custom and judicial decision? As indicated, this seems remote from the reality of late twentieth-century politics. But there is a way of developing the doctrine of the rule of law which does not run aground on brute political fact. I refer to the stress placed by F.A. Hayek (1899-1992) on the character of law, on the formal characteristics which law should embody.

Hayek lists three main characteristics (Hayek, 1960: 207-9). Laws must be:

- general and abstract
- known and certain
- respectful of individual equality

These features require explanation. Generality and abstractness mean that laws must be forward looking, set on future, yet unknown cases, and must omit all mention of determinate individuals, places or objects. For laws to be 'known and certain' the judicial procedures through which the laws are interpreted and applied must be 'predictable'. Respectfulness of individual equality requires mainly that when the law distinguishes a group of people, those inside the group should 'acknowledge the legitimacy of the distinction as well as those outside it' (Hayek, 1960: 209-10). See further Kukathas, 1989: 155-6.

The deliverables of the rule of law are nothing less than justice and freedom. Hayek makes this clear in the following passage:

> It is sometimes said that, in addition to being general and equal, the law of the rule of law must also be just. But though there can be no doubt that, in order to be effective, it must be accepted as just by most people, it is doubtful whether we possess any other formal criteria of justice than generality and equality ... [S]o far as its compatibility with a reign of freedom is concerned, we have no test for a law that confines itself to regulating the relations between different persons and does not interfere with the purely private concerns of an individual, other than its generality and equality (Hayek, 1960: 210; cited in Kukathas, 1989: 156).

We have yet to analyse the concepts of justice and freedom, so we must proceed in a tentative, preliminary way. Take freedom first: Hayek requires laws (1) to be abstract and general, and (2) not to interfere with purely private concerns. The second condition, which is not entailed by the three characteristics of law listed above, is introduced to block the following contingency. A general and abstract law might greatly reduce (say) religious freedom. It need mention no determinate persons, places or objects and may be entirely forward-looking. Hayek realises this point but comments, addressing just this kind of case elsewhere, that 'the fact is simply that such rules are not rules limiting conduct towards others' (Hayek, 1982: 101). They interfere with purely private concerns, invading 'a protected domain of individuals' (ibid.) – protected, that is, within Hayek's political theory.

The problem is that Hayek gives no account of how this domain is to be delimited. What is 'conduct towards others'? If I practise a religion, and you are offended by it, my conduct certainly affects you. In what sense is it not conduct towards you? The question will arise again when we examine John Stuart Mill's liberty principle, but Mill does at least try to define a criterion of harm to others as delimiting the private domain (§22.8.1). Hayek would have been better advised to handle the religious case by appeal to his third feature of desirable law, namely respectfulness of individual equality. For the discriminatory legislation would presumably not be acceptable to those inside the group thus picked out. See further Cunningham, 1979.

In respect of justice the case is much the same. Abstract and general rules can be markedly discriminatory against whole groups of people. A rule that forbade all and only persons between the ages of 19 and 59 from marrying is intuitively unjust, yet it meets the Hayek tests of abstractness and generality. Again, however, the principle of respect for individual equality before the law could be invoked: there is no reason to think that the legislation would be acceptable to those inside the group identified.

The idea of acceptability will return to the picture when we examine Rawls' theory of justice, a theory that aims to base justice on what contractors would agree to on specified conditions (§17.3). The generality of the law causes, we may note before leaving Hayek, a further problem. Laws, as Aristotle observed, 'are unable to speak with precision owing to the difficulty of any general principle embracing all particulars' (P III.11: 68); in §15.1 we met with the same view in Plato. The rule of law will never be fully adequate to the full circumstantiality of social life.

Further reading: N. Barry, 1981: 42-4; Butler, 1985: 31-3, 126-9; Fine et al., 1979; Fine, 1984; Gray, 1989: 91-6, 210-12; J.W. Harris, 1980: ch. 11; Lucas, 1966: 106-17; Oakeshott, 1983: 119-64; Rawls, TJ: 235-43; Raz, 1994: 354-62; Scheuerman, 1997; Scruton, 1984: 91-2; Sinclair, 1951: 176-8, 186-8; Ten in Goodin and Pettit, 1995. In German jurisprudence the rule of law, when combined with the separation of powers (§12.3), is represented by the ideal of the *Rechtstaat*, on which see Fraenkel, 1941; cf. Pasquino, 1998: 198. Logic compels me to insist that the rule of law does not simply combine with the separation of powers; the former positively requires the latter to the extent that, without the separation of powers, there cannot be (as the Diceyan rule of law requires) independent courts. Equality before the law will resurface in Rawls' list of primary goods (§17.3); cf. Rawls in Goodin & Pettit, 1997: 283. For Plato's reliance on his own version of the rule of law in his last major work, aptly entitled the *Laws* (Plato, 1970), see Stalley, 1983: ch. 8.

15.5 Law and morals

The relations between law and morals are complex. It might be more accurate to say 'messy', for there is no likelihood of reducing to consistency the various contrasts and continuities which different writers try to draw out.

One set of complexities I need to sideline. These concern the nature of morality. Morality looks to be rule-governed: types of action are prescribed, proscribed or left optional. 'Stealing' – this type of action – 'is wrong'; 'lying is wrong' and so forth. This puts morality logically in line with law; laws are rules even if Dworkin is right against Hart that the law is not just a system of rules.

This might appear an uncontroversial view of morality but in ethics, the philosophical study of morality, some theorists deny the existence of moral rules. The immediate point is not one of scepticism about the truth or objectivity of morality. Rather the idea is that each situation for action is unique and that there are no general guidelines of the sort that moral rules are intended to provide. This view of morality is sometimes known as 'situation ethics', though it is more commonly called 'ethical particularism'. It is appealing in its suggestion, if only as a counsel of perfection, that we should adjust exactly to the fine-grained circumstantiality of every situation. But its further implications are more problematic. Is there really no place for a moral rule not to cause unnecessary suffering? More to the point in political theory, to glance briefly ahead, the concept of distributive justice (concerned with the proper allocation of benefits and burdens (§17.2)) would need to be reworked from a particularist perspective. Distributive justice currently runs on formulas such as 'to each according to their needs', but such formulas are moral rules for which particularism finds no place.

To go further into the pros and cons of ethical particularism would take us too far afield: see Dancy, 1983; G. Thomas, 1993: 94-6. I shall assume that morality does involve rules, even if more refined and nuanced rules than the textbook crudities of 'stealing is wrong' and 'lying is wrong'. Moral judgements are informed by moral rules. So one alleged disparity between law and morality does not apply.

We have seen how, on Dworkin's account, the positivist distinction between law and morals does not hold good for 'hard cases'; hard cases are resolved by unavoidable appeal to moral considerations. Two further points of connection between law and morals remain to be examined. In the next section we will look at the natural law tradition, which argues distinctively for a tight connection between law and morals. Then in §15.5.2 we will investigate the idea of the legal enforcement of morality. A foundational relationship between law and morals on which all the discussions depend is that we cannot form an idea of the subject of the law, i.e. of an agent to whom the law applies as a rule to be followed, without assuming a moral subject, an agent capable of responsibilities, rights, appropriate liability to censure and punishment (Zarka, 1999).

15.5.1 Natural law

At the heart of the idea of natural law is the simple thought that behind positive law, convention, tradition, folkways and the rest there is a 'fitness of things'. The phrase is from the eighteenth-century moral philosopher, Samuel Clarke, but the assumption is common to all who have invoked the idea of natural law.
Listen first to Cicero, Roman statesman and Stoic publicist:

> True law is right reason in agreement with Nature; it is of universal application, unchanging and everlasting; it summons to duty by its commands, and averts from wrong-doing by its prohibitions. And it does not lay its commands or prohibitions upon good men in vain, though neither have any effect on the wicked. It is a sin to try to alter this law, nor is it allowable to attempt to repeal any part of it, and it is impossible to abolish it entirely. We cannot be freed from its obligations by Senate or People, and we need not look outside ourselves for an expounder or interpreter of it. And there will not be different laws at Rome and at Athens, or different laws now and in the future, but one eternal and unchangeable law will be valid for all nations and for all times, and there will be one master and one ruler, that is, God, over us all, for He is the author of this law, its promulgator, and its enforcing judge (*De Republica* III.22: d'Entrèves, 1951: 20-1; cf. Cicero, 1998: 65).

The tradition of natural law theorising continues to the present day. J.M. Finnis' *Natural Law and Natural Rights* (Finnis, 1980) is perhaps the latest significant contribution to it. The most elaborate development of the doctrine of natural law took place within Scholastic philosophy (§3.9), however. Prime among natural law theorists was St Thomas Aquinas.

On the Scholastic account, natural law has two essential characteristics:

- universality
- immutability

That is, it applies in all circumstances and it never needs to be revised or reformulated, though opinions about its precepts can vary. The Scholastic epistemology of natural law is roughly the following. The precepts of natural law are deliverances of reason; while not necessarily immediately obvious they are self-evident in the sense that we do not have to deduce them from intricate chains of discursive reasoning. Natural law is two-ways 'natural': (1) it is discovered, not invented, by reason and (2) knowledge of its precepts is in principle open to all humankind. Anyone capable of coherent thought can know the natural law. That law itself is not, be it noted, the most fundamental. Beyond even natural law is the eternal law, which is in medieval theological terms the whole of the divine scheme which the universe fulfils.

The precise faculty by which we discover the precepts of natural law is in Scholastic philosophy called *synderesis*. It is the same kind of ability that is at work when we realise that two contradictory statements cannot both be true or that if A is identical with B and B with C, then A is identical with C. The Scholastics recognised that this kind of ability varies between people, as does intellectual capacity in general. Cf. D'Arcy, 1961; Kirk, 1920: ch. 8.

The fundamental precept of natural law is 'Good is to be done', followed by 'Evil is to be avoided'. Evil may certainly not be done that good may come of it; the end does not justify the means. Other precepts are that a being must act in accordance with its nature. For human beings this implies that, qua rational, we must act rationally; as capable of the distinctive human excellences we must pursue truth, act freely, and cultivate virtue.

But if *synderesis* delivers these highly general precepts, something situationally more specific is required if we are to deal adequately with circumstances of real complexity. Here *prudentia* or practical wisdom, sometimes also known as 'right reason' (*recta ratio agibilium*), comes into play. It is what enables us to apply the precept to a particular case or to calculate suitable means to a preceptive end.

Finally, conscience is the (entirely fallible) sense of acting rightly or wrongly that we have when try to follow, or succeed in ignoring, what we understand to be the requirements of natural law.

So much for the 'high theory' of natural law. It is easy to register reservations, not only about the details of the moral psychology but also about the whole idea of universal, immutable moral requirements vouchsafed by reason. Instead of pursuing these points, however, I want to take the theory into its political application, where (under some modification) it is widely thought still to provide a useful legal tool.

'Law', said Nazi jurists, 'is the will of the *Führer*'; and we know to what depths that will declined. The natural law tradition might be read as a riposte to the Nazi dictum. Its cutting-edge gleams in St Augustine's remark, quoted by Aquinas: *non videtur esse lex, quae iusta non fuerit* ('there is no law unless it be just': Aquinas, 1965: 129). This itself is taken to be a deliverance of natural law. There is no moral obligation to obey an unjust law, to heed any legal requirement that bids us violate natural law. In fact, such a 'law' or ordinance is not even law, strictly speaking.

For the Scholastics this view followed from the deliverance of natural law that positive or human law is internally related, conceptually tied, to the common good; positive law has no other rationale or justification. It 'must have as its proper object the well-being of the whole community' (Aquinas, 1965: 111). 'Proper' has here a much stronger sense than simply 'approvable or appropriate'; it means 'logically necessary' in the same way in which the promotion of health is the proper object of medicine. Whatever fails to address the common good, as an unjust ordinance does since it harms those discriminated against, fails to achieve the status of law. Aquinas actually went further. No government has a right to levy taxes beyond the limits determined by the people. All political authority is derived from popular suffrage, and all laws must be made by the people or their representatives. It was this amalgam of views that led Lord Acton to mend Dr Samuel Johnson's remark that the first Whig was the Devil. Not the Devil, said Acton, but St Thomas Aquinas was the first Whig. On the moral obligation to obey the law as an expression of political authority, see P. Harris, 1990: ch. 6. Cf. §17.1 on law and justice in Aristotle's *Nicomachean Ethics*, Bk V.

This political application of the natural law doctrine was resurrected by the Allied prosecutors during the Nuremberg trials after the Second World War. It was felt that the barbarities practised by the Nazi leadership could not go unpunished. But many even of the worst of the leadership's deeds were legal under the German racial laws of 1933-45. 'What positive law have we broken?' The question had its point. The language of 'crimes against humanity' gained currency, but the operative idea traced back to something cited at the start of this section, the thought that behind positive law, convention, tradition, folkways and the rest there is a 'fitness of things'. This is what the Nazis had violated.

One problem is that a full-fledged doctrine of natural law has to elaborate this insight or basic sense. This is precisely what, in their own day and their own terms, the Scholastics did.

Can we provide a modern elaboration? J.M. Finnis undertakes just this task. His basic assumption is that certain things are self-evidently intrinsically good for human beings. He draws up a seven-item list that comprises life, knowledge, play, aesthetic experience, friendship, practical reasonableness – and 'religion', this in a highly diluted sense, merely sufficient to check human hubris and avoid the illusion that humankind are lords of nature (Finnis, 1980: chs. 3-4). The 'basic forms of human flourishing' are those in which such goods are realised.

Finnis supplements his list of intrinsic goods with nine maxims of practical reason-ableness. These are, barely specified: the active pursuit of the intrinsic goods; a coherent lifeplan; no arbitrary preference among the various goods; no arbitrary preference among persons; detachment and commitment; the (limited) relevance of consequences; respect for every action embodying an intrinsic good; the requirement to consult the common good; and following one's conscience. The intrinsic goods plus the maxims of practical reasonableness are the content, as Finnis sees it, of a modern theory of natural law.

Finnis' plain and simple assumption is that we can 'know what is really good for human persons' (Finnis, 1980: 3). This is a matter on which the major ideologies have a good deal to say, and we will return to it in chapter 5.

Fixing on a defensible modern theory of natural law is not, however, the only problem; there is a residual puzzle. Turn back to the question: is an unjust ordinance, law? This is a hard point to negotiate on its own terms. Take a parallel: suppose a doctor to issue a medical prescription which is actually wrong for the patient, seriously wrong to the extent that no benefit will come from it and the patient's life will be put seriously at risk if the prescription is dispensed. A pharmacist, let us further suppose, realises the situation exactly. The key point is, I suggest, that the pharmacist should not dispense the relevant tablets or medicines. Why get into a linguistic-cum-conceptual (or, to attach a more dignified label, a logical) dispute as to whether the prescription in this case is 'really' a prescription?

The vital issue is deeper than this. It connects with a politically more fundamental notion than that of law, namely the idea of authority; there can be no law without authority. The fuller specification of the Scholastic view is that a law is an ordinance for the common good, issued by one who has care of the community (Aquinas, 1965: 111) – that is, a political authority. It is the nature of authority which is at stake here. The Scholastic approach is to tie authority to the substance of its decisions, namely whether these decisions have the right content in relation to the common good. In practice this amounts to the citizen's judgement or perception whether the common good is served by a particular ordinance or body of ordinances.

It is by no means clear that, without serious modification, this is a plausible all-in approach to political authority. An 'authority' that waits upon our reaction to the content of its decisions is arguably not able to fulfil the role for which political authority is needed. A more formal and procedural approach certainly has its place. What the Scholastics have highlighted is the test-case in which form and procedure on the one hand, and perceived content on the other, are so discrepant that a moral crisis results. This is a point which we will take up again when we examine the concept of authority.

In the meantime, on natural law in general see N. Barry, 1981: 25-6; Brierly, 1949: 16-25; D'Entrèves, 1951; T.H. Green, 1986: 47-8; Hart, 1961: 181-95; Hayek, 1982, I: 20-1; G.C. Lewis, 1898: ch. 4; Lloyd, 1964: ch. 4; Lucas, 1966: 332-41; M. Macdonald in PPS 1: 37-40; W.J.M. Mackenzie, 1967: 84-5; McCoubrey, 1987: ch. 3; Pangle, 1989: ch. 9; Ritchie, 1952: ch. 2; Sabine, 1951: ch. 8 & 21; Sigmund, 1971; Stankiewicz, 1976: chs. 5-6; Strauss, 1953. Finnis is reviewed in Tuck, 1981. Among the classic texts you might consult Hobbes, L ch 14-15: 91-111 (for commentary follow up with Hampsher-Monk, 1992: 29-36); Locke, ST ch. 2: 269-78 (on which see Joad, 1938: 484-5; Lloyd Thomas, 1995: 15-18, 96-7; Strauss, 1959: ch. 8; Wolff, 1996b: 19-26). Hume has two brief, drastically critical discussions of the place of reason in ethics: *A Treatise of Human Nature*, II.3.3 & III.1.1. These discussions are relevant to natural law doctrines with their reliance on reason as a moral faculty: see Hume, 1978: 413-18, 456-70. On the link between natural law and natural rights, see §17 below and also Finnis, 1980.

An attempt to reconcile legal positivism with natural law theory would be interesting and might proceed along the following lines. To accept, as a practical commitment, the legal rules in terms of which the validity of laws can be logically deduced (§15.3) is to sign up to a normative judgement that the rules ought to be followed. This is, minimally, to make a connection between law and morals contrary to official positivist doctrine. However, one could make this connection without accepting anything like a full-blooded theory of natural law. In sum, this line of argument rather shows the practical inconsistency of legal positivism than the intellectual plausibility of natural law.

15.5.2 The legal enforcement of morality

In *The Elements of Politics* Henry Sidgwick drew a distinction between positive and ideal morality (Sidgwick, 1891: ch. 13). Ideal morality comprises the ends and principles followed by individuals. This is an area of great variation; and it would probably be impossible to devise a system of law that embodied consistently all the diversities. Positive morality is the body of rules supported by the generality of society, 'recognised morality' in Lord Patrick Devlin's phrase (Devlin, 1965: 11).

Positive morality usually has an area of overlap with law. Some types of action are required or forbidden both by law and by positive morality. One thinks of the prohibitions on theft and murder. But there are matters within positive morality that are not subject to legal enforcement, for instance the courtesy of punctuality and the small deceptions that occur regularly in our day-to-day dealings. Equally there are matters of legal restraint which have no moral content – the requirement, for example, to drive on the left in the UK or the right in the USA.

Morality can still surface in two ways even in these last types of case, however. For one thing, once a law has been passed and a certain kind of behaviour becomes common and expected, there can be a moral dimension in failing to follow it. Abstractly it is morally indifferent whether I drive on the left or the right but if others drive on the left and I do my own thing, I put others' lives at risk; and this is morally significant. Secondly, there is the question of political authority. On one understanding of politics, if I have bound myself to accept the decisions of such an authority, then I have at least some moral reason to comply with what the authority requires regardless of the detail (in this case morally indifferent) of what I am required to do. This last matter belongs to our discussion of political authority (§13.1).

It is in the enforcement of positive morality that problems of interest to political philosophy have mainly arisen. There is an apparent paradox in any talk of the enforcement of morality, namely that morally good action depends on motivation and this cannot be enforced. Say I have borrowed some money: if I return the money only on pain of penalty, my motive is not moral but one of self-interest. For a reflective general discussion, see Bosanquet, 1923: 64 & ch. 8 passim; T.H. Green, 1986: 17-20 (PPO, §§10-14); E. Barker, 1951b: 117-18. To the extent, however, that the law can get actions done or omitted which fit with morality in their external aspect (e.g. returning the borrowed money), morality can be enforced.

But should it be enforced when it conflicts with individual or 'ideal' morality? Extreme ethical individualism aside, mere conflict with individual morality is never a sufficient reason for not intervening to get somebody to do or omit an action. If morality concerns actions that affect people's interests, then we do not need an ambitious theory of interests to recognise that what a person proposes to do may be extremely harmful to others' interests. We hardly have to signal the 'all clear' just because the person concerned is perfectly conscientious in thinking that he or she ought to do the action.

In a work that triggered an animated debate many years back, Patrick Devlin argued that even where obvious harm is not involved society has the right to use the law to enforce its recognised morality. He put his claim as follows:

> If society has a right to make a judgement and has it on the basis that a recognized morality is as necessary to society as, say, a recognized government, then society may use the law to preserve morality in the same way as it uses it to safeguard anything else that is essential to its existence (Devlin, 1965: 11).

Devlin assumes that the safeguarding of a society is permissible; an anarchist would reject this in the case of a state-organised society. His rather metaphorical language of 'society' as having a right is harmless since it can be rephrased in terms of what it is permissible to do in order to preserve a (particular) society. If this is Devlin's thesis, we may now examine it.

Anyone may accept that some shared morality is essential to the existence of any society, though the survival of the Ik (a tribe who live apparently without any consideration of others (Edey, 1975)) might give one pause even here. But this shared, minimal morality is the morality of harm and interests. If no one respected anyone's life, freedom or property (whether privately held or communally shared) it is hard to see how any worthwhile social life would be possible. But Devlin, while he makes this claim, also goes beyond it. The law should also reflect attitudinal preferences and aversions. In particular it should not ignore 'disgust'. Writing at a time when homosexual activity between males was illegal in the UK, Devlin observed:

> Nothing should be punished by the law that does not lie beyond the limits of tolerance. It is not nearly enough to say that the majority dislike a practice; there must be a real feeling of reprobation. Those who are dissatisfied with the present law on homosexuality often say that the opponents of reform are swayed simply by disgust. If that were so it would be wrong, but I do not think one can ignore disgust if it is deeply felt and not manufactured. Its presence is a good indication that the bounds of toleration are being reached. Not everything is to be tolerated. No society can do without intolerance, indignation and disgust; they are the forces behind the moral law (Devlin, 1965: 17; cf. Ryan in Gray & Smith, 1991: 167-8; Stephen, 1873: 162).

The example which Devlin uses to support this contention is that of cruelty to animals. It is one which carries his point that the law should not ignore disgust, though it might be argued that the case of cruelty to animals is not one merely of disgust. The problem is, however, that disgust over cruelty to animals is part of what Oakeshott calls the 'habit of affection and behaviour' which makes up positive or recognised morality in any country to which the reader of this book is likely to belong (Oakeshott, 1991: 467). In this kind of application the enforcement of morality is uncontroversial. What is controversial is any general appeal to 'disgust' as a moral criterion for legislation.

The point is that the objects of disgust are now highly variable in the face of moral, cultural, religious, ethnic, and sexual diversity. The whole issue of the enforcement of morals has swung round. Devlin's situation was one in which there were clearly defined and well-entrenched majority preferences and the question was whether to enforce those preferences against minorities. The current situation is one in which minorities with clearly defined and well-entrenched preferences point-blank do not accept the permissibility of legislation against themselves and do require recognition of their diversity. This reversed situation has wider implications for political theory, as we will see in considering liberalism's 'difference-blindness' in §30.2.

To follow up on the legal enforcement of morality, see N. Barry, 1981: 176-81; R. Dworkin, 1978: ch. 10; Ginsberg, 1965: ch. 12; G. Graham, 1988: ch. 6; T.H. Green, 1986: 159-62; Hart, 1963; Lloyd, 1964: 58-61; Lucas, 1966: 341-51; Lyons, 1984; Mitchell, 1970; J. Norris, 1993; J.F. Stephen, 1873; Wollheim, 1959. We will return to this topic from a different angle when we examine John Stuart Mill's liberty principle.

Before we close this chapter, note the following useful readings on law in general: N. Barry, 1981: ch. 2; T. Campbell in Goodin & Pettit, 1995: ch. 7; R. Dworkin, 1977; L. Fuller, 1969; Summers, 1968; Waldron, 1990. Two approaches to law not examined in our discussion are legal realism and Kelsen's pure theory of law. Legal realism is roughly the view that the law is whatever the courts will in fact enforce. On legal realism and Kelsen, see J.W. Harris, 1980: chs. 6 & 8. Among the classic texts on the nature of law, see Aristotle and Rousseau. The Aristotelian references are: NE V.7: 124-5 (with commentary in Leyden, 1967; also McCoubrey, 1987: 27-30, 49) along with P II.8 1269a20: 39 & NE V.10. For Rousseau, see SC II.6: 66-8 (with commentary in Hall, 1973: 18, 25-6, 61-2, 85-6, 108-25; Wokler, 1995: 39-42, 60-8, 70-4).

3. Justice, Equality, Rights, and Property

16. INTRODUCTION

In this chapter we move on to a new cluster of concepts – justice, equality, rights, and property. Linkages between these concepts are legion. Justice is at least a matter of treating like cases equally, though equality as a substantive social goal involves more than this. Nozick, as will see, regards the pursuit of equality as such a goal actually inconsistent with justice (§18.4). Equality is often claimed as a right; and the violation of rights is commonly taken to be an infringement of justice. As well, there is a widespread view that people have a right to acquire property and that, under a permissible system of property, people have claims of justice to what they possess. First I take the concept of justice.

17. JUSTICE

'None calleth for justice', complains the prophet, Isaiah. *Fiat justitia, ruat cœlum*, runs the Latin tag – 'let justice be done, though the heavens fall'. In Plato's *Protagoras* Zeus, fearing that the whole human race will be exterminated, sends Hermes to humankind, 'bearing reverence and justice to be the ordering principles of cities and the uniting bonds of friendship' (*Protagoras*, 322C: Plato, 1956: 20). 'Justice is the bond of men in states', says Aristotle, 'for the administration of justice, which is the determination of what is just, is the principle of order in political society' (P I.2: 4). St Augustine is terser: 'Remove justice', he asks, 'and what are kingdoms but gangs of criminals on a large scale?' (CG IV.4: 139).

In the main body of our discussion, conceptual analysis will be represented mainly by examining distinctions between distributive, remedial, and commutative justice. Two high-level theories of justice will come under review: Rawls' contractarian theory and Nozick's entitlement theory. The aporia to be investigated is the so-called paradox of affirmative action.

First, a historical survey to get some big figures into the picture. There are four classic theories of justice, those of Plato, Aristotle, Hume, and John Stuart Mill.

The details of Plato's theory of justice are largely of scholarly, rather than of live philosophical interest. We can quickly see why: in the *Republic* Plato argues that justice in the individual is a matter of the correct ordering of the three 'parts' or elements of the mind – reason, emotion, and desire. Reason, with the aid of properly attuned emotion, should control desire. When it does there is 'justice in the soul'. But now, people differ as to their dominant element. Reason rules your life while mine is dominated by desire. Accordingly there is 'justice in the *polis*' when the bulk of the citizenry, those driven by desire, are governed by the group in whom reason holds sway, with the aid of those (largely military and executive types) with well-trained emotions.

This is caricatural Plato, Plato with the arguments, qualifications, and supplementary detail clipped out. A useful word to the beginner is not to read Karl Popper's *The Open*

Society and its Enemies until you know the real Plato well enough to apply a critical filter to Popper's polemic. Try Annas, 1981: ch. 4-5; E. Barker, 1960: ch. 8; Klosko, 1986; Raphael, 1964: 152.

But here and now, on the topic of mind and society, the critics have a point. It is hard to divide the mind plausibly in the way Plato attempts, and harder still to map the results directly onto a theory of social classes. The permanent interest of Plato's theory of justice (and indeed of nearly all his philosophy) is one of perspective rather than of detail. At least from the standpoint of political philosophy, the main point is that Plato's theory introduces the idea of social justice, of justice between groups.

The legacy of the Aristotelian theory of justice to political philosophy is different. In *Nicomachean Ethics*, Bk V, Aristotle conceptualised justice in a threefold scheme that still structures the discussion of the topic. We will examine this scheme shortly (§17.2).

Hume discussed justice in *A Treatise of Human Nature* III.2.1-4. Respect for justice is an artificial, not a natural, virtue. Recall from §13.3.3 that a natural virtue is a morally good tendency that human beings have irrespective of any particular social milieu, the tendency for instance to help children (especially but not only one's own) and to lend a hand in Good Samaritan situations. An artificial virtue is nothing fake but is a morally good pattern of intention and behaviour that depends on an institutional or conventional setting. Without the institution of money there can be no such virtue as financial probity, for instance. (On this distinction see *A Treatise of Human Nature*, III.2.1 – Hume, 1978: 477-84; S.D. Hudson, 1986: ch. 7; G. Thomas, 1993: 145-6.) Minus the institution of private property, on Hume's account, there can be no virtue of justice. Justice is an artificial virtue because it depends on a contingent social institution, that of private property. See Flew, 1976 and D. Miller, 1981: ch. 3. Other aspects of justice, corrective or commutative, are barely a flicker on Hume's screen.

In this coupling of justice and property Hume set a highly modern agenda. Theories of justice such as those of Rawls and Nozick are vitally concerned with the appropriation and command of resources.

In *Utilitarianism* (1863), chapter 5, John Stuart Mill aims to show how utilitarianism can accommodate the requirements of justice. The topic has since become a favourite crux of moral philosophers. Mill's discussion is uncharacteristically dense and opaque. Chapter 5 may well have been a separate exercise (just mind-clearing work in progress) artificially grafted on to the text of *Utilitarianism* (McCloskey, 1971: 87-8). Mill clearly connects justice with rights. This is a highly modern perspective. It is strongly evident in Nozick, whose views will come up for consideration in §17.4.

How might there be a problem for utilitarianism in accommodating justice? To answer the question we need to fill in some background in ethical theory.

Not particularly contentiously, utilitarians take certain states of affairs to be intrinsically good, inherently valuable: certain mental states such as feelings of pleasure (stressed by one of the founders of utilitarianism, Jeremy Bentham (1748-1832)), or certain states of the world in which wants and preferences are satisfied. Utilitarianism is a form of consequentialism for which the rightness or wrongness of anything (an action, an institution, a practice or whatever) can be defined wholly in terms of the merit or demerit of its consequences as these embody or promote the occurrence of intrinsically valuable states of affairs.

But a gloss is needed; the utilitarianism test is always one of *maximisation*. The aim is not to embody or promote such states of affairs in any old way but to maximise. We ask: does an action or a rule produce, through its consequences, inherently valuable states of affairs? And we add: does it maximise the occurrence of such states of affairs? In other words, how well does it aggregate? Does it score better than any alternative when we grade it for how much intrinsic good it brings about? In the classic utilitarian formula: does it promote the greatest happiness of the greatest number? Those are the key utilitarian questions.

Of course, in making moral judgements we have to distinguish between actual, intended and probable consequences, and (in a further refinement to its characterisation, as we will see in §18.5) utilitarianism has traditionally included a rule of distributional equality. But we can sideline these complications for now. What matters is to see that, on a utilitarian account, the line of moral interest runs straight from actions through consequences to the maximisation of inherently valuable states of affairs. In this sense utilitarianism is future-directed; the point (simply said) is to make the future better than it would otherwise be.

We will see shortly that there are various criteria of justice. Examples are: 'to each according to their work, labour contribution or merit'. Let us work with these three for the moment, to see the problem. Work, labour contribution and merit are past-directed considerations. They relate to what has happened – that people have worked, made a labour contribution or acquired merit. There is no guarantee that the best future from a utilitarian viewpoint will be produced by respecting these considerations. If you have worked, perhaps the future will be better if I give your wages to somebody else: your disappointment is one consideration but perhaps on balance more pleasure will be experienced or desires satisfied. That is why utilitarianism is thought to have a problem about justice.

Mill tackles the problem as follows. Injustice occurs when a right is violated. For there to be a right, four conditions have to be met. The first is (1) that there is a rule relating to people's interests. These interests concern physical safety, biological and other basic needs, and the development and exercise of individuality (cf. Donner, 1991: 161) the violation of which causes assignable harm to determinate individuals (see Mill's account of 'harm' under the liberty principle (§22.8.1)). The second condition is (2) that known breaches of this rule attract a demand for punishment. The next condition is (3) that there is a claim on society or the state to protect the individual from such harm. And the final condition is (4) that the requirements of utility are best satisfied by fulfilling this claim to protection. See McCloskey, 1971: 88.

The criteria of justice – in our examples so far, to each according to their work, labour contribution, merit – may be precisely such rules. They are in Mill's phrase 'social utilities' (Mill, 1991: 201). Mill recognises that in particular cases and special circumstances the rules of justice may need to be overridden to secure disproportionate benefits or avoid disproportionate harms. Mill gives little indication of what such cases and circumstances might be. Nor does he tell us exactly which criteria of justice should constitute the relevant rules, though (1) the broad headings of protection from physical harm, security, and freedom of self-development are helpful indications; and (2) the conditions of self-development elaborated in OL add further to the picture. If his theory goes through, harmony of a kind has been restored between utilitarianism and justice.

For further, more detailed and refined discussions of Mill on justice, see Donner, 1991: 165-83; Dryer, 1979; J. Harrison, 1975; Lyons, 1978; Sweet, 1997: 26-9, 49-52. For another angle on utilitarianism and justice, see Godwin, 1971: 321f. See also, on the unsympathetic side, Rawls, TJ: 22-7 in which utilitarianism is accused of not taking 'seriously the distinction between persons' on which justice relies; Nozick, ASU: 32-3.

17.1 Basic distinctions

In NE Bk V, Aristotle distinguishes two senses of 'justice'. The first is that of so-called universal or general justice, which is exemplified by the law-abiding person (*ho nomimos*). The Aristotelian relationship between law and justice is complex but, broadly speaking, in making a close connection between them Aristotle is thinking mainly of law as promoting the common good and as prescribing conduct in line with the moral virtues. In this second regard Aristotle says gnomically that universal justice 'is complete virtue, but not absolutely, but in relation to our neighbour' (NE V.1: 108). He means that the law prescribes and proscribes the same conduct as is enjoined by the moral virtues; in this sense it equates in its requirements with 'complete virtue' but it relates only to one major segment of the moral life, that of our relationship with other people. In this sense it only operates at one level of complete virtue, it is 'complete virtue, but not absolutely'. It leaves out the requirements of the self-regarding virtues.

Two comments are natural, first, that any such role that law may serve in promoting the common good and supporting the requirements of morality is highly contingent; secondly, that this role is ethically too broad to make law-abidingness specifically a form of 'justice'. Most commentators agree (but cf. F. Rosen, 1975: 228-9), and there is a widespread sense that here is another case of failure of precise fit between Greek and modern concepts.

Aristotle is aware that law fails often enough to fulfil this ethical role. There are bad *poleis* whose laws neither promote the common good nor support the requirements of morality (§23.1). But his identification of universal justice with law-abidingness marks the limiting case where the right coincidence between law and morality obtains. What it is important to note is that both universal justice and particular justice (which we are coming on to consider) is 'political' for Aristotle. Only between members of a community can there be relationships of justice; in turn there can be no community without politics, including law (NE V.6: 122).

17.2 Distributive, remedial and commutative justice

If Aristotelian universal justice is only a noise off-stage for present-day philosophers, the case is different with 'particular' justice or fair-dealing. The distinctions that Aristotle draws here form part of the permanent heritage of moral and political philosophy. In regard to particular justice he distinguishes between:

- distributive justice
- remedial or corrective justice
- commutative or reciprocal justice

Distributive (or *dianometic*) justice concerns the allocation, or distribution, of benefits and burdens. Distribution implies division: only the divisible can be parcelled out and distributed. Aristotle recognises this when he says that this kind of justice is about 'things that fall to be divided' (NE V.2: 111). Thus virtue, as a non-divisible good, is beyond the range of distributive justice. Aristotle provides a list, not a complete enumeration of divisibles and the list itself is limited to desiderata (benefits, not burdens): he refers simply to 'honour or money' (NE, ibid.). There is some dispute as to what else he would have included. Acton is right that, on the money side, Aristotle has chiefly in mind the distribution of public property (gifts or windfalls to the *polis*) rather than that of social capital, though Ritchie, 1952: 189 adds some complications to the picture.

Aristotle gives rather unhandy formulas for distributive justice. Note his talk about geometrical proportion (NE V.3). Suppose there are two persons, A and B, with a good (say, an amount of money) to be distributed between them on the basis of personal merit. A possible division is c, d: allocation c going to A, and d to B. This will be just if it reflects the ratio of merit between A and B:

$$A : B = c : d$$

i.e., as A stands to B in respect of merit, so c (the distribution going to A) must stand to d (the distribution going to B). If A's merit is twice that of B, then c must be twice the amount of d. This is a case of geometrical proportion: a certain relation is held constant as the distribution is made. As the parties stood originally in respect of merit, so they stand now in respect of merit-plus-distribution. This means:

$$A + c : B + d = A : B$$

Ross, 1949: 210 will take you through some extra formulaic details. How one could establish a precise ratio of merit, or allocate strictly proportionately a good such as honour, is unclear.

Remedial or corrective justice (*diorthotic* justice) applies when one person has wrongly damaged the interests of another and the resulting disadvantage must be removed. It has two branches, one concerned with contractual relationships such as buying and selling and the other focused on non-contractual activities where one person uses fraud or force against another. Just when we might have thought we were safe from Aristotle's moral mathematics, he tells us that while distributive justice aims at geometrical progression, corrective justice heeds arithmetical proportion. But nothing difficult is involved here. Suppose A has wrongly taken c from B. Their mutual position is now:

$$A + c, B - c$$

If justice requires the remedy of B's mutual disadvantage, the aim is to restore c to B. This is a straightforward piece of moral book-keeping: the wronged person's position is to be restored exactly to what it was before the wrong was done. If the objection occurs, 'but what if one person has killed another, what restoration is possible?', the proper reply is that this question really misses the point. Aristotle is offering a theory of corrective justice, not of crime or punishment. The notion of crime, as contrasted with the righting of wrongs done to individuals, scarcely appears in NE V's discussion of particular justice, though one might note the rejection of suicide as a deprivation of the state (NE V.11: 134). We may punish the wrong-doer in the murder case, but matters here fall outside the scope of corrective justice.

Commutative justice – justice as *antipeponthos*, reciprocity – has to do with fair exchange. It is the origin of later ideas about 'the just price' and the 'just wage' (Acton, 1972: 426); it can perhaps (as David Rees has reminded me) be seen as a development of Platonic justice in the 'minimal city' of R II. Corrective justice is concerned to see if a contract has been broken with resulting harm to someone's interests, but it is a matter for commutative justice to determine whether the exchange, fixed by the contract, is fair.

Aristotle's basic idea is that of proper measurement against a unit of value. If, say, in terms of the time, skill, and materials involved in their construction or manufacture, a house is worth (is equivalent to) a dozen automobiles, then a fair exchange is one that respects that proportion. In return for the house which I have built, I receive either a dozen automobiles (which seems slightly surplus to my needs) or the money that would enable me to buy that many cars. This is Aristotelian commutative justice; 'commutative' because it involves substitution, since where I once had the house I now have cars or money.

Aristotle himself thought that the diverse products of a complex economy differ too much for the necessary comparisons, say of labour and skill, to be made (NE V.5: 120). In a sympathetic discussion Marx takes him to task for this. For Marx, the key comparison precisely is possible: comparison of labour input (Marx, 1976: 151). Marx espouses a labour theory of value (§31.2.1).

For further discussion and details of Aristotle's theory of justice, see Bambrough, 1965; Finley, 1977: 142-50; Hardie, 1980: ch. 10; Joachim, 1955: 126-62; F. Rosen, 1975; J.A. Smith, 1911: xviii-xix. One special feature of Aristotle's theory should be noted before we move on, however. Different theorists have rated the importance of justice differently. For Plato and Rawls in their diverse ways, justice is the supreme desideratum for social institutions; by contrast, some feminist writers have seen justice as gender-biased (§32.2.1). Others argue for orders of priority between the different forms of justice; if the conditions for fair bargaining and exchange were met in market situations, one suggestion runs, a properly enforced commutative justice would pre-empt the call for distributive justice in the shape of benefits having to be provided by the state.

Aristotle is the only theorist in the tradition who, while highly valuing justice, argues for its supersession in particular situations, not by one of the other standard values such as freedom or the common good, nor by any consultation of rules, but rather by equity (*epieikeia*), which is the discernment of the *phronimos* (the practically wise person) in a particular case.

Aristotle's distinctive claim is that we cannot have justice without criteria of justice. Distributive justice allocates by criteria of merit, need or whatever. Corrective justice requires the exact off-setting of an unfair disadvantage caused by another person. Commutative justice requires proportionality between the two sides of an exchange according to a unit of value. In all these ways, justice is rule-governed. And rules, Aristotle is clear, can never be adequate to the full complexity of the moral life (NE II.7: 40).

A whole theory of practical reason is involved in this. For Aristotle, the ideal moral agent, the *phronimos*, apprehends the 'mean' (the neither-too-much-nor-too-little) in particular situations for action. Normally the mean coincides with the rules of justice, which in turn are embodied in the law. When a divergence occurs, justice and law are to be rectified by equity (NE V.10).

One is inclined to regard equity as simply justice running on more refined rules, but Aristotle himself does not see it that way. He tells us that justice and equity are generically different (NE, ibid.). There is indeed nothing rule-governed about Aristotelian equity. It does not apply general considerations but supplies the unique solution to the particular case.

D.D. Raphael argues that Aristotelian corrective (or remedial) justice and commutative justice are both conservative:

> Their object is to preserve an existing order of rights and possessions, or to restore it when any breaches have been made. We may add, though Aristotle does not, that penal justice likewise aims at conserving the position of individuals within that order ... It seems reasonable to say that distributive justice aims at modifying the *status quo*, and so may be called prosthetic justice (Raphael, 1964: 154-5).

Various criteria have been suggested as the basis on which the modification should be made. Some have surfaced already. From Perelman, 1963: 7, here is a sample list:

- to each the same thing
- to each according to their merit
- to each according to their work
- to each according to their labour contribution
- to each according to their needs
- to each according to their rank
- to each according to their legal entitlement

These criteria aim to define 'concrete' justice. To see the point of this label, we need to make a contrast. Formally, justice is a matter of treating like cases equally; of treating different cases differently; and of treating different cases differently to the extent of their differences. These requirements of formal justice, about which there is virtually complete agreement, do not tell us what the relevant likenesses and differences are. This is where the criteria of concrete justice come in; the relevant likeness is (say) neediness. Like cases of need are to be treated alike, different cases differently.

On the criteria of concrete justice, see Perelman, 1963: 7; cf. Lucas, 1980 and MacIntyre, 1988. The list of criteria can be supplemented, as Marx adds a formula for communist justice. 'To each proportionately to their labour contribution' (Elster, 1985: 229) is Marx's formula of socialist justice, as against the formula of communist justice – 'from each according to his ability, to each according to his needs' (PKM, 541; cf. G. Graham, 1988: 66; and §31.2.1 below). The exact sense of all these criteria requires analysis. But without some such criteria, distributive justice has no rule of distribution. If more than one criterion is chosen, then their relationship has to be determined – priorities set or spheres demarcated. The criteria themselves require criteria: by what criterion is someone in need, by what criterion has someone worked, and so on? As well, there is the problem of how to apply the criteria to particular cases, and with what scope for verification. The criteria of concrete justice are sometimes called 'conce*ptions*' of justice, as opposed to the abstract or formal *concept* of justice as treating like cases equally.

A point of terminology should be noted. You may expect to encounter the phrase, 'natural justice'. This should not impress you particularly. 'Natural justice' is simply whatever criteria of corrective, commutative, and distributive justice are (taken to be) morally most adequate. The contrast is with 'positive' justice in the sense of what the law recognises or allows. Cf. Campbell, 1988: 29-30; Scruton, 1983: 316-17.

In political philosophy, theories of justice have typically been theories of distributive justice. We may now proceed to examine two such theories, those of Rawls and Nozick.

17.3 Rawls' contractarian theory: two principles of justice

Rawls' *A Theory of Justice* (1972) is probably the most influential, certainly the most widely discussed, work of political philosophy written in the analytical tradition since the Second World War. TJ was prefigured in a long series of papers, of which the most important are Rawls, 1958, 1963a and 1963b, 1966, 1967, and 1968 (all in Rawls, 1999). In fact, Rawls, 1958 ('Justice as Fairness', reprinted in Goodin & Pettit, 1997: ch. 13 and PPS 2: ch. 7) is a compact, clear statement of TJ's distinctive ideas; if you want to slide gently into Rawls' political theory, this is the text to use. Equally, TJ received commentary and elucidation in a number of Rawls' papers between 1972 and 1992 (also in Rawls, 1999). Something of a watershed occurred with the publication of Rawls' *Political Liberalism* (1993). I say something about the contents of PL below. But there is no point in concealing my real impression. PL bears the same relation to TJ as Plato's *Laws* bears to the *Republic*. It is a late work of comparative mediocrity.

My account of Rawls centres on TJ. This is the text on which lectures, seminars, critical commentary, and (last but not least) examination questions tend to focus. TJ is apt to provoke three kinds of reaction.

The first is a sense of mild disorientation, the kind of unsettlement one might feel in an elongated maze. Even the point of TJ's organisation, the rationale of its three-part structure, often fails to register: and within each part there are excursuses, not really digressive and irrelevant but distractive to the reader. These obscure the lines of argument. TJ is a leaden wheel that spins heavily.

The second reaction is one of paradox and bemusement. Rawls pitches us a long tale about a 'veil of ignorance' behind which rational contractors fix the basic structure of a society – 'the way in which the major social institutions distribute fundamental rights and duties and determine the division of advantages from social co-operation' (TJ 7). The basic structure is the central mechanism of distributive justice. None of the decision-makers knows his or her specific beliefs and attitudes, wants and preferences, desires and inclinations, skills or talents, social position or even gender in the resulting society.

It is not at all apparent to the reader why this fantasy of surpassing strangeness should be invoked. 'Rawls asks us to suppose we are behind a veil of ignorance': 'But we aren't!' This exchange between teacher and student has occurred in more than one classroom. Again, when Rawls delivers his two central principles (the equal liberty principle and, with a view to the regulation of economic inequalities another principle, the so-called difference principle) one readily sees that he is defining a social ideal. But what makes the two principles, principles of *justice* specifically? Lastly, Rawls' portable formula for his theory is 'justice as fairness' but the phrase hardly helps someone new to Rawls. 'Justice' and 'fairness' are too much alike in their ordinary meanings for the formula to convey a distinctive theory. 'Justice as fairness' prompts the same response as 'the real as the actual'.

The third response is one of misplaced partisanship. Rawls is plainly in some sort a philosopher of the welfare state. He allows redistribution in the interests of fulfilling his two central principles; and there is a particularly controversial point in his argument for redistribution of the benefits of natural talents on the grounds that their owners are not entitled to them (TJ 101, 179; cf. Gorr, 1983; Kernohan, 1990; Sartorius in Frey, 1985: 211). He also allows a capitalist market economy if this works out to the maximum benefit of the least advantaged. But there is a common reaction by which these elements of his theory are detached as isolated 'positions'. Rawls supports redistribution, Rawls supports market capitalism. In fact Rawls' preferred mode of social organisation is one that, getting it right first time, prevents the need for redistribution; and his endorsement of market capitalism is conditional. If there are economic inequalities, and if these occur within a capitalist market economy, such an economy can only be justified if it works out to the maximum benefit of the least advantaged. There should be enough 'ifs' in that last sentence to satisfy market capitalism's most sceptical observer. Again, the welfarist label needs to be qualified; in certain moods Rawls is doubtful if his principles of justice can be realised short of a 'property owning democracy', or a 'liberal socialist regime'.

When you tackle Rawls for yourself, you will need to appreciate the structure of his book. TJ is divided into three parts – 'Theory', 'Institutions', and 'Ends'.

In the first part, 'Theory', on which the bulk of philosophical attention has centred, Rawls offers a theory of justice, of which the core can be expressed in two principles (TJ 302):

1. Each person is to have an equal right to the most extensive total system of equal basic liberties compatible with a similar system of liberty for all.
2. Social and economic inequalities are to be arranged so that they are both (a) to the greatest benefit of the least advantaged and (b) attached to offices and positions open to all under conditions of fair equality of opportunity.

In the literature, for quick reference the first principle is called the 'equal liberty' principle; 2(a) is the 'difference principle', 2(b) the 'fair opportunity' principle. The content of these principles is hardly novel. They belong to a left-centre consensus. Rawls' originality is a matter of how he derives the two principles. To begin, he lays down a test of adequacy for moral and political theories. This is that such theories should match our intuitions in a state of 'reflective equilibrium' – that is, at the end of a process of give-and-take between the articulation of our intuitive reactions and the formulation of principles (§5.5). Rawls thinks that he can derive his two principles from a thought-experiment which produces exactly such a match.

The experiment invokes 'the original position'. This is a hypothetical situation in which free and equal members of a society are to choose and agree the basic structure of their social arrangements. They are expected to choose rationally (in the light of self-interest) but also impartially. Rawls assumes that justice is the overriding feature to require of the basic structure (TJ §1: 3); also that the justice of actions by individuals and groups is ultimately dependent on the justice of the basic structure.

The second part of TJ, 'Institutions', explores the concrete implications of the two principles for an assortment of public policy choices as diverse as redistribution through taxation and the justification of civil disobedience. Rawls relates the first two parts of TJ via a distinction between 'strict' and 'partial' compliance theory (TJ §2: 8). Strict compliance theory spells out the ideas in terms of which and the social arrangements through which the basic structure of society will be just. Partial compliance theory covers situations where in certain respects the basic structure is letting us down and not delivering justice; it defines the permissible responses to such situations.

The third part, 'Ends', widely regarded as the least successful (even by Rawls himself), concerns the prospects of stability for a society founded on the two principles.

At the heart of Rawls' theory of justice is a simple idea. It answers the standard examination question, 'Why does Rawls introduce questions about what *would* be agreed on in certain hypothetical conditions?' Suppose we want to determine what would be a just basic structure of society, where this structure is 'the way in which the major social institutions distribute fundamental rights and duties and determine the division of advantages from social co-operation (TJ §2: 7). We could simply appeal, on the one hand, to intuition or, on the other, to utilitarianism as a rule that bids us maximise the occurrence of intrinsically valuable states of affairs.

The appeal to intuition fails to explain why different people's consciences appear to offer conflicting guidance (TJ §7: 34-40); and utilitarianism leaves open the possibility that, in pursuit of the maximisation of happiness, the interests of some persons might be totally subordinated to those of others (TJ §5: 22-7). Rawls takes utilitarianism purely 'aggregatively', as concerned with how much intrinsic good an action, or course of action, brings about irrespective of whether some people benefit at all. He omits the rule of distributional equality with which utilitarianism has been associated historically, as in Bentham's 'one to count for one, nobody for more than one' (§18.5). But it is fair to add that the logical congruence of utilitarianism's aggregative side with its rule of distributional equality is a controversial question.

Suppose, then, that we take a contractualist line, a genuine third possibility beyond intuitionism and utilitarianism. According to contractualism, whatever would be agreed upon by freely contracting, cognitively competent, rational agents under (fair) conditions of equality and impartiality, would be just. This is the basic idea of 'justice as fairness'. A basic structure fixed by these means would be just.

To move down a level of specificity, take a group of people who have to decide on a basic structure for their society. Assume that these people are cognitively competent and rational and that none of them can impose a structure on any of the others. Whatever basic structure these people, as equals, agree on will be just; there is no scope for arbitrariness, because nobody can secure any arrangement that specially favours himself or herself or specially disadvantages others. If we can represent to ourselves in a thought-experiment the nature of such a group's deliberations, we can find out what basic structure is just. That is Rawls' essential thought.

He develops that thought as follows. There is no agreed, known-to-be-shared substantive theory of the human good. But there are certain resources that almost anyone will need, whatever their particular conception of the good – i.e. whatever their specific beliefs and attitudes, wants and preferences, desires and inclinations, as informing their individual ideas about living rightly and living well. (Note that Rawls concentrates on needs to the neglect of desert.) The nature of these resources, known as 'primary goods', will be spelt out later.

There is moderate scarcity, hence some requirement to plan the apportionment of resources; but neither total abundance nor catastrophic shortage of the kind that makes any plan of apportionment either superfluous or pointless (TJ 126-7).

The contractors will fix on a basic structure that, through the provision of needs, will equalise and maximise their mutual freedom to pursue their particular conceptions of the good, and also provide equal opportunity to acquire the resources to put those conceptions into practice, to carry out their lifeplans as Rawls puts it. Since lifeplans can fail, there are likely to be winners and losers and consequent social and economic inequalities. A proviso is set that whatever socio-economic arrangements allow such inequalities, the worst off must do better under these arrangements than they would under different ones.

The thought-experiment by which all this is delivered involves an 'original position' behind a 'veil of ignorance' (TJ 36-42). The idea is to strip away all the personal characteristics that are irrelevant to the decision-making of our group of cognitively competent, rational equals. It is not that any group of people could actually possess only the minimal characteristics that Rawls includes. But just as we quite properly abstract away from many of a person's characteristics when we consider him or her for a job, so Rawls feels entitled to abstract away from many of the group's characteristics when he is considering them as rational, cognitively competent and equally weighted contractors. This stripping away will remove any characteristics by virtue of which anyone might favour himself or herself in violation of impartiality. Note carefully that when, in the story told below, Rawls says his contractors do not know some matter or other about themselves, this simply means that they are not to take such matters into account in a way that might produce a slanted, individually preferential outcome.

To descend to detail. The group do not know what specific desires and inclinations, wants and preferences – ideas about living rightly and living well, 'substantive theories of the good' – they will have in the society whose basic structure they are deciding. (The result will be, on Rawls' reckoning, that the principles that the contractors adopt will neither assume nor favour a particular substantive theory, or set of such theories, of the good. This is important for him in view of the diversity of such conceptions and the lack of an agreed decision-procedure for choosing between them.)

The contractors also do not know their skills and abilities or the social position they will occupy if the society is differentiated. They do not know in what period of history they will live, what race or nationality they belong to, or whether they are male or female. Remember, this is only a thinking-away of irrelevant characteristics, a 'device of representation' as Rawls calls it (Rawls, 1992: 107), with which he has dispensed in later expositions of his ideas. A further gloss on the contractors' impartiality is that Rawls assumes mutual disinterestedness. The contractors are not envious. They are predominantly self-interested in the sense that they will not opt for a basic structure that is likely to harm their interests, but they are not concerned antagonistically about the relative position of others.

The contractors do, however, have certain cognitive and rational resources. They can reason inductively and deductively. They have an elementary knowledge of economics and psychology, by which they realise that virtually whatever their individually variable conceptions of the good and associated lifeplans they are likely to need certain 'primary goods' – which we can now specify as liberties and opportunities, wealth, income, plus (as Rawls interestingly adds) the social bases of self-respect.

The relevant liberties are rights to political participation, freedom of expression (§28.8), religious liberty, equality before the law (§15.4), and so forth. These goods are primary in the sense that it is rational to want them, whatever one's full or substantive conception of the good (TJ 92; and it would be as well to check back to §14.3.2 where the idea of a substantive theory of the good was sketched out).

This claim is Rawls' 'thin' theory of the good (TJ: 395 ff.). The contractors have consistent preferences between the options available to them, they choose in the light of what they estimate will best further their purposes, and they are risk-averse in the limited sense that they are concerned to avoid the worst possible outcome rather than to chance all on the best possible. In game-theoretic language, they follow a policy of 'maximin' (i.e. of maximising or making as 'good' as possible the minimum or worse possible outcome). These are the characteristics of rationality that Rawls ascribes.

When Rawls also attributes to his contractors a sense of justice (TJ 575-7) it is important to note that this is only necessary in order for them to recognise the basic structure on which they agree as just.

With all this in place, Rawls' crucial contention is that the two principles of justice that he delivers in *A Theory of Justice* are those on which his contractors would agree. To repeat the principles (TJ 302):

1. Each person is to have an equal right to the most extensive total system of equal basic liberties compatible with a similar system of liberty for all.
2. Social and economic inequalities are to be arranged so that they are both (a) to the greatest benefit of the least advantaged and (b) attached to offices and positions open to all under conditions of fair equality of opportunity.

Rawls' two principles are 'lexically' ordered. This means that there is an order of priority between them. The first principle, known as the equal liberty principle, concerns political and civil liberties such as the right to vote, the right to run for office, freedom of thought, speech, and assembly, and the right to hold property. It must be satisfied before the second comes into play; within the second principle, (b) has priority over (a). It may be mentioned that, while Rawls assumes the virtual certainty of inequalities, he is not committed to their existence; if there are inequalities, they must be justified in the way he specifies. Inequalities are hypothetical or conditional in Rawls' theory.

'Fair equality' of opportunity might appear a piece of conceptual redundancy. If you enjoy equal opportunities, you must also enjoy fair opportunities: this is a natural thought. But we need to be clear what Rawls is saying. It might be held that getting an education is fairly available only if equally available: for one child to have a better chance of education simply by virtue (e.g.) of its parents' wealth, is arbitrary. Nozick will counter that if this kind of equality of opportunity is financed through redistributive taxation it is unfair because it violates justice in property-holdings. But let us sideline Nozick for now.

Rawls is not thinking crucially of educational provision when he talks of 'fair equality' of opportunity. Consider a different case to lend point to the phrase. You and I are standing for political office. Whoever wins will have more power than the other. Suppose that you have made a close study of political and social issues; you have published your carefully considered views; you have taken part in a great deal of charitable activity which has won you the golden opinions of large numbers of people. I, on the other hand, draw potted opinions from the tabloids, do nothing free for anybody, and am known only the length of my own road (and hardly with affection or respect even there). Come the election in which we are candidates, we do not enjoy equality of opportunity; you are more likely to be elected. But the inequality is fair; it results from the extra efforts you have made. It does not derive from the basic structure. Fair equality of opportunity, as delivered by the basic structure of society, requires only that we can both stand for election.

The facing table may help to summarise the main assumptions and moves in Rawls' derivation of his principles of justice.

More graphically, but with less detail, the Rawlsian contractarian situation can be represented as shown in Figure 7.

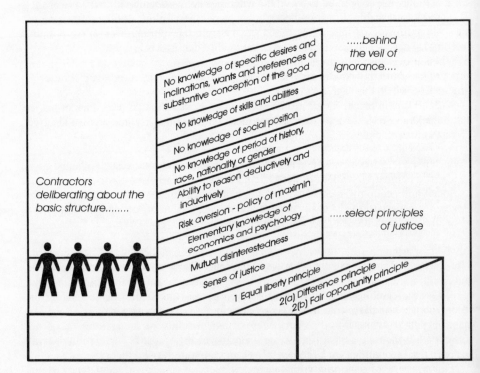

Figure 7. Rawls: the original position and the veil of ignorance

14 steps to justice: Rawls' derivation of his two principles

1.	We want to determine what would be a just basic structure of society – 'the way in which the major social institutions distribute fundamental rights and duties and determine the division of advantages from social co-operation'.	TJ 7
2.	Intuition is an unreliable guide.	TJ 34-40
3.	Utilitarianism is an unreliable guide.	TJ 22-7
4.	Let us take a contractualist line. This is a third possibility beyond intuitionism and utilitarianism. According to contractualism, whatever basic structure would be agreed upon by freely contracting agents who are rational and cognitively competent, under conditions of equality and impartiality, would be just. This is the idea of 'justice as fairness'.	TJ 118-36
5.	How are we to set up the relevant conditions?	TJ 3-192
6.	By resort to an imaginary device – a thought experiment or 'device of representation' (Rawls, 1992) – specified in terms of contractors deciding on the basic structure in an original position behind the veil of ignorance.	TJ §24: 136-42
7.	The idea is to impose on our free, rational, cognitively competent contractors, conditions that ensure equality and impartiality. Instead of saying that they should ignore or neglect certain considerations, else they may take them into account for personal advantage, we will say that they are ignorant of them. Hence the veil of ignorance. In the real world, nobody would be thus ignorant. That is besides the point.	Rawls in PPS 2: ch. 7; TJ 108-14
8.	Our contractors are ignorant of a whole range of things. The original position is simply the base-point of their deliberations. At this stage, the contractors have decided nothing.	TJ §24: 136-42
9.	What the contractors are not to take into account, i.e. are regarded as being ignorant of, are: • their specific desires and inclinations, wants and preferences • their substantive theories of the good • their skills and abilities • their period of history, race, nationality or gender	TJ 136-42
10.	But what we can safely allow them, at no risk to equality or impartiality, is that they have: • an ability to reason deductively and inductively • risk aversion embodied in a policy of maximin • an elementary knowledge of economics and psychology • a sense of justice • mutual disinterestedness	TJ 136-42
11.	With the veil of ignorance in place, we can assume that our equal and impartial contractors, if they are cognitively competent and rational, will opt for two principles.	TJ 60-4
12.	These are the equal liberty and the fair opportunity-cum-difference principles.	Ibid.
13.	They will opt for these principles, in a lexical ordering: the equal liberty principle is to be fully satisfied before the fair opportunity-cum-difference principles come into play. In turn the fair opportunity principle has priority over the difference principle.	Ibid.
14.	The difference principle is wholly contingent. The contractors only agree that, if (IF!) there are differences of status, wealth or power, these will be to the maximum benefit of the least advantaged.	TJ 75-90

Back to more general matters: there is a complex conceptual apparatus in Rawls. We encounter 'the basic structure', 'the original position', 'the veil of ignorance', 'primary goods', 'maximin' and the rest. To see how its various parts interact and with what plausibility to produce his conclusions, is no easy business. Rawls' precise derivation cannot be drawn out here. But the main points are the following. First, agreement to the equal liberty principle is to be expected on the ground that it is not reasonable for any contractor to expect more in a division of social goods, and it is not reasonable for him or her to accept less (TJ 150). Secondly, agreement to the difference principle can be expected on the ground of its being a rational safety-net in case the worst happens to the individual in the play of social chances. The whole position embodies 'justice as fairness' and, now we can say, this formula fixes essentials of Rawls' theory clearly: the two principles of justice are ones that would be agreed on in a situation of fair choice.

The lexical ordering is based roughly on the idea that freedom is basic; without freedom there can be no pursuit of conceptions of the good. So freedom is to be parcelled out in the largest possible equal amounts. What else would rational, impartial equals, pursuing lifeplans informed by personal conceptions of the good, accept? The fair opportunity-cum-difference principles, which apply to all social goods other than freedom, are secondary to this. Principle 2(b), which enables the contractors actually to use their freedom and which again would be endorsed by rational, impartial equals, has priority over principle 2(a) because it is unconditional. Whatever the case, equal access to all social goods other than freedom ensures that we have equal access to the resources to use our freedom. Why, as rational, equal, impartial contractors should we agree to anything less? Principle 2(b), the difference principle, is conditional and therefore secondary. In line with the maximin rule, it ensures that, as different people use their resources with different degrees of success, there is the best possible safety-net for the losers. But it applies only if a system of inequality prevails.

Discussion of Rawls has been sophisticated and extensive, rather like TJ itself. Here I present an abridged version of the main criticisms – a snapshot indication. A fuller, in-depth version ranges across: Mulhall & Swift, 1992: 40-69, 93-100, 119-26, 167-205, 206-26 et passim for an excellent conspectus. Down a level of detail, try Altham, 1973; Altieri, 1989; B. Barry, 1973; N. Barry, 1981: 129-37; A. Brown, 1986: ch. 3; Campbell, 1988: ch. 3; Copp, 1974; Esquith, 1988; Gourevitch, 1975; Gray, 1989: ch. 10; Grey, 1973; Hammond in Hahn & Hollis, 1979: ch. 10; Hampton, 1980; Kymlicka, 1989: 184-7 et passim; Kymlicka, 1990: ch. 3; Levine, 1988: 77-84; McDonald in Nielsen & Shiner, 1977: 71-94; Okin, 1989; Peterson, 1988; Pettit, 1980: Part V; Plant, 1980: 124-31; Plant, 1991: 98-107; Raz, 1986: 117-30; Swanton, 1981; Weatherford, 1983; J. Wolff, 1996b: 167-95; R.P. Wolff (1977). Daniels, ed., 1975 is a useful critical anthology. In the secondary literature there is a point of terminology to note. Rawls is taken to expound a version of 'deontological liberalism'. A brief background needs to be sketched in moral philosophy, where a distinction is drawn between teleological and deontological ethical theories.

Teleological theories look to the effects, results or consequences of actions, states of affairs and so on, measured by some conception of the good. By contrast, deontological theories are more procedural; they are concerned with rules, or how we go about things, rather than with outcomes. In the standard slogan, they centre on what is right, not on what is good. Here as elsewhere there are no absolute divisions, but the broad contrast between these types of theory is clear enough. Utilitarianism is teleological (§17); Kant's ethical theory is deontological (§22.6).

The connection with Rawls is that his theory of justice is seen as a rejection of teleological ethics in its aim to keep clear of any particular conception of the good. It is deontological in the sense that it is concerned with social rules, procedural considerations rather than substantive outcomes. Sandel calls the society depicted in TJ 'the procedural republic' (Sandel in Goodin & Pettit, 1997: 247). Another phrase of Sandel's has become common currency. This is that, for Rawls, 'the right is prior to the good' (Sandel, ibid.). Sandel's point is that, on Rawl's account, without agreeing on substantive theories of the *good*, rational and impartial contractors can agree on principles of justice – rules for the *right* distribution of primary goods as specified by the equal liberty and the difference principles.

Rawls walks a double tightrope. His theory can be two-ways assessed: first within TJ and secondly between TJ and the reader. Otherwise said, his theory can be assessed in two basic ways. That is to say that criticisms of the theory may apply a critique at any point between the description of the original position and the delivery of the two principles; or the two principles may be taken independently and tested by the reader, thinking things calmly over for himself or herself, to see whether they survive the quest for reflective equilibrium (§5.5). For obvious reasons, since the second approach can only be taken by the reader for himself or herself, the first approach will be taken here. Along this line, criticisms of Rawls' theory are of four main kinds:

First, there are objections from rival theorists of justice such as Nozick that the basic structure is not the proper subject of justice. Nozick argues for a ruled-based, more procedural view; it is specific transactional rules that are just, not the social structure. The point will be clearer when we discuss Nozick in his own right (§17.4).

Secondly, there are objections to the statement of the original position – to the terms in which it framed. Some critics allege that the original position is incoherent; others hold that Rawls' characterisation of it includes unintentionally loaded assumptions, i.e. question-begging assumptions that favour the principles he delivers.

Thirdly, the derivation of the two principles has been challenged. It is held that the contractors, even as Rawls characterises them, could rationally choose either different principles or a different ordering of the two principles.

Fourthly, the two principles themselves have been rejected on independent grounds. This has been particularly so with the difference principle; certain egalitarians refuse a principle that allows inequalities to arise. There is also the objection that the difference principle actually conflicts with the equal liberty principle.

17.3.1 First and second objections: shortcomings in the conception of the original position

Setting aside the first objection, as due for separate treatment, we can begin by considering the second. This has it that the original position, as set out by Rawls, is radically flawed. Charges of incoherence and circularity are made. The criticism of incoherence stems particularly from Michael Sandel:

> Sparing all but essentials, the original position works like this: It invites us to imagine the principles we would choose to govern our society if we were to choose them in advance, before we knew the particular persons we would be – whether rich or poor, strong or weak, lucky or unlucky – before we knew even our interests or aims or conceptions of the good. These principles – the ones we would choose in that imaginary situation – are the principles of justice. What is more, they are principles that do not presuppose any particular ends.
>
> What they *do* presuppose is a certain picture of the person, of the way we must be if we are beings for whom justice is the first virtue. This is the picture of the unencumbered self, a self understood as prior to and independent of purposes and ends.
>
> … Can we make sense of moral and political life by the light of the self-image it [Rawls' theory] requires. I do not think we can (Sandel in Goodin & Pettit, 1997: 249).

Sandel's point is that the Rawlsian theory of the self or person is one on which the self can be identified as a rational agent antecedently to the goals, aims and ends – conception of the good – to which it chooses to attach itself. Rawls' contractors will all (once the veil of ignorance has been withdrawn) have conceptions of the good, but they can make an independent, rational choice about the basic structure. Sandel denies this possibility.

Is Rawls here being unnecessarily embroiled in metaphysical issues about the nature of the self? Sandel's view is that the unencumbered self is an illusion; no such creature could exist. The self is constituted by its commitments and relationships. Even if we do not go as far as this, we might sympathise with the idea that only as 'situated' in a society where such commitments and relationships are in place is there anything to be rational about.

But it is hard to see that Rawls really has signed up to any theory of the person as unencumbered. He is simply claiming that whatever one's commitments and relation-ships, whatever one's personal conception of the good, one should rationally value a society that gives one as large an amount of freedom to pursue these things as anyone else has – and that one cannot expect a more favourable share of freedom since there is no reason why others, similarly situated, should agree to it. This is only another way of stating the equal liberty principle. I incline to accept Rawls' own insistence that his theory of justice is, in respect of the matters Sandel raises, 'political not metaphysical' (Rawls, 1992).

For a careful and balanced discussion, see Mulhall & Swift, 1992: 40-69, 158-64, 174-8, and 193-5. Sandel's views can also be found in Sandel, 1982. His stress on the social situatedness of the self is one part of a now standard 'communitarian' critique of liberalism; the other part concerns the liberal promotion of individualism. We will return to these matters in chapter 5.

A different, but equally radical, objection is that in his characterisation of the original position Rawls factors in contestable assumptions which improperly favour the princi-ples he wants to derive. One point may be conceded at once; the primary goods that Rawls identifies are not strictly goods that simply anyone, literally whatever their conception of the good, would need or desire. One can imagine someone whose concep-tion of the good were total mortification of the flesh with a view to extinction. Rawls might reasonably reply that such cases are so exceptional that nothing of general relevance to political theory can be drawn from them.

But the objection can be re-worked. One point, advanced by Thomas Nagel and endorsed by Josph Raz, is that the primary goods are apt enough for (most) individualistic conceptions of the good but less useful in implementing non-individualistic ones (T. Nagel in Daniels ed., 1975: 9; Raz, 1986: 119). Individualism is here a matter of the individual's 'unimpeded pursuit of his own path, provided it does not interfere with the rights of others' (T. Nagel, op. cit.: 10). Moreover even for individualistic conceptions, the further these conceptions diverge from the mainstream the more expensive they are likely to be to pursue, if we assume a market mechanism in which supply and price are mainly a function of extent of demand. Along these lines it is clear that Rawls' hypothetical choice situation behind the veil of ignorance may not favour a particular conception of the good, but it does favour individualistic, mainstream conceptions.

A further point concerns Rawls' account of rationality. In particular, why should his contractors adopt the maximin strategy? Would a rational contractor necessarily be committed to this policy? The complexities of decision-theory beckon here, but (follow-ing Pettit, 1980: 157-8) we can tag three possible prudential strategies the contractors might adopt. The first is 'maximax'. This involves taking the option of which the outcome, if it comes about, is best. Such is typically the strategy of the optimistic gambler. The second is maximin, which looks for the option whose worst possible outcome is the least bad among all the options. The third is to calculate the relative probability of the outcome of all the options, and to plump for the option that best balances risk and advantage. This strategy maximises expected utility. It would apply if, for instance, there were a tiny risk of a terrible outcome but a high likelihood of an extremely satisfactory one.

What is problematic about maximising expected utility is that Rawls' contractors have so little information on which to base the relevant calculations. This results from the way Rawls has set up the thought-experiment. He has deprived his contractors of the information they need in order to apply this strategy. But to provide them with this information would defeat the conditions for impartiality, since it would enable the contractors to calculate their personal chances under projected arrangements. In different circumstances of information, Rawls recognises the limits of maximin (TJ 153-5).

17.3.2 Third objection: shortcomings in the logical derivation of the two principles from the original position

Next we move on to the objection that Rawls' contractors, even as he characterises them, could rationally choose either different principles or a different ordering of the two principles. The difference principle licenses considerable differences between the upper limit (of the best-off) and the lower limit (of the least advantaged). Even with the maximin strategy, why is rational insurance not provided by a principle of highest average utility with only a small difference between the upper and lower limits rather than the difference principle? Again, it is hard to see why there should not be a marginal trade-off between the equal liberty principle and the difference principle, if the latter is accepted. Suppose a great improvement in economic well-being for everyone, including the least advantaged, were possible with just a slight infraction of equal liberty? Rawls discounts this possibility under advanced economic conditions (TJ 542). But the existence of such conditions is only a contingent assumption. See also Reiman, 1990: 264 ff.

A tension between Rawls' two principles has been alleged by some critics. Officially, no such tension should be possible; the equal liberty principle has to be fully satisfied before the difference principle comes into play. But it is hard to see how, once the difference principle comes into play, it does not prejudice equal liberty. It licenses differences in wealth which must impinge critically on the equal liberty of different persons to pursue their substantive theories of the good. Are the 'social bases of self-respect' protected if I recognise myself as one of the least advantaged?

17.3.3 Fourth objection: independent critique of the two principles

Finally there is the objection that the two principles are to be rejected on independent grounds. From some egalitarian standpoints, as mentioned above, the difference principle is a non-starter. But egalitarianism has problems of its own (§18.1-4). Another objection, again in respect of the difference principle, is that Rawls is in the grip of:

a materialistic, consumption-based conception of human welfare. It is impossible, when thinking of the important satisfactions which are derived from involvement in the socially significant activities of a society, to imagine that increased inequality might lead to an enrichment of the lives of the worst-off class. The assumptions required by the principle (the possibility of indefinite expansion of the sum of satisfactions, and the possibility of an absolute, culture-free measure of the well-being of people) do not apply (Watt, 1988: 8).

At the start of our discussion of Rawls I mentioned his later work, *Political Liberalism*. This operates at a more overtly empirical political level than does TJ. Rawls starts from the political fact of pluralism, the existence of an irreducible plurality of substantive theories of the good, of views about living rightly and living well. There is a switch of emphasis from the rational to the reasonable. The aim is no longer to determine what rational contractors would decide behind the veil of ignorance. The problem of PL is to fix the conditions for a 'reasonable pluralism', that is, to discover the terms on which this pluralism can be accommodated within a mutually acceptable, interpersonally justifiable, political order. Most of the conclusions of TJ are retained; Rawls argues for the reasonableness of an 'overlapping consensus' between holders of substantive theories of the good on precisely his two principles of justice. This is 'political liberalism', the mutual accommodation of heterogeneous persons and groups, rather than what Rawls now calls 'comprehensive liberalism' – of which he tells us that TJ is an example. A 'comprehensive' doctrine is one that embraces 'all recognized values and virtues within one rather precisely articulated system' (Rawls, 1993: xvi, 152, n. 17; cf. B. Barry, 1995: 30n.) While this definition is less than luminous, the point appears to be that TJ delivers such a system as a theory to be accepted, not as what is most likely to emerge politically from the search for conditions of mutual accommodation in the real world of Western pluralism.

Certainly the method of exposition is opposite to that of the earlier work. The minimally specified contractors behind the veil of ignorance in the original position become the fully 'encumbered' selves of Sandel's critique. For a detailed discussion, see S. Wolin, 1996. Rawls offers a succinct statement of his new approach in Goodin & Pettit, 1997: ch. 17 ('The Domain of the Political and Overlapping Consensus'). See also Rawls, 1987.

Before we leave Rawls, we should take note of a sub-topic, that of Rawls' relation to Kant in TJ. Rawls' 'Kantianism' – a favourite topic of examiners – rests on two considerations:

- The first, distinctly tenuous connection is that for both theorists 'the right is prior to the good' (Sandel above). On one of Kant's tests for the moral permissibility of actions, the maxim of one's action must be consistently universalisable (§22.6). This is a purely logical test which involves no reference to human benefit or harm. Likewise – in a thin parallelism – Rawls' principles of justice are selected without reference to substantive theories of the human good.
- The second, tighter link is that for both theorists there is an indivisible bond between rationality and morality. Rawls' principles of justice are the product of rational choice under the conditions of the veil of ignorance; Kant's categorical imperative is the product of the rational agent's self-legislation (§22.6). See further Darwall, 1983: 246-9; and O'Neill, 1988-9.

17.4 Nozick's entitlement theory

Nozick's *Anarchy, State and Utopia* is one of the fireworks of political philosophy. Nozick (b. 1938) is caustic and polemical where Rawls is urbane; free-wheeling where Rawls is elaborately and discursively systematic. Capable of deeply subtle twists of argument, Nozick is also a skilful, lively writer, with a deft technique of descending on his opponents with stinging showers of questions, spreading over whole paragraphs, with powerful rhetorical effect. Altogether Nozick is a formidable writer.

Like TJ, Nozick's book is divided into three parts. In the first, 'Anarchy', Nozick tackles what he takes to be the central question of political philosophy: why should there be a state and not anarchy? Against anarchism he argues for the minimal state, a state limited to the functions of protection against force, theft, fraud, and the breaking of contracts (ASU 26). For a brief discussion see §28.5. In the second part, 'State', which incorporates a long critical discussion of Rawls, he defends the minimal state against various champions of a more ambitious style of politics. In Nozick's view, only the minimal state is legitimate. This defence of the minimal state is linked to a particular theory of justice. Finally, in the third part, 'Utopia', he argues for the continuity of his ideas with the utopian tradition. Within the generous social limits of the minimal state, a broad variety of voluntary communities guided by different norms can flourish (cf. Steiner, 1977: 120).

ASU has triggered an extensive and vigorous debate in which the themes of the minimal state and of justice have grabbed the limelight. The themes are connected. Given Nozick's theory of justice, the redistributive policies of the non-minimal, welfare state are unjust. What is redistributed is already 'owned' and through state action can only be coercively, not legitimately, transferred.

Nozick offers a twofold contrast with Rawls. In the first place, he has none of Rawls' complex conceptual machinery of the veil of ignorance, the original position, the thin theory of the good, and the rest. 'Individuals have rights', is Nozick's opening statement (ASU ix). 'People are entitled to their natural assets', and property holding flow from their natural assets. To many, such claims have strong intuitive appeal. Secondly, Nozick ventures a theory of justice which is radically different in kind from that of Rawls. Nozick's theory is historical and unpatterned; Rawls' is end-state or current time-slice. There is a burden of terminology to be discharged here.

Earlier, we noted a range of formulas of justice. Here is the reminder from §17.2:

- to each the same thing
- to each according to their merit
- to each according to their work
- to each according to their contribution
- to each according to their needs
- to each according to their rank
- to each according to their legal entitlement

End-state or current time-slice principles aim at a particular pattern of distribution regardless of what has happened in the past. An example is: 'to each according to their needs'. No matter how needs have arisen, they are to be satisfied. Resources are to be so allocated that society exhibits a pattern, fulfils the description, 'each has resources according to their needs'.

Historical, patterned principles also aim to establish a particular pattern of distribution but they do take into account what has happened in the past: e.g. 'to each according to their contribution', i.e. to each person what he or she has contributed. Nozick's slightly unhelpful phrase is that such principles allocate along a 'natural dimension'.

Historical, unpatterned principles take into account only what has happened in the past and, according to what has happened, allow any pattern of distribution – no particular, pre-set pattern – to emerge. Nozick's own principles of justice are historical and unpatterned. (Cf. Hayek's spontaneous social order (§30.4).)

Rawls' two principles of justice are end-state because Rawlsian distributive justice achieves the end-state of equal liberty, fair opportunity, and (in the event of social and economic inequalities) maximum benefit to the least advantaged. (Or could they be argued to be historical, patterned? The pattern of distribution takes into account what has happened in the past, namely the contractors' adoption of principles to determine the basic structure with the aim of equal liberty, etc.)

In Nozick's view, both the end-state and the historical patterned approaches are to be rejected. The distribution of benefits and burdens is just if and only if it has come about in a particular way, namely through legitimate procedures. Whether a distribution of benefits and burdens is just is a backward-looking, 'historical' matter; the sole question is one of origin and derivation. End-states informed by social ideals are irrelevant. And no particular 'pattern' of distribution is to be expected. Such patterns will emerge as satisfy the procedures.

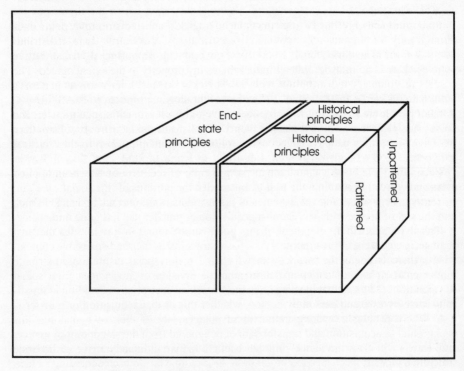

Figure 8. Nozick's classification of principles of justice

The relevant procedures are threefold. Nozick specifies a principle of just acquisition, a principle of just transfer, and a principle of rectification to remedy cases where the principles of just acquisition and transfer have not been respected. The principles, listed in ASU 150-3 and glossed in ASU 32-3, 174-82 & 206, are as follows:

• Principle of just acquisition: I own my body and its abilities and I can come to own various external objects. The condition on which I can do this is that through appropriation I do not, all things considered, worsen the situation of others

- Principle of just transfer: I can trade or give away things that I own; this occurs through uncoerced gift, exchange, or bequest
- Principle of rectification: where acquisition or transfer does not fulfil the preceding conditions, remedies must be applied in the form of restoration or compensation

Nozick objects to end-state theories, Rawls' and others, that they assume, in a now common image, that there is a social cake of benefits, the sum-total of goods and wealth however currently allocated, for the correct distribution of which we have only to specify the right criteria of justice. The knife of redistribution is poised; the cake is in place; we have only to decide how best to cut. But ethically, from the viewpoint of justice, the cake is not redistributionally available; it is already privately owned by those who have acquired their just shares of it through just acquisition and just transfer. Redistribution is like the act of a burglar who has made off with somebody's property and then decides how most 'fairly' to distribute it to friends and family ('Josey had a new PC last week; it's Carl's turn now').

Five comments are due. In the first place, Nozick's anti-redistributive point goes through only for compulsory, involuntary redistributions. Voluntarily done, redistribution is a form of just transfer. If I vote for a government, supporting its redistributive policies, there is no injustice when it redistributes my property to the extent agreed. The politics of voluntary redistribution replaces Nozick's slogan, 'liberty upsets patterns', with 'patterns can be freely willed'. (The point of the slogan, propounded in ASU 160-4, is that if people are free to follow Nozick's principles of just acquisition and transfer, and those principles yield no pre-set pattern, then to establish and maintain a particular pattern we have to restrict people's freedom to follow the principles. For further, critical comments see G.A. Cohen, 1995: ch. 1 & 4.)

Secondly, there is no guarantee that the principle of rectification has been applied often and correctly enough in the past to ensure that the portions of 'the social cake' are currently justly owned. The ethical barriers against redistribution crack and sink an inch into the soil of justice with every unjust acquisition or transfer that has gone unrectified.

Thirdly, a specific development of this point can be found in Rawls' idea that just acquisition and transfer presuppose a just 'basic structure' as their indispensable context. Unless there is justice in 'the way in which the major social institutions distribute fundamental rights and duties and determine the division of advantages from social co-operation' (TJ 7), a total blockage hits the Nozickian enterprise of deciding atomistically, case by case and person by person, whether this or that acquisition or transfer is just. Where people have comparative disadvantages, not of their own making, this background to acquisition and transfer cannot be ignored from the standpoint of justice; and, Rawls will claim, in identifying that background we ultimately arrive at the basic structure of society.

Fourthly, with regard to just acquisition there are difficulties in the idea of not worsening, all things considered, the situation of others – Nozick's version of the Lockean proviso. Nozick does not use the phrase 'all things considered' but the consideration of all relevant things is the strategy of ASU 176-8 (Wolff, 1991: 110). Now take the following example of acquisition. In a state of non-appropriation, situation 1, where some natural resource is held in common, person A receives 10 units of benefit, as does person B. Now A appropriates and arranges a division of labour under which, in situation 2, A receives 15 units and B receives 12. Acquisition here may appear to pass the Nozick test. A has not worsened the situation of B; B is 2 units better off. Situation 2 is the actual situation.

Yet suppose that if B had appropriated, the allocation would have been reversed. A would have received 12 units and B 15 in this hypothetical situation 3. By luck or accident, A pipped B to the post. In the actual situation (situation 2), A has worsened the situation of B vis-à-vis the hypothetical situation – i.e. with the latter situation considered as it should be under the rubric 'all things considered'. In effect Nozick cuts off the argument for appropriation with a comparison between situations 1 and 2, not between situations 1 and 3. Situation 1, in which appropriation does not take place, is the 'base line' (ASU 177). There is no rationale for this. See G.A. Cohen, 1984; Roemer, 1988: 156.

Lastly, Nozick invokes the rule that whatever arises from a just situation by just steps itself is just. Take an initial distribution agreed to be just. If subsequent transactions are voluntary, the new distribution must itself be just. Nozick's Wilt Chamberlain example, famous in the literature, in which from an initial state of financial equality, basketball spectators are willing to make a superb player much better off than themselves (ASU 161; G.A. Cohen, 1995: ch. 1; J. Wolff, 1991: 79-100), is meant to illustrate the point.

Although Nozick's rule has a certain intuitive appeal, it seems to me false as it stands. It needs to be relativised to descriptions. A state of affairs can have more than one description, and can be just under one description but unjust under another.

For instance, the initial distribution, D1, might be just. Voluntary exchanges occur in this society of (let us say) inveterate gamblers. All the transactions are voluntary; and D2, under the description 'new distribution resulting from voluntary exchanges', is just. But relative to another description it is not. A number of families, those of the losers, are now severely under-resourced. Under the description, 'distribution in which children are in a condition of relative disadvantage through no fault of their own', D2 is unjust.

See further B. Barry, 1995: 202-5; A. Brown, 1986: ch. 4; Browning in Axford et al., 1997: 187-8; G. Graham, 1988: 64-71; Kymlicka, 1990: 96-133; J. Paul, 1982; Pettit, 1980: 80-4, 85-93, 94-103; J. Wolff, 1991: 73-117; J. Wolff, 1996b: 189-95.

A final comment. Nozick's theory of justice is premised on the assertion, quoted at the outset, that 'Individuals have rights'(ASU ix) – rights to acquire, rights to transfer, and rights to rectification. This assertion beckons towards a general, rights-based moral theory which Nozick nowhere supplies. His follow-on book to ASU, namely Nozick, 1981, has an extended discussion of ethical value but no attempt to supply ASU's missing moral foundation.

17.5 The paradox of affirmative action

We have noted such formulas of justice as 'to each according to their merit', 'to each according to their work', 'to each according to their contribution', and 'to each according to their needs'. Historically the allocation of benefits and resources has, particularly on grounds of sex, gender, race, colour or creed, violated all these formulas and resulted in injustice. Nor is this so only historically; it continues to be the case. These are not matters of controversy. What is controversial is what should be done about it.

This opens the area of (as it is variously called) compensatory, inverse or reverse discrimination or affirmative action. I will use the last label since the term 'discrimination' has negative associations which can prejudice the discussion.

The paradox of affirmative action arises in the following way. Characteristic X, say, has been used negatively in past times as a control on the allocation of benefits and resources. The result is that the group defined by characteristic X is now in a condition of comparative disadvantage. Characteristic X was morally irrelevant to the allocation. Persons with characteristic X, call them group A, were discriminated against on the basis of an irrelevant difference.

How are we to make good this notion of 'irrelevant difference'? How can we decide which of the formulas of justice was the one that should really have controlled the allocation? I assume that something like Michael Walzer's idea of 'spheres of justice' can be given sufficient substance. This is the idea that advantages and resources fall into types, Walzer's 'spheres', which have internal criteria for their allocation. Now just to put a finger on the fast-forward button, we will meet this notion again in discussing Williams' views on equality (§18.3). One might say, and Williams does, that 'the proper ground of distribution of medical care is ill health' (PPS 2: 121). One might say, and I should, that the proper ground of distribution of education is the need for essential knowledge and understanding (and not the ability to pay); and so on. For a fuller explication see Walzer, 1983; for some difficulties, R. Norman, 1985. For the sake of exposing the paradox we can call the relevant characteristic for some sphere of justice, Y. Fill in 'Y' as you want.

In the case of the disadvantaged group in question, X rather than Y has historically been used as the ground of allocation – or, more strictly, as the basis for non-allocation. If it is proposed now to give group A special advantages to compensate for past discrimination, the question is: does this not involve us in the inconsistency of allocating on the basis of characteristic X which, as morally irrelevant, was the very ground of past injustice? 'Irrelevant in the past, therefore irrelevant now'; this is the objection.

A natural way to answer it is to deny that precisely X is proposed as the revised ground of allocation. Group A should be specially advantaged not on the basis of characteristic X but on that of X^1, namely the characteristic of belonging to a group which has been historically disadvantaged on the basis of X.

This seems to me a proper move, and no kind of moral or logical sleight of hand: X^1 is genuinely the pertinent characteristic. The problem is, however, threefold.

In the first place, X^1 no less than X fails to coincide with Y. Secondly, it does not follow, because a group has been historically disadvantaged, that all current members of the group have been relevantly disadvantaged. To render special advantages to the current group is, as Francis Bacon said of revenge, a kind of 'rough justice'. Thirdly, it equally does not follow that all current members of groups other than A, who have been unjustly *ad*vantaged in the past, have been relevantly advantaged. If, as is historically plainly the case, most men have been unjustly favoured over most women in employment, income and the rest, some men have been unjustly unfavoured to the advantage of other men. A policy of affirmative action in favour of women only adds to the injustice experienced by such disadvantaged men.

The situation is more complex than this, however, because of the overlap of injustice-generating characteristics. One and the same person may have been disadvantaged on the basis of race, creed, and sex or gender (say). It might appear that a disadvantaged man who 'loses out' to such a person in the application for a job for which both are suitable, has a lesser claim because he has experienced the lesser past injustice.

Such considerations take us, however, into the calculus of comparative disadvantage. This belongs to sociology rather than philosophy to determine.

See further N. Barry, 1981: 154-6; Bayles, 1973; A. Brown, 1986: 197-200; Cowan, 1972; Davis, 1983; P. Day, 1981; R. Dworkin, 1978: ch. 9; Goldman, 1975 & 1976; G. Graham, 1988: ch. 4; Nagel, 1973; Newton in Jaggar, 1994: 62-73; Nickel, 1972, 1974a & 1974b; Nunn, 1974; Sartorelli, 1994, with reply by Ruse, 1995; Scruton, 1984: 86-9; Sher, 1974; Shiner, 1973; Silvestri, 1973; Simon, 1974; P.W. Taylor, 1973; J.J. Thomson, 1973; M.S. Williams, 1995.

18. EQUALITY

'The universal and chief cause of ... revolutionary feeling', observed Aristotle, is 'the desire of equality, when men think that they are equal to others who have more than themselves' (P V.2: 112). Making the same point, the American Declaration of Independence of 1776 declared: 'We hold these truths to be self-evident, that all men are created equal ...' (Ritchie, 1952: 289). And yet in the late twentieth century equality is the most questioned of our twelve concepts. It is the only one with powerfully negative associations for large sections of public opinion. The pursuit of equality, once celebrated in the French Revolutionary slogan 'Liberty, Equality, Fraternity', is widely taken to be empirically absurd and morally illegitimate. Moreover, egalitarianism is tightly linked, in the public mind if not in the history of ideas, with socialism. Critics of equality as a political ideal tend to implicate that ideal in all the shortcomings of socialism, theoretical and practical, real and imagined.

Equality is also a topic with a shortfall of high-profile work in recent years. There are distinguished articles by Charvet and Williams but nothing has triggered the sheer extent of debate provoked by (say) Berlin on freedom or Rawls and Nozick on justice. My guess is that the concept of equality has survived under other names that have attracted more positive attention. Thus the rule of law is an ideal of equality – of the equality of all citizens before the law. Democracy is a celebration of political equality – of the equal entitlement of all citizens to take part in collective decision-making or at least to choose representatives. There is no lack of writing (good, bad or indifferent) on democracy or the rule of law.

The plan of the discussion is as follows. Under 'Basic distinctions' we will need to distinguish between equality as an analytical requirement of justice, and equality as substantive social and political ideal. We will also need to be clear about the different forms this ideal can take. Our high-level theories of justice will be the defence of equality of opportunity and Bernard Williams' account of the rationality of equal distribution of health care. The aporia will be the kind of tension between justice and equality that critics of equality, such as Nozick, allege. The high-level theories of equality are, from one point of view, theories presenting grounds on which egalitarianism might be based. What makes equality a value at all? Nozick's argument does not really demolish such grounds. It is not a denial of the value of equality in all circumstances. It is a denial of the primacy of equality over justice, a view that considerations of equality lack countervailing weight in face of 'historical, unpatterned' principles of justice.

18.1 Basic distinctions

A vital distinction is that between equality as analytically an aspect of justice and equality as a substantive social and political ideal (Lucas, 1966: 242). Justice is satisfied if, in the relevant respect, like cases are treated equally and different cases differently. For example, it is a requirement of justice that all those equally qualified are treated in the same way when they apply for a job. In all other respects the condition of the relevant people can vary enormously. Equality as a substantive social and political ideal involves commitment to there being, from one point of view, no relevant differences to justify different treatment. Along some crucial dimension of our lives we are to enjoy identical conditions. This in turn may be seen as a requirement of justice. But there is no conceptual necessity for this linkage back to justice; as an ideal, equality might be promoted on other grounds, for instance utility.

Amartya Sen poses the question, 'Equality of What?' (Sen in Goodin & Pettit, 1997:

476) as the key query for egalitarians. As a substantive social and political ideal, equality (or 'egalitarianism') may involve any of four main positions, namely commitment to:

- systematic removal of arbitrary inequalities
- complete sameness of social and political conditions
- maximum equal well-being
- equality of opportunity

Answers to Sen thus read: equality of exemption from arbitrary inequalities; equality of social and political conditions; equality of maximum well-being; and equality of opportunity. A more detailed account of these matters is as follows.

Justice requires that like cases be treated equally and that arbitrary differences should be excluded from consideration. So much is, as we have seen, part of the internal relation of justice to equality. Arbitrary differences are typically seen as based on nationality, ethnicity, class, gender and sexuality; and they typically produce socio-economic inequalities of exploitation, maginalisation, deprivation, powerlessness and so on (Fraser, 1995: 68-71; I.M. Young, 1990: ch. 2). One ideal of equality requires us systematically to track down, and eliminate or (best of all) prevent and pre-empt discrimination on the basis of arbitrary differences. This is thought to mark a pro-active approach as opposed to the reactive approach of justice to specific cases of arbitrary discrimination as they arise. It is the view of equality as an ideal in Dunn, 1984: 8-9 (§31.2). There is, however, a real question whether this ideal is distinct from that of justice. Why should a proponent of justice not take a pro-active approach?

Commitment to complete sameness of conditions is ambiguous. If it means that everyone is to have exactly the same income, exactly the same food in quality and amount, exactly the same clothing, and so on, then it is a theoretical possibility which has found few actual defenders. By contrast, if it means that all are to have adequate clothing, a sustainable diet, proper medical attention, etc., this 'sameness of conditions' will produce a great deal of diversity. You may need more food than I do and less medical provision. Along this line we approach the third position, that of commitment to maximum equal well-being for all persons.

'Well-being' is by no means a straightforward notion. There are two principal approaches to it:

- subjective
- objective

On the subjective side, well-being is normally counted in terms of the satisfaction of people's expressed or revealed wants and preferences. At most an element of appraisal may be introduced by reference to what people would want or prefer if they were fully or better informed or (more) rational – to their 'criticised' wants and preferences. But on the subjective approach, the basic test of well-being is that of what people say or think they want and prefer. Such theories are sometimes called 'state of the world' or 'success' theories since they measure well-being in terms of the de facto extent of people's success in fulfilling their wants and preferences. Still on the subjective side we also meet with 'mental (or conscious) state' theories for which the emphasis is people's enjoyment of states which they subjectively value – pleasure, enjoyment and so on.

Objective theories rely on assumptions about people's real interests and about what human flourishing truly or properly consists in, irrespective (it may be) of people's actual or expressed wants and preferences or subjectively valued conscious states. Compare Lukes' discussion of real interests in connection with power (§12.2).

On a point of language before we move on: all of the above, and not just the last, may also be called theories of 'interests'. Generally, when a person's interests are said to be harmed, threatened or promoted, the satisfaction of their wants and preferences, actual or expressed, informed or rational, or their being in certain mental states, or their objective human flourishing, is what is taken to be at stake. So whenever the term 'interests' occurs, in this book or elsewhere in your political reading, ask yourself which of the above senses are applicable. Expand the list if necessary.

The idea of equality of opportunity can run on any of these theories. The relevant opportunity may relate to well-being in terms of 'success', 'mental state' or 'real interests'. The image of equality of opportunity presented in Charvet, 1969: 2, that of opportunity to attain superior positions in society, is historically apt through the French Revolutionary idea of the 'career open to all the talents'. Earlier Plato had caught this idea in his educational proposals for the ideal *polis* by which any child of sufficient intellectual and physical merit could reach the guardian class (R III.415B: 182; cf. *Laws* V.744B, Plato, 1970: 214). But recent use of the idea of equal opportunity has had a broader application to well-being. The more specialised notion does, however, re-appear below in the third model for equality of opportunity.

The four positions listed above do not exhaust the options. At the close of the next section we will note variations by Ronald Dworkin and John Charvet.

18.2 Equality of opportunity as a social and political ideal

There are three main models for equality of opportunity. The best guide here is Lloyd Thomas, 1977. The labels are:

- ideal
- non-competitive
- competitive

Under the requirements of ideal equality of opportunity, the chances to achieve subjective or objective well-being must be the same for everyone. I may have different opportunities from you and a different number of opportunities, but when we cast up, across lives, all the opportunities open to different people, those opportunities must be exactly equal in the well-being they make available to each person. The possibility of making the necessary comparisons and interventions is so problematic that ideal equality of opportunity has few proponents. Charvet, 1969: 4 is a classic critique.

Non-competitive equality of opportunity requires only that, along some crucial dimension of life, opportunities for well-being are equal between persons. It could be that a certain range of wants and preferences are judged particularly important (perhaps those for Rawlsian 'primary goods'), or certain 'real interests' are seen as overridingly significant, and in respect only of these our chances for well-being are to be equal. As Lloyd Thomas aptly expresses the idea: 'there shall be some opportunities that are present in everybody's cluster' (Lloyd Thomas, 1977: 390). This is a more plausible, certainly more manageable project than that of ideal equality of opportunity.

Competitive equality of opportunity arises when the access to opportunities is regulated by competitive criteria. For instance, only a small number of training courses is available for astronauts. There are not enough courses to accommodate all those who are willing and able to sign up for them. Therefore the opportunity to join such a course is filtered through a competitive procedure by which only the best-scoring applicants are successful. A good is thus allocated fairly; this appears to reduce competitive equality of opportunity to a form of justice.

Lloyd Thomas has an extended discussion of competitive equality of opportunity, taken as a topic in its own right. But it is fair to say that non-competitive equality is the primary social and political ideal. The relation of non-competitive equality of opportunity to justice is a matter of lively debate. We will listen in to that debate in 19.1.4.

In the meantime, directly on the idea of equality of opportunity itself, see further Arneson, 1989 and 1991; Benn & Peters, 1959: 118-20; Christiano, 1991; Crosland, 1964: ch. 8; Galston, 1980: 177-91; Levin, 1981 & 1982; Levine, 1988: 57-62; Lucas, 1975: 45-50; Plant, 1981: 138-44; Plamenatz, 1963, II: 119-20; Raphael, 1970: 186-90; Williams, PPS 2: 121-31.

On what grounds might equality of opportunity (in whatever form), or the systematic removal of arbitrary inequalities, or maximum equal well-being, to take the most plausible options considered so far, be urged? One ground would be that we are all entitled to equality of treatment (of whatever form) because we are children of God. Another would be an appeal to Kant. Equality of treatment is due to us as 'ends': 'Act so that you treat humanity, whether in your own person or in that of another, always as an end and never as means only' (Kant, 1969: 54).

But these grounds of equality are problematic on their own account; and if we move them into place to support some form of equality as a social and political ideal, we simply relocate and magnify the difficulty of justifying equality. This is not to dismiss either God or Kant; it is simply to recognise the not inconsiderable endeavour required to vindicate the relevant theology and ethics. Compare Galston, 1980: 154-5.

Ronald Dworkin argues for equality of consideration and concern on the basis that this is a basic human right. The substantive equality that this requires is, Dworkin further argues, 'equality of resources' (R. Dworkin, 1981: Parts 1 & 2). This view involves no mazy theological or ethical commitments. It does, however, appeal to rights. So it inherits all the problems intrinsic to the idea of rights and to their place in political reasoning (§19.4). Worse still, it faces internal problems (Raz, 1986: 220-1).

In a valuable contribution Charvet, 1995 advocates respect for the equal worth of persons and their interests by appeal to a procedure of broadly Rawlsian contractarianism. The ground of equality here is rationality; rational contractors would agree on social arrangements that attribute equal worth. The contractarian underpinnings of Charvet's account draw us into a large topic; and the book stands at the mazy centre of so many issues in ethics and practical reason that it belongs to a later stage of your studies. For a first look at the complexities, see Stratton-Lake, 1997: 169-71 and Milne, 1997: 155-6.

Rawls argues for fair equality of opportunity as something that would be agreed on in the hypothetical conditions of the original position behind the veil of ignorance (§17.3). It is worth mentioning, however, that although he lists equality of opportunity separately under principle 2(b), equal liberty (encapsulated in his first principle), is itself a form of equality of opportunity and presumably, since we are dealing with justice as fairness, a fair one at that.

How next to proceed? I opt for considering a defence of equality which draws commonsensically on the inbuilt aims or purposes of a range of activities. The following discussion of a paper by Bernard Williams bears directly on this point.

18.3 Williams on equality

In 'The Idea of Equality' (PPS 2: 110-31; reprinted in Feinberg, 1969: 153-71 and Goodin & Pettit, 1997: 465-75) Bernard Williams (b. 1929) argues that medical care should be equally available to all citizens. We are all equally to be considered, in respect of the distribution of medical care, solely under the description 'person in need of medical care'. This is because, by virtue of the inherent nature of medical care, no other description is relevant to its distribution.

The logic of Williams, argument is capable of extension to cover the distribution of any good that has an inbuilt aim or purpose – education, for example. A development of Williams' argument is Walzer's project of 'complex equality', the aim of applying to each distributive sphere or social good – security and welfare, money and commodities, official positions, work and leisure, education, recognition, political power, medical care and so on – the principles of distribution peculiar to it. Hence Walzer's phrase, 'spheres of justice'. The object is to prevent the illicit domination of one sphere over others, to check (say) money or official position from dictating the distribution of medical care or education. See Walzer, 1983 and R. Norman, 1985.

The 'proper ground of distribution of medical care is ill health'. This, Williams tells us, is 'a necessary truth' (PPS 2: 121). To distribute medical care on any other basis is irrational; in particular it is irrational for 'the possession of sufficient money' to become 'an additional necessary condition for actually receiving treatment' (ibid.).

Andrew Ward has criticised the practical political implication of this argument, namely that medical care should be equally available to all courtesy of a national health service based on redistributive taxation. He attempts a neat rug-pull: if Williams is going to appeal to the irrationality of distributing medical care on grounds other than ill health, it is no less irrational for the rich to pay more for medical care than do the poor. If rich and poor are equally to receive medical care, why should the rich have to pay more for theirs? Are we not presented here with a plain case of distributing medical care on grounds other than ill health, for there is now an additional necessary condition for receiving such care – namely that of paying more money than others? See Ward, 1973: 86.

It is hard to see, however, that on this style of argument Ward could allow any public spending at all. Public spending requires public finance; and that means taxation. Under progressive direct taxation (where the higher one's income, the higher the proportion of it that goes in taxation), the rich pay more for common services than do the poor. Under flat-rate direct taxation (where the rate of tax is the same for all) the rich, with higher incomes, still pay more than the poor. Under a system of indirect taxation (operating on sales or purchase tax), the rich still pay more because they buy more. If Ward's argument goes through, it establishes the irrationality of public finance. But what is the alternative? Even the most ardent advocate of minimal government has been unable to show how public finance can be avoided altogether. See Coady, 1975: 236-7.

A rather different challenge to Williams is mounted by Nozick in ASU 233-5. First Nozick attempts a 'reductio': on Williams' logic, barbering and gardening services should be made equally available to all, since barbering and gardening are, no less than medical care, activities with inbuilt aims or purposes. The natural reply is that barbering and gardening services are less important than medical care, and that this is why in a world of 'ends and scarce means which have alternative uses' (Robbins, §2.2), we should ensure that medical treatment rather than these other services are equally available to all.

Nozick has two replies. The first is to draw a distinction between the inbuilt aim or purpose of an activity and the motivation of those who engage in it. If I am a gardener, I do not feel under any obligation to provide my services primarily to those households that are most in need of them. The purpose of gardening does not dictate my priorities in allocating my services. I can properly go for the best-paying customers or the most interesting work. Why should the same freedom not be accorded to doctors?

Critics are likely to repeat the importance of medical provision. Now Nozick produces his second reply. The 'scarce means' mentioned just now are actually scarcer than Williams and others realise. Where property-holdings are the result of just acquisition and just transfer, they are not resources which are legitimately available to the state in order to make medical care equally available to all. See further J. Wolff, 1991: 123-5.

The cogency of this reply depends on the validity of Nozick's entitlement theory of justice, with its use of 'historical, unpatterned' principles of just acquisition and transfer (§17.4). But note something else: the reply is not pertinent unless the theory is also applicable to the real world of property. If Nozick has produced a valid theory of justice but in fact the great bulk of property-holdings violate his principles, because those holdings have not arisen through just acquisition and transfer, it is hard to see why they should be morally exempt (even on Nozick's own terms) from redistribution by the state. To assert that current property-holdings embody Nozickian justice is little more than wishful thinking in face of the tangled, seamy, and obscure history of private property.

On Williams from an independently critical angle, see Lloyd Thomas, 1979.

18.4 Justice contra equality

In general the promotion of equality, and especially of equality of opportunity, has been criticised on two main grounds:

- efficiency
- justice

On the side of efficiency the main contention is that a policy of equality of opportunity can be pursued only through redistribution. Aside from the ethics of redistribution, the complaint is that redistribution impairs the workings of a market economy and that such an economy is a prime requirement for economic efficiency. There is no guarantee that the workings of the market will lead to a socially optimum distribution of income by the criterion of equality of opportunity; but to redistribute in the interests of securing such equality is to reduce incentive, thrift, savings, investment, the efficient use of labour and the optimal allocation of capital.

Large issues are involved here. Two logical points, however: there is no reason in principle why voluntary giving should not be directed towards achieving equality of opportunity. It is unlikely to do so in practice on anywhere near a sufficient scale, but redistribution does not strictly have to be done by the state. In this case there need be no impairment of market efficiency by reducing rewards. Secondly, we all are capable of different motivations in different areas of our lives. Individuals may conduct their affairs egoistically in the market-place but relatively altruistically at the ballot-box. This divided motivation can counter-act the impairment of incentive when rewards are redistributed. See Kuttner, 1984; Matthews, 1981: 298.

On the side of justice the major challenge is from theories according to which it is morally illegitimate to redistribute resources, already owned through just acquisition or just transfer, in the interests of achieving an end-state or patterned distribution such as that of equality of opportunity. This is familiar Nozick territory recently retrodden in discussing Williams. The challenge applies only to coercive transfers made by the state; Nozick would have no objection to voluntary giving that accomplished the same result.

There are two main comments. The first is that Nozick's entitlement theory of justice, plainly in the background here, only endorses property ownings which satisfy his three principles (§17.4). As I suggested in defending Williams, there is no realistic possibility of validating and vindicating the up-and-running system of private property in these terms. Secondly, Nozick's whole argument runs on the idea of indefeasible property rights. Without any reciprocity or interpersonal agreement, I have the right to exclusive use and control provided I have fulfilled certain conditions. This is a view of 'rights as axioms'. My own view is that this is unsustainable, not only for property rights but for all rights. The point will be discussed in §19.4.

For more general reading on justice and equality, Kane, 1996a and 1996b; Lukes in D. Held, 1991: ch. 2; Sen, 1996; Sidgwick, 1967, Bk III, ch. 5; Vlastos, 1962.

18.5 Utilitarianism and equality

By way of an endnote, the relationship between utilitarianism and equality is often referred to. Utilitarianism assumes that the rightness or wrongness of anything (an action, an institution, a practice or whatever) can be defined wholly in terms of the merit or demerit of its consequences as these embody or promote (and, specifically, maximise) the occurrence of intrinsically valuable states of affairs. There are three standard links between utilitarianism and equality. The first two rest on the historical, Benthamite form of the theory.

The first link runs through Bentham's rule, 'one to count for one, nobody for more than one', which plainly implies some requirement of distributional equality when we are producing inherently valuable states of affairs through the consequences of our actions. The second, more contingent connection is through the idea, also Benthamite, that each person is the best judge of his or her own interests. This entails a natural equality of decision-making at least for 'normal' agents.

The third connection is that there is a utilitarian presumption of equal distribution through considerations of marginal utility. To simplify in order to make the point: if one person has $10 million and another has just $100, there is less benefit in giving $1 to the person with the larger amount. The person with $10 million dollars has already so much capacity to satisfy his or her wants and preferences that an additional dollar – the 'marginal' dollar – creates little benefit. By contrast, the person with only $100 dollars has so little capacity to satisfy his or her wants and preferences that an additional dollar creates a great deal of benefit. So the marginal dollar should go to the person with only $100. The same reasoning applies to the next $1, and so on until marginal utilities are equalised and we cannot benefit one person more than the other in allocating the next available $1. The relation of utilitarianism to equality is considered in A. Brown, 1986: 48-9; McKerlie, 1984 and J. Wolff, 1996b: 167.

On equality in general, see further Arneson in Goodin & Pettit, 1995; Baker, 1997; N. Barry, 1981: ch. 7; Berlin, 1955; Bowie, 1970; R. Dworkin, 1981; P. Green, 1981; Joseph & Sumption, 1979; Landesman, 1983; Lucas, 1965, 1966: 243-50, and 1977; Maitland, 1911a; Mayer, 1977; T. Nagel, 1979: 106-27; Newfield, 1965-66; Raz, 1986: ch. 9; J.C. Rees, 1971; Sen in Goodin & Pettit, 1997; J.F. Stephen, 1873; Vaizey, 1975; Vlastos, 1962; Williams in PPS 2; Wollheim, 1955; R. Young, 1986. On equality and the rule of law, see Fine, 1984: 7, 57, 107-19, 124-6, 161-2, 170-80. A link between equality and democracy will be examined in §23.4.1.2.

19. RIGHTS

'We are now so rich in rights', wrote the Russian émigré Ivan Bunin in his 1920s short story, 'Never-Ending Spring', 'that we could dispense with some of them'. He would have been aghast at the later explosion of rights proclamations and demands, a development which began in earnest with the United Nations Declaration of Human Rights (1948) and now exceeds assignable limit. The 'rhetoric of rights is out of control', one commentator reckons (Sumner in Frey, 1985: 20). By contrast, John Finnis observes that 'the modern grammar of rights provides a way of expressing virtually all the requirements of practical reasonableness' (Finnis, 1980: 198). Both may be correct: the rhetoric of rights may be one thing and the discerning use of rights-talk another, though my own view is that the most discerning use of such talk is to avoid it altogether. One point is clear. If some of our concepts such as sovereignty and the state are on the down-grade politically, this is not the case with rights. Business is booming.

Historically, four languages of rights can be identified. The first was tied to custom. It invoked the idea of 'common law rights' – the rights embodied in a long tradition of legal judgements and social usage (Dicey, 1982: ch. 4; Oakeshott, 1991: 53). The other three languages – of the rights of man, natural rights, and human rights – are of later origin.

Talk of the 'rights of man' flourished roughly in the period 1775-1815, and usually had a theological setting. In 1789 the French Assembly proclaimed the sacred rights of man 'in the presence of the Supreme Being'. The earlier idea of natural rights was less strictly linked to a theological framework. Agreed, this framework is evident in Locke's account of natural rights. God is the law-giver of natural law, the law of reason; and natural rights are rights deducible from natural law. Yet the rational force of natural law and hence of natural rights is independent of God. The theological framework, less definitely present in Hobbes, is missing altogether from Spinoza. Talk of human rights generally assumes a world without God. Human rights also have a more varied content than natural rights. Typical natural rights would be civil and political – supposedly the right to life, the right not to be held in slavery, the right to freedom of thought, assembly, discussion and conscience, the right to vote and to be eligible for public office, the right to hold property. Typical human rights would extend to the socio-economic – the right to education and to work, the right to adequate food and housing, the right to social security (e.g. provision of medical care).

On the history of rights-talk, see Ritchie, 1952; Tuck, 1979; W. Wallace, 1898: 213-64; Zuckert, 1994.

A discussion of rights must cover four topics:

- subjects
- logical form
- basis
- role in reasoning

That is, it must specify the subjects of rights, i.e. who or what can have them. It must unravel the logical form of rights-talk. It must examine the basis of rights; and it must consider the role of rights in political reasoning. I cover the question of logical form under 'Basic distinctions'. H.L.A. Hart's attempt to show the existence of at least one natural right, and Ronald Dworkin's idea of 'rights as trumps' will be our examples of high-level theorising about the basis of rights. An aporia about rights will be explored in connection with political reasoning. I will pose a dilemma: depending on where one sees rights as fitting into political reasoning, either rights-talk is redundant or rights are impossible. Any such sidelining of rights is apt to make the general reader tense in resistance. We live in an Age of Rights. But readers of this book know that in philosophy we have to follow the argument wherever it may lead though the critical reader, as independent thinker and discriminator, also knows that the author is no privileged authority on where the argument does lead.

I can be brief about the subjects of rights. Rights have been claimed for persons and groups. Among groups, think of nations: after the First World War, when the civilised rococo miscellany of the Austro-Hungarian empire gave way to separate states for its component nationalities, the process was endorsed by appeal to 'the right of national self-determination'. Nations aside, women, children, churches, future generations, indefinitely many communities and collectivities have claimed rights or had rights asserted on their behalf. One of the sharpest issues in applied ethics is whether animals have rights. Speculative scientists ponder whether computerised robots, with consciousness and understanding, will have rights.

For our purposes, to allow a manageable discussion, I shall take it that rights are at least assigned to individual persons and to groups (cf. R. Putnam, 1976). To take individual persons as rights-bearers is not to beg any questions about other actual or potential subjects. On nations as subjects of rights, see Freeman, 1996 and Twining, 1991. On group rights in general, see Baker, 1995.

19.1 Basic distinctions

Nearly all present-day accounts of the logical structure of rights start from Hohfeld's pioneering analysis (Hohfeld, 1964). The American jurist, Wesley Newcomb Hohfeld, suggested a four-way classification. Rights, according to Hohfeld, can be:

- bare liberties or privileges
- claims
- powers
- immunities

The table spells out what these labels mean:

Hohfeld's classification of rights		
Right	*Description*	*Correlative*
BARE LIBERTY or PRIVILEGE	Where I enjoy a bare liberty to do action X, I have no duty not to do X.	Others have NO-RIGHT to prevent me from doing X.
CLAIM-RIGHT	Where I have a claim-right to do X, then others (a particular person, the state, some group or whatever) have a duty.	Others have a DUTY to let me do X.
POWER	Where I have a power, I can alter the privileges, claim-rights, powers or immunities of others	Others have a LIABILITY in respect of my power.
IMMUNITY	Where I enjoy an immunity, my privileges, claim-rights, and powers cannot be altered by others.	Others have a DISABILITY in respect of my immunity.

Detaching the interpretative gloss, we can present rights and their correlatives as follows:

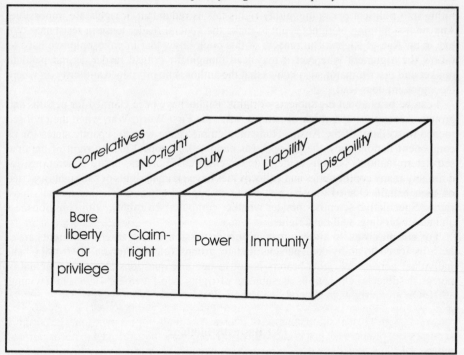

Figure 9. Hohfeld's classification of rights

Two points to note are, first, that claim-rights have duties as their correlates; secondly that bare liberties or privileges do not. If I have a claim-right against you that you desist from phoning me in the small hours, then you have a duty to desist. But if I am at liberty to adorn my home with effigies of *Antinoos Theos*, you have no relevant duty; you have simply no-right that I should desist from this activity.

The relation of claim-rights to duties is a matter of dispute. If, where there is a claim-right there is a corresponding duty, many would resist the contraposition – that where there is a duty there is a corresponding claim-right. There need be no inconsistency in holding that we have duties to animals, for instance, without accepting that animals have claim- or any other rights. Inconsistency is avoided if we equate duty with moral obligation but link claim-rights to 'interests' in a particular way. If I have rights in respect of my interests, and if for me to have interests is for there to be matters relating to my well-being with which I ought to be concerned, then this prescription is inapplicable to animals. They are not moral agents: how can we say that they ought to be concerned about anything? Therefore they do not have interests; therefore they do not have rights.

Still, there is no compelling reason to include the prescriptive element in the idea of interests; we can identify animals' or persons' interests with the satisfaction of their actual or expressed wants and preferences (one of the senses of 'interests' listed in §18.1). Then animals have interests and therefore claim-rights – but, of course, no duties. See Frey, 1977 against animal rights and Regan, 1977 for them.

A further point of clarification about claim-rights is that the corresponding duty 'to let me do X' can range from simple non-interference to positive assistance.

Hohfeld's analysis, to which Chudnow, 1994; Feinberg, 1973: ch. 4; R. Martin, 1993:

29-32; Waldron, 1984: 6-8, are excellent guides, is offered mainly as an account of legal rights. Morally and politically, we can simplify the analysis. In moral and political discourse, rights are typically either protected choices (privileges) or entitlements to provision (claim-rights). They relate either to negative freedoms, matters of personal or group choice in which others may not intervene; or to opportunities and resources to the provision of which persons or groups are entitled.

An important question about such choices or entitlements, supposing them to exist, is their basis.

19.2 Hart on natural rights

A much-cited basis is human nature. Human or natural rights (in this respect we do not need to distinguish between them):

> are the rights that a human being has in virtue of whatever characteristics he has that are both specifically and universally human. Being rational, and being capable of choice, are two such characteristics (or perhaps, after all, one) which are frequently mentioned (B. Mayo, 1965: 219-20).

This suggests a justification of rights in terms of agency. As rational choosers, we should have certain choices protected and certain opportunities and resources provided. The contrast is with a justification in terms of interests; animals, for instance, may have rights as possessors of interests, just because their well-being can be affected, but not as rational choosers. Either way, there is a commitment to the idea (a) that there is a human essence (§§12.2, 13.3.2) among the elements of which is (b) the possession of certain rights.

It may be added that rights argued for on the basis of human nature are often regarded as absolute and indefeasible (which means that they are unconditional and overriding) and also imprescriptible or inalienable (which in turn means that they cannot be forfeited). The following two problems arise about natural or human rights as Mayo characterises them.

In the first place, there is a logical problem of entailment. How does it follow that because I am rational and capable of choice, therefore I should have certain protected choices and entitlements to provision? No known principle of inference will take us from statements of fact ('I am rational and capable of choice') to statements of prescription ('I should have ...'). Hume broke this connection long ago; and no repair job has worked since (Hume, 1978: 469-70; cf. Wiggins, 1987: 95-6).

Secondly, even if the problem of entailment were not to apply, we should still have to deal with the implication that if someone is not rational and is incapable of choice, they have no human or natural rights. This would not mean that they were beyond moral consideration; they might, for instance, qualify for charity or benevolence. But the immediate impression is that on this construction human or natural rights are based on selective characteristics that may be specifically human but are not universally human. Many will see this as the thin end of the discriminatory wedge. But there is always the possibility of widening the set of right-conferring characteristics; if we add (say) limited resources and vulnerability to harm (Hart, 1961: 189-95; cf. Lucas, 1966: 2) it is hard to see how anyone human, from the foetus to the brain-dead adult, would be excluded from the scope of human or natural rights. By the same token, human rights (under a different name) would need to be extended to members of the animal kingdom. 'Same criteria for the attribution of rights + same fulfilment of those criteria = same rights': this moral arithmetic cannot be deflected.

If we restrict ourselves, however, to the original selective characteristics and add a modicum of moral theory, can we establish the existence of natural rights? H.L.A. Hart thinks so (Quinton, 1967: 53-66; reprinted in Waldron, 1984: 77-90 and Goodin & Pettit, 1997: 320-7). It is time to examine his argument, the outline of which is as follows.

Assume that one person can have claim-rights against another. For example, I have borrowed $100,000 from you; other things being equal, I have a duty to repay you. Hart's language for this situation is that you have a 'special' right, one deriving from and relating to our particular situation. Now a right is, from one point of view, a restriction of freedom. Given your claim-right against me, I am not morally free or entitled to do what I want with my money: $100,000 is reserved for you. Hart argues that if my moral freedom, the range of morally permissible choices available to me, is now restricted in this way, then prior to the promise and before the creation of the special right, I had a general moral freedom (a capacity to make moral commitments) which has now been subtracted from. Nobody conferred that freedom; it is in that sense a natural right.

Hart's argument is conditional on there being special rights. It rests on the assumption that one person can have special rights against another. Deny that assumption, and the argument lapses.

Two other points are important. The first concerns the basis of morality. Hart's argument is open to the objection that it is only from within a moral perspective that people have the freedom to enter into obligations that create special rights. If we take the moral point of view, it is natural to think and talk in terms of such freedom. But nothing has been provided to show that this moral freedom is a real entity and not a mere presuppositional construct of the human institution of morality.

The second point is that natural rights on Hart's account are not co-extensive with humanity; we have the exclusion problem again. The capacity to enter into moral obligations may be specifically human but it is hardly universally human. Large segments of humanity, from babies through to psychopaths, do not have this capacity.

On Hart see Frankena, 1955; Finnis, 1980: 204-5, 226-7; also compare Hart's approach with that of M. Macdonald in PPS I: 35-55, reprinted in Waldron, 1984: 21-40; also with that of Gewirth in Pennock & Chapman, 1981. N. Barry, 1981: ch. 9; Benn & Peters, 1959: 95-104; Blanshard, 1961: 389-92; Cranston, 1962; Frankena, 1964; Freeden, 1991: 24-42; R. Martin, 1993: ch. 4; Raphael, 1965; Raphael, 1970: 88, 94, 97, 102-6, 107; Mabbott, 1958: 23, 57-60, 62-3; B. Mayo, 1965 are good basic discussions of natural and human rights. The views of Bentham, Burke, and Marx are collected in Waldron, 1988. A variant of the idea of natural rights is F.H. Bradley's concept of 'ideal rights', held apart from one's social roles (Bradley, 1927: 208, 219; Sweet, 1996: 38). For a distinctive angle on natural rights, see T.H. Green, 1986: 28ff. and (for commentary on Green) Joad, 1938: 550-8 and R. Martin, 1986. For feminist perspectives, see West, 1994. Among the classic texts, Locke's ST assumes natural rights to life, freedom, and property (ST, ch. 2: 269-78). On Locke, see Berki, 1977: 142-50; Chudnow, 1994; Plamenatz, 1963, I: 215-16, 223-7, 247-8; Swanson, 1997. Natural rights also figure in Hobbes, L, ch. 14: 91-3. On Hobbes, see Berki, 1977: 136; Plamenatz, 1963, I: 138-47, 149-50.

19.3 Dworkin and 'rights as trumps'

Ronald Dworkin's view of 'rights as trumps' can usefully be introduced through his distinction between arguments of principle and arguments of policy. Dworkin (b. 1931) lays out the distinction as follows:

> Arguments of policy justify a political decision by showing that the decision advances or protects some collective goal of the community as a whole. The argument in favor of a subsidy for aircraft manufacturers, that the subsidy will protect national defense, is an argument of policy. Arguments of principle justify a political decision by showing that the decision respects or secures some individual or group right. The argument in favor of anti-discrimination statutes, that a minority has a right to equal respect and concern, is an argument of principle (R. Dworkin, 1978: 82).

This is a somewhat appropriative use of 'policy' and 'principle', both of which have other and wider uses than Dworkin's (cf. §2.6.3). That aside, it is important to note that, on Dworkin's account, in the assessment of general welfare, 'external' preferences are to be rigidly excluded (R. Dworkin, 1978: 234 ff.). External preferences are preferences about other people's preferences. In establishing what the general welfare requires, it is perfectly in order to consider your preference for Mozart over Beethoven, and my preference for Ricky Nelson over Elvis; it is out of bounds to consider your abhorrence for my musical taste. With that caveat, the thesis of 'rights as trumps' is the view that principles override social goals or general welfare. I have certain protected choices and entitlements to provision; and the pursuit of social goals and the general welfare, important though it is as a political desideratum, cannot override them.

Three supplementary points are the following. First, rights (unlike community goals or the general welfare) require resources, opportunities or freedoms to be assigned to particular individuals.

Secondly, rights must be accorded a 'threshold value' as against social goals. To say, on the one hand, that people have a right to such-and-such but also to concede, on the other, that this right can be overridden by social goals is self-contradictory. Rights come first; the pursuit of social goals has to accommodate itself to them.

Thirdly, Dworkin's view is that rights must be distributed on a basis of strict impartiality and equality; your rights cannot exceed mine. On the other hand, social goals or the general welfare may dictate an unequal distribution of benefits and burdens; protection of an ailing industry on which the public interest depends may require that particular employers are specially favoured. There are no special favours to be extended or withheld in the domain of rights.

Dworkin's view of rights is two-levelled. At the basic level, rights cannot be seen as mere data. There must be a rationale for them; rights have to be a coherent part of an overall package, a systematic view about politically and morally relevant considerations. We need a systematic account of what the general welfare consists in, and also of why the pursuit of that welfare should be constrained by certain protected choices and entitlements to provision. But once that account is in hand, we can invoke those choices and entitlements without having to argue the case, situation by situation, with those who aim to promote the general welfare. All this is the burden of the following crucial passage:

> Rights cannot be understood as things that people have, come what may, no matter what general justification for political decisions is in play. We construct political theories as a package, and the rights that package assigns individuals must vary with what else is in the package. The idea of rights as trumps is a *formal* idea: it fixes the general function of rights within any particular theory that uses the idea at all. We can therefore think about the content of rights at two different levels of analysis. When we are engaged in constructing a general political theory, we must consider what package – what general justification for political decisions together with what rights – is most suitable .... But on other occasions we must take the general scheme of some political theory as fixed and consider what rights are

necessary as trumps over the general background justification that theory proposes (R. Dworkin in M. Cohen, 1984: 281).

This is clear enough. Dworkin is plainly taking a stand against the kind of utilitarian view that bids us simply maximise (general) welfare or benefit. Such maximisation is blocked where (individual) rights are trumps. Two considerations should qualify our enthusiasm for Dworkin's line, however. On the one hand, there is little definite and substantial indication in Dwokin's extensive writings of how rationally to determine the relevant systematic view about politically and morally relevant considerations – the 'package'. On the other hand, Dworkin's theory tumbles into inconsistency. The trumpet-blast of 'rights as trumps' is followed by the whispered concession that 'to prevent a catastrophe or even to obtain a clear and major benefit' it may be necessary to override individual rights (R. Dworkin, 1978: 192). Is this principle or policy? It is policy. Individual rights are trumps except where society holds a royal flush.

See further Campbell, 1988: ch. 2; Harré & Robinson, 1995; D. Shapiro, 1982. Nozick's view of rights as side-constraints (ASU 28-33; Wolff, 1991: 21, 28) has significant parallels with Dworkin's position.

19.4 Rights and reasoning

If successful, Dworkin's theory of rights as trumps would specify the appropriate role of rights in political reasoning. Policies can be nullified, or acts of governance can be defeated, if they violate rights. But let us start from basics, and work things out for ourselves.

As protected choices or entitlements to provision, rights might figure in any one of three ways in political argument, namely as:

- conclusions
- defeasible presumptions
- axioms

Take 'rights as conclusions' first. I might assess the full facts about your situation, for which (in the words of Hume) 'it is often necessary, we find, that much reasoning should precede, that nice distinctions be made, just conclusions drawn, distant comparisons formed, complicated relations examined, and general facts fixed and ascertained' (Hume, 1975: 173). If at the end of this process it seems to me that you should receive free medical care or help towards getting a job, or that you should be allowed to give your children a religious education though others disapprove, then I can mark this conclusion (underline it, so to say) by talking of your having a right. But the concept of a right does no independent work here; it comes at the end of my reasoning and simply registers how in my view, all things considered, you ought to be treated. Nothing is gained, nothing of moral substance is added, by talking of your rights rather of using the language of moral obligation and talking about what ought to be done. 'Rights as conclusions' are redundant.

As defeasible presumptions, rights feature as generally relevant considerations. This is a pluralist view which has affinities with the theory of prima facie duties offered by Sir David Ross (1877-1971; Ross, 1930: 18-36). Think of the kinds of right that are often claimed: the right to work, to vote, to receive an education, to express opinions, and so on. In relation to indefinitely many people in indefinitely many situations there is a presumption that the relevant choices should be protected and the relevant provisions made. We might even pitch it stronger and say that we are dealing here with considerations that have, as LSE's Paul Kelly put it to me, 'peremptory force'. From a moral point of view, we are obliged to take these considerations into account.

But for the pluralist, one right can clash with another, one person's protected choice can conflict with another's entitlement to provision. In considering how to treat you, I must always take your rights into account but in the full, dilemmatic complexity of real-life decision-making, your rights are only one demand on me. There is a presumption that I (or some other moral agent or the relevant political unit) should fulfil them, but that presumption can be defeated in particular situations for action.

Another way of expressing the matter is to say that rights apply to people under morally significant descriptions. You are ill, unemployed, poor, open to persecution, in need of education, or whatever: and under those descriptions it is morally desirable to protect certain choices for you and to make certain provisions. But no morally significant description, applying to anyone, automatically and without more ado defines overriding moral obligations. How I ought to treat you depends on my total situation, and it cannot be determined by the mere fact that a significant moral description applies to you in yours. No fixed link holds between morally significant descriptions and actual, all-things-considered moral obligations.

As defeasible presumptions, rights may appear to perform a useful role in political reasoning. But we might as well simply cite the morally relevant considerations. Your need for education or a job is a morally relevant description which I ought to take into account. What is added by saying that you have rights in respect of your needs? 'Rights as defeasible presumptions' are no less redundant than rights as conclusions.

Increasingly, however, assertions of rights are put to work ambitiously far beyond the range of defeasible presumptions. Typically in current political discourse, rights are claimed as absolute and indefeasible. These are features from which, we may recall, Hart detached his account of natural rights (§19.2). The current assumption is that of non-negotiable demands creating unconditional, overriding moral obligations. Rights, or more accurately rights-claims, feature as axioms.

Axioms are propositions laid down at the start of an argument or a process of reasoning. Without needing to be deduced or demonstrated, they control the whole subsequent derivation. If rights-claims are taken to be axiomatic, then a corresponding rights-based morality must be assumed, i.e. a morality in which rights are foundational and not deduced from other morally relevant considerations. The possibility of such a morality is discussed by Mackie and Raz in Waldron, 1984: 168-81, 182-200. My own view is that, without implausible appeal to intuition (by which one 'just knows' that A has a right to X), rights must apply to people under morally significant descriptions; it is the descriptions which are basic, and the rights are supervenient on them.

But once we invoke morally significant descriptions, the pluralist argument comes back into play. The idea that a claim-right or a privilege can be invoked at the start of a piece of political reasoning and produce a statement of overriding moral obligation at the end of it, with no scope for rival moral considerations to deflect the derivation – this is not, I submit, the real world of political and moral life. 'Rights as axioms' are impossible.

For further reading on rights, the articles collected in Waldron, 1984 are excellent introductory fare; see also Plamenatz, 1968: ch. 4. William Sweet's historically sensitive and analytically fertile accounts of rights is not to be missed (Sweet, 1997). Sweet gives a luminous exposition not only of Bernard Bosanquet, his main subject, but also of Jeremy Bentham, John Stuart Mill, and Herbert Spencer. Waldron, 1988 has extracts from Bentham, Burke, and Marx. R. Dworkin, 1990 and Finnis, 1985 are helpful on rights and law. On rights and authority, see R. Martin in P. Harris, 1990: ch. 7. On rights and justice, refer back to Mill on justice (§17) and to Nozick (§17.4 ad fin.); note also Campbell, 1974; Galston, 1980: 127-41. Campbell addresses the point that the criteria of concrete justice (§17.2) are seen by some theorists (e.g. Raphael, 1970: 48) as defining rights. Rights and equality are linked in theories of natural or human rights inasmuch as such rights are taken to reflect the universal equality of humankind. Rights and freedom are also connected, since protected choices secure areas of negative freedom. On rights and democracy, see R. Martin, 1993: ch. 7; and §23.4.2.3.

20. PROPERTY

'Who steals my purse steals my Property – and there is no excuse for him. He's *low*, sir!', exclaims Bertram Atkey's 'Smiler Bunn'. The mid-nineteenth century French anarchist Pierre-Joseph Proudhon took a different view. 'Qu'est-ce que la propriété?' he asked. 'C'est le vol', he replied. 'What is property? Nothing but theft!' (Proudhon, 1994). 'Property divides the whole world into parties', observed Gerard Winstanley in seventeenth-century England, 'and is the cause of all wars and bloodshed and contention everywhere ... When the earth becomes a common treasury again, as it must, then this enmity in all lands will cease'. Last word to Rousseau: 'The first man' – 'the imposter' – 'who, having enclosed a piece of ground, to whom it occurred to say *this is mine*, and found people sufficiently simple to believe him (*trouva les gens assez simples pour le croire*), was the true founder of civil society' (DI 161).

Our discussion of property is structured as follows. Once we have drawn some distinctions in the next section (our basic exercise in conceptual analysis), we will examine Locke's theory of property. Two of his arguments will be examined, the labouring-mixing and value-added arguments, with accompanying criticisms. We will end by tackling an aporia in Locke's theory, developed in Nozick's so-called zipping-back argument.

20.1 Basic distinctions

The first requirement in analysing the concept of property is to recognise its internal complexity. This complexity has nothing to do with the distinction between public and private property. It is more basic than that and concerns the network of entitlements which the institution of property involves. Not the least merit of Henry Sidgwick's *The Elements of Politics* among the older textbooks is that, in discussing property, it talks of the right to use, to exclude others from using (the right to possess), to deteriorate or destroy, to alienate and exchange, and only 'perhaps' (he adds) to bequeath (Sidgwick, 1891: ch. 5). This conveys a due sense of a network of distinguishable entitlements.

This distinguishability is important because theories of property which give attractive or plausible accounts of (say) the entitlement to 'use and possess or exclude' often assume that the whole network of entitlements is thereby encompassed. Locke is an example of this. But the right to bequeath (the right of transfer after death) by no means follows directly from arguments which yield the right to use and possess or exclude.

The institution of property – the institution we have to conceptualise – has a centre and a periphery. At the centre is a set of entitlements which are widely accepted as forming 'the essence of ownership' (Christman, 1991: 29). Call these primary entitlements; other entitlements are at best subordinate and contingent. Christman (loc. cit.) draws the line between the primary and the secondary as follows:

Primary entitlements
- the right to possess
- the right to use
- the right to manage
- the right to alienate
- the right to transfer
- the right to gain income from any of the preceding

Secondary entitlements
- the right to security in ownership
- the right of bequest
- the right of absence of term (no time-limits on ownership)

For further refinements, see L.C. Becker, 1977: 19.

20.2 Locke's theory of property

Philosophical explorations of property need to face a number of questions. If we confine ourselves for the present to the core of the primary entitlements – to possess or exclude and to use – there are three vital points to raise:

- what is the rationale of the institution? why and under what conditions is it a good institution to maintain?
- how may individuals (or other property-holders) become entitled to acquire property?
- how much should they be allowed to acquire?

H.L.A. Hart distinguishes these questions (Hart, 1968: 4) under the headings of 'general justifying aim', 'title' and 'amount'; and all of them are addressed by the most famous theory of property, that of John Locke in chapter 5 of his *Second Treatise*.

Note that Locke uses the term 'property' both in a wide and in a more specific sense. In its wide sense, property comprises life, freedom, and estate or possessions (ST §123 350). The theory of property to be considered here centres on the more specific sense in which property relates to possessions. It is debatable how far the wide sense comes back into play through the idea of self-ownership (§20.2.2).

20.2.1 Outline of the theory

The general justifying aim of property as an institution, Locke tells us, is the satisfaction of human needs:

> God, who hath given the World to Men in common, hath also given them reason to make use of it to the best advantage of Life, and convenience. The Earth, and all that is therein, is given to men for the Support and Comfort of their being. And though all the Fruits it naturally produces, and Beasts it feeds, belong to Mankind in common, as they are produced by the spontaneous hand of nature; and no body has originally a private Dominion, exclusive of the rest of Mankind, in any of them, as they are thus in their natural state: yet being given for the use of Men, there must of necessity be a means to *appropriate* them some way or other before they can be of any use, or at all beneficial to any particular Man. The Fruit, or Venison, which nourishes the wild *Indian*, who knows no Inclosure, and is still a Tenant in common, must be his, and so his, i.e. a part of him, that another can no longer

have any right to it, before it can do him any good for the support of his Life (ST §26: 286-7; cf. Sartorius in Frey, 1985: 211).

The title to property is given by labour:

Though the Earth, and all inferior Creatures be common to all Men, yet every Man has a Property in his own *Person*. This no Body has any Right to but himself. The *Labour* of his Body, and the *Work* of his Hands, we may say, are properly his. Whatsoever then he removes out of the State that Nature hath provided, and left it in, he hath mixed his *Labour* with, and joyned to it something that is his own, and thereby makes it his *Property*. It being by him removed from the common state Nature placed it in, it hath by this *labour* something annexed to it, that excludes the common right of other Men. For this *Labour* being the unquestionable Property of the Labourer, no Man but he can have a right to what that is once joyned to, at least where there is enough, and as good left in common for others (ST §27: 287-8).

A student once commented that, by parity of reasoning, God's ownership of the world (which he 'hath given ... to Men in common') is due to his having mixed his labour with it. This is an interesting idea, but theologically unsound since God created the world *ex nihilo*. That point aside, Locke considers that the labour need not be strictly mine for the labour condition to be met. My property includes: 'The Grass my Horse has bit; the Turfs my Servant has cut; and the Ore I have digg'd in any place' (ST §28: 289). The natural sense of 'my horse' is to refer to a horse that I own, which implies the existence of property already; and how that with which my servant has mixed his or her labour becomes my property through a contractual relationship, is a matter quite unexplained.

Furthermore, the preceding passage is an occasion of disagreement through ambiguity. 'At least where' might mean 'only if' and thus mark a necessary condition. Or it might mean 'certainly on this condition but perhaps on other conditions as well' – just 'if', not 'only if', merely a sufficient condition. This ambiguity was first exposed and discussed in Waldron, 1979.

Let us do a retake, slowly. The problem is this. Is Locke saying: whenever you have mixed your labour and left enough and as good for others, then you have the right to appropriate? This is the sufficiency reading, which does not commit him to the view that anybody who has the right to appropriate must have satisfied the 'mixing' and 'leaving' conditions. They are good enough but other conditions yield the right just as well.

On the other reading, Locke is telling us that only if you have 'mixed' and 'left', do you have the right to appropriate. Otherwise said, whenever anybody has the right to appropriate, these conditions must have been met. They are necessary conditions.

A plus point for the sufficiency reading is that gives intuitively the right result in conditions of extreme scarcity. Suppose that, before anyone has appropriated, there is not enough land, or the products of the land are too meagre, to support a given population. Does this mean that appropriation is disallowable? The appropriators cannot leave enough and as good for others. But if no one appropriates, all perish – which is contrary to the Lockean rationale of the institution of property, namely the satisfaction of human needs. I am more impressed with the logic of the argument than convinced that it is Locke's own. See further Lloyd Thomas, 1995: 111.

In the secondary literature the 'enough and as good' condition is widely known as 'the Lockean proviso'. This is mainly contrastive; Nozick has a different version of it, the Nozickian proviso, in his own theory of property. We will return to Nozick in 20.1.3.

The labour-mixing argument is Locke's main account of title to property; it is the argument which is most salient in the text and to which later commentators have paid most attention. There is also something known as the value-added argument, which we will examine in §20.2.3.

We have now looked at Locke's account of general justifying aim and title. What of amount, Hart's three heading for a theory of property? The amount that may be appropriated is set by the limits of effective use:

> It will perhaps be objected ... That if gathering the Acorns, or other Fruits of the Earth, &c. makes a right to them, then any one may *ingross* as much as he will. To which I Answer, Not so. The same Law of Nature, that does by this means give us Property, does also *bound* that *Property* too. *God has given us all things richly*, 1 Tim. vi.17. is the Voice of Reason confirmed by Inspiration. But how far has he given it us? *To enjoy.* As much as any one can make use of to any advantage of life before it spoils; so much he may by his labour fix a Property in. Whatever is beyond this, is more than his share, and belongs to others. Nothing was made by God for Man to spoil or destroy (ST §31: 290).

Locke's theory has been subjected to many criticisms. Under the three headings of a theory of property – general justifying aim, title, and amount – it is his account of what provides the title to property that has attracted long-term interest. It is to this that we turn next, taking in the labour-mixing argument and a second argument, mentioned above, the value-added argument. The conditions assumed are those of the state of nature in all three senses identified in §14.3.3.1 – post-paradisaical, seventeenth-century American, and abstract, ahistorical.

A word before we proceed. Locke's theory of property is set within a theological framework, one that contains three elements. Of these the first and most evident is the account of God-given communal property rights in the state of nature: 'God ... hath given the World to Men in common' (ST §26: 286). The next element is that Locke takes the right of acquisition to be a natural right, deducible from a natural law of which the law-giver is God. The final element is the idea of our property in our own persons, which presupposes (for Locke) a Christian view of the moral status of human beings. To complicate matters, the natural law/natural rights element has a degree of independence. Natural law, which is 'the Voice of Reason' (ST §31: 290), is binding on all rational beings.

In looking at how the theory has been assessed, I will largely detach it from its theological and natural law/natural rights framework. One result of this is that in checking our reaction to Locke's theory and deciding how far, if at all, it succeeds in justifying the acquisition of private property, we are not automatically vindicating the theory on Locke's own terms. We might allow that it does successfully justify such acquisition but we may, all the same and quite consistently, reject (e.g.) the idea of natural law and natural rights (§§15.5.1, 19.2). Otherwise said, in agreeing with Locke, if we do, about the justification of private acquisition, we can yet disagree with him over the precise grounds of justification. We can also, to reverse the process, agree with him over the grounds of justification but, like Aquinas, offer a different account of property (§20.2.4).

20.2.2 The labour-mixing argument

Let us formalise the argument. Versions of the labour-mixing argument are set out in L.C. Becker, 1977: 33-5; J.P. Day, 1971: 109 and Waldron, 1983: 39. You should check out exactly what they have to say for themselves, but here I select from their accounts:

1. Everyone owns their own person
   Therefore
2. Everyone owns the labour of their own person
   Therefore
3. Everyone owns that with which they have mixed the labour of their own person

Naturally (3) has to be set against the background of limitations which Locke has stipulated in the 'enough and as good' and 'not letting spoil' conditions. Even so, precipitous leaps separate the steps in this argument. None of the inferences can be immediate; the 'therefore' need to be supported by sub-premises.

It might be objected that premise (1) is false. This objection could be based on two grounds: one that we are actually owned by God and hence do not own ourselves; and two that under conditions of natural slavery it is not the case that everyone owns their own person. Locke would agree with the first point; self-ownership is to be taken under the proviso of God's ownership of God's creation. (This explains his prohibition of suicide on the ground that we are not our own property, but God's, since God has created us.) Locke emphatically denies any permissible institution of slavery; there are no natural slaves in the sense of persons whose agency is properly, by intrinsic right, under the direction of others (ST ch. 4: 283-5). That is plausible enough; few would defend natural slavery nowadays. But let us look further into the idea of self-ownership.

The idea is an intuitively appealing one. John Christman seeks:

> to articulate what seems so compelling about self-ownership. If decisions about whether and how to use my skills and talents are made by people other than me, even if done for the public good, then I have been denied one of the basic conditions of independence and self-determination – something of fundamental value to me. I have lost an essential aspect of my autonomy in that I cannot, under these conditions, control and plan my life. The basic intuition is that no one should be able to force me to act in any way but that which I choose, except in the enforcement of existing rights on the part of others. Hence, insofar as my body moves or acts, *I* should be the one who has the ultimate say over what it does and where it goes (Christman, 1991: 38-9).

Criticism is never lacking. Here is David Miller with a different point of view:

> We may think, however, that self-ownership is a pretty bad idea all the way down. Suppose there is a large-scale natural disaster, as a consequence of which many victims need blood transfusions if they are to survive. Unfortunately, there are not enough volunteers willing to give (or sell) blood to meet the need. Would it be justifiable in these circumstances for the government to require some people, chosen perhaps by lot, to provide on pain of legal penalty a pint of blood each to the transfusion service? This would be a clear violation of the very core of self-ownership, so if you think (as I do) that the government would be justified in taking this action, then you should reject the idea that we have inviolable rights of property in our bodies. There are other, and better, ways of expressing our abhorrence of rape and torture (D. Miller, 1996: 34).

Miller's example of compulsory transfusion raises hugely controversial issues on its own account. Many would reject the morality of compulsion here, irrespective of the claims of self-ownership. But working with the example for the sake of argument, it does not really overturn the claims of self-ownership. If in this case we are justified in applying compulsion, this just means that the claims of self-ownership are outweighed on this occasion, not that there are no such claims in general. After all, in the passage above,

Christman included the rider, 'except in the enforcement of existing rights on the part of others'. On self-ownership, see G.A. Cohen, 1995: chs. 3, 5, 9 & 10. Later I will briefly indicate a form of the labour-mixing argument that does not draw directly on the idea of self-ownership.

Back to Locke's argument as set out. The move from premise (1) to premise (2) could be challenged along the lines that I might own my person but have obligations under which I am required to labour under the direction and on behalf of others (Grunebaum, 1987: 56). This may on occasion be so, but it hardly affects Locke's argument. Locke's challenge is to show how appropriation could ever be justified; his response is not defeated by showing that there are some conditions in which one of his premises might not be true. If there are conditions in which it is true, this is all he needs.

The move from (2) to (3) might be mediated as follows:

2. Everyone owns the labour of their own person
2a. The object with which they have mixed their labour contains something which they own
2b. To take the object from them without their consent would infringe (2) and (2a)
    Therefore
2c. Nobody may take the object from them without their consent
2d. This amounts to an entitlement in the person over the object
    Therefore
3. Everyone owns that with which they have mixed the labour of their own person

Robert Nozick puts a celebrated objection to this style of argument in ASU ch. 7: 174-5. He attacks (3) head-on. Suppose that you own a can of tomato juice. Now you pour this juice into the sea. You have engaged in activity, done some labour. Does this mean that you own the sea? Hardly: it just means that you have wasted your labour.

Locke would have a straightforward response to this objection, namely that it omits two points. One is that the general justifying aim of property ownership is the satisfaction of human needs and the limits of appropriation are set by effective use. No one's needs require the appropriation of the Atlantic Ocean for their satisfaction; and no individual can, in an exclusionary way, effectively use such a vast resource.

The other point is that Locke may well (in spite of Waldron above) have regarded the leaving of enough and as good for others as a necessary condition for appropriation. Sea-appropriating individuals hardly leave enough and as good for others.

There is, however, another problem that might arise. David Miller describes the circumstances as follows:

> [T]wo people independently and without agreement 'mix their labour' with some object ... [S]uppose that one man fells a tree and a second, coming across the fallen tree, fashions a canoe out of it. The original formulation implies that both have absolute property rights in the transformed object, which is of course absurd (Miller, 1980: 6).

Locke's natural counter-move would be to hold that, since the first has mixed his labour, and also left enough and as good for others and not let spoil, both do not have absolute property rights; the first person has property rights and the second person has wasted his labour. This assumes, however, a right of first occupancy which is not logically entailed by the labour-mixing argument; it is an extra assumption.

After all, the second person can plead, against the first, that they also satisfy all the Lockean conditions: they have mixed their labour, left enough and as good for others, and will not let spoil. Miller draws the anti-Lockean consequence that, in the case described, 'the object should be shared between them in proportion to their respective deserts, or if that is not physically possible that one should compensate the other for the estimated value of his labour' (Miller, 1980: 6).

This suggests a general comment on Locke's approach to property acquisition. Even in the state of nature he neglects the obvious possibility of co-operative labour and hence of joint or public ownership. Locke would most likely reply that private ownership is more efficient than joint or public ownership (Lloyd Thomas, 1995: 101; cf. Nozick, 1974: 177 and Wolff, 1991: 109-10). But the truth of that matter is an intricate one on which political philosophers have no special competence to pronounce.

Now for a form of the labour-mixing argument, suggested by Locke and mentioned earlier, which does not directly rely on the idea of self-ownership but on desert. This is implicit in Locke's statement that God gave the world to the 'Industrious and Rational' (ST §34: 291; Miller, 1980: 6). A justice of deserts is thus invoked. The industrious and rational deserve the product of what they have mixed their labour with. I have my doubts whether even claims of desert will go through without some assumptions about self-ownership, but I turn to a different point. The problem with the desert argument is that, as Marx pointed out, 'one man is superior to another physically or mentally', is more industrious or rational as Locke puts it, but this may be (and must be to some extent) by virtue of morally irrelevant differences of talent, ability, or aptitude for which no credit is due (§31.2.1).

In John Stuart Mill's *Principles of Political Economy* there is an argument, to which L.C. Becker has called attention, which can be seen as developing Lockean desert in an interesting negative direction:

> It is no hardship to anyone to be excluded from what others have produced: they were not bound to produce it for his use, and he loses nothing by not sharing in what otherwise would not have existed at all (PPE II.2.6: 233; L.C. Becker, 1977: 41).

In other words, Mill is saying, when I labour and am under no obligation to surrender the product of my labour to you; and when I produce something which, but for my efforts, would not have existed: then you do not positively deserve to receive the benefits of my labour. So, between the two of us, you have no entitlement that I should *not* have exclusive possession or use of what I have produced. Perhaps the main difficulty which it involves is that the condition, that but for my efforts the product of my labour would not have existed, implies that my exact contribution can be ascertained. But realistically my labour takes place against a whole background of skills which others have helped me to acquire, of tools which others have created, and so on: and but for their efforts, I should not have been able to produce what I did.

It may be stressed, as a point on which to close this section, that the preceding discussion has centred on Locke's theory of appropriation in the state of nature; that is, in a pre-monetary economy. With the introduction of money as a measure and store of value and means of exchange the theory undergoes a subversive change, 'subversive' because it totally inverts the initial conditions of appropriation.

Suppose, Locke argues, that by mixing my labour with unowned natural resources I can produce more than I need or can consume. The 'not letting spoil' condition comes into play, with its stress on use and need. But where is the harm, Locke asks, in my taking money in exchange for my surplus, thereby meeting other people's needs, and (the key point) being allowed to appropriate those natural resources? (ST, §50: 300). More than that, the 'not letting spoil' condition, which limits appropriation in the state of nature, does not apply to money itself; therefore no limits need be set to the accumulation of money (ST §50: 302).

20.2.3 The value-added argument

We have now looked at the labour-mixing argument. Locke also argues for appropriation on the grounds that labour accounts for nearly all the use-value of natural resources. The main texts are ST §§34-45. In §40 he goes so far as to say that 99% of the use-value of cultivated land arises from labour:

> 'tis *Labour* indeed that *puts the difference of value* on every thing; and let any one consider, what the difference is between an Acre of Land planted with Tobacco, or Sugar, sown with Wheat or Barley; and an Acre of the same Land lying in common without any Husbandry upon it, and he will find, that the improvement of *labour makes* the far greater part of the value. I think it will be but a very modest Computation to say, that of the *Products* of the Earth useful to the Life of Man 9/10 are the *effects of labour*: nay, if we will rightly estimate things as they come to our use, and cast up the several Expences about them, what in them is purely owing to *Nature*, and what to *labour*, we shall find, that in most of them 99/100 are wholly to be put on the account of *labour* (ST, 40: 296; cf. Marx on the labour theory of value in §31.2.1).

But how do these considerations create a right of appropriation? The argument seems to be that if I have added value by my labour, I am entitled to the land (or whatever) on which I have laboured. Or as G.A. Cohen puts it:

> His argument says, roughly, that since land without labour produces hardly anything, and land with labour produces an enormous amount, labour contributes vastly more to output than land does, and labour should, accordingly, be appropriately rewarded (G.A. Cohen, 1995: 185).

But why should the appropriate reward be appropriation? Cohen offers a highly sophisticated discussion of the whole matter. My suggestion is that the central problem with the value-added argument is that it does not give me property rights in the land with which I have mixed my labour but only (at most) rights in the added value. See further LLoyd Thomas, 1995: 96-106.

20.2.4 Theology and community: Aquinas versus Locke

Before we shift across to consider an aporia which Nozick finds in 'the Lockean proviso', I want to take a matter which I have sidelined as not being of prime salience to a modern readership but which shows that the theology of property admits of marked differences from the Lockean theory.

Locke's whole political theory sits within a theological framework, a network of theological assumptions. Even his view that, since human beings are moral equals, therefore nobody has natural political authority over anybody else (§13.3.3.1), takes the theological gloss that we are moral equals as independent servants of God (Oakeshott, 1993: 54). The theory of property also finds its place within the framework, but two extra comments are due.

In the first place, ST has not only a theological framework; it also has specifically a divine teleology to which the theory of property belongs as one part. Not only has the earth been made available to humankind, through God's agency, for their sustenance, as the theory of property tells us, but also propagation and self-improvement are incumbent on us as God's creatures. Secondly, within a divine teleology, more communitarian theories of property can be found. A striking example is St Thomas Aquinas' account in his thirteenth-century *Summa Theologiae*.

For Aquinas (1224/5-1274), as for Locke, the general justifying aim of property is the satisfaction of human needs. It is part of God's providence that the natural order is available to us in this way. Unlike Locke, Aquinas considers the possibility of common ownership but decides that there are three reasons why, for the most part, property should be privately owned. These are, first, that we are more likely to be careful in the use of things, and less likely to shirk inconvenient labour, when we personally own them. Secondly, that private property makes for more orderly economic arrangements, since under a regime of private property everyone has specific responsibilities. Thirdly, in general such arrangements also make for civil peace. (Aquinas has not read Marx.) The whole atmosphere of the discussion is quite different from what we find in Locke, where social considerations of the kind that concern Aquinas are marginal. Private property is a conventional arrangement which is justified in terms of the satisfaction of human needs.

On the title to property, the criteria for appropriation, Aquinas is more flexible and more radical. For Locke, the sole basis of appropriation is labour, at any rate in the state of nature. But Aquinas takes a broader view. He allows some entitlement on the basis of labour, but also entitlement on the basis of need. Property is a human institution, consistent with natural or divine law but subordinate to it. Where the actual distribution of property gets out of line with the general justifying aim, namely the satisfaction of human needs, we can appropriate another's property without theft. My need makes your property mine. Aquinas is quite clear on this:

> If ... there is such urgent and evident necessity that there is clearly an immediate need of necessary sustenance, – if, for example, a person is in immediate danger of physical privation, and there is no other way of satisfying his need, – then he may take what is necessary from another person's goods, either openly or by stealth. Nor is this, strictly speaking, fraud or robbery [*Nec hoc proprie habet rationem furti vel rapinae*] (Aquinas, 1965: 171).

Aquinas further stresses that, short of such emergencies, there is a requirement to share if one person is in much easier circumstances than another: 'whatever a man has in superabundance is owed [*debentur*], of natural right, to the poor for their sustenance' (Aquinas, ibid.). On this point at least, Locke is with him: when one person has more than he needs, 'his needy Brother' has 'a Right to the Surplusage of his Goods' (FT §42: 170; cited in Waldron, 1979: 326). But he never goes as far as Aquinas in saying that in case of need, the surplusage actually becomes the needy Brother's property. See further Lloyd Thomas, 1995: 101-2; Swanson, 1997; Winfrey, 1981.

You may not want to slip too far down the by-paths of the history of political thought, but Aquinas is (as John Morrall has reminded me) 'very much of an innovator in asserting property to be a natural right. The vast majority of earlier thinkers (Patristic and early medieval) thought of it as being, like the state, a direct result of the Fall and Augustine even speaks of property as originating in, and being dependent on, the will of the state'. Augustine actually asks, in a striking passage, 'take away rights created by emperors, and then who will dare say, That estate is mine, or that slave is mine, or this house is mine?' (Deane, 1963: 106).

20.3 Locke, Nozick, and the 'proviso'

Nozick is sympathetic to Locke's theory of property, which (like his own) is a 'historical' theory of justice, though (unlike Nozick's) it is also a patterned theory. Property is to go to each, Locke can be roughly represented as saying, according to the labour they have mixed, provided they leave enough and as good for others and do not let spoil. Nozick has drawn attention to a puzzling difficulty, an aporia, in Locke's theory of property acquisition. He sets it out as follows:

> Locke's proviso that there be 'enough and as good left in common for others' (sect. 27) is meant to ensure that the situation of others is not worsened. (If this proviso is met is there any motivation for his further condition of nonwaste?) It is often said that this proviso once held but now no longer does. But there appears to be an argument for the conclusion that if the proviso no longer holds, then it cannot ever have held so as to yield permanent and inheritable property rights. Consider the first person Z for whom there is not enough and as good left to appropriate. The last person Y to appropriate left Z without his previous liberty to act on an object, and so worsened Z's situation. So Y's appropriation is not allowed under Locke's proviso. Therefore the next to last person X to appropriate left Y in a worse position, for X's act ended permissible appropriation. But then the appropriator two from last, W, ended permissible appropriation and so, since it worsened X's position, W's appropriation wasn't permissible. And so on back to the first person A to appropriate a permanent property right (Nozick, 1974: 175-6).

This may be called, following Nozick's own language, the 'zipping back argument'. You would do well to follow up with characteristically able discussion of this argument (Wolff, 1991: 108-9). I offer two comments on my own account.

In the first place, if the argument is valid, its importance for Locke depends on how we resolve the ambiguity over the 'at least where' condition. If the argument goes through, it wrecks Locke's theory if 'at least where' marks a necessary condition; a necessary condition which cannot be met defeats the theory that turns on it. Its significance is reduced if 'at least where' marks a merely sufficient condition; there may be other sufficient conditions quite capable of fulfilment.

Secondly, its significance is also reduced if we break Nozick's conjunction, 'permanent and inheritable property rights'. The long-dead A in Nozick's example would not, or need not, have produced Z's predicament if A's property right had expired with him. Nozick's argument precisely assumes that what is removed from the common stock remains outside it for keeps, through the institution of inheritance.

Inheritance is the flipside of the right to bequeath; and Locke assumes such a right. Call to mind the passage from our discussion of tacit consent (§13.3.3.1) where he refers to possession not just by a person but by 'his Heirs for ever' (ST §119: 348). But how are we to derive the right to bequeath?

The most obvious move is to take the right to bequeath as a particular application of the right to alienate. Now we are on logically tricky ground, however. Anyone might argue that, special circumstances aside, I can relinquish my right to use and possess, and that this involves alienation. So far the right to alienate is secure; but bequest is more than just the bare right to alienate. It is the right to transfer my property (when, incidentally, I no longer exist?) to a specific person, group or whatever. It is logically possible that the general justifying aim of the institution of property licenses use, possession, and alienation but yet not this kind of personal power to 'target' what I alienate.

Does the logic of Locke's theory require the right to bequeath? In my own view the answer is 'no', because it has no resources to deduce this right from its only likely source, the right to alienate. Nozick, however, takes the zipping back argument to be valid and to constitute a refutation of Locke. He offers his own reworking of the proviso. The Nozickian proviso is that nobody, by appropriating, should worsen the position of others, all things considered. Here is what Nozick says:

> Someone may be made worse off by another's appropriation in two ways: first, by losing the opportunity to improve his situation by a particular appropriation or any one; and second, by no longer being able to use freely (without appropriation) what he previously could. A stringent requirement that another not be made worse off by an appropriation would exclude the first way if nothing else counterbalances the diminution in opportunity, as well as the second. A weaker requirement would exclude the second way, though not the first (Nozick, 1974: 176).

This is not the most lucid Nozickian passage on record. But the point seems to be this: on the strong requirement, if my appropriation cuts your chances of appropriating then it can only be justified if something else counterbalances for these reduced chances. On the weaker version, the relevant chances are not those of appropriating but merely of using some natural resource. Nozick's claim is that on both the stronger and the weaker versions, the compensation arises from the system of private property within which the appropriation takes place. This system produces such benefits to all, that the reduced chances of appropriation or use are a price well worth paying (Nozick, 1974: 177; Wolff, 1991: 109-10).

The problem with this argument is that there is no guarantee, under a system of private property, that the position of particular individuals may not deteriorate to a point of deprivation where no such appeals to 'the benefit of all' carry any plausibility. Nozick tries to define a baseline above this point of deprivation, but this attempt saddles him with difficulties which are explored in Sarkar, 1982.

20.4 Other approaches to property

Locke's theory of property and his defence of private property are mainly grounded on considerations of rights and justice. The individual is entitled to appropriate, by right and as a matter of justice, through mixing his or her labour and through adding value. While Locke certainly makes an appeal to utility – he argues that the improving cultivator 'who appropriates land to himself by his labour does not lessen but increase the common stock of mankind' (ST, §37: 294; G.A. Cohen, 1995: 187) – this is not the main foundation of his case. For a different view from Locke's on the relationship between property and justice, see D. Miller, 1980. Note that in the socialist tradition, with regard to the means of production, justice is seen as a ground precisely for public ownership, not for Lockean private ownership.

Utilitarians rest the case for property in general and private property in particular entirely on the utility of the institution. John Stuart Mill observes, for instance, that the rules of distribution (of which property rules are a part) are merely conventional, matters of social choice and contingency about which we should decide on the basis of whatever will produce the best consequences (PPE II.1).

There are two other distinctive approaches. In the first place, there is the argument from freedom. This argument is to be found in the economist Milton Friedman (b.1912) and (with greater sophistication) in F.A. von Hayek (1899-1992). Hayek argues that, unless there is predominantly private ownership of the means of production, the individual is at the mercy of the socialist state which combines economic with political power.

Public ownership is, in Hayek's famous phrase, 'the road to serfdom' (Hayek, 1944; cf. N. Barry et al., 1984; O'Brien, 1994).

Secondly, there is Hegel's argument (prefigured in Aristotle, NE IV.1: 79-85) that moral responsibility and the growth of moral personality require the use, possession, management and so on of resources. The relevant sections of Hegel are PR §§41-71: 73-103. On Hegel see Ryan, 1984b: ch. title 5; Knowles, 1983; Patten, 1995.

On Locke's theory of property see Arneil, 1996; L.M.G. Clark, 1977; Cunningham, 1910: 85-91; Grunebaum, 1987: 53-69; Hampsher-Monk, 1992: 88-95; Lloyd Thomas, 1995: ch. 4; C.B. McPherson, 1962: ch. 5; Olivecrona, 1974a & 1974b; Ryan, 1984b: ch. 1; Wolff, 1996b: 23-6.

General discussions of property include Benn & Peters, 1959: ch. 7; Alan Carter, 1988; Ginsberg, 1965: ch. 5; T.H. Green, 1986: §§ 211-32: 163-78; Hayek, 1982, I: 106-10; Kymlicka, 1990: 96-103, 107-23, 145-51; Lewis, 1898: ch. 19; Oakeshott, 1991: 391-6; Reeve in Goodin & Pettit, 1995, also Reeve in D. Held, 1991: ch. 4. Note also (in historical order) More, 1989: 38-40, 116-18 & 128; Hume, 1978, Bk 3, Pt 2, chs. 2-4: 484-516; Godwin, 1971: Bk 8 and passim; Mill, 1987a, Bk 2, chs. 1-3: 199-241. On Hume, see Miller, 1981: 60-77; on Godwin, Philp, 1986: 134-8; and on Mill, Ryan, 1984b: ch. 6.

Among the classic texts, apart from Locke himself, see in particular Plato, R III-IV, 416D-421E: 184-7. In Plato's *Republic* the ruling class of guardians have no private property; their needs are met solely by communal provision. This arrangement has a double rationale. Under it, the guardians are not distracted from their proper pursuits; they follow reason and justice without scope for satisfying acquisitive desires. This is good for the guardians themselves. Moreover, the *polis* gains by having a ruling class which is dedicated solely to the common good. Aristotle and Hegel had their reservations: P II.5 1263b15-1264a1: 27; PR §46: 77-8. Rousseau has some remarks on property in SC I.9: 54-6 but his main discussion is DI Part 2: esp. 161, 164, 166, 167, 169. 171-4. See Hall, 1973: 43-51; Wokler, 1995: 36-9, 48-52.

4. Freedom, Democracy, and the Public Interest

21. INTRODUCTION

Various linkages and tensions make it suitable to group together freedom, democracy, and the public interest. An instant list, no complete enumeration: democracy has been thought to require a context of constitutional freedoms for its proper working; but equally, freedom has been considered to be at risk from the tyranny of the majority. Democracy, through the formula of majority rule, seems to promote 'the greatest good of the greatest number', to advance the preponderance of interests – which is one understanding of what the public interest consists in.

22. FREEDOM

Freedom receives its meed of praise. 'I know not what course others may take, give me liberty or give me death', said the Virginian statesman and orator, Patrick Henry (1736-99). In the scale of human values the American Declaration of Independence puts freedom second only to life itself. Rousseau goes further. 'To renounce one's freedom', he says, 'is to renounce one's quality as man' (SC I.4: 45). On the darker side there is Madame Roland's cry on the scaffold of the guillotine: 'O liberté! O liberté! Que du crimes on commet en ton nom!' ('Liberty! liberty! What crimes are done in your name!'). Again, there is Plato's sighing complaint in R VIII that in a democracy even the dogs are free.

In discussing freedom we need to draw a number of distinctions – to know how metaphysical freedom differs from political freedom and how, within political freedom, lines have been drawn between negative and positive freedom and also freedom as participation. This will be our exercise in conceptual analysis. Under theories of freedom I shall consider John Stuart Mill's liberty principle. The main aporia is a paradox propounded by Rousseau that we can be forced to be free.

22.1 Basic distinctions

In political philosophy 'freedom' and 'liberty' are interchangeable. You are free, at liberty, to choose which term you will. Who or what can be free? The political subject term, when we say 'X is free', can be a person, a group, or a whole society. For convenience and in line with current practice in political philosophy, I focus on the freedom of persons.

But on what concept of a person? The concept relevant to freedom is that of an agent who can make choices from a range of options and alternatives, and act intentionally in the light of those choices – doing X as a means to Y, or doing W as a case or instance of Z, and so on. The broadest concept of freedom assimilates it to power or ability. We find this in Hobbes' definition: 'Liberty, or Freedome, signifieth (properly) the absence of

Opposition; (by Opposition, I mean externall ḥmpediments of motion;)' (L ch. 21: 145; see further Pennock, 1965; Warrender, 1957: 214-17; J.W.N. Watkins, 1973: ch. 7).

Freedom *is* a kind of power or ability: 'He is free from those bullies now – he can walk down the street in safety.' But to equate freedom with power or ability *simpliciter*, leaves no distinctive work for the concept of freedom to do. The presence of the Alps and the presence of bullies may both affect my ability to act; but the bullies are relevant to freedom, the Alps (qua brute physical barrier) are not. In a quick formula, freedom is at issue when restrictions on the range of options and alternatives available to an agent are brought about, or (as some would add) are removable, by human beings. For this reason the term 'social freedom' is sometimes favoured, as bringing out the vital link between one person's freedom and the actions of other people.

Some philosophers would insert a moral rider at this point. If we are to talk about freedom it is not enough, they would say, for there to be restrictions on the range of options and alternatives available to an agent which are brought about, or are removable, by human beings. Freedom is not, as John Stuart Mill thought, a matter of 'doing what one desires' or wants (OL ch. 5: 96). Listen to Montesquieu:

> [L]iberty in no way consists in doing what one wants. ... [L]iberty can consist only in having the power to do what one should want to do and in no way being constrained to do what one should not want to do (SPL 11.4: 155).

The same view occurs in Locke, for whom simply doing what one wants to do is not liberty but licence (ST §6: 270; cf. Aristotle, P V.9: 129). There is a basis in ordinary usage for this moralistic restriction, as the availability of 'licence' as a contrast term to 'liberty' shows. But the diversity of morals makes the moralistic restriction currently unhelpful.

In political philosophy, three main concepts of freedom have been distinguished. These are:

- negative freedom
- positive freedom
- freedom as participation

But this is not quite all. In the course of your reading you will encounter references to Adam Smith's idea of 'the system of natural liberty'. We will look at it when we have examined the idea of negative freedom (§22.3). This will also be the stage at which to explain the idea of 'republican liberty' which Quentin Skinner traces in the writings of Machiavelli.

Two other concepts will surface in our discussion. The first is autonomy, which stands ambiguously close to positive freedom; telling them apart is not easy. The second is free-will. This is metaphysical freedom. We can usefully look into it straightaway; contrastively it will help get the freedom relevant to political philosophy in clearer focus.

22.2 Political versus metaphysical freedom

Freedom is about choice. Put in headline form, negative freedom centres on the constraints which others impose or allow on our choices; positive freedom centres on the rationality of our choices. These characterisations hold the two notions apart only in a rough and ready way, to give a first impression. The issue of free-will, or of what is also called metaphysical freedom, undercuts both types of freedom with the possibility that (as 'hard' determinists hold) it is causally impossible for a person to do any action other than the one they actually do. For this sort of determinist, my choices explain my actions but are themselves subject to explanation in causal terms. Any thought that, in a situation for action, I could have done otherwise if I had chosen is empty; I could not have chosen otherwise than I did.

Let us see the argument. Make a natural assumption: there are events. Now suppose that for every event or set of events, E2, there occurs another event or set of events, E1, which precedes E2 and is causally sufficient for it. We can call this the thesis of determinism. The notion of causal sufficiency is not yet quite clear, but on a necessitarian view of causation (a view which holds that causes necessitate their effects) we can take the thesis of hard determinism as follows: given E1, E2 cannot but occur.

If we accept that human actions are events, then (quickly and informally) the hard determinist argues as follows:

1. If the thesis of determinism is true, then human actions (events 'done' by human beings) have preceding events that are causally sufficient for them.
2. Among these events are choices.
3. But the thesis of determinism applies to choices themselves, which accordingly (if the thesis of determinism is true) have preceding events that are causally sufficient for them.
4. If choices have preceding events that are causally sufficient for them, then, given that causes necessitate their effects, no one can choose otherwise than they do.
5. The thesis of determinism is true.
6. No one can choose otherwise than they do.

There are many responses to this style of argument. Some philosophers argue that while the thesis of determinism is true, it does not preclude 'alternative possibilities' (in this case the possibility of choosing otherwise) because causes do not necessitate their effects; to assign a causal relation between event A and event B is simply to say that A-type events (say, choices) are regularly followed by B-type events (say, intentional actions). Taking this 'regularitarian' view of causation, John Stuart Mill refers to the thesis of determinism at the start of *On Liberty* as 'the misnamed doctrine of Philosophical Necessity' (OL 5; cf. SL VI.2; and Britton, 1953: 99-100). Other philosophers argue that (at least some) human choices are uncaused. We can make rational or moral choices which are not themselves subject to causal determination. Others again reject the thesis of determinism as unverifiable (how could we check its claims about *all* events, past present and future?) or even as refuted by quantum phenomena, *some* of which are objectively random.

Determinism is a minefield in which some of the ablest philosophers have come to grief. Two good points at which to proceed cautiously into the area are Honderich, 1993 and Wiggins, 1987: 215-37. It is not possible to decide for or against determinism purely from within political philosophy; metaphysical, not political, considerations apply. Whether or not determinism is true, however, there may still be negative freedom, positive freedom, and freedom as participation. To these matters we now proceed.

22.3 Negative freedom

Human beings make choices from a range of options and alternatives, and act intentionally in the light of those choices to fulfil their wants and preferences, desires and inclinations. Call this the minimal metaphysics of agency. Whatever the status of choices as debated by hard determinists and libertarians, there is an analysis of freedom which fixes on the ways that human factors reduce options and alternatives and cut the scope for intentional action. Joel Feinberg has identified four such factors:

- internal positive constraints
- internal negative constraints
- external positive constraints
- external negative constraints

Internal positive constraints are such things as weakness of will, compulsive habits and overmastering impulses, neuroses, obsessions of various kinds. Lack of information or skill, call it 'ignorance', is an example of internal negative constraints. External positive constraints include physical compulsion and coercive incentives. External negative constraints are mainly deficits in resources (Feinberg, 1973: 13; R. Young, 1980: 567).

With these constraints in hand, we can take a look at our first concept of freedom – negative freedom.

The term 'negative freedom' was given currency in the political lexicon by the late Sir Isaiah Berlin in 'Two Concepts of Liberty'. This was his inaugural lecture as Chichele Professor of Social and Political Theory at Oxford in 1958 (Berlin, 1969: 118-72; reprinted in Goodin & Pettit, 1997: 391-417 and abridged in Quinton, 1967: 141-52). Berlin revised the text of his lecture in subsequent reprintings. The 1969 edition contains the last update. Nothing deprecatory is intended by the term 'negative'. It simply indicates a lack or absence of certain kinds of interference or obstruction. Berlin's basic formula for negative freedom is that:

> I am normally said to be free to the degree to which no man or body of men interferes with my activity. [L]iberty in this sense is simply the area within which a man can act unobstructed by others (Berlin, 1969: 122).

This centres firmly on Feinberg's external positive constraints. We could follow Berlin's own exposition of this concept of freedom. But my decision is to take a different course. Berlin was a great historian of ideas, able to sketch large perspectives and to group ideas in important, illuminating ways. His strength was not in the patient refinement of concepts, though he certainly amended his account.

Here then is the plan. Negative freedom is the absence of external positive constraints. We can explore this idea. Berlin will crop up from time to time but the discussion will not revolve round him. If you want to check out the fuller details of Berlin's views, a sound statement of the development of his thinking is given in Parent, 1974: 149-53. Gray, 1995a: ch. 1 contains a longer, textually less close but philosophically deeper discussion. See also Brenkert, 1991: ch. 3 passim; and Macfarlane, 1966.

The first step in probing the view of freedom as the absence of external positive constraints is to look more carefully at the nature of such constraints. These are constraints on intentional action; constraints, that is to say, on the choices we can make in the light of our wants and preferences, desires and inclinations. Examples may help. Let us fix initially on the freedom of agents to do or to avoid doing actions.

Stefan is walking along Half Moon Street, in the shadow of Salisbury Cathedral, daydreaming about things that do not concern us, when the muscular Vincent steps suddenly in front of him and by brute strength marches him into an alley and takes his wallet. With regard to going into the alley Stefan is not free; he is subject to crude force, simple physical compulsion. No practical reasoning in which he engages, no intention that he forms, has any explanatory relevance to the physical fact of his body's making certain movements and taking a certain direction. (This looks like an exercise of Dahl's one-dimensional power (§12.2).)

In no uncertain terms Stefan has been forcibly constrained. Force, then, is one factor that can affect a person's freedom. What of setting physical barriers to action? Suppose Vincent locks Stefan in a room. In this case he does not, as in the street example, render Stefan's practical reasoning and intentions totally irrelevant to action. But he restricts the options or alternatives between which Stefan can choose. Crucially he removes one option entirely, that of leaving the room. (This looks like an exercise of Bachrach & Baratz's two-dimensional power (§12.2).)

Take now a third scenario. The locked room example can be developed. Vincent (whose moral education is possibly beyond remedy) unlocks the door. Stefan steps out, as he thinks, to freedom. But not so: for Vincent presents him with a dilemma. Unless he hands over $10,000 within the week, his long-time companion Sasha will come to serious harm. Stefan knows Vincent too well to suppose this to be an idle threat; and he sees no way of involving the public authorities without the virtual certainty of violent reprisal. Moreover, Stefan can afford this sum, but only just. In the event, to spare Sasha Vincent's grievous attentions, Stefan pays up.

In this case Stefan is subject to a coercive incentive. How are we to formulate this notion? Here is one approach: a coercive incentive is a threat or inducement 'on which it would be unreasonable to expect *any* rational person not to act' (Gert & Duggan, 1979: 203). There perhaps are such incentives, but it is questionable whether we need to make the notion so tight. A less demanding and more realistic approach is in terms of eligibility: a coercive or negative incentive is a threat that renders one course of action (in our example, paying the $10,000) substantially less eligible than another (not paying the money).

Coercive incentives might be overwhelmingly enticing inducements but I will keep to threats. Nozick presents a first formalisation of coercion as follows (Nozick in PPS 4: 102). Person P coerces person Q into not doing A if and only if:

1. P threatens to do something if Q does A (and P knows he is making this threat).
2. This threat renders Q's doing A substantially less eligible as a course of conduct than not doing A.
3. P makes this threat in order to get Q not to do A, intending that Q realise he has been threatened by P.
4. Q does not do A.
5. P's words or deeds are part of Q's reason for not doing A.

In our own example, one person was coercing another into doing an action (handing over some money) while in Nozick's formalisation the coercion is directed towards getting someone not to do an action. The wording can readily be changed, no deep point is at issue. But will the formalisation stand up to criticism?

For one thing, are the conditions sufficient for coercion? Suppose that Q understands the threat in the sense of realising that the relevant evil will befall him if he does the action, but does not recognise it as a threat. Instead he takes it as a warning. Nozick suggests, then, that we need at least to add an extra condition (Nozick, op. cit.: 103):

6. Q knows that P has threatened to do the something mentioned in 1, if he, Q, does A (or, to handle cases of anonymous threats, Q knows that someone has threatened to do something mentioned in (1) if he, Q, does A.

Are (1)-(6) strong enough for sufficiency? Suppose, Nozick continues in his ingenious and persistent way, that Q actually rather likes the thought of what P has threatened to do. Only, he does not want to upset P; and for this reason he refrains from doing A. This is not a case of coercion. Then maybe we should replace 5 with:

5¹ Part of Q's reason for not doing A is to avoid (or lessen the likelihood of) the thing which P has threatened to bring about or have brought about.

Do we now have a full set of sufficient conditions? No, Nozick remarks: there are cases where, unknown to P, Q wants to avoid P's inflicting the threatened consequence only because this will produce some further consequence harmful to P, which Q (mindful, for whatever reason, of P's interests) wants to avoid (Nozick, op. cit.: 103, n. 3).

One's intellectual excitement is likely to wane long before Nozick's ingenuity gives out. The point is taken: an intuitive grasp of the idea of coercion is one thing, its precise conceptualisation quite another. The best plan is to work through Nozick's article and to follow up with V. Held, 1976; Lucas, 1966: 56-72; Lyons, 1975; C.C. Ryan, 1980; P. Wilson 1982. I will work with the idea that P coerces Q to consent to do action A when (a) P threatens to make Q worse off if he or she does not do that action, (b) Q succumbs to the threat, and (c) it is reasonable for Q to succumb to the threat rather than to suffer the consequences. Cf. Wertheimer, 1996: 102. Note that 'coercion' as discussed here is a more specific notion than was involved in our earlier reference to a 'supreme coercive power' (§§9.2.1, 13.3.3) as an ability to quell all opposition and ensure compliance.

We have now identified three factors that can affect negative freedom: the intentional and deliberate use of (1) force, (2) physical barriers, and (3) coercive incentives. These are external positive constraints. But consider a point: how important is the element of intention or deliberateness? What is the conceptual connection with freedom? Does the restriction or removal of options and alternatives, the cutting down the scope for intentional action, have to be intentional and deliberate for a person's freedom to be affected?

On Berlin's first account, in the original version of the 1958 lecture, the assumption was that intention and deliberateness are essential. This would mean that I do not increase your freedom if, e.g. I let you out of a room in which you have been accidentally (i.e. with no intention or deliberateness) locked.

Berlin himself moved away from the requirement of intention and deliberateness. This allowed him to accommodate the locked room example. But he also came up with a new formula for negative freedom: if, as a result of alterable human practices, a person's options and alternatives are fewer than they would otherwise be, then freedom is at issue (Berlin, 1969: xxxix). This brings external negative constraints into play. Obviously enough, indefinitely many deficits in resources are removable by human beings in this extended view of freedom as enablement. The revision was partly motivated by Berlin's acknowledgement that he had originally meant to equate negative liberty with non-interference in a person's fulfilment or attempt to fulfil their desires. On such an equation, freedom might be indefinitely preserved, as the ancient Stoics had claimed, by the contraction of desire; a person who desired absolutely nothing would be perfectly free since nobody could interfere in any way with their desires (Berlin, 1969: xxxviii). This seemed to Berlin paradoxical. 'Stone walls do not a prison make,/Nor iron bars a cage', as Richard Lovelace (1618-58) wrote.

The extended view of freedom poses a number of problems. If we keep to the original idea of negative freedom, with its stress on intention and deliberateness in the restriction of options and alternatives, then we are dealing with factors of a limited and distinctive kind. The constraints practised by Vincent – the intentional and deliberate use of force, physical barriers, and coercive incentives – are markedly different in kind from the constraint 'practised' if I, society or the state fail to provide you with the resources that would expand your range of options and alternatives. Nothing is gained, one might urge, and logical conscience is violated, by assimilating these radically dissimilar constraints (external positive and external negative) in an account of freedom.

If we heed such considerations, we will deny that the locked room example is relevant to freedom; in releasing you from the room in which you have been accidentally locked, I simply increase your power of mobility, your ability to change location. Freedom would only enter the picture if, knowing that you had been accidentally locked in the room, I then deliberately and intentionally kept you there when I had the ability to release you.

The intentional, deliberate use of force, physical barriers, and coercion is something which it is peculiarly important to control. Exemption from the *arbitrary* use of these things is the basic minimum on which civilised life depends; and the originally limited idea of negative freedom, relating it solely to external positive constraints, was a crucial recognition of this precise fact. (To support the original limits in this way is to bring a functional element into conceptual analysis (§3.5.4).)

We have referred to the 'arbitrary' use of force and the rest. This might appear to take us straight back to Berlin's original stress on intention and deliberateness, but it is unlikely that the connection between arbitrariness and intention or deliberateness is sufficiently close. Arbitrariness occurs when we fail to act on a defensible rule in some matter affecting other people's interests. No doubt this is generally intentional and deliberate, but it need not be so. The failure may be unreflective.

Some theorists make a special link between defensibility and coercion. This involves a normative approach to coercion, according to which if I am justified when I apply a negative constraint then I am not acting coercively. Coercion occurs only when defensibility is lacking. (It follows from this that a justifiable law is non-coercive.) Left to myself, I should have said that one can on occasion apply justifiable coercion. (And, to glance back, when we spoke, with respect to sovereignty, of a supreme coercive power, there was the open possibility that one might have an obligation to obey such a power. 'Coercion' cannot plausibly be reduced to a 'boo-word' in the way that the normative approach assumes.) At any rate the normative concept of coercion will not be used here. For further discussion, see C.C. Ryan, 1980.

But if, however, to link back with the main point, there are reasons for tying negative freedom to external positive constraints, there is a problem. Once we admit the relevance to freedom of the accidentally locked room example, there is no obvious way of keeping out all four kinds of constraint from our account of freedom. If I can increase the options and alternatives available to you by opening the accidentally locked room, and thereby increase your freedom, then in other situations I can do the same in principle by countering any one or more of the whole range of constraints, internal negative and positive, external positive and negative. There appears to be no principled point at which we can draw the line and exclude some constraint or other from our concept of freedom.

Does this matter? If we finish up with an omnium-gatherum concept of freedom, where is the harm in that? The harm comes, in the view of some critics, because freedom is so powerfully normative a concept. If we accept that someone's freedom could be increased by adding to their resources, then we must also accept an obligation to provide those resources and to increase their freedom. Few would deny that, other things equal, we have an obligation to refrain from practising external positive constraint. Vincent should not have acted as he did. But if we are to have an equal obligation to redistribute resources, through taxation or charity, to everyone whose lack of resources reduces their freedom, the social and political implications are enormous. These background assumptions exert pressure to resist the extension of the concept of freedom beyond external positive constraints.

But the assumptions can be questioned. Anyone might allow that freedom is a human good. Some grounds for that claim will be examined below (§22.8). But it does not follow, because your freedom is a good and because I could increase your freedom by providing you with resources, that therefore I (or others) have an obligation to secure that increase through the relevant provision. Only if there were an obligation to maximise the enjoyment of a single value, namely freedom, through personal or political action, would the demands of your freedom generate any such simple, straightforward obligation of provision on the part of other people. But no such commitment to single-value politics follows from the extension of negative freedom to include all four kinds of constraint.

A final point may be noted. Negative freedom centres on interferences with an agent's intentional actions, on the choices an agent can make in the light of his or her wants and preferences, desires and inclinations. These wants and preferences, desires and inclinations are nearly always, for defenders of negative freedom, expressed or self-ascribed. One obvious contrast is with 'criticised' wants and preferences (and so on), namely those that the agent would have under 'privileged' conditions of correct information, improved rationality, absence of obsession or whatever – the domain of Feinberg's internal positive and negative constraints. See §18.1. There is a yet stronger contrast with conceptions of the agent's interests which sit loose to wants and preferences altogether and work rather in terms of what is objectively good for the agent, given some theory of the human good. As an ideology, liberalism tends to stress negative freedom, not least because a powerful strand of liberalism rejects the idea of an objective human good in the terms of which expressed wants and preferences might be overridden.

Before we press on to consider positive freedom, there are still the questions of natural liberty and republican liberty to be brought forward from §21.1.1. On natural liberty Adam Smith (1723-90) writes in *The Wealth of Nations* (1776):

> ... the obvious and simple system of natural liberty establishes itself of its own accord. Every man, as long as he does not violate the laws of justice, is left perfectly free to pursue his own interests his own way, and to bring both his industry and his capital into competition with those of any other man, or order of men. The sovereign is completely discharged from a duty in the attempting to perform which he must always be exposed to innumerable delusions, and for the proper performance of which no human wisdom or knowledge could ever be sufficient; the duty of superintending the industry of private people and of directing it towards the employments must suitable to the interest of the society. According to the system of natural liberty, the sovereign has only three duties to attend to; three duties of great importance, indeed, b... plain and intelligible to common understandings: first, the duty of protecting the society from the violence and invasion of other independent societies; secondly, the duty of protecting, as far as possible, every member of the society from the injustice or oppression of every other member of it, or the duty of establishing an exact administration of justice; and, thirdly, the duty of erecting and maintaining certain public works and certain public institutions, which it can never be for the interest of any individual, or small number of individuals, to erect and maintain; because the profit could never repay the expense to any individual or small number of individuals, though it may frequently do much more than repay it to a great society (A. Smith, 1961, I: 208-9).

When we consider Smith's three roles for the state, it is by no means obvious that they would reduce the level of state activity in modern conditions. Smith was mainly reacting against the Mercantilists, economic theorists who looked towards direct and extensive political regulation of the economy for political ends.

Smith's sense of 'natural liberty' is to be distinguished from the freedom which theorists such as Hobbes and Locke ascribe to agents in the so-called state of nature, i.e. the human condition before the emergence of state-organised society (L ch. 14: 91; ST §4: 269). For a further discussion of Smithian natural liberty, see Campbell, 1981: 106-7; Rawls, TJ: 72; also the remarks on *laissez-faire* in Scruton, 1983: 429-30 and Parker, 1982; and Buchanan's article, 'Public Goods and Natural Liberty', in Wilson & Skinner, 1976. Fitzgibbons suggests an interesting identification of Smith's natural liberty with Aristotelian commutative justice (§17.2 above; Fitzgibbons, 1995: 153).

'Republican liberty' is a term coined by Quentin Skinner to identify a political composite of which negative freedom is the essential element. This composite is to be found, he claims, in the work of a range of Renaissance thinkers, centrally including the Machiavelli of the *Discourses*. Upholders of republican liberty place the greatest stress on negative freedom, exemption from arbitrary forceful or coercive intervention by others. From this they infer to the conditions best calculated to secure negative freedom. These conditions turn out to involve membership of a self-governing community in which 'the will of the body politic determines its own actions, the actions of the community as a whole' (Skinner, 1984: 207).

22.4 Positive freedom

There is a common error that the difference between negative and positive freedom is expressible in the two locutions, 'freedom from' and 'freedom to'. If this were so, the distinction would have no philosophical significance. For every 'free from' statement can be translated without remainder into a 'free to' statement. If I am free from interference in crossing the road then I am free to cross the road without interference.

Berlin traces the term 'positive 'freedom' to T.H. Green (e.g. Green, 1986: 200) and explains the idea in the following terms:

> The 'positive' sense of the word 'liberty' derives from the wish on the part of the individual to be his own master ... 'I am my own master'; 'I am slave to no man'; but may I not (as Platonists and Hegelians tend to say) be a slave to nature? Or to my own 'unbridled' passions? Are these not so many species of the identical genus 'slave' – some political or legal, others moral or spiritual? Have not men had the experience of liberating themselves from spiritual slavery, or slavery to nature, and do they not in the course of it become aware, on the one hand, of a self which dominates, and, on the other, of something which in them which is brought to heel? This dominant self is then variously identified with reason, with my 'higher nature', with the self which calculates and aims at what will satisfy it in the long run, with my 'real, or 'ideal', or 'autonomous' self, or with my self 'at its best'; which is then contrasted with irrational impulse, uncontrolled desires, my 'lower' nature, with the self which calculates and aims at what will satisfy it in the long run, with my 'real', or 'ideal', or 'autonomous' self, or with my self 'at its best'; which is then contrasted with irrational impulse. Uncontrolled desires, my 'lower' nature, the pursuit of immediate pleasures, my 'empirical' or 'heteronomous' self, swept by every gust of desire and passion, needing to be rigidly disciplined if it is ever to rise to the full height of its 'real' nature (Berlin, 1969: 131-2).

This characterisation picks out two distinct elements in the idea of positive freedom. The basic element is that components or constituents ('parts') of the individual can stand in the same defeating or constraining relation to choice as can the constraints imposed by other people. Imagine the situation: my view, all things considered, is that I should do action X. This action seems best calculated to satisfy some wants and preferences that are really important to me. I plan to do X, but another person intervenes with force, physical barriers, or coercive incentives. This is the realm of negative freedom. Vary the scenario: suppose that with the intention to do X, I encounter an enticing inducement, some spur of the moment temptation, to do Y instead. I succumb to this temptation. My 'all things considered' judgement has been defeated as effectively by constituents of my own character as it would have been by the intervention of another person. This is the realm of positive freedom.

In Feinberg's terminology, central to negative freedom are external positive constraints. Central to positive freedom are internal positive constraints.

But there is another element, which Berlin brings out when he talks of the higher, real or ideal self. The idea here is that, while any divided self defeats or constrains choice, not just any form of unity will do in place of it. The proper form of unity is that in which (according to various answers) reason rules the passions in a life of rational self-direction, or conscience rules the emotions, and so on.

Two problems attend the idea of positive freedom. Anyone might accept the basic element; the divided self is a patent and inconvenient fact of everyday life. The further element, which we have just examined, involves the sharp difficulty of coming up with a plausible philosophy of mind and normative theory by which to identify the 'higher' self.

That is the first problem; the second concerns the repressive associations of the idea of positive freedom. It is thought (and Berlin makes much of this) that if I, or society, or the state can identify your higher, real or ideal self, we can properly intervene to reinforce it against the beckonings of your lower nature, regardless of your preferences in the matter. Preferences against intervention would, *ex hypothesi*, stem from your lower nature and so would not be worthy of consideration.

This critique of the idea of positive freedom is muddled. In the first place, if the positive theorist is right, your preferences against intervention would indeed stem from your lower nature; the point cannot be returned merely rhetorically against the positivist theorist.

Secondly, there is no necessary connection between a belief in the higher self and the justifiability of intervention in the lives of others. 'Am I my brother's keeper?' There is no moral entailment between my supposing that you are in thrall to your lower nature and my taking myself to be justified in seeking to control you. One can morally disapprove of something, or merely regard it as being of inferior value, without feeling entitled to intervene against it. This is one basis of toleration. John Stuart Mill holds a celebrated view that there are higher and lower pleasures (a favourite crux of ethics examiners) but he never urges this as grounds for suppressing bingo in the interests of Shakespeare and the higher self (Mill, 1991: 136-58). On positive freedom and intervention, see further Cranston, 1954: 29-32; Bosanquet, 1923: chs. 3-7.

The relation between positive and negative freedom is more symbiotic than a merely contrastive discussion brings out. An agent who satisfied the positive theorist on the score of a unified self under the control of reason (say) would still need a fair degree of negative freedom in order to apply their rationality.

In summary: the basic, permanently interesting claim of the positive freedom theorist is that parts of the agent's own character or personality can constrain his or her action as effectively as can interferences by other people. To this we might add, in an account more sympathetic than Berlin's, that it is relevant to freedom (1) if the causal origin of an agent's wants and preferences is such that the agent, X, would repudiate those wants and preferences if he or she realised that origin; and (2) if X wants or prefers Y under a description which is demonstrably false.

22.4.1 Rousseau on being 'forced to be free'

It is informative, finally, to note that while, as a theorist of positive freedom, Rousseau propounds the notorious paradox that one can be forced to be free (SC I.7: 53), he argues this solely in the context of the *Social Contract*'s highly specific arrangements for collective decision-making. The aim of Rousseau's contractors is to preserve 'independence'. This has two components (MacAdam, 1972: 308; cf. Levin, 1970) corresponding respectively to negative and positive freedom:

- not being subject to, or under the control of, another person
- not being subject to, or under the control of, one's negative emotions or divisive, anti-social traits

The emotions in question are *amour-propre*, egoism or selfishness (as distinct from *amour de soi*, a reasonable self-regard or prudence), along with a string of divisive, anti-social traits such as vanity, avarice, envy, ambition, jealousy, shame, and contempt (MacAdam, 1972: 310; Dent, 1988: 21, 53-5: DI passim), all of which Rousseau regards as products of the imperfect, private property-based social arrangements which prevail in the bulk of human history. The causal origins of these negative emotions and divisive, anti-social traits are not transparent to those who are in the grip of them.

Under the arrangements outlined in the *Social Contract*, collective decision-making, in which all voluntarily take part as equals, is constrained by the need to address equally the interests of all. This is the operation of the general will (W.T. Jones, 1987). Nobody can give vent to the negative emotions and divisive, anti-social traits in collective deliberation. In support of a proposal everyone must give grounds for belief that it is to the common advantage. Again, nobody is at the disposal of other persons; decision-makers of equal status have no reason to submit to such treatment.

If, when collective deliberation has taken place and collective decisions have been made, a particular person reneges on what has been decided, they can be forced to be free in the following sense. The collective decision has been made in circumstances calculated to block the adoption of public policies that allow (1) one person to be subjected to another or (2) anyone to give scope to their negative emotions or divisive, anti-social traits. Collective decisions accordingly deliver policies that preserve independence. In enforcing those policies on the recalcitrant individual, we are compelling that person to accept a policies that safeguard his or her independence. This is merely to say that we are forcing him or her to be free. See further Cobban, 1964: ch. 3; Hall, 1973: 94-7; Hampsher-Monk, 1992: 179-80; Noone, 1981: 22, 34-6, 133; Plamenatz, 1972; Wokler, 1995: 66; J. Wolff, 1996b: 96.

Admittedly the kind of case on which Rousseau himself mainly comments is that in which we do not renege but rather differ from the majority over just what is in the common interest (SC IV.2: 124). The majority then forces us to be free. This is distinctly more dubious than the previous case, though there are some interesting assumptions about probability behind it (see §23.4.2.2 on Condorcet; also T. Pateman, 1988; Dahl, 1989: 141-2). But the previous case makes the point. Whatever we may think of the Rousseau-ian scenario, in the case of the reneging individual we are not presented with the spectacle of one person's or group's subjecting another to arbitrary control. See further Cobban, 1964: ch. 3; J.C. Hall, 1973: 94-7; Hampsher-Monk, 1992: 179-80;

Noone, 1981: 22, 34-6, 133; Plamenatz, 1972; J.Wolff, 1996b: 96. The real difficulty in Rousseau's idea of one's being forced to be free is that none of the constraints he imposes on collective decision-making – from the requirement that all citizens participate, to the form in which proposals are phrased, to the emphasis on general rather than specific issues, and so on (see W.T. Jones, 1987: 110-12) – ensure that the conditions of independence are respected. The fact of compulsion, when one is nominally forced to be free, is offset only by the contingent probability, or pious hope, that one's independence is secured.

22.5 Two concepts of liberty or one?: MacCallum's slingshot

The issue is joined between proponents of negative and positive freedom. But perhaps a reconciliation can be reached. Suppose there is a unitary concept of freedom which accommodates both perspectives? Just such a concept is (it seems) advanced by Gerald C. MacCallum, who argues that claims about freedom are best stated as expressing a triadic relation:

> Whenever the freedom of some agent or agents is in question, it is always freedom from some constraint or restriction on, interference with, or barrier to doing, not doing, becoming or not becoming something (PPS 4: 176).

There is no reason why external positive constraints (negative freedom), internal positive constraints (positive freedom), along with internal negative and external negative constraints may not be accommodated within this formula.

My own view is that MacCallum carries his point. Berlin's distinction between negative and positive freedom, and for the matter of that all four of Feinberg's factors which reduce options and alternatives, which defeat or constrain choice and which cut the scope for intentional action, can be fitted into MacCallum's formula.

But I find a critical thought intruding: surely there are shades here of Hegel's night in which all cows are black. The strength of MacCallum's account is also its weakness. It enables us to fit a wide variety of constraints under a single label; by the same token, it does not enable or invite us to distinguish between them. We know quite clearly that, when negative freedom is under review, we are talking about constraints such as physical compulsion and coercive incentives. We know equally clearly that, when positive freedom is under review, weakness of will, compulsive habits, and neurotic obsessions are to the fore. These are useful discriminations.

See further Baldwin, 1984; Berlin, 1969: xliii, Gray, 1989, ch. 4; Gray, 1995a: 18; Parent, 1974: 153-5; Rawls, TJ: 202-4; Simhony, 1991 & 1993; Swanton, 1979.

22.6 Autonomy

The relation of autonomy to freedom is tricky to fix. Let us tick off some points. Negative freedom, as typically understood, means exemption from external positive constraints (physical compulsion and coercive incentives). Positive freedom, on Berlin's account, means exemption from internal positive constraints (weakness of will, compulsive habits and so on). Positive freedom points away from the divided self but we also noted that for the positive theorist, unity must be of certain privileged kinds. What is envisaged is a unified life under the rule of reason, of conscience or whatever the favoured candidate. We saw too that positive freedom needs a degree of negative freedom for its practical exercise. What is left for autonomy?

Approaches to autonomy take two directions. On the one hand, there are highly specific, fine-grained accounts such as one finds in Kant; on the other, there are more open-textured versions. Kant's account of autonomy is a landmark in the Western tradition of philosophy.

Kant starts from two assumptions. One, that autonomy is (whatever its more precise formulation) a kind of independence; and two, that we are rational beings. Rationality is a richly-layered and in many ways ambiguous concept. But for Kant it is primarily 'the faculty of principles' (*Critique of Pure Reason*, A299; Kant, 1973: 301). 'Everything in nature works according to laws. Only a rational being has the capacity of acting according to the conception of laws, i.e. according to principles' (Kant, 1969: 33-4). So a rational being is one who has the ability to act in accordance with his or her idea of laws or principles; and a rational action correspondingly is one that is done in accordance with the idea of a law or principle.

How to combine autonomy and rationality? By prescribing principles, or laws as Kant tends to call them, to ourselves. Self-legislation confers autonomy and meets the conditions of rationality. If I self-legislate, I am exempt from anybody else's prescriptions, and that gives a pretty clear meaning to independence. (The influence of Rousseau is patent here: 'obedience to the law one has prescribed to oneself is freedom' (CS I.8: 54).)

Kant's position develops as follows. Rationality in the theoretical sphere, the sphere of knowledge, is open to everyone without mutual conflict. My using a given rule of logic does not prevent you from using the same rule and does not produce disagreement in our beliefs. We may use logic and disagree but will never disagree because we use logic. Kant looks for an analogue to this compatibility in the practical sphere, the sphere of action. What rules of conduct could rational agents follow, without being drawn into conflict?

We need, Kant argues, to follow consistently universalisable maxims. This requirement, or motivational constraint, follows two routes. On the one hand, I must act on maxims on which it is logically possible for all rational beings to act. On the other, I must act on maxims which it is prudentially possible for all rational beings to act on.

Take two examples. First, suppose I am invited to a bring-a-bottle party. I decide to present a bottle of plonk and to drink the finer wine contributed by the other guests. It is not logically possible for the maxim of my action – my implicit policy, 'always take cheap and drink fine' – to be consistently universalised. If everyone were to follow the same maxim, no one would present fine wine for others to consume.

The second example is the case where I refuse assistance in all circumstances to those in need. When I refuse ever to help the indigent, universalising my maxim ('never help anyone in need') does not generate the kind of logical impossibility that arises in the bottle-party example. It would just mean a rather nastier world than even the one we have if everyone were to follow it. So Kant offers a word to the wise; no rational being could sensibly want a world of no-help and total non-co-operation. We all, foreseeably, need help at times.

As students of Kant's ethics know, if I follow the rational rule of consistent universalisability then I act morally. Kant's challenge is that there is no requirement of morality which is not delivered by the consistent universalisability test and no outcome of the test which is not a requirement of morality. The link between morality and rationality is tight. See further W. Heinemann et al., 1948-49; Gregor, 1996; O'Neill, 1989: ch. 5. Some of the ambiguities of prudential action, relevant to Kant's second universalisability test, have emerged from our discussion of Rawls on 'maximin' (§§17.3, 17.3.1).

The central point for us is that to respect the rule of consistent universalisability on both counts is to act autonomously; the agent lays down this rule for himself or herself and acts accordingly. In all this, Kant is telling us exactly what autonomy requires in fine detail. His idea of rational self-rule is hardly distinguishable from Berlin's account of autonomy as a component of positive freedom (§22.4). And, just to complete the picture, this whole account of practical reason translates straightforwardly across to politics. State law cannot control motivation but it can compel or prohibit action, and the state should require of each citizen whatever actions or omissions are necessary to allow all citizens to act on consistently universalisable maxims meeting the two tests of logical and prudential possibility. The Kantian state creates the external conditions, between citizens, to enable practical reason to be exercised by citizens.

Open-textured accounts, by contrast to that of autonomy as Kantian practical reason, take the idea of independence more loosely. What we have in view is not Kantian self-legislation working through consistently universalisable maxims binding on all rational beings. Rather the autonomous agent is seen as one who is reflective and self-critical about his or her beliefs and attitudes, wants and preferences, desires and inclinations. It is not (realistically) that the agent can 'invent' himself or herself at will, adopting only purely rational beliefs (fully coherent beliefs absolutely consistent with the evidence available and with all other beliefs) and developing a set of attitudes, wants and preferences, etc., exempt from the impact of society, history, psychology or biology.

That is not autonomy but fantasy. Rather the autonomous agent is self-conscious, able to step back and to scrutinise engagements of belief and practice. These engagements are not unbreakable, adamantine personal commitments but are known by the agent to be open to revision. At the level of belief, the quest for Rawlsian reflective equilibrium (§5.5) is an exercise of autonomy, though it is only one option. At the level of practice, I can desire X (e.g. to smoke) and also have a desire not to desire X (to give up the habit). This is why the open-textured approach is sometimes called a 'hierarchical' model; current engagements (e.g. desires) are 'first order' data and their critical review (producing desires about one's desires) represents a 'second order' monitoring. Can one have third-order desires about one's second-order desires about one's first-order desires? Does a regress threaten? My own view is that there is a possibility of indefinite regress, but a harmless one: there are no limits to human self-reflexiveness. For a careful examination of the issue see, first, G. Dworkin, 1988; then Law, 1998.

This open-textured approach to autonomy fills space not taken by the ideas of negative and positive freedom. Kantian autonomy is close to, if not identical with, the rational self-direction involved in Berlin's characterisation of positive freedom. But sliding Kant to one side, the open-textured approach stresses the critical distance between an agent and his or her engagements of belief and practice. The ideal of personal autonomy is that individual persons, self-aware in the ways outlined, ought to be allowed to decide for themselves how to conduct their lives (Raz, 1986: 108). They are viewed as freely choosing, self-determining individuals.

But in the just the same way that positive freedom needs a degree of negative freedom, autonomy needs degrees of negative and positive freedom. Without some exemption from physical restraint or compulsion and coercive incentives, the autonomous agent has no sphere of action in which to be autonomous. What point is there in having critically revised beliefs, attitudes and the rest if there is no scope to act on them? This is one bit of the background to Joseph Raz's claim that to be autonomous is to be 'part-author' of one's life and his view that individual well-being, in its aspect of autonomy requires people to make their own choices as far as possible (§30.5). Again, unless there is a degree of personal unity, of exemption from positive constraints such as weakness of will, compulsive habits and neurotic obsessions, the autonomous agent's critically revised beliefs, attitudes and so on will be practically ineffectual.

On autonomy in general, see further Donner, 1991: 165-83; Double, 1992; Gray, 1996 passim; Levine, 1988: 34-43; Mendus, 1986-87; Raz, 1986: ch. 14. On significant tensions between autonomy and authority, a distinct topic in its own right, see Baier, 1972; C. Carr, 1983; C. Cohen, 1972; G. Dworkin, 1972.

22.7 Freedom as participation: Constant on the liberty of the ancients

Bernard Crick criticises Berlin's account of freedom, both positive and negative, not so much for its internal details as for its lack of explicit connection with politics. 'What is missing in Berlin's analysis, odd though it may sound to say so, is any analysis of the link between freedom and political action ... Freedom is being left alone from politics – is it?' (Crick, 1972: 41). In omitting this link, Berlin's overall account of freedom is incomplete. The French political theorist, Benjamin Constant (1767-1830), would have understood exactly the burden of Crick's complaint.

In *The Liberty of the Ancients Compared With That of the Moderns* (1819) Constant characterises 'ancient' freedom as follows. It consisted, he tells us:

> in exercising collectively, but directly, several parts of the complete sovereignty; in deliberating, in the public square, over war and peace; in forming alliances with foreign governments; in voting laws, in pronouncing judgements; in examining the accounts, the acts, the stewardship of the magistrates; in calling them to appear in front of the assembled people, in accusing, condemning or absolving them (Constant, 1988: 311).

Freedom as participation means that we participate directly in decisions that affect our interests. While this is certainly, as Constant says, a part of the 'ancient' sense of freedom, the issue has effectively been relocated within democratic theory. There are immense difficulties in organising realistic ways for all to take part in collective decision-making. Some of these will resurface when we consider direct, representative, and deliberative democracy (§23.2).

We should, however, note that on Constant's account there is in 'ancient' freedom a direct connection with positive freedom. If positive freedom is, on one version, rational self-direction, 'ancient' freedom can be seen as the collective application of this idea. For a group of rationally self-directed individuals managing their common affairs, positive freedom becomes collective self-rule. See further Gray, 1995a: 20. Conversely, a high degree of negative freedom is perfectly consistent with the absence of self-government. A liberal-minded despot, as Berlin points out, and Frederick the Great is the obvious candidate, could leave his or her subjects with a large amount of negative freedom (Berlin, 1969: 129). See further: Brenkert, 1991: ch. 6; Holmes, 1982; on Constant, see Dunn, 1990: ch. 5.

22.8 Theories of freedom: John Stuart Mill's liberty principle

John Stuart Mill's *On Liberty* (1859) is a celebrated defence of freedom of thought, discussion, and action. 'Discussion' may be taken as 'speech' in the broad sense of any attempt by a person or group to communicate one or more propositions to another (but cf. §32.2.2 for an 'attitudinal' reinterpretation). Mill's defence of freedom of thought and discussion is readily summarised. First, even when our opinions are not revised in the face of criticism, our sense of their distinctness, our grasp of the misunderstandings to which they are open and our realisation of their implications, are all sharpened by their collision with other views. Secondly, an open arena of thought and discussion – a free market for ideas – stimulates new opinions and encourages fresh ideas to emerge. On the assumption that some of these will be true, interesting or otherwise useful, society gains by this freedom. Cf. Aristotle on democratic deliberation (§23.4.2.3).

Mill's case for freedom of thought and discussion is hardly different from the arguments to be found in John Milton's *Areopagitica* (1644), though it has extra vulnerabilities. One of these is Mill's claim that to suppress an expression of opinion is to assume infallibility: 'if any opinion is compelled to silence, that opinion may, for aught we can certainly know, be true. To deny this is to assume our own infallibility' (OL ch. 2: 53). But surely it is not. We may silence an expression of opinion (say, the teaching of Ptolemaic astronomy in schools) because it is, relative to the evidence, almost certainly false. In making this ban we do not need to assume our own infallibility. As Bishop Butler (1692-1752) remarked in *The Analogy of Religion* (1736), 'probability is the very guide of life'. We take and back the view that the Ptolemaic theory is unlikely in the highest degree to be right.

Another weakness is that Mill uses the same defence for freedom of thought as he uses for freedom of discussion. But the two freedoms are not quite on a par. To a first approximation, freedom of thought is hardly critically at risk. Short of brain-washing, who can control what I think about God, the devil, or the family dog? By contrast, nothing could be easier than the public control of discussion. Moreover, my merely privately entertained thoughts have no consequences for other people, but the public expression of views almost invariably has such consequences. Freedom of thought causes at worst a personal headache; freedom of discussion can cause a riot, violence, bloodshed, civil war.

Even so the connections between freedom of thought and of discussion may be deeper than these reflections suggest. As David Rees has pointed out to me, 'to inhibit expression of belief is not merely an infringement of my right of expression; it drastically limits my possibilities of formation of belief, through my not being able to learn what others have to say'. See Benn & Peters, 1959: 224-32; Goldman & Cox, 1996; T.H. McPherson, 1970: 127-8; Rawls (§17.3) includes freedom of expression among his primary goods.

Present-day interest in OL centres on Mill's case for freedom of action. Before we look at this in detail, we need to note three background points.

The first is that Mill was a close and reflective reader of Alexis-Charles-Henri Clérel, comte de Tocqueville's *Democracy in America* (first volume 1835, second 1840) in which the overriding uniformity of American life in the only mass democracy then known was ruthlessly exposed (Laski, 1933; Lively, 1962: ch. 3; F.M. Watkins, 1964: 58; but cf. Brunius, 1960). In Mill's own view, 'Society has now fairly got the better of individuality ... From the highest class of society down to the lowest, everyone lives as under the eye of a hostile and dreaded censorship' (OL 61). The result is a conformity which 'cramps and dwarves' so that we are like trees 'clipped into pollards' (OL 62) – or in yet stronger imagery, maimed by compression 'like a Chinese lady's foot' (OL 69).

The second consideration in the background, one that also derives from Tocqueville (Levin in Forsyth et al., 1993: 156, 160) is that Mill had a vivid sense of 'the tyranny of the majority', both as an idea and as a practical danger (OL 8; cf. Britton, 1953: 99-101). The majority, either directly or through its representatives, can arbitrarily impose severe disadvantages on a minority; it can do this no less readily than a minority can apply the reverse process.

Thirdly, Mill is a perfectionist liberal. He believes, first, that there is, open to investigation, a substantive truth of the matter about human flourishing and, secondly, that political action should be taken to promote such flourishing. But in his view, on the one hand, we cannot yet (if ever) produce a comprehensive theory of what such flourishing consists in; and, on the other, no such developed theory is likely to be monolithic, i.e. to define a single blueprint for everybody. Human flourishing can be expected to take many forms. Mill is clear about the diversity:

> Such are the differences among human beings in their sources of pleasure, their suscepti-bilities of pain, and the operation on them of different physical and moral agencies, that unless there is a corresponding diversity in their modes of life, they neither obtain their fair share of happiness, nor grow up to the mental, moral, and aesthetic stature of which their nature is capable (OL 68; cf. Kirk, 1920: 31 quoted in §13.3.2).

A huge range of possibilities is open to discovery, and we may never scan the whole. Current uniformities and the tyranny of the majority are hostile to the kind of experimen-tation which is necessary if we are to bring to light the diverse forms of human flourishing in all their teeming multiplicity. Nothing contrasts more pointedly with Plato's hostility to cultural innovation (R IV.424B-C: 191) but then, Plato thought that the truth about acting rightly and living well was in outline already known. In OL Mill does not argue for the plausibility of perfectionist liberalism; he simply assumes that radically more is discoverable about a multiform human good. As well, he makes no accommodation with communitarians (§29.5) when they stress how in beneficial ways, without the kind of innovation on which Mill relies, individuals can draw their self-understanding and their conceptions of the good from the network of social institutions and practices into which they have been encultured. For Mill, existing society is largely a moral obstacle, not a moral resource.

It is against the background of these three concerns that we should read Mill's statement about freedom of action:

> The object of this Essay is to assert one very simple principle, as entitled to govern absolutely the dealings of society with the individual in the way of compulsion and control, whether the means used be physical force in the form of legal penalties, or the moral coercion of public opinion. That principle is, that the sole end for which mankind are warranted, individually or collectively, in interfering with the liberty of action of any of their number, is self-protection. That the only purpose for which power can be rightfully exercised over any member of a civilised community, against his will, is to prevent harm to others. His own good, either physical or moral, is not a sufficient warrant. He cannot rightfully be compelled to do or forbear because it will be better for him to do so, because it will make him happier, because, in the opinion of others, to do so would be wise, or even right. These are good reasons for remonstrating with him, or reasoning with him, or persuading him, or entreating him, but not for compelling him, or visiting him with any evil in case he do otherwise. To justify that, the conduct from which it is desired to deter him, must be calculated to produce harm to some one else. The only part of the conduct of any one, for which he is amenable to society, is that which concerns others. In the part which merely concerns himself, his independence is, of right, absolute. Over himself, over his own body and mind, the individual is sovereign (OL 13).

This passage states the 'liberty principle' as it has come to be called, the assertion that we are not to intervene in a person's life and activity except to prevent harm to others, damage to the interests of others (OL 15). The principle, which is an application of negative freedom (§22.3), is as much a rule of social as of state action. It is meant to guide everyday activities as well as the action of the state. As well, Mill nowhere says, implies or could consistently accept that the state has no other role than to implement this principle. The role of the state is to do what only the state can do, or what the state can do better than other social organisations. Mill is open-minded as to what this covers and includes (Greenleaf, 1983: 111-14; see further OL 78-80, 98).

The principle assumes that we are dealing with normal adults, persons of basic cognitive and rational competence (OL 13). Those without such competence may be subject to paternalistic intervention, as under most political systems, in order to prevent serious harm from befalling them. (Those of distinctly superior cognitive and rational competence get separate recognition under 'weighted' political representation (§30.3).)

More work must be done on the notion of 'harm'. Mill's principle supposes, for all agents, a range of possible actions that do, and a range of possible actions that do not, harm the interests of others (cf. §17.1 for Mill's interlinking of justice, rights, and interests). The reference to 'interests' occurs when Mill restates the liberty principle at the start of OL ch. 5:

> the individual is not accountable to society for his actions, in so far as these concern the interests of no person but himself (OL 94).

Harming the interests of other is:

- violating people's security (survival, health, safety and the rest)
- undermining their capacity or potential for individuality
- offending against decency

Though I have included offending against decency, there are special problems about this inclusion which will be considered in §22.8.1.

The notion of individuality is one on which Mill never explicitly elaborates. It appears to be a form of autonomy (§22.6). I think it has two main elements, one theoretical and the other practical.

On the theoretical side it involves the kind of freedom of mind that repudiates intellectual authority and applies the canons of Mill's *A System of Logic* (1843) appropriately. Thus the person of intellectual individuality is an independent thinker and discriminator who employs experimental, abstract, concrete deductive or inverse deductive methods as the subject-matter appears to invite, who is aware of the fallacies of observation and generalisation, who is adept at the calculation of chances, who can tell apart and exercise suitably the four methods of experimental inquiry, and so on.

On the practical side the requirement is a willingness to ignore convention in trying out different conceptions of living rightly and living well in the face (if necessary, here echoing the language in which Mill sets out the liberty principle) of contrary remonstrations, entreaties, and attempts to reason or persuade.

Mill bases his defence of the liberty principle on utilitarian considerations:

> It is proper to state that I forego any advantage which could be derived to my argument from the idea of abstract right, as a thing independent of utility. I regard utility as the ultimate appeal on all ethical questions; but it must be utility in the largest sense, grounded on the permanent interests of man as a progressive being (OL 14).

Literary purists will replace 'forego' with 'forgo', but philosophically a better point is that 'permanent interests' include the discovery of new forms of human flourishing, beyond current surmise. As a perfectionist liberal, Mill wants the liberty principle to provide an area within which people can exercise 'individuality', engage in 'experiments of living' (OL 57) and so discover these new forms. This arrangement will also work against the tyranny of the majority and help resist the trend to uniformity. All of which exactly reflects the three background concerns identified above.

Mill's liberty principle has been attacked on four main grounds, namely his:

- account of harm
- use of two incompatible ideas of freedom
- contradiction of his utilitarian base
- moral authoritarianism

22.8.1 Harm

One problem with the liberty principle is that the harm criterion threatens to nullify it. As David Rees has reminded me, 'Almost everything I do is likely, unless purely trivial, to have consequences for others, some of which will be advantageous and others disadvantageous'. The production of harm, in the sense of whatever is disadvantageous to somebody or other, is inseparable from all significant action. So there appears to be no class of self-regarding actions (of actions that concern only the agent's own interests). The liberty principle is left without application.

A further problem concerns the logical status of the harm criterion. If we take it as necessary and sufficient for intervention, which is the natural way of reading it from the manner in which it is introduced, there is the difficulty that Mill explicitly sanctions economic competition which, as he acknowledges, causes harm to particular groups and individuals. So it looks as if we should take the harm criterion as (at most) necessary for intervention but not sufficient.

I suggest that two points need to be borne in mind in relation to these problems. In the first place, it is plausible to argue (contra Gray, 1996: 12) that Mill is a rule-utilitarian, an ethicist who looks to the justification of institutions and practices in terms of their overall benefit, not in terms of every single outcome they produce. (What is the liberty principle if not a rule to which precisely this justification is meant to apply?) This is plainly how he approaches the justification of competition. All things considered, in Mill's view, competition is not harmful. Since it is not harmful, taken in this way, therefore to allow it is not to allow harm and so does not breach the sufficiency of harm as a criterion for intervention.

Secondly, the harm criterion as formulated and applied in *On Liberty* is precisely targeted. Mill has in mind harm as coming about through personal projects and commitments of the kind he eagerly wants to encourage – exercises in individuality. Only such exercises, and others which it might be practically impossible to block without checking 'experiments of living' as well, fall within the scope of the harm criterion as invoked in OL. The criterion is contextually specific. Harm might quite consistently have a different logical status in relation to other matters in the public realm – only necessary for intervention in some cases, only sufficient in others, both necessary and sufficient in others yet again. Choice, matter by matter, between these different statuses need not be arbitrary; utility, to which Mill has appealed all along, can be the guiding consideration.

A final problem about harm concerns Mill's somewhat ill-integrated inclusion of offending against decency:

> there are many acts which, being directly injurious only to the agents themselves, ought not to be legally interdicted, but which, if done publicly, are a violation of good manners, and coming thus within the category of offences against others, may rightfully be prohibited. Of this kind are offences against decency; on which it is unnecessary to dwell, the rather as they are only connected indirectly with our subject, the objection to publicity being equally

strong in the case of many actions not in themselves condemnable, nor supposed to be so (OL 98).

Serious attention was first drawn to this passage by Jo Wolff (Wolff, 1996b: 140). In face of Mill's reticence, Wolff suggests the example of sexual intercourse between husband and wife. I question the example, since Mill refers to acts which are 'directly injurious only to the agents themselves'; and while sex is no doubt overrated it is, I believe, seldom actually injurious to those who engage in it, even husband and wife. Mill more likely has in mind what the Victorians called 'onanism', an activity on the insanity-producing evils of which contemporary doctors waxed lurid.

But dispute over examples does not detract from the big point on which Wolff is right – in any case, in a later, more elaborate discussion he uses just the example I have suggested (Wolff, 1998: 4). The point is that the liberty principle risks paralysis if offence against decency is a category of harm. 'Indecency' is a matter incapable of eliciting universal rational agreement; it reduces to personal or group reaction, from which no 'experiment of living' would be safe. If, on the other hand and contrary to the natural reading of the passage, offence is not a category of harm, then harm is not necessary for intervention since, ex hypothesi, offence justifies intervention without being harmful.

Perhaps the best approach is to recall yet again the contextuality of the liberty principle. That principle is meant to protect and promote 'experiments of living'. Most cases of indecency, e.g. those of the flasher and the streaker, have no connection with such experiments. They can be regulated, even proscribed, on utilitarian grounds: they cause offence (wounded feelings or annoyance), which causes harm, but have nothing to do with 'the permanent interests of man as a progressive being'.

On Mill and harm, on harm more generally and also on the issue of paternalism (i.e. of intervening politically to prevent people from harming themselves), see Archard, 1990b; Gert & Culver, 1976; Chamberlin, 1988; Hobson, 1984; LaSelva, 1988; G. Graham, 1992; Raz, 1986: 367, 400-1, 412-21. Wolff, 1998 is easily the best discussion so far of the indecency problem in Mill. More widely, see R. Dworkin, 1986: ch. 17, esp. 336-7.

22.8.2 Two ideas of freedom?

A further criticism of Mill is that he starts with a notion of negative freedom, freedom as non-interference, classically stated in the liberty principle, and finishes with a quite different notion – freedom as 'a matter of doing what one desires' (OL ch. 5: 96). There might appear to be no great difference between these notions, but a particular example is of importance. Mill describes the case of someone, X, who wants to get from A to B and is about to step foot on a bridge in order to do so. Unknown to this person, the bridge is unsafe, in fact dangerous. Mill says that we are justified in blocking the person's path because freedom is a matter of doing what one desires and the person does not desire to plunge to his or her doom. J.P. Day insists that in principle this allows us to appeal to a person's 'real will', as we track the implications of wants and preferences, desires and inclinations, perhaps beyond anything the person would recognise (J.P. Day, 1977; Bosanquet, 1923: 65). If Mill is logically committed to any such idea of freedom, then he has gone beyond anything we might expect from the liberty principle.

But it is Day who goes too far. The position is not that Mill announces the slogan that freedom is a matter of doing what one desires, and is then committed to all possible deductions from it. The slogan needs to be taken contextually. The main freedom with which OL is concerned is indeed freedom as non-interference – the non-interference by society or the state in such 'experiments of living' as the individual may care to engage in consistently with non-harm to others.

For the most part, what is to be secured against interference are self-ascribed wants and preferences, desires and inclinations, which inform 'experiments of living'. But Mill recognises that in a range of cases far removed from such experiments, faulty information can lead the agent to desire X as a means to Y, when in fact X is a disastrously irrelevant means to Y. Mill simply acknowledges that we can in such cases cite wants and preferences that the agent would have, or would not have, in the light of improved information. The examples – in fact there is only one example, that of the bridge – are so commonsensical that no one could fairly doubt that the operative notion of improved information is unproblematic: incipient bridge-walker, X, and informed spectator, Y, can agree that bridge-collapsing and death-plunging are not what X desires. There is no doubt that 'not to plunge to my death on this faulty bridge' would be X's self-ascribed preference if the facts were clearly available to him or her.

It would be more plausible to claim that while the liberty principle is an application of negative freedom (§22.3), of freedom as non-interference, Mill's idea of individuality is an idea of autonomy. Autonomy is a form of freedom (§22.6). These are the two, perfectly compatible, ideas of freedom to be found in OL.

22.8.3 The utilitarian base

The next criticism concerns Mill's utilitarian base. The utilitarian thrust of the liberty principle should be clear. Mill is a perfectionist liberal. He believes that there are important, satisfying forms of life yet to be discovered. The liberty principle permits 'experiments of living' which help to flush out these new forms. The liberty principle which, as repeatedly noted, is an application of negative freedom, is never given more than a utilitarian defence by Mill. Where is the problem?

Two difficulties are thought to arise. In the first place, critics assert that freedom is intrinsically important; it is humanly too significant to be served by a merely utilitarian justification. 'No argument based on Utility can maintain or promote liberty except by way of accident, and in a partial manner as a temporary expedient' (Bell, 1908: 86). This kind of claim can be set against the background of Rousseau's view that 'To renounce one's freedom is to renounce one's quality as a man' (SC I.4: 45). Freedom matters too much to be left to the contingencies of utilitarian calculation.

But is this fair to Mill? After all, although the liberty principle is advocated strictly for its utility, nevertheless OL ch. 3 is headed 'Of Individuality, as One of the Elements of Well-Being'. Now if individuality is a form of autonomy, autonomy is a form of freedom (§22.6) – one to which Mill assigns an intrinsic value. For it is, to underline the point, one of the 'elements' of well-being, not merely a means to something else. So freedom as autonomy is here being given just the kind of intrinsic defence the critics say is missing from Mill's account.

Still, this exact point creates a fresh difficulty. If Mill regards individuality (one's being the kind of independent thinker and discriminator who will engage in experiments of living, *contra mundum* if need be) as one of the 'elements of well-being', this is to regard it as a good thing in its own right and not simply for its utility. So what has happened to Mill's utilitarian base?

The following defence is available to Mill. Let us re-tell the story of OL with a new spin. Individuality is valuable for its consequences, for what it produces; it generates 'experiments of living' which have the benefits that Mill tells us about. The liberty principle supplies the social and political condition for such experiments but individuality provides the personal condition. Without individuality, people will not have the qualities on mind and character to make the experiments. But Mill's attitude to individuality quickly undergoes development. Individuality becomes to his mind something inherently desirable, one of the 'elements of well-being'. To possess and to exercise individuality is an integral part of what it is to be a flourishing human being. No contradiction is involved in this development of Mill's attitude. Plato taught us long ago that some things are desirable both inherently and for their consequences (R II.357C: 103).

To take matters back to utilitarian basics. On the utilitarian view, the rightness or wrongness of anything (an action, an institution, a practice or whatever) can be defined wholly in terms of the merit or demerit of its consequences (§17). Then we need a measure of intrinsic value in order to assess this merit or demerit. Said another way, if consequences have instrumental merit or demerit, it is because they promote what is intrinsically good or bad. The classic utilitarian claim is that there is only one intrinsic value, namely happiness or pleasure. Mill himself sometimes says as much, particularly in works such as *Utilitarianism*, where (as noted in §22.4) he also trickily distinguishes between 'higher' and 'lower' pleasures. The point is this: it is open to him to widen the count so that other things besides happiness or pleasure figure as intrinsic values. This seems to me just what he does in OL. The count now includes individuality, which is both an intrinsically valuable human condition and also one that serves 'the permanent interests of man as a progressive being'. The instrumental and the intrinsic are one.

But if we return to utilitarian basics, the reply might come, we should do so thoroughly. Utilitarianism is not only consequentialist in the way described; it bids us *maximise* the occurrence of intrinsically valuable states of affairs (§17). If this requires us, in the old formula, to promote the greatest happiness of the greatest number, what if the greatest number prefer to ignore the liberty principle? Mill has already hinted at the answer in his rider to the liberty principle's utilitarian justification – that 'it must be utility in the largest sense, grounded on the permanent interests of man as a progressive being' (OL 14). Those interests, in which the majority share, are betrayed if we let present majority preferences limit the progressive future.

See further Gray in Mill, 1991: xix-xx; Skorupski, 1989: 343-7; Sweet, 1997: 15; Wollheim in Gray & Smith: 260-76. On a general problem about freedom's 'inefficiency' in maximising utility, see Sen in Hahn & Hollis, 1979: ch. 8.

22.8.4 Moral authoritarianism

In *Mill and Liberalism* (1963) Maurice Cowling launched a broadside against Mill. In Cowling's view, Mill's moral and political theory, including the liberty principle, is a disguised moral authoritarianism. He attributes to Mill the idea that an élite of 'higher minds' and 'more elevated intellects' will lead their more passive and less gifted fellow citizens to a society in which utilitarian thinking wholly prevails (Cowling, 1963a; see Minogue, 1964 and Greenleaf, 1983: 114-17 for a similar style of critique). In Cowling's own words, Mill's 'object was not to free men, but to convert them, and convert them to a peculiarly exclusive, peculiarly insinuating moral doctrine' (Cowling, 1963a: xiii).

The chief basis of this charge is a passage in Mill's *Autobiography* in which he endorses Auguste Comte's view 'that the moral and intellectual ascendancy, once exercised by priests, must in time pass into the hands of philosophers, and will naturally do so when they become sufficiently unanimous' (Mill, 1971: 126). As L.J. Macfarlane points out, however, Mill continues:

But when he [Comte] exaggerated this line of thought into a practical system, in which philosophers were to be organized into a kind of corporate hierarchy, invested with almost the same spiritual supremacy (though without any secular power) once possessed by the Catholic Church – it is not surprising, that while as logicians we were nearly at one, as sociologists we could travel together no further (Mill, ibid.; Macfarlane, 1970: 76).

So Cowling draws Mill too close to Comte. Two further comments are due. In the first place, Mill sees many significant 'experiments of living' as being conducted through self-management by workers' producer co-operatives; he looks to these to generate economic units which (unlike boss-led and managerial capitalist firms) cultivate and encourage individuality (PPE IV.7; Riley, 1996). So the usual social-cum-intellectual associations of élitism wholly fail to apply.

Secondly, Mill's utilitarianism is wide open to innovation. To begin, there is Mill's insistence, in OL ch. 2, on the importance of receptivity to ideas other than one's own. More than that, a major point and distinctive twist of Mill's moral and political theory is the idea that man is a 'progressive being'. He believes that social institutions and human practices of all kinds are to be assessed in terms of their consequences for happiness. But the lode of happiness has yet to be properly mined by 'experiments of living'. Institutions and practices as yet unimagined may bring happiness in forms as yet unconceived.

Final references on Mill: on his utilitarian account of freedom, see Berlin, 1969: 173-206; J.P. Day in Forsyth et al., 1993: ch. 7; P. Day, 1986; Gray, 1996; Hart, 1963: 4-6, 14-18, 75-9; Kurer, 1989; Lucas, 1966: 295-301; McCallum, 1946: vii-xxvii; Mitchell, 1970: ch. 4; Oakeshott, 1993: 78-86; J.C. Rees, 1985: ch. 5; J.F. Stephen, 1873; Ten in Gray & Smith, 1991; J. Wolff, 1996b: 115-46. Alongside Comte's influence should be set that of Samuel Taylor Coleridge (1772-1834), whose idea of a 'clerisy' is similar to that of the Comtean élite: Coleridge, 1972: 36, 38, 42. There is a difficulty in knowing what real difference the liberty principle would make if applied. This is a particular case of the general problem of estimating 'what effect will follow from a given cause, a certain general condition of social circumstances being presupposed'; for Mill's account of this problem and how to deal with it, see 'Of the Inverse Deductive, or Historical Method', SL VI.10; and on a cautionary note, Levin, 1999. On freedom and justice, see Raphael, 1950-51; J.C. Rees, 1985: ch. 6. On freedom and democracy, Mill's worries about the tyranny of the majority, are addressed in K. Graham, 1986: ch. 3. On freedom and rights, see Hohfeld on rights as liberties (Waldron, 1984: 6). On freedom and equality, for a possible tension already noted in §17.4 see ASU 160-4 with response by G.A. Cohen, 1995: chs. 1 & 4; also more generally Carritt in Quinton, 1967; D.J. Fitzgerald, 1976; Hindess, 1987; Maitland, 1911a and 1911b. On freedom and law, see Bosanquet, 1899: ch. 11; Bosanquet, 1923: chs. 3 & 6; Hoggart, 1989; Sweet, 1997: 40-6; among the classic texts, Hobbes, L, ch. 21: 145-54. On freedom and power, see Levine, 1988: 43-9. On freedom in general, see Archard, 1990a; Brenkert, 1991; G.C. Lewis, 1898: ch. 15; and Oppenheim, 1981: chs. 4-5.

23. DEMOCRACY

Democracy has not always enjoyed its present vogue. The Victorian prime minister, Lord Salisbury (1830-1903), a towering intellectual in bluff disguise as 'Remenham' in Lowes Dickinson's *A Modern Symposium* (1905), had nightmares about it. Once, writes A.J.P. Taylor, 'his wife saw him rise from his bed and stand at the open window, warding off an imaginary attack; the forces of democracy were trying to break into Hatfield House' (A.J.P. Taylor, 1976: 127).

Salisbury was not alone among eminent Victorians in his anti-democratic bias. Thomas Carlyle (1795-1881) was equally disdainful. 'To what extent democracy has now reached,' he snarled sarcastically, 'how it advances irresistible with ominous, ever-increasing speed, he that will open his eyes on any province of human affairs may discern. Democracy is everywhere the inexorable demand of these ages, swiftly fulfilling itself. From the thunder of Napoleon battles, to the jabbering of Open-vestry in St Mary Axe, all things announce Democracy' (Carlyle, 1888: 185).

Against these critics is to be counterposed the late twentieth-century publicist, Francis Fukuyama, whose distinctive view is that the institutions of democratic capitalism are 'the final form of human government' (Fukuyama, 1992). The spread of democracy marks 'the end of history'. 'You cannot separate God and Democracy', wrote a fellow American earlier in the century (cited in Inge, 1940: 90). Democracy, ensconced between God at the start of time and Fukuyama at the end of history, seems hardly to need philosophical appraisal. But the habit of analysis dies hard, and I proceed to examination.

The plan of discussion is this: democracy needs to be understood as a contrast-concept; democracy contrasts, and takes much of its point from contrasting, with other forms of government. Within democracy we have to distinguish between direct, representative, and deliberative democracy. Sorting these matters out will be our exercise in conceptual analysis. Defences of democracy are either intrinsic or instrumental; looking at the justification of democracy in these terms will be our foray into democratic theory. The aporias for investigation are Richard Wollheim's paradox of democracy; and the problematic relationship between democracy and the justification of civil disobedience.

23.1 Basic distinctions

'Democracy' is at least partly a contrast term. Plato in his classification of forms of government in *Republic*, Books VIII-IX, distinguishes democracy ('people power', as its Greek etymology implies) from tyranny, one-person rule by the worst type of person, but also from a range of other political forms – oligarchy (the rule of the wealthy few), timocracy (rule by the high-minded military) and, at the top of the tree, rule by philosopher-kings.

In the *Politics* Aristotle offers a different classification, organised by the dual criteria of how many rule and whether they consult the common good or promote more narrow interests. There is also a recognition of an economic dimension; rule by the many will be rule by the relatively poor. If a form of government consults the common good it is 'correct'; otherwise it is 'perverted'. Monarchy, aristocracy, and 'polity' are respectively the rule of one, a few, or the many with a view to the common good. At the theoretical limit, Aristotle appears to give the preference to monarchy – to *pambasileia*, rule by a person of superlative virtue (P IV.17: 80). But his position is ambiguous, because aristocracy, rule by the few of superlative virtue or simply the relatively best, allows alternation of ruling and being ruled which Aristotle regards as a vital part of citizenship (NE V.6: 123).

Democracy, oligarchy, and tyranny are respectively the rule of the many, a few, or one, in their own interests. Democracy is the least bad of the perverted forms; at least the good of the majority is attended to. As a refinement to his analysis, Aristotle produces an elaborate five-way sub-division of democratic forms (P IV.4).

The Platonic and Aristotelian classifications have been widely influential in the history of political thought, but I will only come back briefly to Aristotle in §23.4.2.3. Nor is there space to look at Montesquieu's reworking of the traditional classifications in SPL II.1: 10. I shall, however, return to Plato's criticism of democracy. To follow up

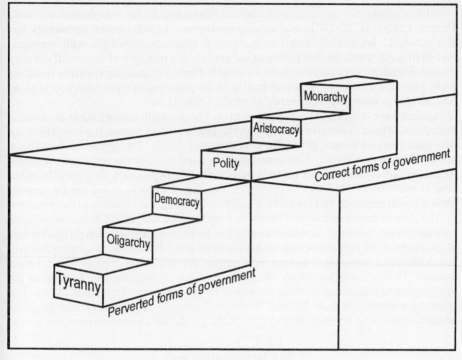

Figure 10. Aristotle's classification of forms of government

on Plato's and Aristotle's classifications for yourself, on Plato see Annas, 1981: ch. 12; E. Barker, 1960: ch. 11; Sinclair, 1951: 159-65. For Aristotle, see P III.6-13: 59-73 and IV.4-6: 85-92; also Morrall, 1977: ch. 4; Mulgan, 1977; Sinclair, 1951: 219-28. On Montesquieu, see Pangle, 1989: 50 and Sabine, 1951: 556.

Away from these historical treatments, few would dispute John May's basic formula for democracy. Under a democracy there is a:

> necessary correspondence between acts of governance and the wishes with respect to those acts of the persons who are affected (May, 1978: 1).

May calls this the 'responsive rule' formula. The qualifier 'necessary' is meant to exclude benevolent dictatorships, where the connection between dictatorial decisions and the wishes of those affected by them is contingent on the dictator's good will. The persons involved who enjoy this correspondence may be the whole citizen body but are more likely to be a majority.

Reservations about the formula are likely to concern its narrowness. To many theorists, democracy includes a range of constitutional elements which R.A. Dahl calls 'public contestation'. These include freedom of speech; freedom of assembly; freedom of association; and regular, free and fair elections: all of which allow freedom of criticism, organisation, and opposition (Bealey, 1988: 2). In the following discussion I will take responsive rule as central to democracy, whilst not denying the extra, contextual elements with which others will want to pack it round. Every regime which claims to be democratic will offer, with whatever plausibility, some account of how it secures correspondence, how it squares acts of governance with the wishes of those affected by them. So taken, responsive rule is a distinctive idea which raises conceptual and normative questions. I will return to the contextual dimension in §23.4.2.3. There are also preconditional, as distinct from contextual, considerations (§23.4.1.2).

It should be underlined that no part of the following discussion endorses the West European or North American status quo. Not only are there other conceptual options besides representative democracy, as we shall see directly below, but also the democratic rhetoric and the political reality of the status quo are markedly different. Writing in 1921, C. Deslisle Burns was and remains right: the West European and North American political experiences 'do not contain more than traces and possibilities of democracy' (C.D. Burns, 1921: 276). That said, a decision has been made not to discuss 'people's democracy' (§4.1.4) as a model. This appears to be a dated concept.

23.2 Direct, representative, and deliberative democracy

Responsive rule involves, to repeat, a necessary correspondence between acts of governance and the wishes (at least of a majority) of those affected by them. If we consider how such correspondence might be secured, we encounter three types of democracy:

- direct, participatory
- representative
- deliberative

In a direct, participatory democracy those who are affected by acts of governance themselves take part in the decision-making by which those acts are made. Their activity directly controls the formulation, adoption, and (to some extent) the implementation of public policy. This is self-government truly at work. Implementation, which calls for special skills of situational perception and the ability to take effective emergency action, has always been a problem for democratic theory, hence the modifier 'to some extent'. Rousseau's remark at SC III.4: 114 (cited in §12.3) that democracy is a form of government suited only to gods is a recognition of this point. He has in mind a political system in which not only the formulation and adoption of public policy is directly done by the citizens themselves (a system of which he approves) but also the implementation (a system of which he doubts the wisdom).

In a representative democracy, this does not occur. Rather, those who are affected by acts of governance choose who shall formulate, adopt, and implement public policy on their behalf – members of parliament, senators and so on. This was the sense of 'republic' in eighteenth-century American political thought. In *The Federalist*, No. 39, James Madison defined a republic as 'a government which derives all its powers directly or indirectly from the great body of the people, and is administered by persons holding their offices during pleasure, for a limited period, or during good behaviour' (F 191). But a representative democracy can contain elements of direct democracy through such devices as the referendum, the initiative, and recall.

In both direct and representative democracy, voting power is equally distributed, with each citizen having one and only one vote. It is on representative democracy that disputes about the correct form of electoral voting systems centre. Should political parties be allocated seats in the assembly in exact proportion to the total votes cast for them in all constituencies (the system known as 'proportional representation' or just 'PR') or should each constituency go to the candidate receiving the highest number of votes within it (as in the British 'first past the post' system) though that candidate may get a minority of the total votes cast? PR can be argued for on grounds of abstract fairness, or on grounds of giving maximum satisfaction (or least dissatisfaction) to voters. John Stuart Mill, who advocated a form of PR in *Representative Government*, ch. 7, linked one part of his defence of it back to the arguments of *On Liberty*; he saw the widest diversity of views, politically represented, as part of freedom of thought and expression (§22.8; Mill, 1958: 102-26; or Mill, 1991: 302-25). Fascinating as these disputes are, our space is too limited to take them up here. On PR see further W.J.M. Mackenzie, 1958: chs. 8-9.

Deliberative democracy, sometimes also called 'discursive' democracy, is best seen as a variant of direct democracy. In the bare idea of direct democracy there are no valuational or appraisive criteria by which to judge the process of decision-making. Under deliberative democracy, by contrast, there are standards of 'public reason', a term to be explained shortly. Deliberative democracy is direct democracy plus public reason. Habermas' 'ethics of discourse' gives some idea of what is involved (§5.4) as does Rousseau's account of decision-making under the conditions of the general will (SC II.3: 59-60; W.T. Jones, 1987).

Two features are central to deliberative democracy. In the first place, theorists of direct and representative democracy commonly assume that voters have wants and preferences which are 'given' – mere data for the political system to process. The question is how and to what extent to reflect these wants and preferences in collective decision-making. Deliberative or discursive democracy rotates this perspective. I will switch briefly to using the term 'discursive' so as to cite a helpful passage from Blaug. For the discursive theorist, Blaug remarks, the voter looks different:

> Her preferences are complicated by pre-commitments, and are both formed and discovered in social interaction. A central difference between liberal [representative: GT] and discursive theories is that the latter place particular stress upon interaction as *constitutive* of individual and collective identity, and of social knowledge itself (Blaug, 1996b: 50).

The second central feature of deliberative or discursive democracy is that it works under constraints of public reason. The idea is that, when proposals are made, choices exercised, options canvassed, justifications take a particular form. There are disagreements among deliberative theorists as to exactly what this form is, but among the possibilities are universality (that proposals should be acceptable to everyone); independence (that justifications cannot take the form of appeals to self-interest); transparency (that justifications are set forth in terms intelligible to all); and reflexivity (that forms of justification can themselves be put under review). These may be termed moral criteria; among the practical criteria are saliency (that people must be able to see the point of conducting public justification in this way); and stability (that sudden shifts in citizens' attitudes do not produces dramatic inconsistencies of public policy). See D'Agostino, 1996; Bertram, 1997: 75.

One point, immediately clear, is that these criteria can conflict. Saliency may be easiest to secure when people can make a straight connection with self-interest, but that connection becomes problematic when justification has to rest on an appeal to the interests of everyone. That aside, the practical problems of deliberative democracy are manifold. The sheer numbers of a modern citizenry, the complexity and technicality of the issues they confront, and the unreliability of citizens' motivation, all give pause to deliberative theorists (Blaug, 1996b: 51; cf. J. Cohen in Goodin & Pettit, 1997).

See further on deliberative democracy: Benhabib in Rosenblum, 1991: ch. 8; Blaug, 1996a. Check out the related notion of communal democracy with A. Black, 1997. Among the classic texts, for public reason in Hobbes and Rawls, see Ivison, 1997.

Rousseau offers his own version of public reason through the requirement to put matters for collective decision-making in a special form (not 'do you favour such-and-such?' but 'do you believe that such-and-such will promote the common good?'). See SC IV.1: 122.

We have drawn apart the ideas of direct, representative, and deliberative democracy. Where are the examples? On the surface fifth-century BC Athens was a direct democracy in full working order. All major political decisions were taken by mass meeting of the Assembly or *Ekklesia*, which met not fewer than forty times a year. Any citizen could contribute to the discussion or propose a motion. The Assembly legislated and decreed, voted for war, peace or military alliances, controlled the civil and military magistrates, scrutinised public finances, and generally oversaw matters concerning the welfare and security of the city. Voting power was equally distributed; each citizen had just one vote.

The deeper realities of the Athenian political system were less democratic. It lacked inclusiveness. The exclusions were severe. Only adult males could be citizens; women were excluded from the political no less than the intellectual and artistic life of Athens. Not all adult males were citizens. Resident aliens were banned from political participation, and the process of 'naturalisation', by which citizenship was conferred, was made extremely difficult. Perhaps the most striking exclusion in modern eyes was that of slaves, who represented probably a quarter of the entire population of Attika (Athens and its surrounding land). See further Forrest, 1966; Glotz, 1929; Hatzfeld, 1962: ch. 17; Rodewald, 1974. It may be mentioned that A.H.M. Jones, 1957 is a learned and lively defence of Athenian democracy against modern critics. Jones' view is that, given the circumstances of its time, Athens made a creditable shot at democracy. A similar endorsement, from an unexpectedly marxist quarter, is made by Ellen Meiksins Wood (Wood, 1988).

Whatever our judgement on Athenian direct democracy, all the present-day regimes called democratic, whether parliamentary or presidential, are at best representative democracies. But the distinction between direct and representative democracy is open to refinement, for the idea of representation admits of various interpretations (Birch, 1971: 15; cf. Pitkin, 1967; McLean in D. Held, 1991: ch. 7). A representative may be:

- an agent or spokesperson acting for a principal
- a person typical of some category of persons
- a symbolic figure

A symbolic figure is someone whose character or fate highlights in a vivid, dramatic way a situation or state of affairs. Such was Louis XVI, King of France, who in his show trial of 1793 was not Citizen Capet, a man of limited virtues and faults, but a symbol of absolute monarchy. This is not a sense of 'representative' that bears much relation to democratic theory, though it raises questions of political ethics (Fehér, 1989; Walzer, 1974; Watts Miller, 1993).

Nor is there any necessary connection between representative government, in the second sense of 'representative', and democratic government seen in terms of the responsive rule formula. Even a dictator is representative of some category of persons.

It is the first sense of 'representative' that is of primary importance to democratic theory. As agent of the electorate, under democratic theory, a representative holds political authority by consent (§13.3.3). But note the ambiguity of this term, 'agent'. An agent might be a mere delegate, someone strictly required to act on prior instructions. In this sense a representative is mandated to express pre-defined views, and to take pre-defined actions, on behalf of a principal. On the other hand, an agent might be an independent thinker and discriminator, someone who is licensed to make his or her own judgements on behalf of the principal. Call this the 'envoy' view.

Edmund Burke (1729-97) was emphatic that members of parliament should be envoys. He made his views clear to the voters *after* being elected to parliament for Bristol:

> Certainly, gentlemen, it ought to be the happiness and glory of a representative to live in the strictest union, the closest correspondence, and the most unreserved communication with his constituents. Their wishes ought to have great weight with him; their opinion, high respect; their business, unremitted attention. It is his duty to sacrifice his repose, his pleasures, his satisfactions, to theirs; and above all, ever, and in all cases, to prefer their interest to his own. But his unbiassed opinion, his mature judgment, his enlightened conscience, he ought not to sacrifice to you, to any man, or to any set of men living. These he does not derive from your pleasure; no, nor from the law and the constitution. They are a trust from Providence, for the abuse of which he is deeply answerable. Your representative owes you, not his industry only, but his judgment; and he betrays, instead of serving you, if he sacrifices it to your opinion (Hampsher-Monk, 1987: 109; cf. Barker,1951a: ch. 6; and ch. 12 of *Representative Government*: Mill, 1958: 174-85 or Mill 1991: 373-83).

The more a representative democracy approximates to the delegate view, the closer it stands to direct democracy, because the delegate representative is taking decisions 'for' the citizens much less than the envoy.

Even in the third sense of 'representative', whether as delegate or envoy, there is only a contingent connection between representation and democracy. English medieval monarchs sought the advice of the 'estates of the realm', whose interests were represented in Parliament by the Lords Spiritual, the Lords Temporal, and the Commons. But no one would regard Edward I, II or III as a May-type responsive ruler. If Athenian democracy was democracy without representation, medieval England was representation without democracy.

To look now at deliberative democracy. If ancient Athens serves as an example of direct democracy and the USA and UK count as examples of representative democracy, deliberative democracy is harder to exemplify; it remains more of a theoretical construction than a practical reality. But on a more optimistic note, deliberative democracy can apply at a variety of levels. It is not confined to the deliberations of national or international bodies – the level at which mainstream political theory pitches the discussion of direct and representative democracy. It can descend to the local, neighbourhood, small group level, where its conditions are likely to be easier to fulfil. If the scope for deliberative democracy is limited – or currently looks limited – this is not to rule out its practicability altogether.

23.3 Democracy and majority rule

Democratic decision-making aspires to unanimity, settles for majority rule, and often achieves even less than that. Intuitively the idea of majority rule is clear enough; one fixes on the magic number, 51%, and if 51% or more get what they want, we have a working notion of majority rule. But there are hidden complications.

Consider the following voting puzzle derived from Gorman, 1978: 48. There are five voters and three policy choices, A, B and C, are put to the voters in the form of Yes/No questions. The results are as follows:

Complexities in the idea of majority rule

Voter	Questions		
	A	B	C
1	Yes	Yes	Yes
2	Yes	Yes	Yes
3	Yes	No	No
4	No	Yes	No
5	No	No	Yes

We can assume that A, B and C are mutually compatible; all three can be adopted. Whether a policy choice is adopted or not depends on a Yes/No majority vote. On this basis A, B and C are all adopted by a 3-2 majority. But note that – take the phrasing carefully – a majority of the voters are in a minority on a majority of the issues. Voters 3, 4 and 5 (a majority of the voters) all said 'No' on 2 out of 3 (a majority) of the issues (B and C for 3, A and C for 4, A and B for 5). The will of this majority has been deflected on most of the issues. Does the notion of the will of the majority still seem straightforward?

An ambiguity is evident. Our criterion for majority rule might be: for each policy choice, that choice is adopted if and only if a majority of the voters choose it. In this sense the preceding result – the adoption of A, B and C – satisfies the will of the majority. Or our criterion might be: the majority of the voters get their way on a majority of the policy choices. In this sense the result frustrates the will of the majority.

There are further problems connected with majority rule. The paradox of cyclical majorities was discovered by Marie Jean, Marquis de Condorcet (1743-94). Matters readily run into mathematical technicalities but a simple example will serve. Take an electorate of sixty voters, who have the following preferences between three options:

23 voters: A>B>C
17 voters: B>C>A
 2 voters: B>A>C
10 voters: C>A>B
 8 voters: C>B>A

One simply has to cast up the results to see that there is a kind of incoherence. A majority (23+17+2 = 42 voters) prefers B to C. And a majority (17+10+8 = 35 voters) prefers C to A. By the logic of transitivity, if B is preferred to C, and C to A, then B should be preferred to A. But that does not happen here: a majority (23+10 = 33 voters) prefers A to B.

The problem can be side-stepped, as a student (David Walter) once insisted, if one just asks the electorate to enter one vote for A or B or C and states that the votes will be used to rank A, B and C with the top-scoring option being adopted. In this case, assuming that the voters keep to their first preferences as expressed above, we find that A receives 23 votes, B 19, and C 18. Option A is adopted, a minority choice if ever there was one; it has 37 votes against it. See further B. Barry in PPS 5: 164 ff.

23.4 The justification of democracy

Democracy attracts two kinds of high-level theorising – philosophical and empirical. Two influential empirical theories are the élitist and the economic. Elitist theory, linked particularly with the names of Gaetano Mosca (1858-1941), Vilfredo Pareto (1848-1923) and Roberto Michels (1876-1936), holds that all political systems, democratic no less than others, are dominated by ruling minorities. Michels coined the phrase, 'the iron law of oligarchy', to depict his position. See further Frankel, 1997: 58-9; Parry, 1969; Schwarzmantel, 1987: ch. 2. Related to élite theory, 'consociational' democracy occurs in societies with deeply divided sub-cultures where stability is secured through power-sharing between the political élites of the various groups (see Kaiser, 1997: 427-9). The most obvious, if past, example is 1945-90 Jugoslavia.

The economic theory of democracy is stated by one of its proponents, Anthony Downs, in the following terms: 'parties in democratic politics are analogous to entrepreneurs in a profit-seeking economy. In order to attain their private ends, they formulate whatever policies they believe will gain the most votes, just as entrepreneurs produce whatever products they believe will gain the most profits for the same reasons' (Downs, 1957: 295-6). This viewpoint is commonly identified with so-called public choice theory.

Philosophical theories usually concern the justification of democracy. The point of departure is normally consent; the assumption is made that consent is the basis of political authority (§13.3.4) and that democracy is government by consent. As we saw in discussing authority, however, many forms of government might enjoy consent. The question is why democratic government is preferable to the others.

In a famous article, 'The Priority of Democracy to Philosophy', the American philosopher, Richard Rorty (b. 1931), denies that democracy needs a philosophical foundation (Rorty, 1988). His point is that any attempt to discover some timeless truth about the desirability of democracy is wasted labour. The most that can be achieved are specific, adequate replies to whatever criticisms are raised against democracy by one opponent or another. The point is well taken that, in the welter of arguments for and against democracy, there are endless possibilities of qualification and reply. Here and elsewhere, no once-for-all discussion and resolution are to be expected. To justify a moral or political theory is to meet whatever challenges have actually been made to it.

Arguments to justify democracy, whether heeding Rorty's caution or not, take two routes: instrumental and intrinsic. The claim may be, in other words, that democracy makes certain desirable outcomes more likely and certain undesirable outcomes less likely. This is in broad terms a policy-orientated approach. Intrinsic defences, by contrast, are policy-neutral in the sense that democracy itself is held to be desirable. A democratic decision-procedure is worth having on its own account.

23.4.1 The intrinsic defence

I will consider two intrinsic and three instrumental defences. The intrinsic defences rest on the values of autonomy and equality respectively; the instrumental defences relate to utility, probability, and Aristotelian deliberation.

23.4.1.1 Democratic autonomy

If we value autonomy, and its celebration of the freely choosing, self-determining individual (§22.6), then democracy readily appears to be the form of government uniquely appropriate to autonomous persons. Just as, in the private realm, the autonomous individual determines his or her own affairs, so democracy is the political medium through which autonomous individuals manage their collective affairs. A link can be made back to our discussion of authority, since democracy is widely accepted as a form of government that confers or embodies de jure authority through consent (§13.3.3).

What form of government could better embody authority for autonomous individuals than democracy as self-government?

This approach plainly relies on democracy's allowing the individual significant influence over collective decisions. If as an autonomous person I take part in democratic decision-making but have a negligible impact on its outcome, then the special link between democracy and autonomy is broken. What particularly matters here is the kind of democratic system involved. Autonomy may be well-served by small-scale direct or deliberative democracy, but under a mass, representative democracy the prospects for autonomy are bleak. Such democracy may have other virtues, but the promotion of autonomy is not among them.

See further Breiner, 1989; G. Graham,1983: 100-1; Mill, 1991: 238-56.

23.4.1.2 Democratic equality

Under democratic decision-making, voting power is equally distributed; each voter has an equal say. Consider, then, the following line of argument adapted from Nathan, 1993, suggesting that democracy embodies two inherent goods:

1. One enjoys a good by having those policies adopted which one wants to have adopted.
2. The equal distribution of goods is itself a good.
3. The chance of enjoying a good is itself a good.
4. Under democracy, voting power is equally distributed.
5. If voting power is equally distributed, then so are voters' chances of having those policies adopted which they want to have adopted.
6. Under democracy, voters have a chance of having those policies adopted which they want to have adopted (this is a good) and that chance is equally distributed (and this is a further good).

Three points call for comment. To begin, the first premise appears to rely on a particular view of what a person's interests consist in. Only if one's interests are defined in terms of one's uncriticised wants and preferences can one necessarily be said to enjoy a good by having policies adopted which one wants to have adopted. (On interests, see §18.1.)

Next, in regard to the second premise, it is hard to accept the flat statement that the equal distribution of goods is itself a good. Suppose, for instance, that an unequal distribution would make everyone better off; everyone would get more under an unequal distribution than under an equal one (cf. Rawls' 'difference principle', §17.3). Certainly the claim that the equal distribution of goods is itself a good cannot go through on a simple assertion.

Finally, the fifth premise is doubtful. Only on special assumptions is there any plausibility in holding that under democracy all voters enjoy an equal chance of having their preferred policies adopted – a form of competitive equality of opportunity (§18.2). Policies favoured only by minorities, and policies widely seen as impracticable or as unduly costly, are less likely to be adopted than those that are mainstream. (A further point is that if mainstream policies are likely to be adopted anyway, and I support such policies, is it rational for me, on a tally of returns against costs, to vote or indeed to participate politically at all? If I am in a minority, my influence is negligible; and if, as in this case, I belong to a majority, my influence still is negligible. See Benn in PPS 5.) Of the different kinds of democracy, the deliberative version seems best fitted to promote equal chances, as policies evolve through intersubjective understanding and agreement.

Nathan offers an extended and nuanced discussion of the egalitarian argument. Also worth reading is K. Graham, 1986: chs. 2 & 4. A further connection between democracy and equality runs through the idea that when there are acute economic inequalities, democracy remains a largely formal mechanism because economic power countervails the political process. (See Wolff, 1996b: 93). From this angle, equality or limited inequality is an essential precondition for democracy. The point is quite different from the claim in the argument considered by Nathan that democracy embodies equality. Non-competitive equality of opportunity (§18.2) may be seen as the minimum safeguard against great extremes of wealth and poverty.

23.4.2 The instrumental defence

To turn now to the instrumental defence of democracy. We will go through three defences concerning utility, probability, and Aristotelian deliberation respectively.

23.4.2.1 Utility

One defence of democratic decision-making uses the idea of a social welfare function. The essential notion is that sets of individual preferences ('utilities') can be aggregated and translated into social alternatives, i.e. orderings of policy choices for the public realm. See Samuelson, 1947 and Sen, 1970. Democracy is seen as the translation device. Voters express their policy preferences; and their individual sets of preferences indicate, on aggregation, the policies which will maximise voters' satisfaction. The task of representatives is to ensure that those policies are adopted.

Aside from the fact that 'satisfaction' and 'social welfare' – in effect, voters' interests – are here being equated with uncriticised wants and preferences, there is the further point that the logic of aggregation can produce incoherences. We glimpsed this possibility when we noted the Condorcet problem of cyclical majorities (§23.3). A powerful development of basically the same problem is to be found in Arrow, 1963. It is probably best to look first at Arrow's brief and informal, 'Values and Collective Decision-Making' in PPS 3: 215-32. Bonner, 1986: ch. 4 is also helpful.

Apart again from the logical problem another point concerns the simplistic view of democratic processes on which this utility approach rests. Representatives are projected as mere delegates, purely concerned accurately to mirror voters' preferences. The phenomenon of non-decisionalism should be recalled from our discussion of power (§12.2). Not the least activity of representatives in a democracy is to prevent certain options from appearing on the political agenda. The social welfare function is depleted accordingly. There are also the distortions produced by the impact of special interests, lobbyists, Madison's 'factions' (§12.3), on representatives. (Plato knew the parallel problem in a direct democracy; in the simile of the captain, the factionalism of special interests is caught in the image of the crew who 'spend all their time milling round the captain' – the *demos*, the sovereign people – 'and doing all they can to get him to give them the helm' (R VI.488B-C: 282).)

Next to consider the classical utilitarian defence of democracy. On this approach, democracy is a guard against 'sinister interests', thought Bentham and James Mill. Whenever a political class is not answerable, or is imperfectly answerable, to the wider population, it will pursue its own interests rather than the greatest happiness of the greatest number. Democracy, by making government accountable to the people, renders the interests of government and governed identical. The theory of élites and public choice theory (see above) cast doubt on this cosy picture. See further Hampsher-Monk, 1992: 328-33; Lindsay, 1943: 136-46.

23.4.2.2 Probability

Condorcet drew a particular result from probability theory to support the correctness of majority decision-making. If each voter has a better than evens chance of being right (i.e. a probability of > .5), then the chances of a majority's being right increase exponentially with the size of the majority. For example, in a group of 100 people, a majority of 51 has a 52% likelihood of being right; but a majority of 60 has a likelihood of almost 70%. See Dahl, 1989: 142, 355-6; also more technically D. Black, 1971: 163ff.

Significant as this result is, its democratic relevance is problematic. On the one hand, in valuational matters, unless we accept value objectivity, it is hardly proper to speak of anyone's getting things 'right', let alone of their having a better than evens chance of doing so. On the other hand, in matters of fact, there are two worries. For a whole range of economic, environmental, military and other issues, technical, intricate and uncertain, the assumption that a majority of voters actually does have a better than evens chance of being right looks distinctly shaky. Moreover, there is the so-called mixed-motivation problem. Someone highly knowledgeable on an issue, with a near certainty of being right, may not vote on that knowledge: their motivation may be divided between others' and their own benefit. (I know pretty well how policy X will affect most others, but I discount this knowledge when I vote; I vote for my own reasons.)

On the mixed-motivation problem see B. Barry, 'The Public Interest' in Quinton, 1967: 112-26; K. Graham, 1996; J. Wolff, 1994. As to the 'rightness' of voters, their capacity for correct and insightful belief, it is relevant to point back to Plato's view of knowledge as the basis of authority (§13.3.2). Plato has a three-level critique of democracy in this regard. At one level he complains of democratic debate as inherently superficial and uninformed. This is the image of democracy conveyed at large in the parable of the ship (R VI.488A-489A: 282-3). In this vein anyone with a sharp sense of the mediocrity of current democratic debate will agree with Plato. At one level up, Plato argues for the existence of an objective human good, knowledge of which should inform political action; democracy pays no heed to the possibility of such a good. Plato compares democratic citizens to self-appointed sailors who ignore the art of navigation (op. cit.: 282). Finally, as outlined in Book V-VII of the *Republic*, knowledge of the objective human good is intellectually so demanding to acquire that only a small class of citizens can realistically aspire to it. They alone, and not the bulk of the citizenry, are fit to rule.

23.4.2.3 Aristotelian deliberation and the epistemic justification

> For the many, of whom each individual is not a good man, when they meet together may be better than the few good, if regarded not individually but collectively, just as a feast to which many contribute is better than a dinner provided out of a single purse. For each individual among the many has a share of excellence and practical wisdom, and when they meet together, just as they become in a manner one man, who has many feet, and hands, and senses, so too with regard to their character and thought. Hence the many are better judges than a single man of music and poetry; for some understand one part, and some another, and among them they understand the whole (P III.11: 66).

Aristotle is describing a situation in which, unlike that depicted by Cordorcet, most or all voters have a less than evens chance of being right, of taking an adequate view. His basic idea is that political issues are multi-faceted and that no individual's knowledge encompasses more than a part of the whole matter (Waldron, 1995: 568; cf. Saunders in Aristotle, 1981: 201-2). A diversity of impressions and ideas, fragments of knowledge, surface in discussion; and from them can be drawn a comprehensively informed view. The claim has been made that a master-synthesiser is needed to collate the information, to reduce the diversity to order (Nichols, 1992: 66). But the point is contentious; consider how a process of the Aristotelian kind occurs in the deliberations of a jury or how at Quaker gatherings 'the sense or mind of the meeting' emerges.

Aristotle's picture of the cognitively challenged democratic electorate is more realistic than the >.5 Condorcet assumption. There was a famous diplomatic crux in the mid-nineteenth century, the Schleswig-Holstein question concerning Danish sovereignty over two predominantly German duchies. Of this problem Lord Palmerston said that only three people had understood it: the Prince Consort, who was dead; a German professor, who had been driven mad by it; and himself, who had forgotten all about it. The Schleswig-Holstein question is emblematic of the problems which a modern democratic electorate faces. Probably even fewer people than Palmerston's select threesome know whether monetary union will achieve European integration, yet in the closing years of the twentieth century the matter was an electoral issue throughout the European Union. In face of such involved issues, increasingly common in contemporary politics, Aristotelian deliberation seems a plausible democratic option. The alternative to having the electorate pronounce on involved issues is for them, still under the conditions of Aristotelian deliberation, to vote on priorities and to leave the details to technicians. This is the suggestion of Eyal, Szelényi & Townsley in §31.4. But the problems of technical expertise should be recalled from our discussion of Berlin (§2.3).

The Aristotelian picture tallies well with the 'contextualist' approach, by which democracy is seen as a matter not merely of outcomes (May's 'necessary correspondence') or procedures ('majority rule') but as embedded in a whole constitutional context of 'public contestation': freedom of speech, assembly, association and the rest (§23.1).

The connection is that, if we want the multi-faceted truth to emerge, these constitutional freedoms are sound enabling mechanisms. Simply said, the more viewpoints that are expressed, the greater the chance of our getting insights which embody the facts and considerations that are needed for informed decision-making. Constitutional freedoms thus stitched on to democracy might also serve to allay some of Mill's fears about the tyranny of the majority; although Mill sees such tyranny as extending deep into social life, beyond the kind of deliberative context we have been discussing.

Aristotle's justification of democracy is limited and qualified, since he has distinct worries, particularly about democracy's proneness to produce class-based legislation. In any event, the aspect of democracy on which he dwells in the foregoing passage seems best accommodated by deliberative democracy. See further Robinson in Aristotle, 1962: 39-40.

23.5 Wollheim's paradox of democracy

In PPS 2 Richard Wollheim (b. 1923) propounds the following paradox. Suppose that in an election I believe that policy X is the right policy but that in the event the majority prefer policy Y. Under a rule of majority decision-making I accept that policy Y should be pursued. Then I am committed to this position: that it is right to pursue a policy which is wrong.

I suggest the following response. At the election, and subsequently, I believe that, all else equal, policy X is the policy which will maximise the general happiness, promote social justice, reduce pollution, advance gender equality, or whatever the criterion I apply. By this criterion policy X is in my view the right policy, preferable to Y. This is my valuation of policy X. But after the election all else is not equal: the majority prefer policy Y.

Now, I value policy X and I value the majority principle. In this situation the two valuations can be fulfilled only through incompatible practical prescriptions: namely that policy X ought to be pursued, policy Y ought to be pursued. But I am not committed to either prescription until I have assigned priority to one or other of my valuations. Forced to choose, I opt for the majority principle. I give priority to this valuation. Accordingly I give priority to the practical prescription that policy Y ought to be pursued, to which I am now committed.

At the level of valuations there is no incompatibility: valuing policy X and valuing the majority principle are formally consistent. At the level of practical prescriptions there is no inconsistency either; I prescribe policy Y. I do this because I assign valuational priority to the majority principle.

See further B. Barry, 1965: 58-66, 293-4; Dommen, 1964; R. Harrison, 1970.

23.6 Democracy and civil disobedience

A particular issue has arisen over the relation of democracy to civil disobedience. Some conceptualisation is due. Civil disobedience typically covers situations in which: (1) a person or group, X, acts in a way that infringes a law, Y; where this infringement is (2) intentional, (3) public; (4) non-violent; (5) done without resisting the penalty; and (6) done because X objects to Y on grounds of integrity, justice or policy. These grounds, identified in R. Dworkin, 1985: 107-13, include cases such as the following. On grounds of integrity or conscience, of my commitment to a particular ethical code, I personally cannot do an action required by law; on grounds of justice I cannot support a law that unfairly discriminates against particular groups or individuals within society; and on grounds of policy I must take a stand against a policy that I regard as ruinous to all. See also Dworkin, 1978: ch. 8.

Refinements of conceptualisation readily suggest themselves. Law X may be disobeyed, not because it is itself objectionable under Dworkin's three grounds, but in order to draw attention to another law or political decision that *is* – as in jaywalking in order to get publicity against military policies. Again, civil disobedience may or may not assume that the political authority responsible for the law to which objection is taken, is actually entitled to rule. Mahatma Gandhi's campaign of civil disobedience against the salt tax in India in the 1920-30s hardly assumed that the British had de jure authority in India. By contrast, UK civil disobedience by members of the Campaign for Nuclear Disarmament in the 1960s did not normally reject the de jure authority of the British government, only the prudence of its military commitments.

Unless some form of constitutionalism prevails (§30.3), blocking certain illiberal majoritarian outcomes through contextual arrangements (§23.4.2.3), it is hard to see how, depending on the issue and the occasion, democracy can pre-empt the moral validity of civil disobedience on grounds of integrity or justice. The question of policy-based civil disobedience is the really tricky issue. There are arguments that such disobedience breaks the rules of the democratic game. When we take part in democratic decision-making, there is always the possibility of reversing any resulting policy with which we disagree, namely by persuading the majority to change its mind at the next election. Not only, however, does this not answer those, perhaps the ones committing civil disobedience, who do not take part in democratic decision-making; there is also the brute, non-rational entrenchment of opinion that makes talk of 'persuading the majority' sound like facile optimism.

On democracy and civil disobedience see further April Carter, 1973: esp. ch. 5 & 7; R. Norman, 1986; Rawls in TJ: 356-91 (for comment, see Sumner in Nielsen & Shiner, 1977: 1-48); Schlossenberger 1989; Scruton, 1983: 64; Singer, 1973. On civil disobedience more generally see Plato, *Crito*, especially the Dialogue between Socrates and the Laws of Athens (*Crito*, 50A-54D; Plato, 1960: 174-91: for commentary see Sinclair, 1961: 127-8; E. Barker, 1960: 141-2); Henry David Thoreau's 1849 essay, 'On the Duty of Civil Disobedience' (Thoreau, 1960: 222-40).

On democracy and justice, see I. Shapiro, 1996; Bader, 1995a and 1995b; Hunold & Young, 1998; Walzer, 1995. Waldron, 1998 discusses the relation of democracy to rights through the idea of a right to political participation which democracy may be taken to embody. On democracy and equality, see K. Graham, 1986: ch. 4. On democracy and freedom, see K. Graham, 1986: ch. 3. For some sceptical remarks on the relation of democracy to consent, see Lloyd Thomas, 1980. On democracy and law, see Bobbio, 1987: 31-2, 94; Dahl, 1989: 17-18, 108; Dean, 1966; Fine, 1984. On democracy and the common good, see the references to Aristotle, Schumpeter, Plamenatz and others in §24.1.

For further reading on democracy in general see Arblaster, 1987; B. Barry in PPS 5; Bealey, 1988; C.L. Becker, 1941; Britton, 1953: ch. 3; Burnheim, 1985; Held & Pollitt, 1986; Hirst & Khilnani, 1996; G.C. Lewis, 1898: ch. 9; Lindsay, 1943: ch. 5; Maine, 1976; Mansbridge, 1983; H.B. Mayo, 1960; Offe & Preuss in D. Held, 1991: ch. 6; C. Pateman, 1970; Pennock, 1979; Plamenatz, 1973; Sartori, 1965. Dahl has introduced the term 'polyarchy' for the conditions necessary in his view for democracy to work on the scale of the nation state and of large federal systems such as the United States and the European Union: see Dahl, 1989: 220-2. Polyarchy is essentially a combination of public contestation (§23.1) and inclusiveness (§23.2).

Among the classic texts, note in particular Rousseau's view that no one can be bound by a representative's decisions, whether delegate or envoy: I am bound by my will, by my voluntary decisions, and 'will cannot be represented' (SC III.15: 114). Locke does not appear to be committed to universal suffrage as ST stands. It is hard to say precisely who Locke's original contractors are, but it is unlikely that he saw them as the whole adult population. Women were excluded from the franchise in Locke's day; he says nothing about extending the franchise to them. And even in the case of the male population, the only constitutional change he proposes is the rectification of some seats (ST, ch. 13). As noted earlier (§14.6), Hobbes prefers monarchy to other forms of government, including democracy, because one-person rule reduces the risk of division in the management of the state. Machiavelli's republican freedom (§22.3 ad fin.) is, like Constant's liberty of the ancients (§22.7), democracy under another name.

24. THE PUBLIC INTEREST AND THE COMMON GOOD

[A] public is ... an abstract void which is everything and nothing ... the most dangerous of powers ... the public is also a gruesome abstraction through which the individual will receive his religious formation – or sink ... More and more individuals, owing to their bloodless indolence, will aspire to be nothing at all – in order to become the public (Kierkegaard, 1962: 63-4).

'The public interest', 'the common good', 'the common weal', 'the national interest': these terms figure widely in political discourse. All of them are vague enough as they are standardly used. 'The common weal' we can dismiss as an archaic variant on one or more of the others. The language of the 'common good' is older than that of 'public interest' and 'national interest'; I examine it first. Sifting through these distinctions, and noting

Virginia Held's three-way conceptualisation of 'the public interest', will be our essay in conceptual analysis. The issue between the civil association and the enterprise association view of politics will be our main examination of theories of the public interest. The aporia will be the teasing issue of whether different moral standards are applicable in politics, in pursuit of the public interest, from those in ordinary life.

24.1 Basic distinctions

The common good contrasts with a private good – a good which, if consumed by one person, cannot be consumed by others. Beyond this, the common good is capable of a double interpretation, collective and distributive (Gilby, 1953: 89, 203-13). On the collective interpretation a common good is one which is enjoyed by every member of a group or society, but which is in no way shared between them. It is a private good enjoyed by all, as everyone might have a house or a car from which they individually benefit and in which no one else shares. On the distributive interpretation a common good is a good which, if consumed by one person, can still be consumed by others. Clean air, defence, and civil peace, the 'public goods' of §§2.5, 13.2, 14.2, would be cases in point. (A pure public good is one of which all consumers consume the same amount, although they may derive differential satisfaction from it.) For further analysis of the idea of a common good, see T.H. Green, 1986: 263-79; Hollis, 1985: ch. 8; Jordan, 1989; Joseph, 1931: ch. 10; Jouvenel, 1957: ch. 7; Plamenatz, 1968: ch. 3; Runciman & Sen, 1965; Sweet, 1997: 104-7. On the connection between the common good and democracy, see Aristotle, P III.7: 61-2; Dahl, 1989: chs. 20-1; Plamenatz, 1973: 7-8, 96-7; Schumpeter, 1947: ch. 21 (reproduced in Quinton, 1967: 153-73). On links between the common good, law, and authority, see Gaus in P. Harris, 1990: ch. 2; and refer back to Aquinas and the Scholastics in §15.5.1. On the common good and justice, see B. Barry in Quinton, 1967: ch. 10. I leave you to consider how far the 'utility' served by Mill's liberty principle is a common good and in what sense (§22.8).

If we turn to the public interest, there are three influential approaches (V. Held, 1970). The first is the preponderance approach, a frankly majoritarian, no-nonsense application of 'the greatest good of the greatest number'. What is in the public interest is what will advance the preponderance of interests on any of the subjective constructions of well-being identified in §18.1. The second approach is the common interest one. This essentially coincides, if ambiguously, with the collective and distributive interpretations of the common good: 'ambiguously' because these two possibilities are not always clearly distinguished by theorists who take this approach to the public interest. The third approach is 'unitary'. It differs from the common interest approach in appealing to the fact or possibility of 'real' or 'objective' interests (§§12.2, 18.1).

While Held's account has its merits, it omits a key element. Perhaps a false 'reification' is involved but the idea is unavoidable, in much public interest talk, of society's or the public's having an interest which does not reduce, at least directly, to the interests of its members in any of the preceding three ways. For instance, it might be in the public interest that our economy rely on renewable resources. What may be at stake are the interests of future generations – 'the invisible community' (Lippmann, 1955: 41) – in which none of the living participate.

We have already seen that there are three main constructions of 'interests' (§18.1):

- expressed or revealed wants and preferences
- criticised wants and preferences
- real interests

On the first approach, a person's interests are simply his or her expressed or revealed wants and preferences. Interests are satisfied if wants and preferences are fulfilled; there is no conceptual space between the two outcomes. One might call this the market economy theory of interests, with the minor catch that the market responds only to wants and preferences expressed in the convenient form of effective demand. Instead I shall call it the expressive theory.

Two objections are put to this theory. In the first place, it provides no opening for error. People often feel that they have previously been mistaken about their interests. 'I thought a career in banking would be really stimulating but in the event it was a great disappointment, so boring.' The expressive theory can here only say that one's interests, alias one's revealed wants and preferences, have changed. But the idea dies hard that one can be simply wrong about one's interests in the sense that what one thought would satisfy the person merely satisfied a preference.

Next, the expressive theory is radically non-contextual. It is indifferent to the causal ancestry of people's revealed wants and preferences (cf. Lukes contra Dahl in §12.2). A social system that satisfies people's interests seems to have a high order of validity, but that impression is reduced if the relevant wants and preferences have been formed to a significant extent through misinformation, indoctrination, or coercive incentives of one kind or another. This is not to say that those who promote the expressive theory are unconcerned about such things. The point is rather that the theory gives us no language, in its own terms, for taking revealed wants and preferences at other than face value.

This is not a problem for the second construction of 'interests', which precisely does enable a criticism of the processes of want and preference-formation. By identifying interests with those wants and preferences which a person would have if they were fully or better informed or (more) rational, we can accommodate the idea of people being mistaken about their interests and the idea of wants and preferences as arising in ways that lessen or remove their normative force.

The third construction of 'interests' relies on a substantive theory of the good. We have met with such theories, Platonic and Christian, in §13.3.2. There is also an Aristotelian version (§2.2): when Aristotle tells us that *eudaimonia* (happiness, well-being or flourishing) can only come to those who possess and exercise the intellectual and ethical virtues set out in his *Nicomachean Ethics*, he takes himself to be identifying our real or objective interests. To be a flourishing human being is, totally non-contingently, to possess and exercise those virtues. The Marxist does the same when, in different language, he or she tells us about exploitation and alienation under capitalism and about the era of freedom in the communist society of the future (§31.3).

On the different constructions of 'interests' see further K. Graham, 1986: ch. 2. For further discussion of the concept of the public interest, see B. Barry, 1965: chs. 12-15; also B. Barry in Quinton, 1967: ch. 6 (with commentary in Hall, 1973: 146-8); Stankiewicz, 1976: ch. 2. On the connection between the public interest and authority, see Milne in P. Harris, 1990: ch. 1.

The idea of the national interest can be set out largely in terms of the aspirational and operational preferences of governments (J. Frankel, 1970: ch. 2). It is mainly a term of high politics; the national interest is appealed to in order to justify foreign policy as it ranges from treaty-making through trade agreements to declarations of war. Aspirational preferences are normally long-term goals, ambitions or vague hopes, often with a strong ideological component. Operational preferences are short-term plans, tactical goals, dictated by expediency or necessity.

The national interest is, from one point of view, the pursuit of the public interest in international affairs through foreign policy. The idea of the public interest is thus more basic.

24.2 The civil association versus the enterprise view of politics

Different understandings of the proper relation of the public interest to collective decision-making are marked by Michael Oakeshott's distinction between the civil association and the enterprise association views of politics. Oakeshott does not believe that modern American or European politics has ever exemplified these two views as pure types. They are messily mixed in the practicalities of collective decision-making. But they do represent distinct understandings of politics and the proper ends of political action; conceptually there is no blur between them. So Oakeshott holds. The main texts for the distinction are Oakeshott, 1975a: 108-84; 1975b; and 1991: 438-61.

If we regard political society as an enterprise, then the idea is that there is either a unitary or a common interest (to use Held's terms), a social ideal or goal (Dworkin's 'collective goal of the community as a whole' (§19.3) or a Nozickian 'end-state', deplored by Nozick himself of course (§17.4)), to the pursuit and promotion of which collective decision-making is properly to be directed. This interest may be to achieve 'socialism in our time', or Islamic renewal, or the *Respublica Christiana*, or any of a variety of ideals. Enterprise association views of politics are typically tied, to revert to language used before, to substantive theories of the good. This is a teleological approach to politics (§2.2).

On a civil association view, substantive theories of the good, if they occur at all, are confined to the activities of citizens acting individually or in groups. They do not inform collective decision-making. Such decision-making simply provides the conditions to enable citizens to pursue their self-ascribed interests. In the language of §2.6.3, this is a procedural politics, a politics of principle. Policy choices for the public realm, typically embodied in laws, are not (to use a metaphor) a vehicle by which we reach a common destination but a turnstile through which we pass to our separate destinations. The rule of law (§14.4) is emblematic of a civil association; and Oakeshott has his own account of precisely what this involves (Oakeshott, 1983: 119-64). Hayek's views are also relevant at this point. In Hayek's view the rule of law is inconsistent with an enterprise association approach to politics. Abstract and general rules will never have pliant aptness enough for a political system intent on the promotion of social goals (Hayek, 1982: 119-20).

Essentially the civil association view is a liberal position and some of its ramifications will be traced when we examine liberalism in its own right (§30). For now we may note that Oakeshott's distinction has been criticised on a number of grounds. Seeing that the enterprise association view assigns an overarching purpose to politics, some commentators have taken the civil association view to entail that politics has no purpose. And much of Oakeshott's language lends support to this claim. He frequently stresses that the laws of a civil association are purely procedural; they have no purpose, they are simply instrumental to the purposes of citizens.

Plainly this just means that the laws have the purpose of serving citizens' purposes, so the laws are purposive after all. The point can hardly be denied. But I doubt whether it really affects the substance of Oakeshott's distinction. In a civil association the laws do not have the specific purpose of promoting a substantive theory of the good, a particular view of people's real interests. That is the main differentia between a civil and an enterprise association.

The reply is open that some theory of the good is involved in supposing that people are best left to pursue their substantive theories of the good through a neutral framework of law. But Oakeshott could argue that the institutions of a civil association are merely a practical response to the fact of an irreducible plurality of substantive theories of the good.

See further Auspitz, 1976; Franco, 1990: 179-99, 222-9; Grant, 1990: 79-83; Liddington, 1984; Pitkin, 1976; Spitz, 1976; Wolin, 1976. Oakeshott replies to Auspitz, Pitkin, Spitz, and Wolin in Oakeshott, 1976. The civil/enterprise association distinction is presented in slightly different form in Oakeshott, 1996.

24.3 Ethics and public office: the problem of 'dirty hands'

The phrase 'dirty hands' became popular as a translation of the title of a 1948 play by Jean-Paul Sartre (1905-80), *Les Mains Sales*. The problem of dirty hands is the question whether actions can be morally required of, or allowable to, individuals in their public capacity which are not morally permissible to 'private' individuals. The architect of Italian unity, Camillo Cavour (1810-61), made the agonised confession: 'If we had done for ourselves what we have done for Italy, what scoundrels we should be.' The American naval commodore, Stephen Decatur (1779-1820), uttered the aphorism, 'Our country, right or wrong'. So as a citizen I can and should support my country in its wrong-doing when wrong-doing in my private life would be ruled out. Sartre, Cavour, Decatur, all recognise the problem of dirty hands.

The problem presupposes a 'forum' or 'arena' view of politics. To someone who holds the contrasted 'process' view that politics is omnipresent, because power relationships are omnipresent, the requisite distinction between public and private will not hold good. It is when we assume that the central institutions of a political system are peculiarly important, with large responsibilities attaching to their place-holders, that we begin to think that the magnitude of responsibility may create a gap or rift in the moral life between private and public life.

This is one of the themes of Machiavelli's *Prince* – that the ruler makes the world safe for morality. In doing so, he or she properly abandons the ethical code applicable to private individuals:

A prince must not worry about the reproach of cruelty when it is a matter of keeping his subjects united and loyal (PCE 55).

Hence it is necessary for a prince who wishes to maintain his position to learn how not to be good (PCE 52).

[H]e need not worry about increasing the bad reputation of those vices without which it would be difficult for him to hold his state (PCE 52-3).

[W]hether it is better to be loved than to be feared, or the contrary. I reply that one should like to be both one and the other; but since it is difficult to join them together, it is much safer to be feared than to be loved when one of the two must be lacking (PCE 56).

[O]ne sees from the experience of our times that the princes who have accomplished great deeds are those who have cared little for keeping their promises (PCE 55).

This is not a paean to amoral power-seeking. We are dealing here with two moralities on Machiavelli's account. By making possible the conditions of civil peace – freedom from internal disorder and external interference – in which private honour can flourish, the ruler has chosen a different but equal path of honour. Machiavelli as the cynical proponent of unethical *Realpolitik* is a caricature, far removed from the real thinker.

The Machiavellian perspective, and the whole problem of 'dirty hands', assumes a particular view of the moral life. At stake is a rule-bound conception of morality. Any action has indefinitely many descriptions. The question is whether there are some descriptions which, when they apply, morally silence all other considerations. If, for instance, we accept a rule (or principle) that innocent lives are never to be taken, that a promise is always to be kept, that a lie is never to be told, or that we should always so as to promote the greatest possible happiness, then other descriptions are morally insignificant. It is hard to see how public roles and private or personal conduct can be answerable to different moral requirements from this kind of perspective.

Such a perspective is not unproblematic, however. Rules can be either specific to types of action such as lying or promise-keeping or they can be single and overarching such as the rule to promote the greatest happiness. Take the specific rules. If we accept more than one of them, they plainly can clash in particular situations for action. More than that, none of them seems really adequate to the complexities of the moral life even in the private sphere. No mature moral agent really accepts an unqualified rule of truth-telling or promise-keeping. Circumstances alter cases. So this way of keeping the ethics of public life to the same standards as private life, through identical rules, looks unpromising.

If, however, we go up a level and consider a single, overarching rule such as the greatest happiness principle, the adequacy of such a rule to private life again runs into trouble. Is happiness to be pursued inconsistently with justice? If so, translating the rule across to public life might appear to license (say) punishment of the innocent. The 'same rules' approach may produce the same standards for public and private life but unsatisfactory standards in both cases.

However, if we take a view of morality akin to that of situation-ethics or ethical particularism, and quit a rule-based approach to morality, then the line will not be between public and private or personal life but across the whole range of an agent's actions. Every situation is, or may be, relevantly unique; and nothing will specially turn on whether an action has been done in a public or a private capacity. There will be no absolute stance that lying is wrong, or that an innocent life is never to be taken (in situations of tragic dilemma even such a taking of life may have to be contemplated).

Situation ethics has powerful attractions. Aristotle thought that while there are moral rules, these are only rules of thumb – presumptions to guide us in typical situations. There are moments of insight in which one 'sees' that one's situation is non-standard and decides what to do here and now in the unusual, perhaps even unique, circumstances.

The problem is that the further one moves away from presumptions, the greater the scope for arbitrariness. This finds its principal political expression in the invocation of 'reasons of state'. A politician decides 'in the public interest' (in any of Held's three senses) to remove an opponent, to order the bombing of enemy civilians, or whatever, all within a fog of lies and disinformation for 'reasons of state'.

The only solution appears to be through answerability. The indefinite range of descriptions applicable to any course of action means that, in public and private life alike, the morally most significant description may be unusual or even unique, something for which the Aristotelian rules of thumb do not prepare us. Here we have to act on and in the situation as we perceive it. The main trouble with reasons of state is that, adopted in secrecy, they prevent at the time and even afterwards the scrutiny through 'public reason' (§23.2) to which moral decisions should be answerable in political and personal life alike.

See further Coady in Goodin & Pettit, 1995; Downie, 1964; French, 1972; Hampshire, 1978; Kultgen, 1988; C.A.W. Manning, 1962 ch. 12; D.F. Thompson, 1987. For another perspective, due to Foucault, see §32.1.2. Among the classic texts, see Hegel's views in PR, §§257-340: 275-371; cf. Bosanquet, 1923: 300-5. While Hegel and Bosanquet are emphatic that the standards of public and private ethics are not answerable to the same standards, Plato might appear to be equally emphatic that they are: justice in the individual and justice in the polis are related as small letters to large (R IV: 116). But Plato also makes clear his view that the rulers of the ideal *polis*, the Guardians or philosopher-kings, know the real nature of justice while the citizens, incapable of a full, philosophically grounded education, can at best have approximately true beliefs about it (R VI-VII passim). This introduces a fresh angle on public and private ethics and the disparities between them (cf. §§14.3.2, 23.1). The 1970s *cause célèbre* of Lieutenant Calley, architect of the 16 March 1968 My Lai massacre in Vietnam, who was only 'obeying orders', is also crucially in point (French, 1972).

Dworkin's discussion of rights as trumps (§19.3), and Nozick's view of rights as side-constraints (ASU 28-33), are relevant to the relation of individual rights to the public interest.

5. Ideological Frameworks

25. INTRODUCTION

Our programme till now has been simple. It has been to analyse our twelve central political concepts, to check out some high-level theories about them, and to probe aporias – conceptual and theoretical tensions or difficulties that are specially hard to resolve. In this chapter we leap up a level. Ideologies are now in view. These are a particular kind of high level theory.

26. THE NATURE OF IDEOLOGY

Ideologies as they come under review in political theory have two distinguishing features. They represent, in the first place, a total perspective, value-laden and action-guiding, on social and political life. This feature has been captured by Bernard Williams:

> In its broadest sense, I take the term 'ideology' to stand for a system of political and social beliefs that does two things. First, it embodies some set of values or ideals, and, conse-quently, some principles of action: though such principles will be of necessity very general, and in some cases mainly negative, being concerned more with limitations on political action, for instance, rather than an overall aim of it. Secondly, an ideology connects with its values and principles of action some set of very general theoretical beliefs which give the values and principles some sort of backing or justification. The generality of these beliefs must, moreover, be of a special kind, if we are to speak of 'an ideology': they must, I think, be general beliefs about man, society, and the state, and not merely about some aspect of man in society. For instance, a belief in Free Trade or federalism, even though supported by general economic or political reasons, could not by itself constitute an ideology. The distinguishing mark of an ideology is that its general beliefs concern man and society as such, and hence concern things that are presupposed in any political or social situation whatsoever (Williams, 1967: 162-3).

To many, talk of such a system of belief carries associations of 'intellectual robotry' – of fixed, unresponsive thinking and of closed systems of ideas (Palma, 1986; cf. G.A. Cohen, 1997: 33-4). Such associations are not relevant here. The ideologies under review may be robotically followed. This shows the limitations of particular adherents. The systems of ideas themselves are living and capable of growth.

Williams' sense of 'ideology' has two, head-on historical contrasts. One, which we can practically discount, is that of Destutt de Tracy, who coined the term '*ideologie*' in 1795. For Tracy, ideology was to be the systematic study of the origin of ideas, where 'ideas' are the whole contents of the mind – mental objects or events of all kinds, anything known, believed, imagined or entertained. The other contrast is with Marx, who adopted the term 'ideology' for a specific purpose. In Marx's vocabulary of politics an ideology is a system of ideas that serves class interests and has a distinctive role to play in class struggle (Nielsen, 1983: 140). We will look further into Marx's concept of ideology when we examine Marxist socialism (§31.4.1).

The second distinguishing feature of ideologies is that different ideologies cluster concepts differently. Some they put in pole position; others they sideline and downplay, and they apply their own interpretative gloss throughout (Freeden, 1994). Thus anarchism finds no place for the state. Marxist socialism finds a place, but only a temporary one, pending the emergence of a classless society. Liberalism sees the state in some form or other as a permanent political fixture, as do conservatives. But liberals and conservatives typically differ over the proper ends and limits of state action. Again, liberals have traditionally stressed rights – centrally the right of the individual to pursue his or her own conception of the good. Socialists, particularly Marxist socialists, have tended to regard rights-talk as the product of an alienated individualism arising from the tensions of bourgeois society. These are only illustrative examples.

For further discussion of the nature of ideology, see Adams, 1989; Ball, 1996; Bambrough, and also Mackie, in Körner, 1975; Carver, 1988; Goldie in Ball, Farr & Hanson, 1989; Hamilton, 1987; D.J. Manning, 1980; Markovic, 1984; Parel, 1983; Plamenatz, 1970; Susser, 1988 & 1996; A. Vincent, 1992: ch.1.

27. THE RANGE OF IDEOLOGIES

'Out there', in the real world of politics, what would people widely count as ideologies? Even a quite modest list would have to include at least the following:

- fascism
- nationalism
- environmentalism
- anarchism
- conservatism
- liberalism
- socialism
- feminism
- postmodernism

In what follows I discuss anarchism, conservatism, liberalism, socialism, feminism, and postmodernism. Why exclude the others? For two main reasons, the first of which is that in contemporary political philosophy these still dominate the discussion. The second reason is that, while fascism, nationalism, and environmentalism are high profile in public discussion, they fall short of the others in their depth and complexity of perspective on social and political life. Fascism, though a sinister and portentous twentieth-century phenomenon, has no philosophical apparatus of any sophistication. Nationalism is on the rise but the principal question about nationalism, aside from the teasing question 'what is a nation?', is its relation to conservatism, liberalism and socialism. Environmental issues are of grave concern but green political theory still has far to go in providing a really distinctive perspective on politics and society which does not basically assume an anarchist, socialist or similar context.

On these matters I am simply taking a view; and that view is particularly tentative in the case of green political theory, of which the ideological credentials improve by the day. There is every reason why, from intellectual curiosity or personal involvement, you should follow up on the ideologies that I omit. To help towards that, I include some pointers in the Endnote (§34.2.1-4).

A further restriction should be noted. In a full discussion of the six ideologies on which we are concentrating, we would examine the relationship of each ideology to all twelve central political concepts. This would, however, require a book in its own right. Moreover, there would be a degree of artificiality about it. Take two examples, anarchism and postmodernism. Anarchism is primarily and overwhelmingly a critique of the state. Anarchist views on rights, equality, and justice are as diverse as anarchists themselves; there is no distinctive, *en bloc* anarchist position on rights. Postmodernism is critical, on grounds of intellectual coherence, of all the central political concepts. There is no special postmodernist critique of justice that does not apply also to rights or the public interest. So the aim will be to highlight the concepts, variable between them, on which the six ideologies take a distinctive line.

27.1 Left/right: a dispensable dichotomy?

If ideologies represent clusterings of concepts, can ideologies themselves be usefully clustered? Ideologies are commonly ranged on a scale from 'left' to 'right', with fascism on the extreme right and marxist socialism on the extreme left. The left/right dichotomy is so entrenched in political discourse as to be ineliminable. But how valuable is it?

The origin of the distinction is French revolutionary. Its history is straightforward enough. At the ill-omened meeting of the Estates-General in 1789 the nobility took the place of honour, on King Louis XVI's right; and the Third Estate, the commoners, took a subordinate place on his left. Later, in the revolutionary assemblies and beyond, seats were arranged in a semi-circle, with the radicals on the left and the traditionalists on the right. This made sense; it defined illuminatingly distinct differences when the range of political issues was relatively small and apparently simple. Are we Legitimists or Orléanists, set on re-establishing the monarchy and the old social order? Or do we want to keep the republic and press ahead with social change for equality?

How does the distinction work nowadays? One view is that the main axis of the distinction is the now opposition between socialism and capitalism. Parties and movements which support socialism are left-wing, parties and movements that support capitalism are right-wing. Roughly, capitalism is an economic system in which:

- there is predominantly private ownership of the means of production
- the rate and direction of economic growth are the outcome of spontaneous interactions of supply and demand
- the means of production are used principally for the pursuit of personal profit
- there is a market for consumer goods amounting to consumer sovereignty
- prices for all goods are fixed by the interactions of supply and demand, prices adjust spontaneously to consumer demand

A market economy requires features 2-5, not necessarily the first. Capitalism, to which the first feature is vital, may entail at least some elements of a market economy; a market economy does not presuppose capitalism. If the market can be shared between socialism and capitalism (§31.4), the gap between the two economic systems is reduced and the gap between left and right along with it.

At a different level of political debate the right is often seen as committed to national sovereignty and to the preservation of exclusive national and even racial identities. This, rather than its commitment to capitalism, puts fascism on the far right.

My own view is that when we are inclined to use the left/right distinction, we should switch to more precise contrasts instead. See further Browning in Axford et al., 1997:

230-1; Kolakowski, 1969: 67-83; MacRae, 1961: 208; Oakeshott, 1939: xxii-xxiii; Scruton, 1983: 260-2, 408; Spitz, 1964: 175-87. The language of 'left' and 'right' will not feature further in our discussion.

A final point before we begin. Broad contrasts hold between the ideologies but lucid distinctness can go only so far. We should have no thought of encasing each ideology in a tidy box of necessary and sufficient conditions, of features common and unique to it. For one thing, ideologies show up too much internal diversity to be neatly capturable in this way. For another, different ideologies share particular features: both conservatism and socialism include an element of communitarianism, and liberalism shares egalitarianism and rationalism with socialism. (One of these elements, rationalism, offers a precise antithesis to the anti-rationalism of conservatism.) It is then the specific mix of features that separates one ideology from another.

The term, 'New Right', emerged in the USA and UK in the early 1980s to identify theorists such as F.A. Hayek and Milton Friedman who espoused a free-market, anti-welfarist politics. The New Right became more distinctive in the UK when this style of politics was joined with an emphasis on tradition and hierarchy and on the political need for a broadly homogeneous 'common culture'. Leading figures of the British New Right were Maurice Cowling, John Casey, Roger Scruton, and Enoch Powell. The free-market element was perhaps more qualified in Casey. See further M. Barker, 1982; Cowling, 1978; Duffield, 1984; Levitas, 1986.

28. ANARCHISM

Anarchism is a predominantly modern doctrine, though there are traces of anarchist ideas in ancient and medieval political thought. The ancient Greek sophist, Antiphon, qualifies as a proto-anarchist with his idea that coercive political authority is unnatural and should therefore be circumvented wherever possible (Havelock, 1957: ch. 10; cf. E. Barker, 1960: 76-9, 95-8). Among the medievals the extreme radical wing of the Hussite movement in Bohemia came nearest to anarchism; they rejected all coercive government in church or state. But their 'anarchism' rested on a basis of religious dissent which separates them from the main body of modern anarchism.

The first fully-fledged anarchist is generally taken to be William Godwin (1756-1836). In *Enquiry Concerning Political Justice* (1793) Godwin's view is that economic conditions, and specifically the excessive accumulation of private property in the means of production, have undermined social justice, and that the state takes its rationale from this economic unfairness which it maintains ultimately through force and coercion. Remove the state, and the way is open to restoring a fair distribution of private property. See Godwin, 1971; Philp, 1986; Woodcock, 1962: ch. 3. Other names in the early anarchist pantheon include Thomas Hodgskin (1787-69) and Pierre-Joseph Proudhon (1809-1865). But let us move from history to analysis.

28.1 Anarchism as the mono-politics of the state

The state is the focal concept of anarchism. Anarchists not only prefer life without the state; they regard the abolition of the state as the prime and direct goal of policy. This gives us the basic two-part anarchist claim:

Thesis 1. We would have a better society without the state
Thesis 2. The removal of the state should be the prime and direct goal of policy

Thesis 2 divides anarchism from the anti-state element in the socialist tradition (§31.3.1), in which the disappearance of the state has generally been regarded as the natural outcome of broader social and economic developments, not a direct goal of policy. Relatedly, the anarchist emphasis on the state contradicts a common socialist assumption that the state is of instrumental and secondary significance. From a standard socialist viewpoint, other social configurations, reinforced indeed by the state, are the main players and therefore their abolition, not that of the state is the prime goal. An anarchist, in rejecting the state, need not reject also the idea of political authority. It is to the combination of authority and supreme coercive power – to the state as sovereign (§14.6) – that the anarchist classically objects. But what if supreme coercive power, in the sense of an unconditional ability to quell opposition and ensure compliance, should prove to be a chimera, a possibility that surfaced in §14.6.2? Even without *supreme* coercive power, the state is still objectionable to many anarchists because it employs an apparatus of coercive power, involving deliberate acts or threats of violence (§2.5).

Some would add negative freedom as equally central to anarchist concerns. But this is not distinctive to anarchism, nor is it common to all forms of anarchism. It belongs particularly to individualist anarchism (§28.2). Liberalism also takes negative freedom as a central value. But the liberal does not normally construe freedom as solely or mainly a question of freedom from the state. Some liberals have wanted a minimal state but no liberal has thought seriously of abolishing the state.

Here, then, is a major point. Antagonism to the state is the only point of convergence, the single common factor, in the anarchist tradition: hence the phrase 'mono-politics' in the title of this section. While many anarchists have repudiated the state largely or wholly on grounds of its being inimical to freedom, there is no necessary connection between anarchism and freedom. An anarchist is someone who wants to abolish the state, to remove it as an institution from social life. He or she is not necessarily someone who wants to abolish the state specifically in the interests of freedom. As an anarchist once expressed the point to me: 'Whatever problem you think the state is a solution to, you would be better off without the state.' For the bulk of the discussion and except where indicated, the state will be taken to be a political unit exercising supreme coercive power.

To note some elementary points before we go further: *arche* is the Greek word for rule. *Anarchia* is its negative, indicating the absence of rule. But what does the absence of rule mean, conceptually and practically? There is a common view that 'anarchy means chaos'. Certainly Hobbes, 'the apostle of toughness', thinks that there is no stable halting place between the supreme coercive power of the state and the violence and degradation of the state of nature (§14.6). If anarchists abolish the state, they will inevitably produce chaos if Hobbes is right. But it is fair to say that most anarchists do not see, let alone desire, the abolition of the state as the prelude to chaos. (Those who do are commonly termed 'nihilists'.) The usual idea is rather that voluntary mechanisms are sufficient to resolve the issues of social life. Or if an element of coercive power is allowed, it is not to be contained predominantly or monopolistically in a single political unit such as the state but in a plurality of protective agencies.

28.2 Individualist and communalist anarchism

There is no consensus among anarchists on the social forms that will support the relevant voluntary mechanisms or embody acceptably some element of coercive power. Smaller social units, the diffusion of power, self-management, and federalism are favourite options for the new social organisation. Human beings are seen as social animals, capable of creating a spirit of mutual amiability and cooperativeness to achieve agreed ends.

But this approach describes only one, communalist branch of anarchism. There is also individualistic anarchism, strongly marked in twentieth-century American writing, though also clear much earlier in the European tradition in a theorist such as Max Stirner.

1. Choice and (negative) freedom are supreme values
2. Coercive power may be exercised by one person or group, A, over another, B, only if this is necessary to prevent B from constraining either A (the case of self-defence) or some other group C, but
3. Such coercive power may not be exercised by the state, other protection agencies must be found

On a more extreme version, (2) would be amended to read that coercive power is never to be exercised by one person or group over others. This is 'moralism', which is considered below. But we will run with the current version. Individualist anarchists typically support market institutions. In a genuine market there is non-coercive interaction between buyers and sellers. The greater the area of social life covered by the market, the less scope there is for coercive power.

D. Miller, 1984 illuminatingly explores the communalist/individualist divide. Varieties of communalist and individualist approach are examined in Woodcock, 1962. A key point on which the individualist must satisfy us is whether the market can operate without the state. The individualist faces three problems.

In the first place, it is unclear how the market (once established) can be maintained without the state. How are its would-be subverters to be handled? If Nozick is right, protection is a natural monopoly – which is just to say that we need a state. Nozick's claim will be examined shortly. Secondly, there are difficulties in passing over to the market all the functions now performed by the state, crucially including the protection of person and property. What if I cannot afford the market price? Thirdly, there are familiar troubles about market failure in the case of public goods. However, here I would point back to an earlier discussion (§13.2). It cannot be simply assumed that public goods will be produced at inefficient levels by the market; and even if the claim can be made good, the anarchist can point out that it does not follow that we need specifically the state to supply the deficiency.

Communalist anarchism may rely on the social-mindedness of the anarchist citizenry to provide public goods if the market does fail. Problems of economic co-ordination are still likely to occur, however; and it is uncertain how the various productive units' activities are to be aligned without the summoning into existence of a proto-state. Market socialism is one approach, but then we return to the problem of maintaining the free market without the state; Proudhon's federationism (*Du Principe Fédératif* (1863)) is another.

28.3 Immediate versus long-term anarchism

Aside from the rift between the individualist and the communalist traditions, anarchists can also be grouped according to whether they propose the immediate abolition of the state or its piecemeal replacement as a new social organisation arises.

The 'immediate versus long-term' debate is well represented in Alan Carter, 1993. Carter defends a long-term approach. While accepting the basic anarchist stance, namely theses 1 and 2, he denies two further theses:

Thesis 3. The state must be smashed or abolished prior to the formation of any truly desirable society; and

Thesis 4. In order to bring about a desirable society it is merely sufficient to smash or abolish the state.

Carter counters thesis 3 with the logical point that one political and social form can be destroyed, as state-organised society should be destroyed, by a process of transformation. To use a slightly mundane parallel, if I take a glass of water and add lime juice cordial to it, I create a glass of lime juice. I have 'destroyed' the water, but only by transforming it – not by throwing it away. The practical point arises, however, whether an anarchist transformation can take place in this gradual way, with the state evanescing on the margins of social and political life. Carter replies that this is an empirical matter; there is nothing to show that it is impossible. Thesis 3 is represented by writers such as Mikhail Bakunin: see Limond, 1996; Woodcock, 1962: ch. 6.

Thesis 4 comes under attack in Carter's argument that 'the state may well be the immediate cause of social problems', but 'not the ultimate cause' (Carter, op. cit.: 198). The point is that if, as Carter suspects, there are deeper factors that cause social problems, these factors may continue to operate when the state has been abolished. In that case they could either recreate the state or cause greater problems than we face at present. Among such factors Carter identifies, diversely, authoritarian and hierarchical attitudes and the kind of technology (particularly nuclear power) which has statist implications.

Carter's positive view is that anarchists should cultivate forms of co-operative autonomy, such as workers' co-operatives and other collaborating groups on a level of equality, in which authoritarian and hierarchical attitudes would be planed away and in which alternative technology would be used. The model here is Prince Peter Kropotkin's *Mutual Aid*, 1902. Such forms already occur bittily; the aim should be to extend them whenever and wherever possible.

28.4 Pragmatic versus moralist anarchism

Pragmatist anarchists argue that any form of state is unnecessary. They object, not to the use of coercive power as such, but to its predominant or monopolistic concentration in a single political unit, the state as supreme coercive power. This they regard as unneedful for any function we look to the state to fulfil. Their attitude is 'negative' (Horton, 1992: 124) or 'a posteriori' (Simmons, 1996); they argue simply that in fact no sufficient case for the state has been made out. They do not foreclose in principle the possibility of such a case, as (by contrast) moralist anarchists do. The latter take the 'positive' or 'a priori' line that any form of state is immoral and hence unjustifiable. Coercive power, any ability to quell all opposition and ensure compliance, is never to be exercised by one person or group over others. From this standpoint, it would not matter if supreme coercive power should prove to be a chimera; the state undoubtedly employs an apparatus of coercive power, and this is enough to condemn it. Both positions are attacked by Robert Nozick, though he does not use these labels, in ASU Part 1, where he maintains the need and legitimacy of a minimal state.

One need for which the state is meant to provide is the adjudication of disputes. There are other needs the state aims to meet – co-ordination and free rider problems for example. But I keep here to the adjudication of disputes. Disputes may arise for at least three reasons.

The first is cognitive; under conditions of risk and uncertainty, two or more people may make different judgements of probability about the consequences of some proposed course of action.

The second has to do with the conceptual indeterminateness of morality, where for instance it is not clear (and no agreed decision procedure is available to determine) whether Christian morality sanctions euthanasia or whether affirmative action is consistent with justice.

The third centres on substantive differences of moral theory, between (say) Kantians and utilitarians. When, in totally good faith, people embrace such divergent moral theories, there is once again no agreed decision procedure to resolve the matter. (I should myself be inclined to add a fourth source of dispute, when one party bucks all considerations of morality and seeks to impose its self-interested will on another person or group. Since this prompts the question of how far 'natural goodness' would prevail under anarchist conditions, I set aside this source of dispute. The argument can run without it.)

The role of the state in such cases is not to provide truth where others have mere opinion; it is to establish a *modus vivendi* where some accommodation has to be made in the interests of civil peace.

28.5 Nozick contra anarchism

But, counters the pragmatist anarchist, we do not need the state to secure this accommodation. Fine, then: let us 'think away' the state, and project ourselves imaginatively into a social condition that Nozick calls the state of nature, an abstract, ahistorical model of the condition of humankind prior to the advent of political authority (§13.3.3.1). In this condition disputes of the foregoing kinds may still be expected to arise. It would be a brave anarchist who argued that such disputes are wholly the product of the state, which seeks to justify its existence by negotiating these very disputes.

In face of such disputes, appeal to third parties is a natural resort, not only for adjudication but for enforcement when adjudications are rejected or ignored. Nozick's term for such third parties is 'protective agencies' or 'protective associations'. Suppose a plurality of these: Nozick's argument is that there is an inherent tendency for the number of such agencies to dwindle. Some will prove stronger and more efficient than others. As well, adjudication is stymied if the parties to a dispute belong to different protective agencies. Using an economic model, Nozick says that protection is a natural monopoly. A dominant protective agency will emerge.

Resting his case on these points, Nozick considers that he has proved the need for a state, albeit a minimal state because one limited to an adjudicatory-cum-protective (basic safety and security) role. We only have to grant the need for agencies to adjudicate and protect, and we arrive at the need for a single such agency – the dominant protective agency alias the minimal state.

This is Nozick's response to the pragmatist anarchist. The moralist anarchist still awaits a reply. The moralist might object that the natural monopoly argument neglects a vital ethical consideration. What of those individuals whose protective agency has lost out, or gone under, to others? Or those who do not want to join a protective agency at all? What obligation is there on such individuals to obey the resulting dominant protective agency or minimal state? They never consented to be members of it.

Nozick's answer is that such individuals may be forced or coerced on condition that the minimal state performs all that they might accomplish on their own behalf. In this case, they are no worse off.

Whatever the cogency of this answer, the moralist anarchist will object that, qua source of forcible and coercive constraint, the state is inherently immoral. But this view places the moralist on a lonely promontary, easier to occupy briefly in argument than consistently in practice. If the main point of morality is to promote human (or sentient) well-being, it is hard to see what consistent moral theory would rule out the use of coercive power in all circumstances. If, without provocation or other valid excuse, you decide to kill me, is my use of force or coercion in self-defence not to be allowed?

The moralist may reply, relaxing full rigour of position, that the two cases – action by the state and action in self-defence – are different. The use of coercive power in self-defence is one thing; its use on behalf of others is another. Agreed, my inclination is to reply, there is a distinction but does it make a moral difference? What plausibility is there is holding that the use of coercive power, permissible in self-defence, is never allowable on behalf of others? If you are overpowered by an assailant, is it actually immoral for me to intervene to help you? And when I do intervene, what I do the minimal state might do instead: where is the moral problem? Cf. J. Wolff, 1991: ch. 2.

Sylvan in Goodin & Pettit, 1995: ch. 8 provides a sound, wide-ranging discussion of anarchism; and this is probably the best text to take next. Sylvan also has a useful bibliography. D. Miller, 1984, will take you down a level of detail. Other texts to be recommended are N. Barry, 1981: 56-63; Bookchin, 1974; Cahm, 1989; April Carter, 1971; Dahl, 1989: ch. 3; Angus MacCarthy's speech in Dickinson, 1905: 63-74; P. Goodman, 1977; Joll, 1979; Kropotkin, 1970; Limond, 1996; Marshall, 1992; Perlin, 1979; Schwarzmantel, 1987: ch. 7; Scruton, 1983: 14-16; Todd, 1986; A. Vincent, 1992: ch. 5; J. Wolff, 1996a, also 1996b: 32-6, 50-3; R.P. Wolff, 1976. Among the classic texts containing only limited, negative views of what absence of government entails, see Hobbes, L ch. 19: 130 and Locke, ST §§124-7: 350-2. A curiosity of philosophical literature is Feyerabend's *Against Method*, which represents itself as an anarchist philosophy of science. This gives a new spin to the connection between science and politics. See Feyerabend, 1975a and 1975b; and for commentary Sankey, 1994; Lugg, 1977. Finally, for a graphic eyewitness description of how anarchism has worked (or not worked) in practice on one of the rare occasions when the anarchist movement has been in control, you might look at George Orwell's *Homage to Catalonia* (Orwell, 1938; Woodcock, 1962: 365-6).

29. CONSERVATISM

'Given the nature of life', Kingsley Smellie (1897-1987), LSE's veteran political theorist remarked to me in June 1965, delivering a testament just days before his retirement, 'I don't see how there can be any philosophy except a conservative one.' 'Conservatism' can be taken in three main ways (cf. Huntingdon, 1957: 454-5):

• historically specific
• indexical
• general

In the first place it identifies a diverse range of ideas – feudal, aristocratic, agrarian, ecclesiastical, papalist, monarchist, authoritarian – united only by their convergence of reaction against the French Revolution. The high-profile thinkers are Edmund Burke (1729-97) whose *Reflections on the Revolution in France* (1790) looms huge, abiding and 'awful' over all subsequent conservative thought; Joseph de Maistre (1753-1821, author of the exquisitely perceptive and nuanced *Soirées de Saint-Pétersbourg* (*St Petersburg Dialogues* in Lively, 1965: 183-290)); the Marquis de Bonald (1754-1840); and Hugues-Félicité Robert de Lamennais (1782-1854).

Secondly, there is a socially and politically variable, 'indexical' conservatism. If someone believes that the central institutions of a particular society embody a high degree of value and that any amount of peripheral or incidental change may be allowed, consistently with preserving the continuity of the central institutions, that person is conservative in relation to the society in question. On this basis, we can count as a conservative someone who, in the former Soviet Union, wished to preserve the essentials of Communist Party rule; and equally someone who in the latter days of the Dual Monarchy wanted to keep the Austro-Hungarian empire intact.

Thirdly, there is a general body of ideas typically regarded as conservative. These ideas are sceptical, they involve a reliance on tradition, they stress the limited, role-based nature of government, and they take an organic or communitarian view of the individual's relation to society. This is the conservatism that Kingsley Smellie had in mind.

Often the same thinkers crop up under all three references, but a cautionary note should be struck. Thinkers can move in and out of conservatism, as with other ideologies. Lamennais started his intellectual life as a critic of the Revolution but moved on to essentially non-conservative positions in both church and state, going through liberalism to end up as a radical socialist and near-anarchist. It is a standard view that something like the same process applies to Burke in reverse, that he started as a radical Whig and became conservative only late in life under the impact of the French Revolution. My own view is that Burke's politics was largely consistent throughout his career. A final point is that Walt Whitman's remark applies superabundantly to all major thinkers: 'I am large. I contain multitudes.' Their ideas at any given time do not belong *en bloc* to a single ideology. There are elements of liberalism in Burke; and it is not implausible to see, intermixed with de Maistre's conservatism, some prefiguations of fascism (Berlin, 1990).

The present discussion follows the third way of taking conservatism, as a philosophical body of ideas. The (possible) relation of this body of ideas to the principles, policies, and programmes of the British Conservative Party is a point to be looked into, but not here. British readers should note that identity of ideas is not secured by sameness of name.

There is little point, as suggested earlier, in trying to pin down an ideology in terms of necessary and sufficient conditions. The messy reality cannot be so neatly caught. There are, however, typical features – lines of assumption and argument that are characteristic of particular ideologies. Ideologies thus appear as family resemblance concepts (§4.1.3). In the case of conservatism, we can identify five such features:

- scepticism and the complexity thesis
- rejection of the politics of ideals
- limited, role-based government
- reliance on tradition
- organicism and communitarianism

If these features are not to be taken as defining necessary and sufficient conditions, other relationships between them are worth bearing in mind. The features are not a bare conjunction, four lines of thought or assumption that merely chance to have been put together under a single label. But then, on the other hand, is the relationship between the features tight enough to yield entailment? Can we really say that to subscribe to one feature and to reject the others is to fall into self-contradiction? My guess is that in putting together and moving between the four features we are dealing with less tight, logically informal relationships of coherence or mutual appropriateness.

29.1 Scepticism, anti-rationalism, and the complexity thesis

A useful introduction to conservatism as a philosophical body of ideas is given by John Plamenatz:

> A conservative is not someone who denies the fact of social and cultural change, or even who seeks to slow it down; he is either someone who wants to preserve the advantages of privileged social groups or someone who, on broader and more philosophical grounds, believes that the ability to make large social changes according to plan is severely limited, and that the attempt to make them ordinarily does more harm than good (Plamenatz, 1975: vii).

This quotation from Plamenatz introduces the first feature of conservative thought, the sceptical idea that we do not have a predictive science of politics. Large-scale social planning is always a leap in the dark, a mere pretension to knowledge. Oakeshott quotes a Latin dictum, *Spartam nactus es; hanc exorna* (Oakeshott, 1991: 60 – 'Sparta is what you have been allotted; do what is best with it' in David Rees' free translation). Society is simply too complex; too many variables, local and ephemeral, are at work for us to be able to practise what Marx called exuberantly the 'revolutionary reconstitution of society at large' (PKM 204). Aims are only incompletely accomplished, and unforeseen side-effects always cause results to be markedly different from intentions.

The conservative gloss on this is to add that normally the results of large-scale social planning are on balance negative and harmful. We are worse off overall than if the planning had never been attempted. This is, Plamenatz is right, not an argument against all attempts at social change or improvement. Change, always inevitable, is often desirable: 'A state without the means of some change is without the means of its conservation' Burke said (Hampsher-Monk, 1987: 168; E. Burke, 1900: 23). Lord Rosebery observed of Burke that 'He hated revolution because he loved reform'.

Small-scale, incremental changes should be the norm. We can present this as a form of anti-rationalism, though we need to be careful about language.

In looking at epistemology in §3.9 we met with Rationalism as the view that reason is a source of knowledge independent of sense-experience. The conservative might want to draw out connections between this epistemological rationalism and the kinds of large-scale social planning to which he or she is opposed. Oakeshott, 1991: ch. 1 (the title essay of *Rationalism in Politics*) is just such a linking exercise. But advocates of large-scale social planning need not be epistemological rationalists; and in opposing their projects the conservative may simply object to means/end or (as it is sometimes called) 'instrumental' rationality as applied systematically and globally to politics. It is in opposition to this kind of rationalism that typically the conservative is anti-rationalist. Social complexity will always, in the conservative view, defeat the calculation of efficient means to clearly conceived, large-scale political ends.

The conservative faces an objection that, if the consequences of large-scale social planning are thus unpredictable, the logic of the argument is that we never know what we are inaugurating – and this applies just as much to what are taken to be piecemeal, incremental changes as well. There is the famous 'butterfly-effect' by which the beating of the wings of a butterfly in Europe can produce, by its contribution to successive chains of causation, a hurricane in the Caribbean. Who could predict such an outcome from such a trivial event? For a related argument against the apparent caution of incremental change, see Goodin, 1982: ch. 2.

The conservative's reply is likely to be twofold. In the first place, that this unpredictability of consequences is no positive argument in favour of large-scale social change. Secondly, that as we may recall from Bishop Butler in §22.8, probability is the very guide of life. Certain consequences of policy x or action y are probable, particularly within a tradition of behaviour (§29.4); as rational agents this is the most we can take into account.

29.2 Rejection of the politics of ideals

This scepticism connects with a further characteristic of conservative thought. This is the idea, first, that politics has no intrinsic purpose or end (recall Scruton from §2.2); and next, that secondary teleology is also to be rejected. We are not to inject a contingent purpose or end into politics, fixing our sights on social goals, informed by ideals, which are to be realised through political action. Society is not an enterprise association (§24.2). The realisation of social goals is precisely the politics of large-scale social and political change. There is, as a refinement, a second application of scepticism here: the epistemology of ideals is greatly questioned by conservatives. The normative theories in which ideals are encapsulated have a highly problematic status. Can they plausibly claim to be true, or such that any rational person must subscribe to them? We saw some of the difficulties that Rawls encounters on the last count. (On the score of justice, conservatives are likely to promote corrective justice (§17.2), looking to restore the *status quo ante*. Certainly if one puts distributive justice at the service of a social goal or political ideal, the conservative will repudiate that.)

Conservatives are apt to say, in a glancing and teasing phrase, that politics is not a particularly important activity. The point of this is generally just that politics does not have the importance attributed to it by enterprise association theorists, the importance of being a vehicle by which society is to be transformed to embody an ideal.

29.3 Limited, role-based government

Another characteristic of conservative political thought is that government is seen as a limited, role-based activity. Two points emerge here: (1) government must be limited if large-scale social change and the politics of ideals are 'out'. Because the role of government is so limited, (2) the democratic idea of authority's being an attribute of persons (namely of representatives holding political authority by consent and particularly of delegates elected with a mandate 'to create a better Britain' or whatever (§23.2)) is uncongenial. Authority is an attribute of institutions, roles and offices, of those political institutions, roles and offices that have to be in place if citizens are to be provided with the means of living together. Government approximates to administration; and the typical framework of government is the rule of law. On the one hand, the tension between the rule of law and the pursuit of social goals (§24.2) is irrelevant to conservatism, since it is not committed to the pursuit of such goals (§29.2); and on the other hand, the rule of law gives clarity and predictability to the workings of limited government. See further Oakeshott, 1975a: 149-58, 189-93; Oakeshott, 1991: 441-6; Scruton, 1991: 11-13, 91-2; Singh, 1967.

29.4 Reliance on tradition

This leads on readily to yet another characteristic of conservative thought, namely the reliance on tradition. Tradition is the vague mystery at the heart of conservative thought. The word 'tradition' derives from the language of Roman law in which *trans-dare* means 'to hand across, to hand over'. From its original legal reference to objects of gift, barter, and inheritance it came to refer to ideas, customs, and laws. Its further characterisation is elusive. Here is a suggestion. Where there is a (valuable) tradition of political activity:

1. There are institutions, roles, and offices
2. Within these, reasons for action and standards of expectation are selected from a recognisable, diverse, but limited range of considerations
3. The institutions, roles, and offices work with acceptable efficiency in providing citizens with the means of living together
4. These institutions, roles, and offices are capable of change, even of improvement, but the reasons for changing them, and the standards of expectation to be used in trying to improve them, must be selected from the same limited range of considerations that apply in (2) above.

Probably the most puzzling element here is the idea of the 'recognisable, diverse, but limited range of considerations'. This refers to entrenched forms of political discourse, the kinds of considerations – the common moral and political currency – to which anyone in a society can appeal in order to argue for or against a political proposal. (There are echoes of 'public reason' here (§23.2).) Thus, for instance, 'law', 'authority', 'rights', 'property', 'freedom', and perhaps the whole bulk of our twelve central political concepts in §4.1, are part of the common currency. But other concepts and controversial applications of these common concepts – 'political correctness', 'affirmative action', 'the One True Religion', 'natural law' and 'human rights' – are not. These latter ideas are too contested to form part of a shared vocabulary of politics.

To see what style of political argument this produces, consider a British example: the extension of the franchise to include women in 1918 and 1928. For the conservative the case for extension was historically specific. Women formed an extensive part of the workforce. Without the contribution of women workers, the British economy would have been in dire straits during the 1914-18 war. Women were property-owners; the Married Women's Property Act of 1882 and subsequent case-law had amended centuries-old anomalies. All this, and yet no franchise. Withholding from women the right to vote was an anomaly within the British political system.

These in outline were the conservative arguments for reform. We might talk of law and rights. But these were the law and rights of a specific, evolving historic community. No reference to natural law, or to supposed civil rights based on natural or human rights possessed by historically abstract individuals, was pertinent. No such talk was part of the British tradition of political discourse. Alien, it was also redundant. Every comparative disadvantage that women wished to remove could, in principle, be critiqued by sound argument *within* a tradition of political discourse and public reason that eschewed such terms. So Oakeshott argues: see Oakeshott, 1991: 11, 57. For an opposing point of view, see B. Barry, 1965: 152.

The conservative reliance on tradition marks a contrast with a rationalist approach to politics. The scope for rational intervention in social life, through the smooth execution of clearly conceived schemes with foreseeable, controllable consequences, is either nil or negligible in the conservative's view. But we should not miss the coda that, given this view, tradition for the conservative takes on its own aspect of rationality. Where tradition is the only reliable resource, its disregard is irrational. Following on from this is a view of tradition-based politics as involving a set of skills, a mode of practical reason, by which a tradition can be interrogated and applied. This means, further, that for the conservative we are always dealing with a reflective tradition, not an inert pattern of habitual behaviour. To reflect on a tradition, to 'pursue its intimations' in Oakeshott's language (Oakeshott, 1991: 57-8), requires, moreover, to make a back-connection, the Burkean independent thinker and discriminator, the envoy not the delegate (§23.2). Finally, there is nothing external to a tradition in terms of which, for the conservative, it can be appraised. 'Every rational tradition' – i.e. every tradition reflectively followed and revisable – 'fixes and applies its own internal criteria, methods, distinctions, standards of cogent argument, etc., its own immanent standard of epistemic weight regarding its methodological, conceptual, or empirical problems, and its own conception and standards of rational superiority to rival and predecessor traditions' (Colby, 1995: 54 on MacIntyre, 1988: 350).

On tradition see further Casey, 1978; S. Coleman, 1968; Dowling, 1959; Oakeshott, 1965; Oakeshott, 1991: 54-62; Parry, 1982; Popper, 1963; Singh, 1967; Tate, 1997. The legal enforcement of traditional morality is seen by some conservatives as a proper part of the reliance on tradition (§15.5.2; cf. Scruton, 1983: 75-9 on 'social continuity'). Dworkin's 'great network' account of judicial decision-making in 'hard cases' as articulating the moral and political vision embodied in a community's law is also relevant (§15.3) even if Dworkin would not himself care to be seen keeping conservative company. Conservatism offers a tradition-based account of authority (§13.3.3.1 ad fin.) since the institutions to which authority belongs are elements of a tradition.

29.5 Organicism and communitarianism

The final features of conservative thought, for our purposes, are organicism and communitarianism.

The organicist idea is that a society is in some respects an entity in its own right. In recognising myself as a British or an American citizen I identify myself with both past and future, feeling (as it may be) pride or shame for what my forebears have done, and looking also to the interests of future Britons or Americans. Burke captures this aspect of conservative thinking in a famous passage:

> Society is indeed a contract. Subordinate contracts for objects of mere occasional interest may be dissolved at pleasure – but the state ought not to be considered as nothing better than a partnership agreement in a trade of pepper and coffee, calico or tobacco, or some other such low concern, to be taken up for a little temporary interest, and to be dissolved by the fancy of the parties. It is to be looked on with other reverence; because it is not a partnership in things subservient only to the gross animal existence of a temporary and perishable nature. It is a partnership in all science; a partnership in all art; a partnership in every virtue, and in all perfection ... a partnership not only between those who are living, but between those who are living, those who are dead, and those who are to be born (E. Burke, 1900: 107-8; Hampsher-Monk, 1987: 193).

Organicism of this sort does not commit the conservative to the more speculative uses of organicist models in politics. The conservative need not hold, for instance, that just as the parts of an organism have no value other than in their contribution to the proper functioning of the whole, so society is or ought to be an end for its individual members. Nor need the conservative liken the development of societies to the growth and decay of organisms.

Neither of these uses of organicist models is now influential in political theory, though historically they are often to be found and the huge prestige of nineteenth-century biology gave them a new lease of life. See Bosanquet, 1898; Deutsch, 1966: 30-4; W.J.M. Mackenzie, 1979; McCloskey, 1958: 321-6; McTaggart, 1918: ch. 7; Spencer, 1969:

195-233; Weldon, 1962: 34-45. Cf. Plato, R IV, 419C-421C but also 342E, 346E-347A, 465D-466A and 519C-520E and Aristotle, P I.2 1253a20-5: 4. Currently the main link between biology and political theory is through sociobiology and the emphasis on human nature, explicated by evolutionary biology, as the foundation of politics. Follow up with Masters, 1989; and cf. §2.6.2 on the causal autonomy of politics.

Communitarianism is a label for a range of views. It is associated with a group of writers of whom the leading names are Michael Sandel, Charles Taylor, Alasdair MacIntyre and Amitai Etzioni. Primary sources are Sandel, 1982; C. Taylor in Rosenblum, 1991: ch. 9; MacIntyre, 1985 and 1988; Etzioni, 1996. Good general guides to communitarian thinking are provided by Avineri & de-Shalit, 1992; Mulhall & Swift, 1992; and in the exchange of views in Lacey & Frazer, 1994; Lowe, 1996; Lacey & Frazer, 1996. See also Charvet in P. Harris, 1990: ch. 3; Charvet, 1995; Dunn, 1990: ch. 11.

Note that including a communitarian element in conservatism does not make communitarianism as such a conservative position. Conservatism distinctively combines communitarianism with other views – scepticism and the complexity thesis, the preferability of limited, role-based government and the rest. We will find communitarianism surfacing also in socialist thought.

The two main characteristics of communitarianism are (1) its stress on the social situatedness of the self and (2) its rejection of what may be termed focal individualism. Social situatedness means that individuals draw their self-understanding and their conceptions of the good, their 'constitutive ends', from what is conceptually to hand in historically specific societies or civilisations. The projects and ambitions of a medieval European Christian are not possible for a twentieth-century Briton; the view of one's place in the world, and the psychology of faith, are wholly different between the two. As Scruton puts it, 'society is in some sense antecedent to the individuals which compose it, the individual being a social artefact, the product of historical conditions that ally him to customs, values and expectations without which' – and this brings in a normative element – 'he is seriously damaged or incomplete' (Scruton, 1983: 90; Bevir, 1996b; cf. Aristotle, P I.2 1253a19-20: 4). To accept social situatedness is also to reject abstract individualism, the idea that human drives and behavioural characteristics are socially and historically invariant (§2.6.1).

Repudiation of focal individualism, the second characteristic of communitarianism, is a rejection, in the first place, of the intense concentration (taken to be typical of liberalism) on the individual person with his or her rights and, secondly, of the market-based culture of predominant self-interest which undermines social solidarity. Communitarians widely deprecate the tendency for the market to become the dominant model for all social relationships and institutions; they argue that the market needs to be 'embedded' in a network of non-market relationships without which social breakdown threatens.

Conservative communitarianism has often gone along with a morality of social roles and an ethics of special obligations. There are general obligations – the obligation, say, to help in Good Samaritan situations or not to return evil for good. But conservatives not uncommonly see conceptions of the good, the cultural stock on which individuals draw in giving meaning to their lives, as embedded in social roles and practices. The requirements and expectations associated with these roles and practices define to a large extent my rights and duties. This is not implausible; my day-to-day moral conduct is wholly tied up with my determinate identity as a son, writer, teacher and the rest. Through this identity I have special obligations to this student, that friend, this parent, that neighbour. By the same token I have special entitlements too.

The conservative does not reject the idea of rights – bare liberties, claims, privileges or immunities (§19.1). But conservative rights are 'prescriptive', tradition-based rights: they are in Burke's words 'an entailed inheritance derived to us from our forefathers' (E. Burke, 1900: 36; Hampsher-Monk, 1987: 172). There is no talk of natural or human rights (§19.2) but only of the rights of members of historically specific cultures and social organisations (Burke has in view 'the rights of Englishmen'). The logic is clear: natural or human rights could only belong to abstract individuals; whichever of our characteristics are socially and historically specific cannot be possessed by humankind as such. And the abstract individual 'is a delusion of theory' (Bradley, 1927: 174; cf. Scruton, 1984: 49, 52).

The most vivid presentation of this conservative vision of the moral life is to be found in F.H. Bradley's essay, 'My Station and its Duties', from which this quotation comes, though it is fair to add that Bradley was not fully content with it (Bradley, 1927: 160-213). Bradley's essay was strongly influenced by Hegel's account of *Sittlichkeit* or 'social morality', 'ethical life' in PR §§142-258.

See further on conservatism in general: Allison, 1984; N. Barry, 1997; Buck, 1975; Cecil, 1912; Gilmour, 1978; G. Graham, 1986: ch. 10; Greenleaf, 1983: ch. 6-9; Hayek, 1960: 397-411; Hogg, 1947; Kedourie, 1984: 29-83; J.S. Mill on Coleridge in Mill, 1950: 99-168; O'Sullivan, 1976; Quinton in Goodin & Pettit, 1995: ch. 9; Schwarzmantel, 1987: ch. 6; Scruton, 1991; Tännsjö, 1990; A. Vincent, 1992: ch. 3; R.J. White, 1950; Vierek, 1962. An attempt to wed conservatism specifically to free market economics is in Willetts' contribution to Gray & Willetts, 1997. This attempt is foredoomed to failure since the market generates a spontaneous social order which dissolves tradition (§30.4). The logic of conservatism requires an economic system based on customary behaviour, whatever that behaviour might be. On Burke, see the Introduction to Hampsher-Monk, 1987; Keens-Soper in Forsyth et al., 1993; Plamenatz, 1963, I: ch. 9. But Oakeshott's remark should be noted that there is more to be learnt about conservatism from Hume than from Burke (Oakeshott, 1991: 435). Initially try Hume, 1987: 512-29 ('Idea of a Perfect Commonwealth'). The whole of Hume's writings is relevant.

30. LIBERALISM

'A Conservative', wrote Ambrose Bierce in *The Devil's Dictionary* (1911), 'is one who is enamoured of existing evils, as distinguished from the Liberal, who wishes to replace them with others.' Like 'conservatism', 'liberalism' has numerous senses, some of which we need to exclude from a philosophical discussion. Setting aside the irrelevance of liberalism as identified with political parties calling themselves 'liberal', we may note four senses of the term:

- historically specific
- polemical
- economic
- general

In its narrowly historically specific sense, 'liberalism' is the viewpoint of the liberales, the group of Spanish politicians who, in the Cortes or parliament of March 1810 (the bequest of the mildly populist Junta to the traditionally-minded Regents), looked for British-style constitutional monarchy and parliamentary government – more precisely, 'a representative body that should combine the virtues of the French revolutionary assembly, the British House of Commons, and the sixteenth-century Cortes of Aragon or Castille' (Butler Clarke, 1906: 18; Cranston, 1954: 67).

The polemical sense of 'liberalism', dear to British tabloid journalism, is that of a relativistic, permissive, 'don't blame the individual', 'let's be supportive to everyone', attitude to life and society. Liberals are people (usually identified with 'the chattering classes', talkers and thinkers rather than real doers) who side automatically with the criminal as victim of society; people whose 'children's rights' educational ideology is responsible for ill-discipline in schools; people again who defend the rights of minorities irrespective of the public interest. A whole demonology of 'liberal' beliefs and attitudes has been created, which I mention only to exclude from philosophical consideration.

Economic liberalism largely means *laissez-faire*, the core idea of which is that, beyond a minimum consistent (on the one hand) with compassion in the event of humanitarian catastrophe and (on the other) with market failure in the supply of public goods (§13.2), the government should not intervene in the economy.

The term *laissez-faire* was first used by an eighteenth-century French merchant, Gournay, pleading for relief from the dense network of state economic regulations: 'laissez faire, laissez passer' ('leave things alone, let them through' (Lippmann, 1937: 185)). The term was taken up and developed into a doctrine by the eighteenth-century school of French economists, the Physiocrats, though the idea may go back to Italian economists of the seventeenth century. The Physiocrats opposed Mercantilism, the theory and practice of regulating the economy by tight governmental controls to create national wealth. Instead of the state's regulating the pricing and manufacture of goods, the location of industry, and the movement of trade, the Physiocrats backed people's operating as they pleased, consistently with public security and the protection of property rights. All that was needed, for society to find its 'natural and essential order' (in the phrase of one of the Physiocrats, Mercier de la Rivière) was to leave things alone, *laissez-faire*.

Gradually, to this core idea of governmental non-intervention in the economy, *laissez-faire* added the related idea that the government should abstain from welfare politics. Welfare goods such as unemployment insurance, health care, pensions and the rest, should be left to self-help and voluntary agencies.

This expanded concept of *laissez-faire* is captured in John Stuart Mill's phrase that, subject to exceptions which he noted, 'the business of society can be best performed by private and voluntary agency' (PPE V.xi, §16: 977-8). This fits with Adam Smith's 'system of natural liberty', though Smith's role for the state is potentially large (§22.3) – a veritable time bomb for *laissez-faire*. There are also affinities with 'libertarianism', which generally means a commitment to cutting drastically the political constraints on economic activity and in particular to lessening, or even withdrawing, welfare-based redistribution.

Mill's voluntary agencies are the institutions of a market economy. To be clear on terminology:

- a market exists wherever there is interaction between buyers and sellers for a good or service
- in a market economy, demand (the amount of a good or service that consumers are willing to buy at a given price) and supply (the amount of a good or service that producers are willing to sell at a given price) depend on consumers' and producers' choices and are not under the control of a central authority
- in such an economy producers are in a competitive situation – sales are made through a process of competitive price-setting by producers, and no consumer is constrained to buy from any particular producer

Mill hoped that the market producers would eventually be, not capitalist firms but workers' co-operatives (§22.8.4).

The way in which 'liberalism' is used in this economic sense opens up a divergence between American and British political discourse. American usage, which points in a quite different direction from *laissez-faire*, is captured by William Safire's entry on liberalism in his political lexicon:

> LIBERAL: currently one who believes in some government action to meet individual needs; originally, one who resisted government encroachment on individual liberties.
>
> In the original sense the word described those of the emerging middle classes in France and Great Britain who wanted to throw off the rules the dominant aristocracy had made to cement its own control.
>
> During the 1920's the meaning changed to describe those who believed a certain amount of governmental action was necessary to protect the people's 'real' freedoms as opposed to their purely legal – and not necessarily existent – freedoms (Safire, 1972: 343-4).

This reverses the British economic sense of 'liberalism'. In the UK, just to add difficulty, economic liberalism was espoused in all but name by the Conservative Party in the nineteen-eighties and early nineteen-nineties. Welcome to the giddy world of transatlantic discourse.

As a general body of ideas, liberalism has already made its appearance in earlier discussions. In considering Hayek's defence of the rule of law, Mill's liberty principle, Rawls' theory of justice, Locke's account of individual property rights, and Dworkin's view of rights as trumps, we were dealing with liberal viewpoints. Other figures in the liberal pantheon include Adam Smith (1723-90), Immanuel Kant (1724-1804), Jeremy Bentham (1748-1832), Benjamin Constant (1767-1830), Alexis de Tocqueville (1805-59), T.H. Green (1836-82), Bernard Bosanquet (1848-1923), Benedetto Croce (1866-1952).

Our discussion will centre on liberalism as a general body of ideas, though economic liberalism will find its way in (§30.1). Although, as usual, we are not to look for necessary and sufficient conditions, it is reasonably safe to identify seven typical features of liberalism. I will take five in one group, then bring in the remaining two. The theorists just mentioned exhibit enough of these features to be significantly grouped together; they should not taken as producing an identical body of doctrine.

John Gray picks out four typical features of liberalism as a political theory:

- individualism
- universalism
- egalitarianism
- meliorism

He outlines these features as follows:

> Common to all variants of the liberal tradition is a definite conception, distinctively modern in character, of man and society. What are the several elements of this conception? It is *individualistic,* in that it asserts the moral primacy of the person against the claims of any social collectivity; *egalitarian,* inasmuch as it confers on all men the same moral status and denies the relevance to legal or political order of differences in moral worth among human beings; *universalist,* affirming the moral unity of the human species and according a secondary importance to specific historical associations and cultural forms; and *meliorist* in its affirmation of the corrigibility and improvability of all social institutions and political arrangements (Gray, 1995b: xii).

In going over these features I will add rationalism to meliorism, since I take liberal meliorism to have a rationalist component. This brings the list of typical features now up to five. The sixth and seventh features, missing from Gray's list, are the exclusion of ideals and political neutrality. I will change Gray's order of presentation, taking universalism immediately after individualism. Why, will be clear as we proceed. Finally, the exposition is my own gloss, and is not to be taken as representing what Gray himself would say.

30.1 Individualism

'Individualism' has a wide range of meanings (see Lukes, 1973a). We earlier encountered methodological individualism – the idea that statements about political (and other) institutions are reducible to statements about individuals and their interactions (§2.6.1). The individualism of immediate relevance here is ethical. Three main liberal theses are:

1a. Individual persons are the ultimate units of moral value
1b. Society has as its proper end the good of individuals; there is no social good over and above that of individuals
1c. Individual well-being requires people to make their own choices so far as possible

Kant and Green provide glosses on (1a). Kant does this in his injunction noted in §18.2: 'Act so that you treat humanity, whether in your own person or in that of another, always as an end and never as a means only' (Kant, 1969: 54; O'Neill, 1989: 113-14, 136-40). Green also does it in his claim that: 'Our ultimate standard of worth is an ideal of personal worth. All other values are relative to values for, of, or in a person' (T.H. Green, 1986: 256). Lockean self-ownership (§20.2.2) is often taken to be a further implication of the moral ultimacy of individuals.

(1b) contradicts a view, once 'in the air' rather than definitely attributable to particular thinkers, that society is or ought to be an end for its individual members. We encountered this view in connection with conservative organicism, noting that the conservative is not committed to this particular application of organicist thinking.

Finally, (1c) takes very much the view of the individual that Beran presented in §14.3.3, when we were considering consent as a basis for political authority. It carries rather more tangled implications for liberalism than might at first appear.

Many liberals have seen (1c) as requiring what was characterised above as economic liberalism – *laissez-faire* and a predominantly market economy. Aside from defences of *laissez-faire* which assume the comparative efficiency of the market as against the inherent defects of central planning (§31.4), many liberals have seen the economic freedom which *laissez-faire* and the market involve as:

> the most precious temporal freedom, for the reason that *it alone* gives to each one of us, in our comings and goings in our complex society, sovereignty – and over that part of existence in which by far the most choices have in fact to be made, and in which it is possible to make choices, involving oneself, without damage to other people. And for the further reason that without economic freedom, political and other freedoms are likely to be taken from us (Buckley, 1968: 156; quoted in R. Goodman, 1974: 237).

Much the same conclusion has been drawn from a further interpretation of (1a), which is taken by some liberals to entail Lockean self-ownership. With discernible disapproval, David Miller comments:

To enjoy self-ownership is to enjoy rights over one's own body that are like the property rights standardly held in, say, a pocket calculator or garden spade: that is, we can decide how to use the thing, enjoy the fruits of using it, hire it out, sell it, give it away. ... We have strong moral intuitions about the importance of bodily integrity: rape and torture are perhaps the worst evils that humans can experience. These intuitions can be framed in the language of self-ownership: it is because we are rightful owners of our own bodies that such violations stand condemned. But if we are indeed self-owners, must it not follow that we have the right to use our bodies as we wish, which will entail having the freedom to make whatever contracts we choose, the right to retain whatever we work to produce, the right to kill or injure ourselves etc.? In this way a whole political philosophy – essentially, a defence of laissez-faire capitalism – can be spun out of a single concept (D. Miller, 1996: 34).

However, when we consider liberal egalitarianism we will note a quite different direction in which liberal politics can move, one far remote from economic liberalism.

The comment can be expected that ethical individualism is not unique to liberalism. Do conservatives and socialists not equally accept (1a)-(1c)? Are they not equally respectful of the individual? It depends on what we mean by 'individual'. Liberalism's individual is a person seen in relatively abstract, universalist terms. Conservatives and socialists tend to respect persons in a communitarian perspective, under 'richer', histori-cally and socially more specific descriptions than liberalism allows. This aspect of liberalism is just what we have to look at in the next section.

Many liberals have added to (1a)-(1c) the universalist moral claim:

1d.   Individuals are the possessors of natural or human rights (§19.2).

Bentham was a notable exception here, dismissing talk of natural rights as 'simple nonsense: natural and imprescriptible rights – nonsense upon stilts'.

30.2 Universalism

There are three dimensions to liberal universalism – psychological, ethical, and political.

We can take our bearings on the first dimension from the contrast between abstract individualism and social holism (§2.6.2). Abstract individualists hold, and social holists deny, that the explanatorily decisive attitudinal states and behavioural characteristics are historically and socially invariant. It has been typical of liberalism to view persons under just such states and characteristics:

2a.   Human beings are self-interested utility-maximisers
2b.   Human beings are inherently competitive, acquisitive and possessive
2c.   Human beings are fundamentally motivated by the pursuit of pleasure and the avoidance of pain (Bentham)
2d.   Human beings are rational, self-determining, free choosers (i.e. possessors of free-will (§22.2)), responsible for their actions
2e.   Human beings are free, equal, rational choosers of lifeplans (Rawls)

All of these conceptions, and others besides, have been fed back into the theses of ethical individualism, (1a)-(1d) above, as giving content to the idea of the individual. The image of the rational, self-determining, free chooser as the ultimate unit of value has been particularly influential and has some claims to be the dominant liberal conception of the abstract individual.

Such an image fits well with consent as the basis of political authority (what but consent could create such authority over such an individual?). It integrates with the view of rights as trumps (if the freely choosing individual is the final locus of value, then limits must be set to the pursuit of aggregative social goals). It suits Mill's liberty principle, which creates a protected area of negative freedom within which choices can be made. These are only quick connections, not tight entailments. But their plausibility is evident.

The second dimension of liberal universalism is the view that it is by virtue of such characteristics as (2a)-(2e) that the ethical theses, (1a)-(1d), go through.

Liberal universalism's third and final dimension has two aspects. The first is what has come to be called 'difference-blindness' (M.S. Williams, 1995: 67). In general, liberal political theory talks of 'citizens', 'voters', 'consumers'; Rawls talks of 'rational contractors', Mill views us as 'progressive beings'. These descriptions apply to us all, and distinguish none of us. Notice in particular that it is hard for any idea of justice as affirmative action or positive discrimination to find a purchase here, because such action or discrimination requires more specific levels of description, of nationality, ethnicity, gender and sexuality, by which groups can be identified (§17.5). Social contract theory (§13.3.3), is often rejected by feminists, reformist and radical alike, precisely because it runs on a difference-blind notion of 'citizens' with mutual rights and obligations (on feminism and difference-blindness, see §32.1.1; on feminism and contract theory, Coole, 1993b: 200).

The second aspect is the idea of a universal form of politics. We have met this in Rawls' account of justice (§17.3). His rational contractors agree on a timelessly appropriate basic social structure informed by the two principles of justice. You might significantly recall that they do not even know what in what period of history they will live. The idea occurs again in John Stuart Mill's view that representative government is the uniquely right form of politics for all societies which have reached a certain level of development (*Representative Government*, chs. 3-4: Mill, 1958: 36-67; Mill, 1991: 238-68; cf. Oakeshott, 1991: 63-4). Again, there is Locke's assumption that only consent-based government has de jure authority (§13.3.3.1). Again, if people are inherently self-interested, competitive, acquisitive, and possessive, political authority will always have the predominant task of reconciling conflictive interests and preserving civil peace. Lastly, those liberals who believe in *laissez-faire* typically regard it as the timelessly correct relation of government to the economy. If we start from abstract individuals there is nothing to stop a universalist politics. There is nothing to differentiate the politics of individuals who are relevantly similar.

Historians of political thought would be justified in a criticism at this point. The account so far of liberalism's commitment to the abstract individual is fair enough for a large part of the liberal tradition, they might point out, but it omits those liberal theorists who precisely have insisted on the social situatedness of persons. One need only mention T.H. Green and Bernard Bosanquet, and the case is made.

As may be expected, however, this view of the situated person as opposed to the abstract individual cannot be introduced without creating distinct divergencies within liberalism. Some of the implications for liberal egalitarianism will be explored in the next section.

30.3 Egalitarianism

For abstract individuals, ultimate and equal units of value, rational, self-determining and freely choosing, the traditional liberal institutions of the rule of law and *laissez-faire* have a natural appropriateness. The Hayekian rule of law, as we recall from §15.5, posits general and abstract laws, which are known and certain, and also courts which respect individual equality before the law. Such a legal system is tailor-made for such abstract individuals. Again, *laissez-faire* can be seen as a celebration of free choice, as the §30.1 quotation from William Buckley makes clear.

If, however, we turn to Green's view of situated persons as distinct from abstract individuals, the picture starts to change. Green, no less than any liberal, accepts the moral ultimacy of persons; we had a citation from him to that effect in §30.1. But he also has a strong sense of the historical specificity of the culture and social organisation in which persons find themselves. On the one hand, he subscribes to an ethics of social roles, believing that the moral life is primarily a matter of fulfilling our obligations as parents, teachers, doctors, lawyers, accountants, labourers or whatever our precise commitments and occupations. On the other hand, he realises that persons are differentially situated within the culture and social organisation. He mentions the examples of 'an Athenian slave, who might be used to gratify a master's lust' and 'an untaught and under-fed denizen of a London yard with gin-shops on the right hand and on the left' (Green, 1986: 233). The London example might need to be updated from the late 1870s, but Green's point still stands that people are unequally placed to fulfil their own conceptions of the good or even to consider a broad range of such conceptions.

With this view of situated persons, the role of the state begins to change. Liberal egalitarianism requires equality of opportunity for well-being (§18.1); and an idea of freedom as enablement (§22.3) may emerge as functional (§§3.5.4) to it. No one is to be disadvantaged through the 'accident' of their social placement. But the pursuit of equality of opportunity is the promotion of a social goal; and we have noted the tension which Hayek sees between a politics of social goals and the rule of law (§24.2). Moreover, since the market and *laissez-faire* will produce losers as well as winners, the pursuit of equality of opportunity is in effect a commitment to welfarist, redistributive taxation to help the unfairly disadvantaged (e.g. the children of market losers). So *laissez-faire* is no longer a realistic option for the 'new' or 'social' liberal. These two wings of the liberal movement, roughly Green's and Hayek's, are not finally compatible. That Green himself did not draw the full implications of his revised liberalism is easily conceded. Green's is very much the American sense of 'liberalism' as noted by Safire above.

Political equality has often been espoused by liberals under the form of representative democracy running on universal and equal suffrage. It may be mentioned that John Stuart Mill broadly supported universal but not equal suffrage; in *Representative Government*, ch. 8, he sought extra votes for individuals of 'superior qualifications' (Mill, 1958: 139; Mill, 1991: 337). Equal suffrage is in any case more formal than real. We noted earlier that if voting power is equally distributed, it does not follow that so are voters' chances of having those policies adopted which they want to have adopted (§23.4.1.2). There is also the danger of the tyranny of the majority, which so alarmed Tocqueville and Mill (§22.8). Consequently, liberals have tended to favour a contextualist approach (§23.4.2.3), seeing democracy not as an untrammelled majority-based procedure for collective decision-making but as operating in a context of freedom of speech, assembly and association along with the separation of powers and the rule of law (§§12.3, 15.4). 'Constitutionalism' is the name usually given to the view that such arrangements define the basic rules under which the political system should operate.

30.4 Meliorism and rationalism

Much of nineteenth-century liberalism ran on the issue of progress – technological progress, democratic progress, progress in rationality, progress in material social well-being and morality. Anyone might have asked sceptically, though few did, (1) whether progress in one sphere might clash with progress in another; or (2) how, beyond reference to such vague formulae as 'the greatest happiness of the greatest number', overall progress was to be calculated if such collisions occurred; or again (3) what explanatory mechanisms underlay such progress as could be recognised and gave reassurance that it would continue.

The idea of progress as the automatic direction of history has long since ceased to be a hallmark of liberal thinking in general, though it survives vestigially in Fukuyama's *The End of History* (1992). See further G. Graham, 1997: ch. 3; Plamenatz, 1963, II: ch. 7.

A standard liberal assumption remains, however, that society is indefinitely improvable. Historically this assumption derives in no small part from liberalism's de facto association with utilitarianism. Many of the early liberals – Bentham, James and John Stuart Mill among the major names – were utilitarians. Utilitarianism measures the merit or demerit of actions, institutions, and practices wholly by their consequences as these maximise the occurrence of intrinsically desirable states of affairs. In the case of these early liberal utilitarians, the relevant consequences were those for happiness. If social institutions or practices fail to maximise happiness, by whatever criterion of happiness, we should work to amend or replace them. In principle, there is every reason to expect success. This was the (highly activist) approach.

Not all liberals have been utilitarians; Green, for example, was a powerful and persistent critic of utilitarianism, as is John Rawls in our own day. But liberals typically assume that the social and political system can and should be revised to reflect liberal values of individualism and egalitarianism. This is a form of rationalism which we can add to Gray's list; it is the politics of conscious, organised change. Certain values are desired in our social and political life, and we are to use effective means of achieving them. Even a theorist such as Hayek who believes that, under the rule of law and a market economy, unpredictable interactions with unpredictable consequences produce a 'spontaneous order' (Hayek, 1982: 41-2), is committed to the wholesale if gradual reform of government and the economy to create the rule of law and a freely functioning market.

It is right to add that liberals have tended to favour piecemeal, incremental reform, and this for two main reasons. In the first place, liberals (unlike marxist socialists) lack a philosophy of history of the kind that might enable them to create a predictive science of politics. A tentative and cautious approach to major change has seemed appropriate. Secondly, the largest programmes of social and political change have generally been motivated by an enterprise association view of politics; and this, as we will see directly below, is no part of the liberal perspective.

A puzzle might present itself. If in favouring incremental and in repudiating large-scale social change, conservatism is anti-rationalist, how can liberalism, which equally favours incremental change, be rationalist? The puzzle is solved as follows. From a conservative standpoint, liberalism is a form of rationalism. The liberal has a clearly conceived, large-scale political end, namely the transformation of society to embody liberal values; and incremental changes are for the liberal the efficient means towards it. In sharing a common incrementalist approach, liberalism does not shed its rationalism.

30.5 Exclusion of ideals and political neutrality

The features that Gray lists are typical of philosophical liberalism. But his tally omits a recognisably liberal view, that of state neutrality. This is not a point against Gray; to say that there are four – or, with rationalism, five – typical features is not to say that there are only these features. Moreover, a major liberal theorist, Joseph Raz, distances himself from state neutrality. He distinguishes two positions within the state neutrality viewpoint (Raz, 1986: 108):

> Thesis 1: exclusion of ideals. Governments should not heed the truth or falsity of moral ideals, or of conceptions of the good − neither the validity, cogency or truth of any conception of the good, nor the falsity, invalidity or stupidity of any other may be a reason for any governmental action.
>
> Thesis 2: political neutrality. Governments must be neutral regarding different people's conceptions of the good − no act of governance may either improve or hinder individuals' chances of living in line with their conception of the good.

By 'conceptions of the good' we are to understand the substantive theories of the good defined earlier, specific views of human flourishing, of what it is to live rightly and well (§13.3.2). The two theses are connected. If the state ought to be neutral in respect of conceptions of the good then, if you and I have different conceptions, the state should be impartial between us. Raz presents both theses as putatively derivable from an ideal of personal autonomy − (1c) above − that individual well-being requires people to make their own choices so far as possible (Raz, 1986: ibid.). This, note carefully, is a minimalist account of autonomy, given the discussions of §22.6. That point aside, the supplementary clause of Thesis 2 does not follow from the opening clause. One could accept that governments must be neutral regarding different people's conceptions of the good. One could insist also that governments may not *differentially* improve or hinder the chances individuals have of living in accord with their conception of the good. But one could hold further that governments should equally promote those chances − not that governments should neither improve nor hinder them.

There are difficulties with this revised version of Thesis 2, not least because different conceptions of the good are logically inconsistent, and practically competitive, with one another. But it is a theoretical possibility.

The exclusion of ideals, which can be seen as requiring an area of negative freedom in which individuals are exempt from interference in pursuing their personal conceptions of the good on condition that they respect a like restraint towards others (recall Mill's liberty principle (§22.8)), is a point of connection between liberalism and conservatism. Conservatism also rejects the politics of ideals, the promotion of social goals. This means in turn a further agreement, common acceptance of a form of limited government. There is, however, an ambiguity on the liberal side. Although exclusion-of-ideals liberals will not accept a style of politics that aims at a transformation of social and political life to reflect substantive theories of the good, so-called 'social liberals' want equality of opportunity (practically equivalent to a view of freedom as enablement (§22.3)) for people to achieve their personal conceptions of the good. This itself is a kind of ideal, and its realisation or even its resolute pursuit brings social liberals into conflict with the conservative ban on the political promotion of social goals.

To return to Raz, who presents the two theses as putatively derivable (as noted) from the ideal of personal autonomy. Notice that Raz himself accepts this ideal but he denies the derivation; the ideal does not entail the two theses. In rejecting political neutrality and the exclusion of ideals, Raz commits himself to what is sometimes called, not specially aptly, 'perfectionist' liberalism − the view (1) that there is a truth of the matter about human flourishing and (2) that political action should be taken to promote such flourishing. Notice also that though Raz puts forward the two theses as putatively based on the ideal of personal autonomy, the theses might be grounded in other ways. Even, therefore, if he breaks the connection between the theses and the ideal, the theses might still be otherwise defensible.

At least three such alternative grounds are on offer in the broad liberal tradition that extends from Locke down to the present day.

One view, admittedly not widespread among liberals nowadays, is that there is known to be an objective human good and that its nature is also known, or is at any rate a matter of reasonable belief. But, the point is, this good can be realised only if it is freely acknowledged in an act of genuine intellectual assent and conscientiously acted on accordingly. Locke takes this view of Christianity. He is genuinely convinced of 'the reasonableness of Christianity' (that very phrase is the title of one of his books). The state cannot create the relevant assent or enforce conscientious action. The point is one of morality, concerning the conditions on which an action can have moral value. Though Locke himself did not follow up the full implications of this viewpoint (he is politically hard on atheists, for example), it does contain grounds on which one might support Theses 1 and 2. For the rather fuller complexities of Locke's views on toleration, see Creppell, 1996. Note the non-accidental link between Locke's requirement here that the state not be implicated in spiritual concerns and his confinement of political authority to the (secular) role of protecting our natural rights to life, liberty and property, and of adjudicating on their infringement. The delicate balance between this political 'hands off' attitude and ST's divine teleology (§20.2.4) is a fascinating juncture in the history of political thought.

Yet another view, quite removed from Locke, is that there is an objective human good but that we do not yet have anything amounting to full knowledge of its nature. This is John Stuart Mill's position (§22.8). The recommendation in *On Liberty* to encourage 'experiments of living' is meant to create the conditions (rather like laboratory conditions in experimental science) in which people acting innovatively may bring the objective human good in any number of unexpected forms and dimensions to light. Although there is firm evidence that Mill accepts the ideal of personal autonomy, the logic of his argument does not require it. He could support Theses 1 and 2 on the basis of utility, which is in fact his official stand.

The final view, which has enjoyed most support in the present century, is that there is no such thing as an objective human good to be known. A person's interests are definable in terms of the satisfaction of his or her actual or expressed wants and preferences, desires and inclinations, with possibly an element of appraisal fixed by reference to what would be wanted or preferred if the person were better informed or more rational. Some liberals would reject even this element of appraisal as the thin end of the objectivist wedge. The relevant 'liberal view of the mind' is spelt out in Lawrence, 1989: 37. Liberalism of this stamp tallies well with market capitalism: given a person's actual or expressed wants and preferences, desires and inclinations, about which we cannot judge, the capitalist market will non-judgementally satisfy them.

A subjectivist construction of interests, without or without the element of appraisal, might lead to the adoption of Theses 1 and 2. There is certainly no incompatibility, but no entailment either. For I might decide, contrary to Theses 1 and 2, to enforce politically my own subjective preferences (cf. G. Harrison in PPS 5: ch. 12). But whatever the case, support for the two theses on a subjectivist construction of interests need have no ideal of personal autonomy behind it.

On all three grounds Theses 1 and 2 are defensible (or might be successfully defended) without recourse to the ideal of personal autonomy. Thesis 2 runs into difficulties of practical plausibility if taken in full strictness; virtually any policy choice, or bundle of policy choices, will facilitate or privilege certain lifestyles, certain conceptions of the good, over others. But let us switch from practice to theory and consider why Raz accepts the ideal but rejects the theses.

The main point is that, on Raz's account, the value of autonomy turns on the ability to choose between *valid* conceptions of the good (Waluchow, 1989: 480). As Raz himself puts it: 'Autonomous life is valuable only if it is spent in the pursuit of acceptable and valuable projects and relationships' (Raz, 1986: 417). All conceptions are not valid, and there is no reason for the state to assume that they are. The state should take a benign, facilitating attitude towards valid conceptions; and it has every reason to treat us differently, you and I, if my conception of the good is a valid one and yours is not. 'The autonomy principle permits and even requires governments to create morally valuable opportunities, and to eliminate repugnant ones' (Raz, ibid.). Theses 1 and 2 are thus rejected.

Raz faces two problems. The first is to establish his claim that there are genuinely valid and invalid conceptions of the good. The other is to explain to us how his position is liberal. If the state is not to be neutral in regard to conceptions of the good, how is this consistent with the ideal of personal autonomy?

On the first problem, the difficulties facing an objectivist account of the human good are appreciable. Objectivist theories of the good normally specify ways of living rightly and living well of which the preferability does not depend on the actual or expressed wants and preferences of individual agents. The objectivist might argue that such preferability is a matter of truth or rationality. How to argue this plausibly in view of the extent of disagreement and the intractability of disputes is not readily apparent. The question arises whether there is a satisfying spine to Raz's perfectionist liberalism if it depends on an objectivist theory of the good.

My own view is that Raz's best recourse is to something like John Stuart Mill's account of desirability and higher pleasures in *Utilitarianism*, chs. 2 & 4. Mill argued famously that the only proof that something is desirable is that people do actually desire it. This is not to say that actual desire is a sufficient condition of desirability. In some parts of the world, people desire to see harnessed bears boiled alive in preparation for soup. No humane person could endorse the link between desire and desirability in this or in indefinitely many other cases.

This is not the connection Mill has in mind. His point is twofold. On the one hand, if X were presented to us as desirable this would be an odd claim if, in any imaginable circumstances, nobody would actually want X. On the other hand, the real issues are about relative preferability. The fact that most readers prefer Jeffrey Archer to Henry James is not a total clincher: if the Archer-readers have never seriously attempted Henry James, and the James-readers prefer James to Archer on the basis of acquaintance with both, it is not implausible to avow the superior literary virtues of Henry James. See Mill, 1991: 139-42 and 168-9.

This is, in my view, how Raz should argue for the principle of personal autonomy. Those who have experienced autonomy would not, for the most part, want to give it up; and the rejection of autonomy by those who have not experienced it and do not want to have it, is a secondary consideration. Problems beckon: a parallel argument could be mounted in favour of those who have received a reality-recessing injection that makes them deliriously happy as against the rest of the population. Those who have had the injection and experienced the happiness would not, for the most part, want to relinquish their state: is the rejection of this pathetic state by those who have not experienced it and do not want to do so, also a secondary consideration? Unless Raz can show a plausible, relevant difference between the two cases, his perfectionist project is in trouble.

Raz's second problem concerns the status of his political theory as a genuine form of liberalism. If the state is not to be neutral in regard to substantive theories of the good, how does it respect personal autonomy? The state is pre-empting the options.

On this point we can be briefer. Raz's key idea is that of value-incommensurability. For any values, X and Y (friendship and justice, knowledge and health, or whatever), X and Y are incommensurable if and only if they are (1) conceptually independent, (2) nor subject to a common metric that enables relative assessment in the abstract; and (3) capable of clashing situationally. We cannot, in general and in the abstract, order these values lexically, deciding that (non-contextually) health is more important than knowledge, or friendship more important than justice. Nor can we analyse them in terms of one another; health, for instance, is not a form of knowledge, nor is justice a variety of friendship. Nor are these values always practically reconcilable. People have to decide, through their goals, projects, plans, aspirations, and commitments, what ordering to give to which values. In the process, without irrationality, different values are weighted and traded-off differently by different people. 'We lack any grounds for judging a career as a graphic designer to be intrinsically better or worse for those engaged in it than a career as a livestock farmer or a gliding instructor, assuming that [people] are likely to be equally successful and content in them' (Raz, 1986: 343; cf. Gray, 1995a: 34-6, 49-50, 52 & 63; Waluchow, 1989: 482-5).

Raz's idea stands right with Mill's rejection of the single blueprint for human flourishing (§22.8). It may also be mentioned that Raz, like Green, has a strong sense of social and historical specificity. The pursuit of goals, projects and so on is possible only within the context of existing social forms, with all the network of relationships and responsibilities involved. With regard to the social situatedness of the self, Raz is a communitarian liberal.

A further form of liberalism, also running on the idea of incommensurability, is the 'agonistic' liberalism associated with the late Sir Isaiah Berlin. 'Agonistic' here derives from the Greek *agonistikos*, 'relating to a combatant in an athletic contest'; the central idea is that of there being plural values between which a strictly rational choice cannot be made. While Raz emphasises how, in the life of the individual, diverse and competing values can be balanced and reconciled in valid and specific goals, projects, plans, aspirations, and commitments, Berlin puts the accent on how at the level of collective decision-making these goals, projects and so forth, like the values they differentially embody, are incapable of joint realisation:

> One freedom may abort another; one freedom may obstruct or fail to create conditions which make other freedoms, or a larger degree of freedom, or freedom for more persons, possible; positive and negative freedom may collide; the freedom of the individual or the group may not be fully compatible with a full degree of participation in a common life, with its demands for cooperation, solidarity, fraternity. But beyond all these there is an acuter issue: the paramount need to satisfy the claims of other, no less ultimate, values: justice, happiness, love, the realization of capacities to create new things and experiences and ideas, the discovery of truth. Nothing is gained by identifying freedom proper, in either of its senses, with these values, or with the conditions of freedom, or by confounding types of freedom with one another (Berlin, 1969: lvi).

Situational choices between freedoms, and choices between freedom and other values, are ineluctable and incapable of rational determination. Values are neither mutually entailing conceptually nor practically consistent; and nor, when one value must be traded-off against other, is there an objective scale of values by which one value can be given priority over another. See further Berlin, 1969: 169; Gray, 1995a: 6-8 & 141-68. I suspect that the intellectual pedigree of Berlin's agonistic liberalism runs through, first, Sir David Ross' theory of prima facie duties – a theory that posits moral considerations which are relevant to a broad variety of situations but which can clash circumstantially and which are not capable of lexical ordering (Ross, 1930: 18-36); secondly, J.L. Austin's moral ideas as instanced in his footnote on 'simply disparate ideals' (Austin, 1961: 151).

There need be, to scotch a false inference, no connection between value pluralism and incommensurability on the one hand and relativism on the other (Gray, 1995a: 149-50). 'Relativism' is a term of diverse meanings but Berlin is not committed to holding that values ultimately rest on feelings of approval or disapproval and psychological attitudes to which no question of truth applies. (For a different view, see Lukes, 1998.)

To make a back-connection, the conservative response is likely to be that a tradition of political behaviour in effect embodies a scale of value preferences at the collective level and that this is the only coherent way in which values can be balanced and reconciled.

Before we close our discussion of liberalism, a number of general sources may be indicated. Ackerman, 1980; Browning in Axford et al., 1997: 231-5; R. Dworkin in Hampshire, 1978; Flathman, 1989; Galston, 1991; Gray, 1989, 1993 & 1995b; D.J. Manning, 1976; A. Vincent, 1992: ch. 2 will repay study; Alan Ryan's discussion in Goodin & Pettit, 1995: ch. 11 should not be overlooked. On liberal neutrality, see Caney, 1992; Dunleavy & O'Leary, 1987: 44-7; Nagel in Raz, 1990; Newey, 1997 (dense, complex, sophisticated, highly worthwhile).

31. SOCIALISM

Socialism, enthuses MacCarthy in Lowes Dickinson's *A Modern Symposium*, is 'the dream of the world, the light of the grail on the marsh, the mystic city of Sarras, the vale of Avalon! Socialism the soul of liberty, the bond of brotherhood, the seal of equality!' (Dickinson, 1905: 63-4). On the eve of the October Revolution of 1917, Lenin announced: 'All nations will arrive at socialism – this is inevitable.' The Victorian statesman, Sir William Harcourt, thought the journey already accomplished. Introducing death duties, he shrugged his shoulders: 'We are all socialists now'. For the 1980s British prime minister, Margaret Thatcher, socialism was neither desirable nor inevitable. She set herself to destroy it as a social, political, and economic evil. But what is this thing called 'socialism'? 'Socialism is what the Labour Party says it is', Herbert Morrison, an early twentieth-century British politician, once said. This dictum has its limitations, more especially since the British Labour Party now says nothing about socialism. We must take a longer way.

The term 'socialism' dates from the early nineteenth century. It has a double origin. Among the Saint-Simonians in France (followers of Claude-Henri de Rouvroy, comte de Saint-Simon, 1760-1825), it slipped into print in 1832 in a journal edited by Pierre Leroux. Leroux himself used it unfavourably for the view that society is or ought to be an end for its individual members, whose interests are thus to be subordinated totally to those of the collectivity (cf. organicism in §29.5). The term was also used, independently and a shade earlier in UK, by the Owenites (followers of the mill-owner, philanthropist and social theorist, Robert Owen, 1771-1858). For the Owenites it meant co-operation, the co-operative principle as the basis for a new society. This usage dates, as far as we can tell, from 1827.

As a body of ideas, socialism emerged as a reaction to the rise of capitalism in the eighteenth and nineteenth centuries. It had its prefigurations; strands and anticipations are traceable in the medieval schoolmen such as St Thomas Aquinas. Jarrett, 1913, is still worth reading on these; note also Marx and Engels on 'feudal socialism' (PKM 228-30). Few would go so far as the late Alexander Gray in identifying a socialist tradition from Moses to Lenin (A. Gray, 1946). Gray saw socialism everywhere and merit in it nowhere. We can sideline Gray. As a distinctive set of ideas, socialism is a modern phenomenon.

Like the other ideologies we have examined – anarchism, conservatism and liberalism – socialism has proliferated into a diversity of schools and tendencies. It has also passed through at least four broadly distinct phases.

In the first phase, represented by the Owenites, by some of the followers of Saint-Simon, by Charles Fourier (1772-1837) and by Étienne Cabet (1788-1856) among others, the aim was to create centres of co-operation within existing society. Socialists were to find their own salvation within the existing system. Co-operation would catch on; a gradual transformation of society would ensue. The state was to play no central role in this process. We can call this the 'islands of socialism' approach. Owen funded a socialist commune in Indiana, called 'New Harmony', a idealistic venture which cost him £40,000, four-fifths of his fortune. On Owen, see Berki, 1975: 48-9, 52-3; Morton, 1969; Scruton, 1983: 339; Tawney, 1964: ch. 2; J. Wolff, 1992: 36-7.

Karl Marx (1818-83) dismissed Fourier, the Owenites and the rest as 'utopian socialists' whose ideas and activities would never bear fruit. Marx's revolutionary, 'scientific' socialism, the second phase of socialist theorising, is a body of ideas to which I will return shortly.

In the third phase, 'state socialism' emerged. This was reformist and welfarist. It was associated in France and Germany with the names of Louis Blanc (1813-82), J.K. Rodbertus (1805-75) and Ferdinand Lassalle (1825-64), and in the UK with the Fabians, whose leading lights were George Bernard Shaw, Beatrice and Sidney Webb, Graham Wallas, G.D.H. Cole, and R.H. Tawney. (Lenin once described George Bernard Shaw as a good man who had fallen among Fabians. The Fabians took their name from the Roman general Quintus Fabius Maximus, who defeated Hannibal by cautious harassment rather than full confrontation. While Lenin invoked the inevitability of revolution, Sidney Webb spoke of 'the inevitability of gradualism'.) State socialism stressed nationalisation, economic planning, and a high level of social welfare. There was no intention of overturning the state apparatus through revolution but also no reliance on the 'DIY' socialism of Fourier and the 'utopians'.

The fourth phase, the current stage of the socialist venture, looks beyond state socialism. 'Market socialism' has been mooted, the idea that the means of production might be owned or leased by workers' producer co-operatives which would compete under market conditions. A foreshadowing of this idea is to be found in John Stuart Mill's *Principles of Political Economy*, IV.7, 'On the Probable Futurity of the Labouring Classes', and in his posthumous 'Chapters on Socialism'. See Mill, 1987a: 752-94; and OL 222-79; cf. Ashcraft in Rosenblum, 1991: ch. 6.

Talk of 'phases' needs to be taken with a reservation. Although historically the utopians were followed by the Marxists, who preceded the state socialists, who were succeeded by market socialists, none of these socialist schools has run dry. All remain as streams of tendency and influence within the socialist movement.

In face of such untamed liveliness, as with conservatism and liberalism, nobody should be tempted to foist a set of necessary and sufficient conditions on socialism – as well try to clamp a saddle on Pegasus. The point remains that there are typical features of socialist thought. Broadly following Berki, 1975: ch. 2 but altering some of his labels, we can identify the following four:

- egalitarianism as a requirement of justice
- liberationism
- rationalism
- communitarianism and public participation

These features are typical in two ways. Historically they have been influential in the socialist tradition; also in our political culture they are part of the image of socialism. Before we discuss them, however, there is a complication to notice. Socialism has the peculiarity that, within its diversities, one of its variants, namely marxism, is virtually an ideology in its own right. Marxism is a part of the socialist tradition but it is so distinctive, developed and sophisticated a part that it deserves to be taken separately. The plan is as follows. In the next section I will briefly introduce marxism; then, as our main discussion of socialism proceeds, tracking the four typical features one by one, at each stage I will sketch in a sub-section marxism's special angle on the topics in hand.

31.1 Marxism

'Marxist' and 'marxism' are here confined mainly to the ideas and writings of Karl Marx (1818-1883). Be warned, however, that, in face of representations of his views, Marx said that he was no marxist.

More widely, 'marxism' includes the elaboration and recasting of Marx's ideas by a highly numerous class of later writers. Particular mention should be made of Eduard Bernstein (1850-1932), Karl Kautsky (1854-1938), Vladimir Ilyich Lenin (1870-1924), Rosa Luxemburg (1870-1919), Grigory Lukács (1885-1971), and Antonio Gramsci (1891-1937) along with, in more recent times, Herbert Marcuse (1898-1979), Theodor Adorno (1903-69), Louis Althusser (1918-90), and Jürgen Habermas (b. 1929). Current 'analytical' marxism, represented diversely by G.A. Cohen, Jon Elster, John Roemer, Adam Przeworski, Erik Olin Wright, and Philippe Van Parijs, is an attempt to present and develop Marx's ideas with the clarity and rigour of analytical philosophical method.

'Marxism' also has an institutional reference, especially to the regimes which, for a large slice of the twentieth century until 1991, dominated Russia and Eastern Europe and which still prevail in parts of the Far East.

The recovery of Marx's social and political theory presents two problems. We need to negotiate but not to resolve them in the kind of introductory discussion offered in this book. The first problem is that Marx produced no single work containing a full statement of his central and most characteristic views, namely his:

- critique of religion, philosophy, and reformist politics
- theory of history
- analysis of the capitalist economy
- account of bourgeois society and the state
- down-to-earth guidelines for the workers' movement and revolutionary action

Instead we have to turn to a variety of writings, the most famous of which is *The Communist Manifesto*, co-authored with Friedrich Engels and published in 1848. (For Engels without Marx, talent without genius, see Arthur, 1996, reviewed in Diamanti, 1998, and I. Hunt, 1997.) Almost as famous as the *Manifesto* is *Capital*. To the task of writing this huge book Marx said that he had 'sacrificed my life, my happiness, and my family'. The first volume appeared in 1867. Two further volumes, compilations from Marx's manuscripts, were published posthumously in 1885 and 1894 respectively.

Earlier than *Capital* is *The German Ideology*, another work written with Engels, produced in 1845-6 but not published until 1935. Earlier yet are the *Economic and Philosophic Manuscripts of 1844*, unpublished until 1927. *A Contribution to the Critique of Political Economy*, published in 1859, succinctly states many of Marx's best-known doctrines. It is a sketch drawn from a larger picture, the *Grundrisse der Kritik der Politischen Oekonomie* (*Foundations of the Critique of Political Economy*, usually just called the *Grundrisse*) of 1857-58, not published until 1939-41. It may be mentioned that 'critique' in Marx generally means the refutation of views and arguments, not by flat-out external assault, but through internal criticism, showing that they contain incoherent assumptions or involve inconsistent consequences.

A range of pamphlets, articles, and memoranda also spreads sharp light over Marx's ideas. 'On the Jewish Question' and 'Contribution to the Critique of Hegel's *Philosophy of Right*', both dating from 1844, are of leading importance. Then at least the three great pamphlets on French politics should be singled out: *The Class Struggles in France* (1850), *The Eighteenth Brumaire of Louis Bonaparte* (1852), and *The Civil War in France* (1871).

Marx is a writer of contrasts. He can be vivid, pungent, and epigrammatic. Yet much of his work has an opaque atmosphere, hardly thick enough to be termed a fog but sufficiently dense to be inconvenient.

So much for the first problem, that of the lack of a single major text. The second problem is one of periodisation. Marx's anti-capitalist critique varied over time. Karl Löwith was right that Marx engaged capitalism philosophically in his *Contribution to the Critique of Hegel's Philosophy of Right* (1844), politically in *The Communist Manifesto* (1848), and economically in *Capital* (1867: Löwith, 1934-35: 235). Althusser fixed on key stages along a more clearly developmental direction (Œglart, 1970: 108):

- 1840-44   works of Marx's apprenticeship
- 1845   works of Marx's intellectual coming of age
- 1845-57   works of Marx's maturation
- 1857-83   works of Marx's maturity

My account of marxism accommodates Marx's central and most characteristic views, regardless of the precise period to which they belong or the texts from which they are drawn. This is how I negotiate the two problems.

A word of caution before we move on. Discussion of Marxism is nowadays clouded by the experience of 'the collapse of socialism' in the late 1980s and early 1990s. Many students feel that Marxism has been refuted by the logic of events. This verdict goes too far.

It is unclear how far the political systems of Eastern Europe and the former Soviet Union were genuine versions of Marxist politics (Plamenatz, 1954). It is also not clear to what extent their fall is to be explained by any kind of self-refutation on Marxism's part, though John Gray's point should be noted that these systems represented a triumph of the political over the economic, of 'superstructure' over 'base' in language shortly to be explained, which should have been impossible on Marx's own account: Gray in Mount, 1992: 219-20. I suggest a reply to this point in §31.4.1. All this aside, I shall examine Marxism as a body of ideas without heeding its fortunes in practical politics.

My overall assessment of Marx's theory of history and society, for anybody interested in a personal reaction, is threefold. As diagnosis, with its account of exploitation, alienation and estrangement, it remains a powerful tool: *de nobis fabula narratur*, it is to our own story that we are listening. As prescription, in the form of a policy science enabling us to intervene effectively in social formations/processes to achieve liberation, its credentials are thin. As prognosis, with its predictive theory or speculative philosophy (§3.2) of history, its success is limited. Despite this, Marx is the only genius the social sciences have produced.

I take up now the four typical features of socialist thought highlighted in §31: egalitarianism, liberationism, rationalism, and communitarianism plus public participation. I will take these features one by one, adding to the discussion of each feature a sub-section on its specifically marxist construction.

31.2 Egalitarianism

Recall that John Gray identified egalitarianism as a typical feature of liberal thought (§30). But there is a difference between socialism and liberalism. Gray characterised liberal egalitarianism in the following terms. Liberalism is:

> *egalitarian*, inasmuch as it confers on all men the same moral status and denies the relevance to legal or political order of differences in moral worth among human beings

While socialist egalitarianism is no less than this, it is also more. Socialists have traditionally insisted that where wide differences of power, wealth or status prevail, liberal legal and political equality yields only 'empty' or 'formal' rights and freedoms. This criticism assumes the liberalism of abstract individualism rather than the new or social liberalism' of Green. Another point is that the insistence on rights as claims and immunities against other people (§19.1), has been widely regarded by socialists as anti-communitarian (Levine, 1988: 146-52). Marx berated natural rights as 'nothing but the rights of ... egoistic man, man separated from other men and from the community' (PKM: 107).

Where liberals have pressed for equality beyond the limits of merely political and legal equality, they have generally stopped at equality of opportunity in one or other of its forms. This is because, to go beyond equality of opportunity to the next likely option, namely maximum equal well-being (§18.1), is to risk moving into the realm of objectivist assumptions about real interests which liberalism, certainly in its main twentieth-century versions, is wary of entering (§30.5).

In the socialist tradition there has been a greater readiness to identify people's real interests and hence to think in terms of maximum equal well-being; this is clearly so in the case of Marx, whose views will be examined shortly (§31.3.1). That aside, there is a strong sense within the socialist movement that, whatever differences of wealth, status, power or opportunity might be justifiable in an improved society, the present distribution of these goods between individuals and groups is without legitimacy. Socialists, moving down a level from the categories of liberal abstract individualism to historically and socially more specific descriptions concerning people's wealth, their privileges, their status and so on, have seen the systematic removal of arbitrary inequalities as a requirement of justice:

> Some forms of egalitarianism certainly are silly, objectionable and hazardous. A society which insisted on regarding all its members with equal respect and patience irrespective of the character of their actions would not be so much deplorable as simply incomprehensible – it would also be extremely short-lived. Any real society requires effort and restraint of its members; and the actual members of any real society will vary dramatically both in their capacity for restraint or effort and in the use which they elect to make of these capacities. ... Where the value of equality does play a major and a more cogent role in specifying a

socialist conception of the good is not as the overall goal of social organization. Rather, it is in the systematic criticism of arbitrariness in the distribution of social, economic or political advantages. In this context, as the trajectory of western political and social theory since the sixteenth century makes very evident, egalitarian principles possess considerable critical power. The demand for justification in terms of right or contribution has been levelled against one feature after another of the feudal political, economic and social order of late medieval Europe and one feature after another has duly succumbed to its ideological impetus. The main brunt of the attack has fallen upon the possession of privileges which cannot plausibly be represented as earned by the efforts or attainments of their possessor: privileges of political choice, or social status or inherited wealth (Dunn, 1984: 8-9).

The arbitrary distribution of advantages is generally taken to be mainly due to exploitative property relationships, especially the private ownership of the means of production. This viewpoint is most systematically developed in Marx.

31.2.1 Marxism and egalitarianism

If we think of socialist egalitarianism, running on equality of opportunity, on maximum equal well-being or on the systematic removal of arbitrary inequalities, as a requirement of justice, matters become more complex when we look at Marx. Marxism's relation to justice, in fact to morality in general, leads so often to misconception. We need to tread carefully, for the evidence pulls in contrary directions.

In the first place, many see marxism as a determinist philosophy, and there are well-known questions about the compatibility of determinism and moral judgement or responsibility (§23.2). Secondly, there is the textual explicitness of Marx's dismissal in the *Critique of the Gotha Programme* of 'obsolete verbal rubbish' and 'ideological nonsense about right' (PKM 541). We can add to this the point that 'The moment anyone started to talk to Marx about morality, he would roar with laughter' (Vorlander in Lukes, 1985: 27).

To be offset against this is Marx's ethically-laden language of capitalist 'exploitation' and his readiness to talk of 'theft' and 'robbery' in discussing the extraction of surplus value. How are we to negotiate Marx's apparently divided attitude?

Marx's determinism is a tricky issue. He is widely taken to be a historical determinist, charting the play of iron laws of history. His language sometimes suggests this, the language for instance of the first German edition of *Capital* where Marx talks of 'tendencies working with iron necessity towards inevitable results' (PKM 434). But 'tendencies' and 'necessity' are an odd juxtaposition which should give us pause. In any case, even if there is a law-governed, non-random, non-accidental direction to human history by which one stage succeeds another, it does not follow that at the level of individual action, the prime focus of moral responsibility, no one can do otherwise than they do. We will look at Marx's theory of history in §31.4.1.

The determinist interpretation can, however, draw on other sources. Of principal importance is Marx's Sixth Thesis on Feuerbach: 'the essence of man is no abstraction inherent in each separate individual. In its reality it is the *ensemble* (aggregate) of social relations' (PKM 157). I take Marx's meaning to be that human beings are the products of society in the sense that their attitudinal states and behavioural characteristics are socially and historically context-dependent (cf. Geras, 1983: ch. 2). This, which is in all but name our 'social holism' of §2.6.2, represents a kind of determinism, reflected further in the Preface to the first German edition of *Capital* where Marx says: 'My standpoint ... can less than any other make the individual responsible for relations whose creature he socially remains, however much he may subjectively raise himself above them' (PKM 435-6).

But we need to be careful in reading off implications. For Marx also holds that we have a 'species-being', an essential nature which identifies us as distinctively human. At the heart of that nature is the need for free, creative activity. This is not the natural language of a determinist viewpoint. Moreover, the social origin of my language, beliefs, knowledge and the rest does not automatically entail that I am not morally responsible for my actions.

My own view is that Marx never fully worked out his ideas on determinism at the level of individual action. There is not sufficient evidence, when he talks deterministically, to exclude a moral perspective from his work.

What, though, of Marx's apparently explicit repudiation of moral judgement? Here again matters are less straightforward than they appear at first sight. Marx was sure that capitalism depends on causal mechanisms, resting on entrenched social relationships of power and exploitation, which resist the impact of moral denunciation. Capitalism will not fall, Jericho-like, before trumpet blasts of moral indignation. This is so, not least because among the mechanisms that support it is an ideological morality which ensures that capitalists and even workers will see the relevant social relationships as ethically valid: employers have the right to hire and fire, the right to a profit on their investments, and so on. Such beliefs, however sincerely held, are forms of 'false consciousness', because they rest on an incorrect understanding or interpretation of the social context and, to recall a notion from way back (§§12.2, 13.3.2), of real human interests. None the less, as part of an entrenched mind-set, they are likely to be highly effective against talk of the evils of capitalism. These claims are a curtain-raiser for the discussion of ideology, which follows in §31.4.1.

Exploitation for Marx is principally a matter of the extraction of surplus value. Marx's theory of surplus value is a part of his general theory of value; it fits in as follows. A traditional distinction is made between use-value and exchange-value. A commodity's use-value is its efficiency in satisfying a want or range of wants. Exchange-value, Marx's main interest, is the relative value of commodities against a common measure. The obvious measure is money but Marx looks elsewhere, to labour input. On Marx's account the market value of a commodity, the price at which it can sell vis-à-vis other commodities, is a reflection of the amount of labour that has gone to produce it.

But what of slackers who spin out their hours? They cannot thereby automatically increase the price at which their products can sell. Marx handles this objection by calling up the idea of 'socially necessary labour' time. If we abstract from such special circumstances and go for the average there is, he thinks, a broad comparability between price and labour input. This part of Marx's theory has always drawn a sharp fire of criticism and it now has few defenders.

Not much of his theory of exploitation actually depends on it, however. For that theory relies on the claim that non-workers, i.e. capitalists who are able to work, share in the returns on workers' labour products; they do not produce but take unfair advantage of those who do. For all the argumentative detail that Marx weaves round the idea of exploitation, there is at the centre of it a simple sense that those who can work ought to do so and not derive unfair benefits from the work of direct producers. How far this moral intuition illuminates the workings of capitalism is another matter; it highlights the shareholder who has no productive part in a business but not the 'working capitalist' or the worker who holds shares in the company. (Surplus value is also extracted by the state in the form of taxes, though this is not a matter to which Marx pays much direct attention (C. Barker, 1997: 59).)

Marx embodies his moral intuition in his formula for socialist justice: 'to each proportionately to their labour contribution', but that formula is easily misunderstood in what it presupposes. Many think that Marx is endorsing the so-called 'Labour Principle': 'to each according to their labour product', i.e. that view that each worker has the right to that product. This has strong resonances of Locke's idea that one is entitled to appropriate that with which one has mixed one's labour (§20.2.2). In a way Marx is endorsing the Labour Principle, but only for the first stage in the transition from capitalism. What socialist justice will do is to ensure that workers get the benefit of their labour product, and that capitalists do not. This is a moral advance in Marx's view, but it is still a highly imperfect state of affairs.

It contains two flaws. Its basic injustice is that what workers are able to contribute is partly dependent on morally irrelevant differences of talent, ability, aptitude, however we express it (cf. Rawls on the collective ownership of natural abilities (§17.3)). Here is Marx on the subject:

> But one man is superior to another physically or mentally and so supplies more labour in the same time, or can labour for a longer time ... This equal right is an unequal right for unequal labour ... [I]t tacitly recognises unequal individual endowment and thus productive capacity as natural privileges (PKM 540).

The other flaw in socialist justice is that it embodies an individualistic, 'bourgeois' morality, with its fixed focus on the individual person with his or her rights within a culture of predominant self-interest. This is an aspect of Marx's communitarianism (§31.5.1; cf. §29.5). It is expressed when he observes that socialist justice is 'stigmatised by a bourgeois limitation' (PKM 540).

In the second stage of the transition from capitalism, the 'higher phase of communist society' (PKM 541), a different type of justice will prevail. Its formula will be: 'From each according to his ability, to each according to his needs' (ibid.). With a different psychology produced by the end of exploitation and (its inseparable attendants) alienation and estrangement, people will voluntarily work according to their abilities. There will be no inclination 'to calculate with the coldheartedness of a Shylock whether one has not worked half an hour more than somebody else, whether one is not getting less pay than somebody else – this narrow horizon will then be crossed' (Lenin, 1969: 165). Moreover, the legacy of capitalism will be a post-scarcity world made possible by a technology of abundance. So there will be no need, to quote Lenin again, 'for society to regulate the quantity of products to be received by each; each will take freely "according to his needs" ' (Lenin, 1969: ibid.).

This is an attractive vision, millennial in its sunny optimism. One's confidence in its plausibility will depend on the view one takes of competitive self-interest as a spur to work and also of the malleability of human psychology. Further aspects of Marx's psychological views will emerge when we discuss his liberationism (§31.3.1).

For further discussion of this section's topics see Campbell, 1988: ch. 7; Chitty, 1993; Gould, 1980: ch. 5; Ollman, 1971: 43-51; Roemer, 1988; Wood in Mepham & Ruben, 1981: ch. 6. A short, focused and excellent account of Marx on justice is available in S. White, 1996. On Marx's relation to Locke see Lloyd Thomas, 1995: 90; again S. White, 1996: 91-6. The theory of surplus value is also a part of Marx's theory of history. Exploitative modes of production such as feudalism and capitalism differ in 'the form in which surplus is pumped out of direct producers' (C. Barker, 1997: 43).

31.3 Liberationism

Unjust inequality is not all that is amiss, according to the socialist view of society. A standard socialist assumption is that, relative to human potentiality, the existing political, social and economic order is deviant and pathological. The point is not simply that an improved society is conceivable and attainable. Rather, something (or a whole diversity of things) has gone wrong in the course of human history, and needs to be remedied.

The evil concerns not only the distribution of wealth, status, power and opportunity. It also has a dimension of moral psychology. The psychological qualities of human beings are less and lower than they could and should be. People are subject to estrangement, a tendency to harmful competitiveness, and other undesirable traits from which a socialist order will liberate them. This involves an idea of positive freedom (§22.4). The key to current human psychology lies in a social structure with an economic base that fails to meet the egalitarian requirements of justice.

As in the case of justice and equality, the root of the problem is an economic order based on exploitative property relationships. In Marxism there is a distinctive, 'dialectical materialist' story to be told about the course of human history and how it has produced this outcome. An equally distinctive story comes from Christian socialism and liberation theology with their messages of Fall and Redemption, individual and social. On the secular side, Rousseau's speculative anthropology in DI (1755) is particularly congenial to socialist thinking (§22.4; cf. Springborg in R. Fitzgerald, 1980).

31.3.1 Marxism and liberationism

On Marx's account capitalism is exploitative, involving the appropriation of surplus value. It also involves two further phenomena – alienation (*Entäusserung*) and estrangement (*Entfremdung*). Under capitalism the worker is compelled, i.e. has no realistic option but, to alienate his or her own labour in exchange for wages. When, in legal terminology, I alienate a property to another, I completely transfer all ownership of that property. The same thing happens with regard to labour under capitalism; I surrender my labour to my employer, who now owns it. I am accordingly estranged both from the product of my labour, which becomes my employer's property, and from the activity of work, which I have sold as labour. Along with this estrangement goes a mistrustful psychology in which each person tries to get the best deal in their relations with others, the Shylock mentality which Lenin identified above.

In the background of this anti-capitalist account is Marx's idea of human flourishing, his substantive theory of the good. The relevant part of this theory, already glimpsed in Marx's stress on free, creative activity, is well-caught in the following quotation from R.P. Wolff when he refers to:

> a ... tradition, going back to Aristotle and finding its most powerful expression in the writings of the young Marx, according to which creative, productive, rational *activity* is the good for men. Consumption is essential to life; its gratifications form a component of the good life when properly integrated into a healthy and well-ordered psyche. But consumption is not, and cannot be, the end for man. For Marx ... labour of the right sort is an indispensable element of the good life (R.P. Wolff, 1977: 208-9).

Labour of the right sort is precisely what capitalism cannot provide:

> Supposing that we had produced in a human manner; in his production each of us would

have doubly affirmed himself and his fellow men. (1) I would have objectified in my production my individuality and its peculiarity, and would thus have enjoyed in my activity an individual expression of my life and would have also had – in looking at the object – the individual pleasure of realizing that my personality was objective, visible to the senses and therefore a power raised beyond all doubt; (2) in your enjoyment or use of my product I would have had the direct enjoyment of realizing that by my work I had both satisfied a human need and also objectified the human essence and therefore fashioned for another human being the object that had met his need. ... In such a situation our products would be like so many mirrors, each one reflecting our essence. Thus, in this relationship what occurred on my side would also occur on yours. My work would be a free expression of my life, and therefore a free enjoyment of my life. In work the peculiarity of my individuality would have been affirmed since it is my individual life. Work would thus be genuine active property (Marx, *Comments on James Mill's Elements of Political Economy*, 1844; cited in Kitching, 1988: 131-2).

None of this is possible under conditions of capitalist alienation and estrangement. What I produce, how I produce it, and the use made of what I produce, are all beyond my control under those conditions. Everything is down to what my employer, or alternative employers, decide. Marx has a particular animus against the capitalist division of labour by which work is atomised into distinct, segregated tasks to which workers are exclusively assigned. To Marx's mind, the principle of the division of labour, though celebrated in the opening chapters of Adam Smith's *The Wealth of Nations* (1776), the first modern textbook of economic theory, treats the worker as a tool. A passage in *The German Ideology* celebrates the end of this regime under communism:

as soon as the distribution of labour comes into being, each man has a particular, exclusive sphere of activity, which is forced upon him and from which he cannot escape. He is a hunter, a fisherman, a shepherd, or a critical critic, and must remain so if he does not want to lose his means of livelihood; while in communist society, where nobody has one exclusive sphere of activity but each can become accomplished in any branch he wishes, society regulates the general production and thus makes it possible for me to do one thing today and another tomorrow, to hunt in the morning, fish in the afternoon, rear cattle in the evening, criticise after dinner, just as I have a mind, without ever becoming hunter, fisherman, shepherd or critic (Marx & Engels, 1965: 44-5).

In Marx's view only a system of public ownership of the means of production will deliver the conditions for the kind of spontaneous, creative, productive activity that he envisages. Reflection suggests, however, that such ownership is not a sufficient condition for the kind of labour that Marx wants to see. We will consider this side of his economic thinking in §31.4.1.

A connected point is that since exploitation, alienation, and estrangement are the centrally important things from which human beings need to be freed, there is a distinction to be drawn between 'human' and 'political' emancipation. Marx uses this contrast in *On the Jewish Question* (PKM 96-114) to criticise the idea that political reform such as universal suffrage, representative democracy, political and civil liberties of all kinds, will produce the changes he wants to see in society's economic base. Given his predominant view that political power reflects economic power, over which it has no significant control, Marx regarded reformism, political emancipation, as an irrelevance to the real task of human emancipation. The time for effective political action will come when the economic conditions are right for revolutionary intervention by the proletariat, the main body of workers (Harding, 1998).

Truly important political emancipation awaits the conditions of communism under which the state will 'wither away'. 'So long as the state exists', remarked Lenin, 'there is no freedom' (Lenin, 1969: 163). The state is functional to class conflict, as we will see in §31.4.1. Since communism means a classless society, the state will have no role to play; it will step quietly into history. Not all socialists sympathetic to Marx has been able to subscribe to this scenario. G.D.H. Cole refers to:

> the destiny of the State, after the revolution had consolidated itself, to 'wither away.' But this assumes that, when there is but one class left in society, or rather no classes at all, there will be no difference of views deep enough to make one group wish to coerce another. It assumes the solidarity of the class, and consequently the solidarity of the whole society when classes no longer exist, to a degree which I cannot believe in (Cole, 1947: 638).

Cole is correct against Marx in this respect at least. Marx does not claim, or at any rate argue, that with the passing of capitalism all sources of human individual and group conflict will be removed. All that will happen in the future communist society is that certain basic and humanly impoverishing conflicts based on exploitation, alienation, and estrangement will cease. There is nothing to prevent Cole's deep differences of views from continuing and requiring a state apparatus for their containment. Cf. Elster, 1985: 401; Plamenatz, 1963, II: 373-83; Schwarzmantel, 1987: ch. 3.

For further reading on the nature, causes, and forms of alienation, see Plamenatz, 1975: chs. 4-6, 8 & 11. But note that Baxter, 1982: 127-9 is more reliable than Plamenatz on the distinction between alienation and estrangement; see also Ollman, 1971; Holloway, 1997; Walliman, 1981. We will return to Marx's views on the state in capitalist society in §31.4.1. On the link between freedom and creativity, see O'Sullivan, 1998: 82-3.

31.4 Rationalism

While there is spirited controversy among socialists on the remedial action needed to secure equality as a requirement of justice, and to gain liberation, socialist theory has regularly assumed that projects of social change can be planned, carried out by successive steps, with reliable foresight, on a large scale. Hence the term, 'large-scale social engineering', applied by one of its keenest critics, Karl Popper (see Popper, 1957; Shearmur, 1990). This is rationalism in the sense of an assumption that society is open to conscious, efficient alteration according to plan. Here the socialist makes exactly the opposite assumption to the conservative. Rewinding to §29.1, we note:

> the first characteristic of conservative thought, the sceptical idea that we do not have a predictive science of politics. Large-scale social planning is always a leap in the dark. Society is simply too complex; too many variables, local and ephemeral, are at work for us to be able to practise what Marx called exuberantly the 'revolutionary reconstitution of society at large'. Aims are only incompletely accomplished, and unforeseen side-effects always make the results markedly different from the initial intention.

A common idea has been that to accomplish the changes necessary for a socialist transformation of society, an economic order must be in place with the following features:

- public ownership of the means of production
- central planning, controlling the extent and direction of economic growth
- a market for consumer goods (though not necessarily 'consumer sovereignty')
- prices fixed by the central planning agency

We can call these the full conditions of economic socialism. Some of the rationale for such an economic order is spelt out in the following passage:

> Under socialism, capitalist private ownership of the means of production is replaced by social ownership; the operation of market forces is replaced by socialist economic planning. Social ownership enables exploitation to be abolished; socialist economic planning enables the anarchy of production to be replaced by conscious social control of the economy. The two dimensions are connected in that market forces operate through the interaction of numerous separate decisions over the use of discrete parcels of society's productive forces, which are therefore de facto privately owned whatever the de jure position, whereas economic planning involves a single set of co-ordinated decisions over the use of society's productive resources as a whole, which necessarily precludes private ownership and fragmented decision making (Adaman & Devine, 1997: 54-5)

Yet public ownership and central planning have run aground in recent socialist thinking. They have suffered by comparison with an ideal market in which, under perfect competition, resource allocation is Pareto-efficient: for a given set of consumer wants and preferences, expressed in effective demand, it will be impossible to move to another allocation that makes some people better off without making anyone worse off. But (1) perfect competition is a fantasy; (2) wants and preferences are answerable to a theory of well-being (§18.1); (3) some persons may be too poor to express their wants and preferences in effective demand; and (4) others may deserve to be made worse off because their current holdings are unjust. So much for the ideal market; two factors are more relevant to the appraisal of public ownership and central planning. Both are closely connected with the work of the Austrian economist and political theorist, F.A. Hayek.

One is the perception that, given public ownership and central planning, the state embodies an overpowering, freedom-damaging concentration of power. The other is the epistemological critique of planning (Hayek, 1948; commentary in Butler, 1985: ch. 3). Alec Nove also deserves mention. Nove was keen to point out that the autocratic-cum-bureaucratic nature of planning, most evident in Soviet-style economies, is not the key problem. Suppose that, by whatever criteria (direct, representative or deliberative), we democratise the process. Still an epistemological barrier arises:

> Nove liked to ask, how can workers vote on how many ball-bearings to produce, or what kinds? Or on how much sulphuric acid, and by when? And so on. 'Obviously', said Nove, the centre can never know all the myriad needs, as well as capacities at the base, or know them in time. So rational planning cannot be top-down, by command. It requires constant feedback from the base, information on productivity and changes in capacity. It requires, furthermore, unplanned spontaneous initiative at the grass-roots to constantly correct central planners. In short, '*the centre does not know* just what it is that needs doing, in disaggregated detail, while management in its situation *cannot know* what it is that society needs unless the centre informs it.' So economic planning must inevitably founder on this intractable epistemological dilemma (Eyal, Szelényi & Townsley, 1997: 39).

The reply is swiftly forthcoming. Eyal and his fellow contributors comment:

> Nove is certainly right that the centre should not have to micro-manage every detail of the economy 'specifying every journey of every lorry'. That would be absurd. But an intelligent, informed citizenry can vote on broad priorities – whether to build nuclear power or solar power, or take stronger measures to conserve power. Whether to make private cars or public transit the mainstay of urban transport. Whether to fish tuna to extinction. Whether to cut down the last of the old-growth forest to make cedar desks for suburbanites,

disposable chip-board furniture, paper towels and phone books. I see no practical reason why ordinary citizens cannot make such decisions. To plan in this way does not require that ordinary citizens have total and instant knowledge of every aspect of an impossibly complicated economy. They can vote on priorities and leave the details to technicians – that's what capitalists do (Eyal, Szelényi & Townsley, 1997: 40; cf. B. Frankel, 1985 and Nove 1985).

This reply is fine from one point of view. It outlines a coherent possibility which escapes the epistemological dilemma. But then, we ought to recall the problematics of technical expertise that came to light in our discussion of Berlin at the start of the book (§2.3). Scepticism about an informed, intelligent citizenry is also important, as is the mixed motivation problem, both of which were important in our examination of democracy (§23.4.2.2).

You need to adjudicate this see-saw of argument for yourself. For now, let us consider a socialist option which:

- rejects central planning, and therefore
- does not have prices fixed by a central planning agency
- does have public ownership of the means of production, but licenses out the means of production to workers' producer co-operatives, which compete in
- a consumer goods market

This is 'market socialism'. The assumption is that the objectives of equality as a requirement of justice, of liberation, and of public participation and communitarianism can either be promoted by market mechanisms or at least are not incompatible with them.

There are two central problems. The first is that there appears to be a tension between socialist communitarianism, with its rejection of a restless, acquisitive spirit of predominant self-interest, and an embracing of the market, which has just such a culture as its natural setting. The point is sociological rather than logical; logically it is perfectly possible for successful market operators to be motived largely by a desire to devote all their profits to charity. Sociologically, by contrast, the evidence points in a rather different direction.

The second problem is that it is not plausible to expect a socialist society to run on a wholly or predominantly market economy. The reason lies in the nature of socialism and the nature of markets. Take Marx's formulas of justice, which have enjoyed wide support in the socialist movement: 'to each proportionately to their labour contribution' and 'from each according to his ability, to each according to his needs'. These are in Nozickian terms 'patterned' principles (§17.4); they specify end-states that meet these descriptions. But the market, as F.A. Hayek never tired of insisting, produces a 'spontaneous order' (§30.4), of winners and losers, which cannot be guaranteed to satisfy any such particular descriptions as Marx's or anybody else's formulas lay down.

There is the further point, with regard to Marx's second formula, that the market responds not to needs (construed on whatever model of well-being (§18.1)) but to effective demand – to the willingness and ability to pay. A socialist economy would have to 'house' institutions and agencies that provided, funded or subsidised where there was (as why should there not be?) a gap between the fulfilment of needs and the satisfaction of effective demand.

On market socialism see further B. Frankel, 1985; Levine, 1988: 110-20; Miller, 1977 & 1989; also Miller in Reeve, 1987: ch. 8; Nove, 1985; Self in Goodin & Pettit, 1995: 345-7; A. Vincent, 1992: 109-12.

31.4.1 Marxism and rationalism

Marx believed in the full conditions of economic socialism outlined in the last section: public ownership of the means of production, a planned economy and the rest. This side of his thought is well-covered in J. Wolff, 1992. At a level of generality one can see how public ownership removes exploitation; there are no capitalist non-workers to extract surplus value from workers. Alienation and estrangement are removed by the self-managing nature of socialist enterprises, while central planning prepares the ground for the second, key part of Marx's formula of communist justice: 'to each according to his needs'. How the division of labour, one of Marx's bugbears, is to disappear in a complex modern economy requiring specialist skills, is never made clear. The full conditions of economic socialism do not appear sufficient to end the division of labour. On this point compare O'Hagan in Mepham & Ruben, 1981: 99-103 with Plamenatz, 1975: 169-72. Note also Walliman, 1981. Marx's hostility to the division of labour was shared, incidentally, by William Morris (1834-96) in *News from Nowhere* (1890; cf. §6.2). Since Morris was one of the contemned 'utopian socialists', the agreement had perhaps better not be pressed.

Marx's belief that the economy can be remodelled comprehensively so as to achieve socialist objectives, is an aspect of his rationalism. A further aspect is his view that human history has an underlying intelligibility. Its past course and future direction can, within limits, be penetrated by reason; and Marx's socialism in making this penetration is 'scientific'.

The older commentators represented Marx as a believer in iron laws of history, a rigid and comprehensive economic determinism. At any time, every social phenomenon (from diplomatic events and legal decisions down to the most trivial interpersonal motivation) is to be explained economically; and across time, the coming to be and passing away of every historical stage is causally determined by economic events, in accordance with laws which, of necessity, admit of no exception. So Marx was presented.

But in the first place he certainly did not believe that every least diplomatic event, legal decision or personal motivation is economically pre-determined. His claim was that economic structures, turning on the 'forces of production', provide the ultimate explanation of the rest of the social system: 'More than this neither Marx nor I have ever asserted' (Engels in Marx & Engels, 1942: 475).

What Marx's economic determinism amounts to, across time, is the view that *from the stage of feudalism* onwards there is an inherent tendency, which will not be defeated overall and in the long run, for an ordered sequence of changes to occur – for feudalism to pass over into capitalism, for capitalism to yield place to socialism, and for socialism to be superseded finally by communism. We will examine this pattern of historical change shortly.

Marx did suppose that economic structures basically determine the rest of the social system. Changes in the 'forces of production' (mainly raw materials, skills, and technology) induce new patterns of ownership, 'relations of production' as Marx calls them, without which they cannot be fully used. 'The hand-mill gives you society with the feudal system; the steam-mill, society with the industrial capitalist' (Marx, quoted in Heilbroner, 1970: 147). The social system changes non-accidentally to accommodate the new relations of production.

In Marx's writings, and even more in those of his collaborator, Friedrich Engels, this process is set against a whole philosophy of nature – dialectical and historical materialism. (The phrase does not derive from Marx himself, but from Engels.) The idea is that throughout nature, change comes about by the successive and progressive struggle of opposites, 'thesis' and 'antithesis' producing a 'synthesis' which in turn becomes a new thesis. The influences of Hegel (§3.5.4) and Darwin are equal in this area of marxist thought.

That is the dialectical side of dialectical materialism. The historical side is the pattern that Marx thinks he can identify in human history, the development of successive economic systems, of which the latest is capitalism. Historical materialism is only 'materialist' in its stress on the economic; Marx is not committed to the metaphysical view that all that exists is matter or states of matter. See further Ruben, 1977 and Lenin, 1947.

Marx's finer-grained account of the historical dialectic is that the relevant struggle of opposites is that between social classes. Hence the famous opening lines of *The Communist Manifesto* (1848):

> The history of all hitherto existing society is the history of class struggles. Freeman and slave, patrician and plebeian, lord and serf, guildmaster and journeyman – in a word oppressor and oppressed, stood in constant opposition to one another, carried on an uninterrupted, now hidden, now open fight (PKM 203-4).

Marxist social classes are defined in terms of relationship to the forces of production. Those who own those forces constitute the dominant class. Their ownership enables them to extract surplus value from direct producers, i.e. the proletariat, or working class, who do not own any (significant) forces of production but must sell their labour in order to live – or at least, even under the welfare state, to live well. Later Marxist analysis has recognised the need to distinguish between the (private) ownership and the (managerial) control of capital. This only complicates, without invalidating, Marx's concept of a dominant class. See Miliband, 1973: ch. 2.

Marx claims that the dominant class uses the state as supreme power, pseudo-legitimate under the false appearance of promoting the public interest or the common good, to maintain its rule. This it does partly through its control of the economy and partly through a socially pervasive ideological false consciousness or mind-set (see below) which fixes the scope and limits of political action in line with its interests. The modern state is the product of a class-divided society; and it is set to 'wither away' when, under communism, there is only one social class. There will be no more class conflicts for the state to 'manage'. We noted Cole's scepticism that the end of class conflict will necessarily mean the end of the state (§31.3.1; on marxist classes in general, see G.A. Cohen, 1978: 24-6, 69-70, 170-1, 207-15, 241-3; Kitcher, 1988: 151-3, 155-61, 164-85; Plamenatz, 1963, II: 293-322).

The state is one part of the 'superstructure'. Marx uses the metaphor of base and superstructure to represent the relationship of the fundamentally important economic system (of forces of production and patterns of ownership, his version of Hegelian *bürgerliche Gesellschaft* (§14.4)) to the rest of the social system. The superstructure contains, besides the state, the legal system, and (depending on one's interpretation) either (a) all non-economic institutions or (b) all such institutions whose features are explained by the economic base (G.A Cohen, 1979: 216). These are functional to the needs of the dominant class (under capitalism, the *bourgeoisie*), against the interests of the dominated class (the proletariat; on the definition of which see Harding, 1998).

On the (a) interpretation, even where these institutions pre-date capitalism, the fact that they survive and the forms in which they survive are to be explained by this economic functionality. These institutions also have an expressive quality. The law, like the state which issues and enforces it, assumes and expresses a culture of predominant self-interest of the kind which, in the first transition from capitalism, socialist justice has to accommodate (§31.2.1), 'a world of ... egoistic, antagonistic individuals whose relationships it seeks to regulate' (Sypnowich, 1990: 2).

The norms, values, and ideas which keep the superstructure intact and which are in this sense distinct from it – legal, religious, moral, economic beliefs and assumptions and the rest – are 'ideology' in Marx's terminology. Ideology is 'false consciousness' for Marx; it is essentially distortive, a form of miscognition. In the grip of an ideology one makes assumptions about what is good, right, or desirable, and about what is possible. None of this has any objective correlate. The content of an ideology is epistemologically valueless; the 'value' of the ideology is its economic functionality. Ideology, which colours the whole language in which the public interest or common good is thought about and discussed, even by dissentients, primarily serves the interests of the dominant class – which is largely itself taken in by it. Dissentients like Marx are effective only in times of revolutionary transition such as Marx took his own era to be, when base and superstructure become discrepant. Quite how all this functionality arises and operates, Marx never explains, but Marxists will insist on the non-accidentality of (e.g.) the fact that current economic theory, celebrating the 'efficiency' of the market and its embodiment of 'consumer sovereignty', ignores the unequal property relationships on which real-world markets rest and the great differences of power both between consumers and between workers and owners of capital. See further Nielsen in Parel, 1983: 144-5.

Marx claimed in these matters, incidentally, to have turned Hegel rightside-up. The Hegelian dialectic is couched in terms of concepts or ideas embodied in a developing pattern in human institutions and practices (§3.5.4). Marx concentrates on the development of economic institutions and practices that produce (ideological) concepts or ideas.

Here is Marx's own broad account of matters so far. It is taken from the Preface to *A Contribution to the Critique of Political Economy* (1859):

> In the social production of their life, men enter into definite relations that are indispensable and independent of their will; these relations of production correspond to a definite stage of development of their material forces of production. The sum-total of these relations of production constitutes the economic structure of society -- the real foundation, on which rises a legal and political superstructure and to which correspond definite forms of social consciousness. The mode of production of material life determines the social, political and intellectual life process in general. It is not the consciousness of men that determines their being, but, on the contrary, their social being that determines their consciousness (PKM 159-60; cf. Engels, III.2, 1969: 300).

There is, then, an economic base and a dependent superstructure serviced by an ideology, but also there is a dynamic of social change. History is basically the growth of human productive power. The forces of production are continually changing and developing, mainly through technological innovation, and these innovations induce changes in patterns of ownership (the relations of production), which in turn alter the superstructure.

It is easy to gain the impression that, in his theory of history, Marx is taking us through stations on a fixed route. Thus there is 'the Asiatic mode of production' in which, under conditions of great scarcity, governmental control of key resources is necessary (Elster, 1985: 58-9, 274-5). Next comes 'ancient slavery' in which (large populations of) direct producers have no control over their activities. Ancient slavery in turn is followed by feudalism, capitalism, socialism and eventually communism. 'Feudalism' Marx uses as a name for the hierarchical social and economic system, prevalent in Europe between the eleventh and seventeenth centuries, in which relations of service and subordination held between each class and the class above it. Under feudalism the lowest class, the serfs, were not without legal and customary rights but they had no power of independent activity and only a limited entitlement to retain their labour products.

More likely, however, the sequence which is the focus of Marx's intense interest is that from feudalism onwards; and it is within this sequence that the principal lawlike correlations hold. There *may* be a broad and crude directionality from the Asiatic mode of production, through slavery, to feudalism; and I have allowed this to show under the 'Direction of History' arrow in Figure 11. But do not let this dominate your attention. The Asiatic mode of production shows rather the influence of geography on economic structures – Marx instances ancient Egypt, Mesopotamia, India, China, and Peru – than some stage through which all economic systems are likely to pass on their way to a slave-based economy and then feudalism. It is on the sub-set of historical stages – feudalism, capitalism, socialism, communism – that Marx clamps his theory of history. Marx also refers to primitive communism, in which there was common ownership and distribution according to needs. But this formation preceded class-divided society and it plays no significant role in Marx's theory of history.

The changes from feudalism onwards have been, or will be, triggered by a dysfunctionality between the forces of production and patterns of ownership. In the case of capitalism, Marx expressed the emerging failure of fit between forces and patterns by saying that 'The conditions of bourgeois society are too narrow to comprise the wealth created by them' (PKM 210). The immense growth of productive power under capitalism is literally uncontrollable, with ever greater pressure to capture new markets and extend old ones, technological innovation introduced haphazardly without thought of social consequences, trade and stock market crises a commonplace as different parts of the system get out of alignment.

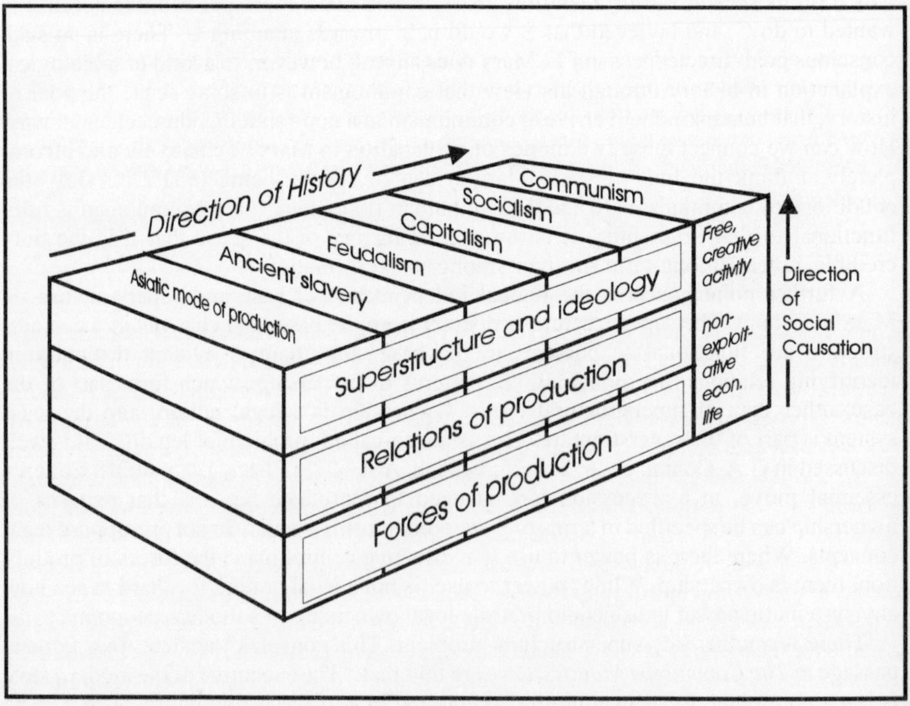

Figure 11. Marx's theory of history and society

Marx expected the exploitation, alienation, estrangement and (his famous false prediction) increasing impoverishment that are inseparable from capitalism to provoke a proletarian revolution ('the dictatorship of the proletariat': PKM 550; Forbes, 1990: 212; Plamenatz, 1963, II: 381-3), the passing of the forces of production into public ownership in the transition to socialism, and eventually the emergence of a classless society under communism – the era of freedom and 'truly human history'. For the revolution to occur, there has to be a shift of consciousness on the part of the proletariat. Though marxist classes are defined in terms of their relationship to the forces of production, an added element of self-consciousness supervenes. The proletariat, in the course of its exploitation by the dominant class, realises its position and potential within society. Already a class 'in itself', it becomes a class 'for itself' (C. Barker, 1997: 44).

In reviewing the present range of ideas, we can only glance at some major points. The first is that, methodologically, Marx's account of the relation of base to superstructure appears to rely on a form of functional explanation (FE). FE explains the recurrence of some event or the persistence of some state of affairs in terms of its being functional, through its consequences, to something or other. Thus in evolutionary biology, where a trait is initially due to random variation, its persistence as a characteristic of the species is to be explained in terms of its functionality to the species' survival. In the same way Marx explains, for example, the emergence of new patterns of ownership as functional to the full use of expanded forces of production. The best discussion of marxist functional explanation is G.A. Cohen, 1978: 160-3, 169-71, 249-96, although Cohen has since switched to the language of consequence explanation (G.A. Cohen, 1982). Cf. Elster, 1985: 27-37, 109-15, 267-72; Scruton, 1983: 183-4. Some of Marx's main functional dependencies are summarised in Figure 11. FE contrasts with teleological explanation, which (in its standard form) identifies goal-directed behaviour: e.g. A did B because A wanted to do C, and believed that B would help towards attaining C. There is no such conscious goal-directedness in FE. Marx does appeal, however, to a kind of teleological explanation in history through his view that communism is in some sense the goal of history, that humankind will arrive at communism in a non-random, non-accidental way. How can we connect these two modes of explanation in Marx? Tentatively and incompletely, I think the link runs via Marx's idea of species-being (§31.2.1). Only the conditions of communism are adequate to human flourishing; only communism is fully functional to that flourishing. It is the goal of history in the sense that it is the only credible, potential long-term survivor among social formations.

A further point concerns the logical independence of base and superstructure on Marx's account. The superstructure is distinct from the base, and changes in the superstructure are functional to changes in the base. But there is evident difficulty in identifying relations of production, i.e. patterns of ownership, which form part of the base, other than in superstructural terms. Ownership is a legal notion; and the legal system is part of the superstructure. This is the so-called 'problem of legality'. It is well discussed in G.A. Cohen, 1978: 217-25; Nozick, ASU: 273; Elster, 1985: 403ff. Cohen's essential move, in a discussion too nuanced to reproduce here, is that patterns of ownership can be specified in terms of power relationships which do not presuppose legal concepts. Where there is power to use (i.e. effective control over) the forces of production, there is ownership. While 'power to use' is not a legal notion, it is hard to see how any systematic power to use could precede legal ownership in a modern economy.

There is another key superstructural problem. This concerns the state. In a famous passage in *The Communist Manifesto* we are told that: 'The executive of the modern state is but a committee for managing the common affairs of the whole bourgeoisie' (PKM 206). In line with the general picture of the relation of superstructure to base, this is a state-dependency thesis. It has two parts. Negatively the state, as part of the superstructure, cannot act (except occasionally by accident or mistake) contrary to the interests of the dominant class, defined in terms of ownership of the forces of production; and positively the state is instrumental to the interests of the dominant class.

Elster, who offers perhaps the best discussion of this part of Marx's theory, suggests that after around 1850 Marx began to see a more autonomous role for the state. As a distinct set of institutions and personnel (§14.1), it had a real capacity for independent action. The clearest acknowledgement of this capacity is made in a passage in *The Eighteenth Brumaire of Louis Bonaparte*, written in the wake of Louis' 1851 *coup d'état* (Louis Bonaparte, 1808-73, was the future Emperor Napoleon III). It will only take a moment to explain Marx's title. Under the French Revolutionary calendar, the Eighteenth Brumaire was the occasion, on 9 November 1799, when Louis' uncle, the great Napoleon, had overturned the republic and established his military dictatorship. History over, now for the text:

> [U]nder the absolute monarchy, during the first revolution and under Napoleon, the bureaucracy was only a means of preparing the class-rule of the bourgeoisie. Under the Restoration, Louis Philippe and the parliamentary republic it became the instrument of the ruling class, strive as it might for independent power. Only under the second Bonaparte does the state seem to have become completely autonomous. The state machine has established itself so securely, as against bourgeois society, that it needs as leader only the head of the Society of December 10 [Louis Bonaparte], a fortune-hunter from foreign parts, chosen as leader by a drunken soldiery bought with drams and sausages (PKM 310-11).

Marx's revised view, accommodating state autonomy, seems closer to the facts than his earlier, complete dependency view. How close it stands to the facts is, as Elster remarks, 'a strictly empirical issue'. But we should recall John Gray's point from §31.1 that the former regimes in Eastern Europe and the Soviet Union revised the entire economic base of their societies through state action, exactly the opposite of what the dependency thesis allows. On the state autonomy thesis, Gray's point can be accommodated. But the accommodation *is* at the expense of the dependency thesis, which alone makes marxism distinctive. See further Elster, 1985: 398-428.

The shift of viewpoint from state-dependency to state-autonomy – a qualified shift, since it did not apply to every state at every stage of its history – caused an ambivalence in Marx's attitude and that of marxists in general to representative democracy. On the state-dependency picture, representative democracy (the elements of which were slowly expanding in nineteenth-century Britain and in other capitalist countries) was a sham. It conferred political rights and freedoms without adequate means of exercising them; it affirmed the fiction of popular sovereignty (§14.6) while leaving intact the political domination of private capital; etc. (Proudhon: 'universal suffrage is counter-revolution'.)

Assume the state-autonomy thesis, however, and things start to look different. If the proletariat can, through their representatives, take over the state apparatus, then the state's capacity for independent action *vis-à-vis* the dominant class becomes an instrument for the socialist transformation of society. Engels developed this line quite clearly in his Introduction to Marx's *The Class Struggles in France* (Marx, 1979: 7-29). See further Hindess in Hunt, 1980: 21-54.

A final point to consider is the predictive power of Marx's theory of history. It looked closest to the facts in the 1930s in the United States and Western Europe when capitalism tumbled into the Great Depression, a downturn from which the socialist economy of the

Soviet Union was largely exempt. But the large-scale collapse of capitalism has not occurred; and state socialism on the Soviet model is in retreat.

I offer just two observations. In the first place, while Marx finds a place for revolution in the transition from capitalism to socialism, he sees revolution and in fact any form of drastic political action as best intervening when capitalism is in a state of terminal collapse. Revolution then simply eases the birth-pangs of history. As an economic system, capitalism must have reached virtually its quietus; revolution is then just the kick that causes the final smash. At this stage the proletariat, having suffered under the successive crises that mark capitalism's decline, will have unity and self-confidence as a class. Socialism will be the obvious next step; capitalism will certainly no longer be an option.

If this is Marx's projection, then it may still lie in the future. The socialist experiment in the Soviet Union, conducted in a country of barely developed capitalism, is of limited relevance to Marx's predictions. We may still witness the collapse of capitalism but on a much longer timescale than Marx anticipated.

Secondly and contrarily, there are perhaps good marxist reasons why marxism cannot possess predictive power. This involves the issue of technological determinism. If technological change is the fundamentally explanatory factor in the economic base, then if technological invention is unpredictable (who foresaw the word processor in 1900 or space satellites in 1945?), we cannot predict the relations of production which it will induce. In that case we cannot have a predictive theory of history of the kind that Marx wants and believes, within limits, that he has.

On the general matters discussed in this section, see Kitching, 1988: chs. 2 & 6. 'Technological determinism' involves the assumption that, within the forces of production, it is primarily technological innovations that provide the motor of history. See further Heilbroner, 1970: ch. 8; Callinicos, 1997; Carling, 1997; and (most emphatically) G.A. Cohen, 1978: passim. But not all marxists accept technological determinism; see in particular C. Barker, 1997: 29-31 commenting on Wood, 1991 & 1995. On Marx and ideology, see Bevir, 1996a; Centre for Contemporary Social Studies, 1978; Drucker, 1972; Mepham, 1972; Nielsen, 1983; Plamenatz, 1970; M. Rosen, 1996; J. Wolff, 1996c. On Marx and the state, see Avineri, 1968: 202-3; C. Barker, 1997: 58-9; Carnoy, 1984: ch. 2; Miliband, 1973; Plamenatz, 1954: 135-51; Plamenatz, 1963, II: 351-73. Macfarlane, 1970 adjudicates between Averini, 1968 and Plamenatz, 1954. The metaphor of base and superstructure is questioned, and alternative metaphors from the *Grundrisse* explored, in C. Barker, 1997: 27-9.

I have kept to Marx's own account of ideology. But there is an original development of this concept, well worth considering, by the Italian marxist, Antonio Gramsci, in his theory of cultural hegemony. See Bobbio in Keane, 1988: 73-99; Brandist, 1996; Carnoy, 1984: ch. 3; Rosamond in Axford et al., 1997: 86-8.

31.5 Communitarianism and public participation

We have already noted the nature of communitarianism and seen how conservatism embodies a communitarian element (§29.5). Assuming that socialist communitarianism show some difference from its conservative counterpart, we need to identify that difference.

The problem is stated by Susan Mendus in a passage which is worth quoting in full:

by its emphasis on such concepts as 'fraternity' and 'solidarity' socialism draws attention to the ties which bind members of a community to one another and, by contrast with liberalism, it construes these ties as constitutive of individual identity. However, and by contrast with many other forms of communitarianism, socialism is also committed to a concept of identity which is malleable and changeable. For socialists, the past, and its role in the creation of identity, is not something which can simply be taken on board unconsciously; it is also to be appropriated and formed anew. Individuals are indeed (partly) constituted by their membership of communities, but they are not merely the passive recipients of that identity, they are also able to mould and reform it. For socialists, therefore, the question 'who am I?' is peculiarly problematic, for it requires an answer which can acknowledge both the situatedness of people within a particular community and their ability to reflect upon and transform their relationships to that community. Is such an amalgam of activity and passivity, distance and situatedness possible? (Mendus, 1992: 5; cited in M. Parker, 1996: 208).

The key to the problem appears to be that socialists can separate off the *de facto* from the normative in a way that is refused by conservatives. For the conservative, society is in an important sense as it ought to be; there is no point in saying that it ought to be radically different from how it is, because we lack the rational instrumentalities for changing it on a large scale by deliberate action. This is the complexity thesis back at work (§29.1).

The socialist, by contrast, can accept the social situatedness of persons. This amounts to no more than the position of social holism outlined in §2.6.2. It is without the normative implication that the social situation – the current condition of society – is predominantly desirable. Since the situation is also capable of radical change through rational political action, it ought to be changed. And we already know in what directions: towards equality as a requirement of justice and towards liberation. Situatedness and distance are both fulfilled.

If socialist communitarianism differs from the conservative variety, it also stands opposed to liberal individualism (§§30.1-2). The abstract descriptions under which liberalism regards the citizen body – as self-interested utility-maximisers, as inherently competitive, acquisitive and possessive, as possessors of rights, etc. – are taken to be socially and historically specific descriptions which are part of capitalism's ideology. Even the attractive image of human beings as rational, self-determining, free choosers is seen as a fantasising of the real conditions of life for the vast majority of liberal citizens under capitalism. Here we catch the tendency of socialism, quite consistently on its own terms and most pronouncedly in its marxist version, to explain away rival ideologies as rationalisations of the current social and economic system.

Along with communitarianism goes a stress on public participation. The idea is that in collective decision-making, process is as important as outcome. That is to say, it matters not only that equality as a requirement of justice, and liberation are secured; it matters how they come about. Everyone should take part in decisions that affect their interests. More than that, the community as a whole is seen as debating and adopting the projects for social change which, as a socialist society, it carries out.

How to secure this participatory style of collective decision-making is a real question. It prompts the interest of many socialists in devolution, decentralisation, self-management through workers' producer co-operatives, and similar ideas. On a cautionary note, see J. Wolff, 1996b: 99-103. If the typical style of liberalism has been representative democracy, that of socialism should be deliberative democracy (§23.2; cf. Dunn, 1984: 36-70; B. Frankel, 1997: 80-90; Levine, 1988: 127-32, 204-6, 209-10; Sypnowich, 1990: 135-54, 159-62; Schumpeter, 1947, Part 4: 232-302; and, for commentary on Schumpeter, Coe & Wilber, 1985: passim).

31.5.1 Marxism, communitarianism and public participation

In §31.2.1 we encountered Marx's idea of humankind's 'species-being' at the centre of which is the need for free, creative activity; as a natural kind we have this as one of the conditions of our flourishing. Also intrinsic to our species-being is the need for co-operative existence. We have a 'communal nature' (PKM 104). Marx waxes eager over the economic conditions of communism, where 'bourgeois' competition, acquisition and possession are superseded and workers recognise 'a new need – the need for society' (Marx, 1977: 109). The prefiguration of this new social attitude is already to be observed, he tells us:

> whenever French socialist workers are seen together. Such things as smoking, drinking, eating, etc., are no longer means of contact or means that bring them together. Association, society and conversation, which again has association as its end, are enough for them; the brotherhood of man is no mere phrase with them, but a fact of life, and the nobility of man shines upon us from their work-hardened bodies (Marx, 1977: 109-10).

The picture is not wholly idyllic, however. Under communism, our species-being will be fulfilled – our need for a co-operative existence in which we can engage in free, creative activity. But this does not necessarily reach down to our individual being. I have, as an individual, not only a species-being but also personal abilities, talents, and potential. Communism may not accommodate all of these. (Have we turned full-circle to a description as abstract in its way as those under which liberalism regards the citizen body?) Walliman brings out this point well:

> Although communism enables individuals to associate freely, it cannot be conceived of as providing *the* social environment conducive to the pecularities of an individual. Thus, individuals cannot be compared with a plant which, in order to grow, must be provided by nature with water, soil, sunshine, and the like. Communism must not be envisioned as a society in which each individual has a claim to be nurtured according to the peculiarity of his person (Walliman, 1981: 108; quoted in Forbes, 1990: 180).

What political forms are appropriate to men and women as 'communal beings'? A distinction must be drawn between the first stage of transition from capitalism, that of the dictatorship of the proletariat, and the higher stage of communism in which (as already noted (§31.3.1)) the state will wither away. The political institutions of communism, presumably mere administrative mechanisms, are never precisely indicated by Marx. But his reaction to the 1871 Paris Commune gives a slight index to how the state might look under the dictatorship of the proletariat. There is evidence that Marx's public account of the Commune veiled some of his personal reservations about its proletarian credentials (R. Thomas, 1997; Avineri, 1968: 247-9). This does not reduce the suggestiveness of Marx's description of its political features.

The short-lived Commune arose in the aftermath of French defeat in the Franco-Prussian War of 1870-71. The brief background is as follows. In the wake of the January 1871 armistice, a French national assembly was elected in order to make terms with the Prussians. The character of the assembly and some of its measures were widely unpopular in Paris. A city assembly was elected, calling itself the 'Commune of Paris' in memory of the eighteenth-century Commune of Paris which had overthrown Louis XVI. The Commune, self-proclaimed on 18 March, elected on 26 March and lasting till 28 May 1871, rejected the authority of the national assembly. It was crushed, violently and vengefully, by the national government of Adolphe Thiers.

At most a handful of marxists were involved in the Commune but Marx himself saw this political experiment as a blueprint for the socialist state, though he criticised the Commune for tactical mistakes and for excessive symbolic re-enactment of the French Revolution. Marx noted five politically relevant features of the Commune (PKM 513-15):

- direct election of the assembly on the basis of universal suffrage, mandate, and short-term revocability
- no separate police force or army but public militias
- combination of legislative and executive powers
- disestablishment of the church
- all public servants directly elected by the assembly

Of these it was perhaps the first and last that struck the deepest chord in Marx, who felt revulsion at the idea of a state apparatus able to raise itself above society. The mandated members of the assembly were nothing like Burkean representatives (§23.2). Nor could a permanent and entrenched bureaucracy gain a foothold. There was no need for the separation of powers (§12.3). For further commentary, see Blackburn, 1977: 48-53; Kitching, 1988: 145-9; Lenin, 1931; Mészaros, 1986: 16; Plamenatz, 1963, I: 381-6; R. Thomas, 1997. For a distinctive, conservative view, see Salisbury, 1871.

Feminism stands next in line but, before we move on, you might note that for socialism, broadly viewed, the following are particularly useful: Browning in Axford et al., 1997: 238-42; D.A. Crocker, 1983; Crosland, 1964; Harrington, 1993; Kolakowski & Hampshire, 1977; Levine, 1988; Luard, 1979; Parekh, 1975; Plant, 1981; Pimlott, 1984; Self in Goodin & Pettit, 1995: ch. 13; Shalom, 1983; Soper, 1990: ch. 3; A. Vincent, 1992: ch. 4; Wright, 1996. O'Sullivan, 1998 explores the Russian thinker Nikolai Berdyaev's attempt to reformulate socialism in the light of 'a tragic vision' of the human condition.

For marxism in general, try Aron, 1965, I: 107-80; N. Barry, 1981: 17-21; Berki, 1983 & 1988; Berlin, 1960; A. Brown, 1986: ch. 5; J. Coleman, 1990: ch. 7; Hampsher-Monk, 1992: ch. 10; Hindess in Goodin & Pettit, 1995: ch. 12; Kedourie, 1984: 137-41; Labriola, 1908 (a classic older work, now a little dated but still worth reading); McLennan, 1989: chs. 3-4; Mills, 1963: ch. 2-6; Plamenatz, 1963, II: chs. 5-6; Plamenatz, 1975; Smellie, 1939: ch. 5; E.P. Thompson, 1978; J. Wolff, 1992; J. Wolff, 1996b: 164-7. Leszek Kolakowski's three-volume *magnum opus* (Kolakowski, 1978) is thorough in tracing the philosophical origins of marxism. It has the additional interest of being an 'insider's' critique – the work of a writer who was at one stage a marxist intellectual. On analytical marxism, see M. Roberts, 1996.

I might as well record my own view that four of the items to which earlier reference was made provide between them as clear, accurate, and compact a view of Marx's central and most characteristic ideas as you are likely to find: Callinicos, 1997; Carling, 1997; Chitty, 1993; S. White, 1996.

Since my account of Marx's ideas has been spread over a number of sections, a summary (opposite) may help pull things together before we leave this part of the chapter.

32. FEMINISM

Feminism is no less internally diverse than any other ideology. A basic distinction is customarily drawn between radical and reformist feminism, a distinction I shall follow here. But radical and reformist feminism are not uniform blocks of antithetical opinion. There is commonality between them, even while a rich variety prevails within each.

Karl Marx's basic ideas about history and society

1. An economic foundation underlies historical development.

2. This foundation is, in its first main element, the forces of production = labour power, machinery and equipment, scientific knowledge, and technical expertise.

3. Production occurs only under certain relations of production = patterns of ownership and control. These relations are the second main element of the economic foundation.

4. The forces of production are subject to development.

5. For any given level of development, X, a given system of relations of production, Y, is functional to X: it allows X to develop.

6. This functionality explains why Y exists.

7. People belong to social classes, defined by whether they significantly own or control the forces of production. The dominant class under capitalism, the owning and controlling class, is the bourgeoisie; workers who, lacking such ownership or control, can only sell their labour, are the proletariat.

8. Capitalist relations of production are (a) alienated, they destroy the possibility of free, creative activity, and (b) exploitative through the extraction of surplus value (i.e. the difference between what workers are paid and what their product sells for).

9. The forces and relations of production together constitute the economic base of society. Relative to this base, a given superstructure is functional.

10. This functionality explains why the superstructure exists.

11. The superstructure comprises the state and the legal system and either all non-economic institutions or all such institutions as are explicable through functionality to the economic base. The superstructure is legitimated, if only at the level of false consciousness, by ethical codes, economic theories, and systems of religious belief, the relevant body of ideas constituting an ideology.

12. Different bases and superstructures combine to constitute different types of economic system. The main systems in which Marx is interested are:
- Asiatic mode of production
- ancient slavery
- feudalism
- capitalism

13. The dynamic of history, what explains the transition from one system to another, is the ongoing development of the forces of production. This development means that particular relations of production – patterns of ownership and control – become dysfunctional to the productive forces. This dysfunctionality reaches a point of strain where merely reforming the relations of production or the superstructure is ineffectual: a revolutionary transition occurs. Feudalism gives way to capitalism, for instance.

14. Capitalism, the current system in Marx's day and ours, is inherently unstable for reasons that Marx explains in his economic theory, particularly in *Capital*.

15. It will give way to socialism, a system of public ownership of the forces of production, and to the dictatorship of the proletariat.

16. Under a complete system of public ownership, only one class will remain in society, namely the proletariat. The state will disappear as redundant for managing class conflict. This will be the era of communism, an era of free, creative, unalienated and non-exploitative activity.

Feminism engages comprehensively with philosophy. First there is the feminist attack on philosophy as (in its projected self-image and assumed current practice) gender-neutral, purely rational. Elizabeth Grosz tackles, head-on, just this view in Gunew, 1990: ch. 5. Next, feminist ethics and feminist epistemology supply part of feminism's wider philosophical reach. Thus the Western tradition's stress on reason is seen as exclusionary of women as when, in precision and reliability of knowledge, (male) reason is taken to contrast with and excel over (female) intuition and emotion. See J. Thompson, 1983. Ethical issues are considered separately in §32.2 with regard to the ethics of justice versus the ethics of care.

Within the Western tradition only two central figures, separated by millennia, have paid distinct, sympathetic attention to women – Plato and John Stuart Mill. Plato's feminism is ambivalent. *Meno*, 72D-74A, assumes the identity of virtue in women and men. And in the *Republic*, membership of the guardian class (§13.3.2), the political and intellectual élite, is open to women. Nor is this so merely in Justice Darling's ironical sense when he said that the courts, like the Ritz hotel, are open to all. Plato expects women to become guardians. Yet the best men surpass the best women both mentally and physically, though the best women surpass many men (*Rep.* V.455D: 232). Plato also pronounces women inferior at *Timaeus*, 41B and 90E, despite 18C; and note also *Laws*, VII.802E (Plato, 1970: 291). Overall impression? Mine is that the limitations of Plato's assumptions about the relative merits of women are less important than his 'inclusive' attitude to women, an attitude which breaks decisively with the main cultural norms of ancient Greece (cf. §23.2 on Athenian democracy).

Aristotle, by contrast, takes over essentially a traditional Greek position at NE VIII.10, 1160b32-1161a3 and VIII.11, 1161a22-5. The criticism of Plato's Republic in *Politics* II says quite a lot about the community of property and wives, but nothing about the identity of functions between men and women. *Politics* I.13, 1260b8ff, in spite of the promising remark that women make up half the *polis*, leads nowhere. It is worth noting even so that some feminists, such as Martha Nussbaum, have found Aristotle sympathetic on general philosophical grounds distinct from the specific issues of feminism.

For criticism of Plato, see Annas, 1976; in defence, see Lesser, 1979 and Levinson, 1953: 85-6, 104-6, 125-38. A typically balanced view is taken in Coole, 1993b: ch. 2. Bluestone, 1987, more detailed, is also well worth consulting. Okin, 1980 is alert to Plato's radicalism about women, though she contrasts the *Republic*'s forthrightness with the somewhat understated position taken in the *Laws* (on which see also Stalley, 1983: 104-6).

How much of John Stuart Mill's political theory derives from his relationship with his friend, lover, and eventual wife, the feminist Harriet Taylor (1807-58), is a crux for historians of ideas. Mill makes fulsome acknowledgement to Harriet in *On Liberty* (1859) and in his posthumous *Autobiography* (1873). The foreword to *On Liberty* refers to her as 'the inspirer, and in part author, of all that is best in my writings' (OL 4). Extravagant laudation or simple truth? Nobody knows; I am glad to be writing philosophy and not the history of ideas. The safest comment is that while Mill's humane, informed intelligence might have been expected to seize unaided on the fact of injustice to women, there is little doubt that Harriet Taylor's advocacy set the problem in sharp relief for him. Coole, 1993b: ch. 6, informed and fair, is the best all-round discussion; also useful is Okin, 1980. For an account of Mill which undervalues him for failing to anticipate twentieth-century radical feminism, see Annas, 1977. This article prompted Stove, 1993; and in turn Brecher, 1993; cf. Britton, 1953: 37, 40. Mill's main feminist text is *On the Subjection of Women* (1869), printed in Stefan Collini's edition of *On Liberty* which have used throughout this book.

If Plato and Mill are saints of feminism, the German philosopher and essayist, Arthur Schopenhauer (1788-1860), is its Lucifer. In 'On Women' (Schopenhauer, 1951: 464-77) we find a wide-ranging depreciation. Women are 'by nature meant to obey'; they are 'the unaesthetic sex' and 'have, in general, no love of any art; they have no proper knowledge of any; and they have no genius'; the 'sympathies that exist between them and men are skin-deep only, and do not touch the mind or the feelings or the character'; women are 'incapable of taking a purely objective interest in anything'; and 'they have no sense of justice'. Admittedly, one of the few female pluses is that 'women show more sympathy for the unfortunate than men do' but this is owing to their fixing on what immediately presents itself to their attention. Significant reasoning and abstraction are beyond them. It may be added that Schopenhauer, a notable misanthrope, took a dim view of men also. Some have seen Nietzsche (1844-1900) as even more anti-feminine than Schopenhauer. But his much-quoted remark, 'If you are visiting a woman, remember to take the whip', is typically ambiguous: it does not say whether visitor or visited is to use the whip. On Nietzsche see Oliver, 1988.

The title of first female feminist philosopher is normally accorded to Mary Wollstone-craft (1759-97), wife of William Godwin (§§17, 20.4, 28) and author of *Vindication of the Rights of Woman* (1792) – primarily an attack on Rousseau's treatment of women and their education in *Emile*, Book V. She had previously written, as a counterblast to Burke's *Reflections on the Revolution in France* (§§9.2, 29), a *Vindication of the Rights of Man* (1790) and, some time before, *Thoughts on the Education of Daughters* (1787). Woll-stonecraft's 1792 work is available in paperback as Wollstonecraft, 1975. For commentary, see Coole, 1993b: 91-101; Grimshaw, 1989.

I mentioned the distinction standardly drawn between reformist and radical feminism. It will be helpful to have a characterisation of feminism in terms of which we can align these two wings of the feminist movement. A useful formula is that of Denise Réaume. Feminism involves:

> a broad commitment to women's equality, a sense that the injustice women face is systematic or widespread, and a generally critical stance toward traditional power structures and the existing state of affairs (Réaume, 1996: 271).

But the formula is adequate only if revised from the conjunctive to the disjunctive. We can take it that there is no feminist who does not either have the commitment, or share the sense, or take the stance. Not all feminists share a sense of systematic injustice; in fact some query the requirement of justice as androcentric. Still, vague though it is in parts (what does 'the existing state of affairs' cover and include?), and disjunctively rephrased, the formula can launch our discussion.

32.1 Reformist feminism

A first flavour of reformist feminism is captured in Janet Radcliffe Richards' view that feminism involves essentially simply the belief that women suffer injustice because of their sex, though Millett, 1969 has some claim to be the first in the modern reformist field. Feminism is mainly about the elimination of sex-based injustice (Richards, 1982: 13-14). If we take any of the conventional formulas of justice from §17.2 – to each according to their merit, work, labour contribution, needs, or legal entitlement – we find that histori-cally and in the present day, in the West, the East and the Third World, women are relevantly disadvantaged.

32.1.1 Reformist feminism and justice

It might appear that, if this is the basic feminist complaint, then it can be accommodated within liberalism. The liberal state, with its penchant for abstract descriptions (§§30.1-2), cannot discriminate against women under any of the formulas of justice, because it is 'difference-blind'; it pays no heed to what differentiates one citizen from another but treats all equally and therefore cannot tilt the scales against women. This is the subsumptive view; feminism can be subsumed under liberalism.

A number of points are involved here. The first is that a particular word has been lost in the course of our discussion. Réaume spoke not simply of injustice but of *systematic* injustice, a term also used by Richards (Richards, 1982: 13). To invoke systematicity is to call on a social theory; we need a social theory to explain why this law-like correlation holds between sex or gender and disadvantage. Liberalism is, from this point of view, a political theory without a social theory; there are no conceptual resources within liberalism, as we characterised it in §§30.1-5, to deliver the requisite social analysis.

Partly for this reason, many feminists have looked to socialism, particularly in its marxist form, for the appropriate social explanation. This is not without its irony. While the early socialists, pilloried by Marx (§31), seized on the close connection between the family and property, especially hereditary property, and were thus keenly alert and sympathetic to the social situation of women (Plamenatz, 1963, II: 61-6), marxism sees class division as the primary social division and has not traditionally paid specific attention to the social situation of women. But socialist feminists have found illumination in the idea that women's systematic disadvantages can be identified as a by-product of class-divided society. The line of explanation runs through a link between capitalism and patriarchal social structures which give pride of place and systematic advantage to men. In fairness to Marx, see the remarks on the bourgeois family and prostitution in *The Communist Manifesto* (PKM 223-4; cf. Coole, 1993b: chs. 8 & 9).

Richards is lukewarm to the socialist-feminist approach. Although she lays emphasis on the systematic nature of women's disadvantages, she thinks it relatively unimportant to identify the systematic social causation behind it. '[H]ow it came about' can be separated from 'what should be done to put matters right' (Richards, 1982: 14). Jean Grimshaw is not alone in wondering whether the two things can be quite so neatly separated. There is a clear possibility, even a definite likelihood, that matters cannot be put systematically right if a systematic pattern of social causation continues to operate unaddressed (Grimshaw, 1982: 2-3).

A different angle on justice is to be found in the work of Nancy Fraser. A major injustice of which feminists complain is one of distribution. In the allocation of benefits and burdens, women have been systematically disadvantaged. Exploitation, marginalisation, and deprivation have been the result of this kind of socio-economic injustice. Redistribution is called for. But another kind of injustice has also prevailed:

> The second kind of injustice is cultural or symbolic. It is rooted in social patterns of representation, interpretation, and communication. Examples include cultural domination (being subjected to patterns of interpretation and communication that are associated with another culture and are alien and/or hostile to one's own; nonrecognition (being rendered invisible via the authoritative representational, communicative, and interpretative practices of one's culture); and disrespect (being routinely maligned or disparaged in stereotypic public cultural representations and/or in everyday life interactions) (Fraser, 1995: 71).

Here the requirement is for 'justice as recognition', in a now common formula. One contrast is that, under justice as redistribution, at the limit the relevant groups will disappear from specific concern; under successful redistributive policies they will no longer feature as needing distinct attention. This is not the case with justice as recognition, which aims permanently to brighten the spotlight on previously 'invisible' groups. Fraser is concerned at the danger, as she sees it, that justice as recognition may act as a distraction from justice as redistribution; and she tries to show ways in which the dichotomy can be deconstructed.

I.M. Young takes this approach quite thoroughly. For Young, it is not justice but rather oppression that is the focal concept. Oppression extends across the phenomena of exploitation, marginalisation, powerlessness, cultural imperialism, and violence (I.M. Young, 1990: ch. 2; and 1997: 151). In combating these phenomena we necessarily take into account the requirements of both the justice of redistribution and the justice of recognition.

32.1.2 Reformist feminism and freedom

We have not done with the concept of justice, which is the subject (shortly to be considered) of radical feminist critique. But it is time to move on to consider another concept on which reformist feminists have fixed their attention, that of freedom.

Recall MacCallum's formula for freedom (§22.5): whenever the freedom of some agent or agents is in question, it is always freedom from some constraint or restriction on, interference with, or barrier to doing, not doing, becoming or not becoming something (PPS 4: 176). We saw how different theories of freedom group and arrange these constraints, restrictions, interferences and barriers to define negative and positive freedom according, roughly, to whether they are external to the agent (and relevant to negative freedom) or internal (and relevant to positive freedom).

Reformist feminists have discussed both negative and positive freedom, but their main contribution has been, not to re-analyse these ideas at a basic conceptual level but to stretch our understanding of what can constitute constraints, restrictions, interferences and barriers. Thus, for instance, Nancy Hirschmann argues that in respect of negative freedom:

> the existing patriarchal context – not only its genderically inegalitarian customs and practices but also its language, conceptual framework, and epistemology – could be seen as a socially constructed external barrier to women's freedom (Hirschmann, 1996: 53).

To this we can add, on the side of positive freedom, internal (psycho-cultural) impediments: for example, the limiting self-images which women may derive from the ways in which they are trained and educated (Coole, 1993a: 84). Adding in these extra internal and external factors does not re-conceptualise the relation between freedom and barriers, but extends our sense of what barriers there might be. Such extension is seen as increasing the functionality of the concept of freedom relative to feminist concerns.

Since epistemology was mentioned just above in the extract from Hirschmann, it is worth saying something about feminist angles on this topic. To many, and not only men, the notion of a feminist epistemology is a baffling one: knowledge is knowledge, surely? But matters are not quite so straightforward. The project of a feminist epistemology has evolved along two paths.

One is the identification of types of sources of knowledge to which women have sole or special access either through their social situation or through the particular nature of 'female subjects as more contextual and relational, less defined by rigid ego boundaries' (Coole, 1993a: 86). We will return to develop this perspective on female subjects in §32.2.2.

The other path is the exposure of male-centred assumptions about the conditions and privileged forms of knowledge. The key points concern the way in which (1) standard analyses of knowledge seek for universality: 'S knows that p if and only if ...' and (2)

scientific knowledge, centring on exceptionless generalisations about law-bound relationships between phenomena, is regarded as knowledge *par excellence*. The disregard
for particularity implicit in these two points is seen by some feminists as typically
androcentric. We cannot go further into these matters here, but see Duran, 1995; Gunew,
1990; Halberg, 1989; Richards, 1995.

To return to the concept of freedom. A further feminist issue centres on the public/
private distinction. In §22.3 negative freedom was presented by Berlin as an area of
non-interference: 'the area within which a man (*sic*) can act unobstructed by others'
(Berlin, 1969: 122). This area can be seen as defining a private or personal sphere, exempt
from public intrusion. Such a sphere is also protected by Mill's liberty principle (§22.8).
The feminist counter-comment is that 'the personal is political'. This slogan needs
careful interpretation. At least four points are involved:

1. If a private or personal sphere is to be defined, then its scope and limits are politically
   determined. The personal is the political in the sense that a political decision has been
   made that this sphere, thus delimited, is to exist.
2. Much historical feminist critique has highlighted the ways in which women have
   suffered injustice or oppression because a range of matters were consigned to the
   private sphere and so sealed off from political remedy. 'An Englishman's home is his
   castle' and within its walls, secure from public scrutiny, his wife and daughters have
   often been rawly dealt with. It is only fair to stress that Mill's liberty principle, given
   Mill's feminism and his special concern to encourage 'experiments of living', was
   never intended to license this kind of 'privatisation' of women's interests. See further
   Okin in D. Held, 1991: ch. 3.
3. The same kinds of patriarchal, autocratic structures which dominate the 'private' life
   of the family are replicated publicly in ideas about leadership and 'image', coercion
   and manipulation, which are the common coin of politics.
4. On a process as opposed to a forum or arena view of politics (§§2.4, 24.3), power
   relationships (usually detrimental to women) are omnipresent and so therefore is
   politics. No purely personal sphere, released from such relationships, can be isolated.

For a further discussion of the slogan, without predominant stress on feminism, see Craib,
1988.

32.2 Radical feminism

Reformist feminism is the politics of equality. The categories of justice and freedom are
central to political evaluations and demands; and the aim is to secure equal justice and
equal freedom for women. Radical feminism is the politics of difference. To mention two
specifics: (1) as a masculine 'virtue', justice is a gender-biased category; it stands
opposed to an female ethics of care. Also (2) the idea of negative freedom involves spatial
metaphors which do not stand right with women's experience. The start of this style of
thought, without its full elaboration, is perhaps Firestone, 1970.

32.2.1 Radical feminism and justice

The distinction between an ethics of justice and an ethics of care derives from Carol
Gilligan's *In a Different Voice: Psychological Theory and Women's Development*
(1982). Gilligan herself repudiates any direct, precise mapping of the justice/care distinction on to the male/female divide. Nor does she recommend the abandonment of justice

as a pseudo-virtue. But her work has been found illuminating by some radical feminists. Justice, a rule-bound virtue, is seen as a moral parallel to knowledge as that concept features in traditional, androcentric, law-bound epistemology. However that may be, the argument about justice is that women are given more to context-relative thinking, i.e. to 'caring' about the particular case with which they are confronted, and less inclined to subsume complex situations under fixed formulas of justice such as the criteria of concrete justice listed in §17.2 (cf. §15.5 on ethical particularism).

Such a view provokes the question whether this preference for caring, if indeed it is typical of (i.e. broadly common and distinctive to) women, is a natural or a socially mediated phenomenon. Is it the case that there is a 'female essence', a distinct female human nature? This might mean that, while women share some characteristics with men, there are states of mind and character and kinds of activity which are distinctive to women. This is a 'naturalist' approach; and the specific idea is that a greater tendency to care is among those states and activities. Or is the tendency to be explained rather in terms of the fact that women and men are raised differently, with women being directed more into the 'caring' occupations and activities?

It will be useful at this stage to refer to the now common distinction between sex and gender. Here is a canonical formulation of the distinction by Robert Stoller:

> With a few exceptions there are two sexes, male and female. To determine sex one must assay the following conditions – chromosomes, external genitalia, internal genitalia, gonads, hormonal states, and secondary sex characteristics ... One's sex, then, is determined by an algebraic sum of all these qualities, and as is obvious, most people fall under one of the two separate bell curves, the one of which is called 'male', the other 'female'.
>
> Gender is a term that has psychological and cultural rather than biological connotations; if the proper terms for sex are 'male' and 'female', the corresponding terms for gender are 'masculine' and 'feminine', these latter being quite independent of (biological) sex. Gender is the amount of masculinity and femininity found in a person, and obviously, while there are mixtures of both in many humans, the normal male has a preponderance of masculinity and the normal female a preponderance of femininity (Stoller, 1968 quoted in Plumwood, 1989: 2).

Sex is a matter of biological differentia; as such, it may be added, the sexual line between men and women is largely common ground between reformist and radical feminists, liberals, socialists, conservatives, anarchists. It should be noted, however, that Stoller identifies a number of conditions for sexuality; and, as some radical feminists have pointed out, it not entirely a neutral matter what relative weight one gives to the different conditions in the determination of sexuality as a category.

But the centrally controversial question concerns gender. Traditional thinking has assumed an indivisible, intimate link between sex and gender. Women are intuitive, emotional, disinclined to logical thinking, and (the item under the spotlight) 'carers', and so on through a catalogue of stereotypical features. Those who believe that there is a female essence need not endorse the traditional account in all or any of its details, but they do appear to be committed to there being a distinct link between sex and gender. Talk of certain states of mind and character and kinds of activity as distinctive to women is talk of women's psychology and culture. Gender-features are being correlated with a sexually identified group.

The opposite view that gender is wholly a social product, the result of conditioning, is (one version of) 'social constructionism'. The truth is probably undramatically in the middle. Roughly, it seems likely that gender-tendencies run on a causal link with sex-qua-biology but that precise gender-result is socially induced. See further Grimshaw,

1996; Parsons, 1987. For more on the ethics of care, see Clement, 1996 reviewed in Bubeck, 1998; and B. Barry, 1995: 246-55.

32.2.2 Radical feminism and freedom

The main impact of radical feminism on the concept of freedom relates specifically to the idea of negative freedom. Theorists of negative freedom, as we saw in §22.3, attempt to map out an area of non-interference around the individual. Radical feminists have offered two kinds of critique here.

In the first place, they emphasise the masculine imagery involved in the idea of negative freedom, that of an 'area' of non-interference. The language is that of a binary divide between self and others; and this divide, some radical feminists claim, is the kind of rigid ego boundary that tallies well with masculine experience. Against such experience should be set:

> the greater permeability of the female *body*, where experiences like sexual penetration, pregnancy, childbirth and gynaecological examination transgress its thin pellicle of putative privacy, opening women to relations of consent and coercion in the most intimate recesses of the flesh (Coole, 1993a: 86).

In other words, for (most) women an area of negative freedom is an unreal abstraction.

Secondly, if a connection is made (one that many radical feminists make) with postmodernism, then we can bring Foucault into the picture (cf. §14.6.2):

> Foucault locates a fragmented, multiple, circulatory power of which we are all both vehicles and victims. It is impossible to formulate a notion of liberty as freedom *from* such power, because its 'capillary' form is anonymous and ubiquitous, reaching into 'the very grain of individuals', where it 'touches their bodies and inserts itself into their actions and attitudes, their discourses, learning processes and everyday lives' (Coole, 1993a: 88; quotations from Foucault, 1980: 39).

On this basis, even without the preceding assumptions about the female subject, no area of non-interference can be defined. It is worth mentioning that, using Foucault's idea that the political covers anything that has to do with power, we may add to the senses in which the personal is the political (§31.1.2). All personal relationships are power relationships to whatever degree, therefore all are political. This also alters our angle on the issue of 'dirty hands', an issue which precisely presupposes that there is, distinct from each other, a personal and a political sphere and a question of whether the moral standards of one are applicable to the other (§24.3).

One issue about freedom falls squarely across the reformist/radical divide, namely the issue of pornography. Some liberal theorists defend the legal publication of pornography on grounds of freedom of speech while others, along with both reformist and radical feminists, are ready to apply Mill's 'harm' condition (§22.8.1): freedom can rightly be restricted when it causes harm, and pornography harms women in many ways, not least by reinforcing dismissive attitudes towards them.

Mill's position is strong as it stands and capable of entrenchment. Three noteworthy points are, first, that to present a contemporary Millian (à la A. Thomson, 1993: 123) as resisting a legal ban on pornography on the basis that pornography is insulting and therefore offensive but not harmful, is to read OL strangely. Mill includes offences against decency in his category of harm (§22.8.1). In any case, why should he not accept that to cause any offence, whether or not indecency is involved, is to cause some harm?

A sharp separation between offence and harm is without any textual or intellectual warrant. Secondly, Mill's defence of freedom of speech ('discussion') is conducted mainly with a view to the emergence of truth (§22.8). To defend the publication of pornography, e.g. in Ronald Dworkin's way, as a form of respect for liberal individualism (cf. 1c in §30.1) is leagues away from Mill's intentions. Mill would never attempt to bring pornography under the aegis of free speech; free speech serves truth in a manner to which pornography is irrelevant. Thirdly, Mill could extend his understanding of 'speech' (as interpreted in §22.8) to include the communication of *attitudes* as well as propositional content (cf. Hornsby, 1996). It would then be a short task to expel pornography from the realm of free speech by reference to the harmful attitudes it supports.

Further on the pornography debate between liberalism and feminism, see Benn, 1993; P. Davis, 1991; Dworkin, 1993; Hornsby & Langton, 1998; Langton, 1990; MacKinnon, 1993; A. Thomson, 1993; Willis in Jaggar, 1994: 161-4. On feminism generally: Fricker, 1991; Kymlicka, 1990, ch. 7; Lovibond, 1994; Lucas, 1973; Mansbridge & Okin in Goodin & Pettit, 1995: ch. 10; McCabe, 1998; Mellor, 1996; J. Thompson, 1983; A. Vincent, 1992: ch. 7; J. Wolff, 1996b: 202-21. On postmodernism and feminism, see Soper, 1990: ch. 10. On the public/private divide, see Craib, 1988; Elshtain in Goodin & Pettit, 1997, ch. 37; A. Vincent, 1992: 201-4. On the state, law, sovereignty, authority, and power, check out J. Coleman, 1990: ch. 9; Kingdom in Adlam, 1981: 97-114; MacKinnon, 1989; Richards, 1995. On justice, try Dancy, 1992; Grimshaw, 1982; Richards, 1982. On equality: Coole, 1993b; Jaggar, Littleton, MacKinnon, and Crenshaw in Jaggar, 1994: Part I. On property: Coole, 1993b. On rights: again Coole, 1993b; West, 1994. On democracy: Phillips, 1992; Rowbotham in Held & Pollitt, 1986.

33. THE POSTMODERN PERSPECTIVE

'Postmodernism', often abbreviated to 'POMO', is a style of thinking which dates at least from Friedrich Nietzsche (1844-1900) and which in recent decades has included the names of Gilles Deleuze, Jacques Derrida, and Michel Foucault.

Derrida has also come under review for his deconstructionist approach to textual interpretation (§9.2.3); and we have already examined a portion of Foucault's ideas in considering his views about the pervasiveness of power, and hence of political, relationships throughout society (§14.6.2). These views have widespread implications for the topics of this book. We saw one such implication in the case of negative freedom (§32.2.2).

The usual disclaimer applies with extra force in the case of the postmoderns. We cannot pin down their ideas, assumptions, and attitudes in a set of clear-cut, necessary and sufficient conditions. But this is not only because styles of thinking – postmodernism as much as conservatism, socialism, and liberalism – have too much internal diversity. It is also because the postmoderns resist the clear-cut in general. If they could define their viewpoint in this hard-and-fast way, it would count against that very viewpoint.

Two features are typical of postmodern discourse. The first is a rejection of structural linguistics of the kind associated with Ferdinand de Saussure (1857-1913) in his *Cours de linguistique générale* (1916).

33.1 Rejection of structural linguistics

Saussure departed from the standard view of language as referential. A typical such referential view is the Fregean distinction between sense and reference; words have meanings in the context of sentences and they refer (often at least) to extra-linguistic items in the external world. 'The morning star' refers to a heavenly body, the planet

Venus; 'meaning is the route to reference' as Frege put it. Saussure broke this referential link. Meanings are wholly linguistic. A word, phrase or sentence, or 'sign' in Saussure's terminology, means what it does, not by virtue of its relationship to a referent, but through its relationship to other signs.

This relationship is mediated by systems of convention; and structuralism undertook to map or model these conventions. At the heart of such models the structuralists saw certain binary oppositions: subject and object, infinite and finite, relative and absolute, true and false, literal and metaphorical, confused and clear, intuitive and discursive, reason and passion, end and means, man and woman, necessary and contingent, substance and accident, actual and possible, and so on.

The post-structuralists, particularly Derrida, seek to deconstruct these foundational oppositions. When probed, they are shown to be ambiguous, arbitrary, and conventional (historically and socially specific). In political philosophy, there are implications for such oppositions as ruler and subject, state and society, freedom and coercion.

The post-structuralists keep the Saussurean view that words have meaning purely by relationship with other words. But they interpret it differently. For Saussure, words can have stable and precise meanings through their place in a delimited network of relationships; for the post-structuralists, in contrast, these relationships are too intricate, numerous, and variable to define. This confers an ineliminable degree of indeterminateness on word meanings. It is as if meanings were objects caught in a vast, undulating and tangled net from which we cannot extricate them. To pick out 'the' meaning of any word, phrase or sentence is an impossibility. Even authors do not fully know what they mean. This has consequences for the interpretation of classic texts such as Plato's *Republic* and Hobbes' *Leviathan*, as noted earlier (§9.2).

33.2 Rejection of a metaphysics of the person

The second feature of postmodern discourse is a rejection of metaphysical characterisations of human agency.

In the modern era, that is, from the seventeenth century to the present century, human beings are characterised through a range of descriptions in law and politics, ethics and economics. Certain assumptions about the nature of human beings come to the fore. Human beings are self-interested utility maximisers, rational self-determining free choosers, responsible for their actions (§30.2), bearers of natural rights (Locke), moral equals with no natural political authority over one another (Locke again, §13.3.3), and so on. These are the dominant descriptions on which political, legal, ethical, and economic discourse runs.

It is not exactly that the postmoderns want to eliminate these descriptions. But they deny that they have any metaphysical validity. All these are ways of viewing people, but to assume that they are a genuine metaphysics of the person, that they identify the real nature of human beings, and tell us the truth about the human condition, that for instance people really are rational subjects or individual choosers or whatever, is unsustainable. All these dominant descriptions merely identify socially defined roles, images under which people are treated and regard others and themselves in historically specific societies. I am an individual chooser or a rational subject, to the extent that I am so, not because this is my human essence, but because this is what I have grown into in a social system that categorises human beings under these (and many other) descriptions.

Two diverse categories outside this list have separate interest: madness and homosexuality. Foucault made a famous study (*Madness and Civilisation*, 1961) of the way in which 'the mad' are recognised as a separate category only in the modern world. There were no asylums in ancient or feudal times. Individuals were recognised as deranged, disturbed, erratic, and so on. But no one thought of the mad as a group requiring social response.

Again, while homosexual *behaviour* has occurred and been recognised throughout recorded history, the category of the homosexual *person* and the idea of homosexuals as a distinct *social group*, is entirely modern. Social relations, language, and culture have created a category where none existed before.

To return: Foucault tells an elaborate, speculative story of how dominant descriptions occur within a process of 'normalising' behaviour in a modern, rationalised world and of enabling the prediction and control of behaviour by public and private bureaucracies.

Some or all of the foregoing dominant descriptions rest on binary oppositions of the kind that the postmoderns reject. But they are not suggesting that we can avoid such descriptions altogether. They argue, however, that if we value individual choice or responsible agency, for example, these values are misserved by thinking of them under a spurious metaphysics of the person. If we think that people *just are* individual choosers or responsible agents, as a matter of brute fact about humankind, then we will not attend to the conditions, often quite difficult to contrive and requiring sustained political action, on which people can actually fulfil these descriptions, and realise these values.

Postmoderns face problems in the philosophy of language on which they rely, but this is a question on which something has been said already (§9.2.3) and of which the further consideration would take us too far beyond political philosophy. There is also a question of how far postmoderns are able to take the collapse of distinctions. Here is Steve Fuller on a key case in point:

> Postmodernists may talk a lot about blurring 'genres', but I do not recall any of their number ever saying they wanted to blur the difference between true and false. Their claim, rather, is that the difference between true and false – however clearly one wishes to draw it – does not explain either the initial acceptance or the subsequent persistence of beliefs. The reason is that the embrace of truth and the avoidance of falsehood are things that everyone claims for themselves and can usually demonstrate to their own satisfaction. The deeper question is how does a particular way of drawing the true/false distinction come to predominate over other possible ways. An adequate answer transcends the resources of logic, and requires some understanding of the history and sociology of knowledge-production (S. Fuller, 1996: 17; see further S. Fuller, 1988.)

On postmodernism in general see further Blaug, 1996b: 54 ff.; Downing & Bazargan, 1991: Part IV; Heller & Fehér, 1988.

6. Endnote

34. REVIEW AND PROSPECT

Twelve key normative political concepts have been examined. We have explored conceptual analyses of the state, sovereignty, law, authority, power, justice, equality, rights, property, freedom, democracy, and the public interest. We have checked out some high-level theories involving those concepts, and *en route* have investigated aporias, puzzles or difficulties, in which the concepts and theories are caught up. What is there for you to do next?

Fresh from an introductory text, everything! I have given pointers, a structured route, through political philosophy. That has been the sum of it. All your detailed work is before you. According to time, inclination, and the pressures of the weekly essay, there are five future tasks.

34.1 References in the text

The immediate task is to go down a level of detail and follow up the references to further reading. The Cambridge Latinist, A.E. Housman (1859-1936), once rather dauntingly observed that a scholar 'must spend much of his life in acquiring knowledge which for its own sake is not worth having and in reading books which do not in themselves deserve to be read'. I have tried in the references to suggest only what will genuinely add depth and refinement to the slight sketch of topics and issues given in the text.

It will also be useful for you to check out the articles appearing in a number of journals. This will keep you up to date in a way that no bibliography in this or any other book can hope to do. Do not be overwhelmed by the sheer number of journals or by the relentlessness of their output. You do not have to read everything unless you have Housmanic ambitions. A regular scan through, say, *Political Theory*, *Political Studies*, and the *History of Political Thought*, will keep you in touch with new material of assured quality. *The Philosopher's Index*, held by most university libraries and often available on-line, is a good guide to the journal literature, usually with helpful summaries by the authors.

34.2 Filling in the gaps

I have had to make exclusionary decisions. In the chapter on ideologies I left out fascism, nationalism, and environmentalism. My original intention, defeated by considerations of space, was to look at the relations of politics to religion in Christian and Islamic political theory. A full education in political philosophy will make good these omissions. To move towards this is the second task. I will talk just briefly about the three missing ideologies.

34.2.1 Fascism

Fascism was a distinct early twentieth-century ideology, though 'fascist' has long since degenerated into a vapid term of political abuse. The primary reference is to the fascist movement formed in Italy in 1919 under the leadership of Benito Mussolini (1883-1945). The Italian fascist regime held power between 1922 and 1943/5 with clear prefiguration in the regime established in 1919-20 in the northern Adriatic port of Fiume (present-day Rijeka) by the poet-soldier Gabriele d'Annunzio (1863-1938). Mussolini was over-thrown in 1943 but headed a German puppet regime, the Social Republic (*Repubblica Sociale Italiana*), controlling parts of Italy till 1945. Francisco Franco (1892-1975) is another figure in the fascist pantheon. He ruled Spain from the late 1930s till 1975. Apologists of the regime claim 1936 as its date of inception, but this is merely Franco's bogus date of de jure authority; he won the Civil War, which he himself had illegally started, in 1938-9. In Portugal the Salazar regime (1932-68), an altogether more intellec-tual affair, has been widely regarded as fascist. The fascist label is also commonly attached to the 1946-55 regime of Juan Perón (1895-1974) in Argentina. A host of smaller fascisms have had bit-parts on the stage of history.

I should exclude Salazar from fascism. The body of ideas expounded and institution-alised by Dr Antonio de Oliveira Salazar (1889-1970), economist, political thinker, ascetic, devout Christian, and prime architect of the Portuguese *Estado Novo* (New State), had numerous sources. If Salazar was a man with 'a serious idea', that idea had distinct bases. He was influenced, in the first place, by the writings and activities of Charles Maurras (1868-1952), who found a vehicle for the political values of order, discipline, and stability in the movement, *Action Française*, in 1899. The maverick thinker Georges Sorel (1847-1922) also exerted an impact. Sorel despised capitalism. As an anarcho-syndicalist, he agitated for a General Strike and the reorganisation of the economy into associations of workers. Salazar hardly went so far in his support for workers' self-management, but the idea of running the economy through 'corporations' of workers and employers had distinct appeal for him. These influences aside, Salazar's political ideas bear the clear and overriding imprint of Catholic social teaching – in particular of the two Papal encyclicals of Leo XIII (1810-1903; *Pontifex Maximus*, 1878-1903) and Pius XI (1864-1939; *Pontifex Maximus*, 1922-39) – *Rerum Novarum* (1891) and *Quadragesimo Anno* (1931). To say this is not to commit the Catholic Church to the idiosyncrasies of Dr Salazar but only to separate Dr Salazar from the *corpore vile* of fascism (cf. Payne in Laqueur, 1979: 310-11). As always we must discriminate; back now to the central ground.

The Italian term, *fascismo*, derives from the insignia of political authority in ancient Rome – the *fasces*, a bundle of punitory rods encasing an axe (a symbol of unity, discipline, and the power of death), which marked the authority of the Consuls.

As an ideology fascism has definite philosophical shortcomings. How far this would worry fascists is another matter; Mussolini exhorted fascists to 'think with their blood'. At all events, fascism has failed to produce any text of the order (say) of Mill's *On Liberty* or Burke's *Reflections*. Even as a broad body of ideas, it lacks conceptual refinement and theoretical rigour. Admittedly, we encounter something genuinely philosophical in the *Genesis and Structure of Society* (posthumous, 1946) of Giovanni Gentile (1875-1944) but if the philosopher is fascist, the book is not. Gentile just re-treads Hegelian ethics and politics.

The hallmarks of fascist ideology are the following:

- anti-rationalism (shared with conservatism) and ⅎ corresponding reliance on instinct (contrasting with the conservative reliance on tradition)
- positive acceptance of violence as an instrument of politics
- pressure for a hierarchical organisation of society
- emphasis on a common, national culture as the basis of politics ('Nationalism was the central appeal of fascist movements' (Linz in Laqueur, 1979: 47))
- support for complete social and economic integration and control in the interests of promoting political ideals (fascism's totalitarian aspect)

To check out fascism further see: Allardyce, 1979; Berlin, 1990 on de Maistre (§29); Griffin, 1993 & 1995; Ignatieff in Margalit, 1991; Joad, 1938: ch. 16; Laqueur, 1979; Neocleous, 1997; Oakeshott, 1939: Part V (esp. 'The Doctrine of Fascism', 164-79, published in 1932 under Mussolini's name but written by the philosopher Giovanni Gentile); O'Sullivan, 1983 (brilliant and profound, the reflections of a deep-minded conservative on the fascist heresy); Schwarzmantel, 1987: ch. 5; Scruton, 1983: 169. On a literary note, Thomas Mann's short story 'Mario and the Magician' (*Mario und der Zauberer*) has been seen as a parable of fascism (Crick in PPS 3: 201).

'Why no mention of nazism?', you might ask with pertinent curiosity. Nazism was one form of fascism. The whole image of fascism should not be subsumed under it. The special mark of nazism was its racism. There is nothing specifically racist about fascism; any loyal citizen can be a good fascist. The argument for this differentia between nazism and the main body of fascism is as follows.

Racism of the standard kind – unlike 'the new racism' (M. Barker, 1982) which relies on the biological 'naturalness' of xenophobia at the level of the nation state – has five components. The first is the idea that human beings can be grouped into distinct natural kinds (§4.1.2) identifiable by the possession of specific physical characteristics. The second is that these characteristics have a genetic base; the third, less innocuous, is that this genetic base also explains the level and value of culture which the different groups exhibit. Add, fourthly, an adverse judgement on the level and value of particular groups' culture and, fifthly, a practical imperative to act against those advesely-judged groups, and there one has standard racism. The five hallmarks of fascism, listed above, neither entail nor presuppose any or all of the five components of racism.

It was nazism, a particular variety of fascism embodied in the 1933-45 German dictatorship of Adolf Hitler (1889-1945), which stressed egregiously the racial basis of the common, national culture. Nazism has given fascism, if not its bad name, a worse name than it would otherwise have. For the distinctiveness of nazism, see E. Weber, 1964. The intellectual links between nazism and the thought of the ambiguously great philosopher, Martin Heidegger (1889-1976), are unlikely ever to be agreed. My own view is that, while Heidegger collaborated eagerly with the nazis in their early days of power, and whatever his later attitude towards them, his fascinating and obscure philosophy is too remote to entail nazi political theory in any direct way. Heidegger's nazism, like Gentile's fascism, was a personal leap of faith not a logical deduction from philosophical doctrine. See further Safranski, 1998.

34.2.2 Nationalism

Nationalism is no single thing. It has a double existence, as movement and ideology. As movement, a trend of political events, it embraces a great diversity of loosely associated phenomena from at least the First Partition of Poland (1775) and the American Declaration of Independence (1776), through the Latin American wars of liberation in the early nineteenth century, down to the dismemberment of Yugoslavia in the mid-1990s – and doubtless far beyond into the future.

As an ideology, nationalism has no less diversity. Early theorists of nationalist ideology include J.G. Fichte (1762-1814) with his *Addresses to the German Nation* (1807), G. Mazzini (1805-72), and Heinrich von Treitschke (1834-96). In earlier writers, some of them significant thinkers in the classic tradition – Rousseau, Burke, and Hegel among others – nationalist ideas and arguments occur prefiguratively, though none of them could be properly called ideologues of nationalism. See, for example, Rousseau's proposals for constitutional reforms in Corsica (1765) and Poland (1771) in Rousseau, 1953 (for Poland, SC 177-260); and Hegel, PR §347.374-5.

The diversity of nationalism as an ideology diversity has two sources. One is that the concept of a nation is open to incompatible interpretations, and so the ultimate point of reference is contestable. The other is that, however the nation is conceptualised, different normative claims are made on its behalf.

Ernest Renan (1823-92) probed the concept of a nation, famously, in 'What is a Nation?' (1882). Essential to nationhood are common memories and a shared past along with a sense of the importance of sharing a form of life that preserves this inheritance. Renan wrily adds that collective forgetfulness is no less important than common memories. This joint amnesia lets the relevant group fashion a selective image of past triumphs and ordeals – its national mythology or *mystique*. See Renan, 1939; Gellner, 1982.

Renan's main idea is that people constitute themselves a nation. Nationality is not an independently discoverable fact about a group of people. You cannot surprise me by telling me, as a matter of truth, that I belong to a nation to which I recognise no affiliation. A distinguished theorist of nationalism, Ernest Gellner, expresses the Renanian view as follows:

> Two men are of the same nation if and only if they recognise each other as belonging to the same nation. In other words ... nations are the artefacts of men's convictions and loyalties and solidarities (Gellner, 1983: 7).

The usual label for this approach to nationality is that nations are 'ideal communities', where 'ideal' = 'based on ideas'. The idea of the nation as ideal community was prefigured more than twenty years before Renan by John Stuart Mill:

> A portion of mankind may be said to constitute a nationality if they are united among themselves by common sympathies which do not exist between them and any others – which make them co-operate with each other more willingly than with other people, desire to be under the same government, and desire that it should be government by themselves or a portion of themselves exclusively. This feeling of nationality may have been generated by various causes. Sometimes it is the effect of identity of race and descent. Community of language and community of religion greatly contribute to it. Geographical limits are one of its causes. But the strongest of all is identity of political antecedents: the possession of a national history, and consequent community of recollections; collective pride and humiliation, pleasure and regret, connected with the same incidents in the past (Mill, 1958: 229; 1991: 427).

To avoid circularity, Mill should refer to a 'common' rather than to a 'national' history. Otherwise his account is a fine statement of the ideal community view. The contrast is with the objective identity view, expressed again by Gellner:

> Two men are of the same nation if and only if thet share the same culture, where culture in

turn means a system of ideas and signs and associations and ways of behaving and communicating (Gellner, 1983: 7).

The objective identity view attaches no importance to the individual's recognition or acceptance of his or her 'belonging'. If I share the relevant system of ideas and the rest then I am a member of the relevant nation independently of any recognition or assent on my part.

The distinction between ideal community and objective identity (a major wrangle among political scientists) does not exhaust the role of the concept of the nation in political discourse. 'Nation' also figures as a contrast term. The contrast is not between one nation and another but between the nation and other social categories. The nation is set over against social classes.

Along this line one encounters the idea that the nation covers all social categories without limitation or reserve. We may belong to different social classes but we are all (say) British or Americans. Alternatively the nation may be identified with a segment of the population: only 'the workers' or the 'British-born' or somesuch are 'really' British nationals.

A particular conception of the nation arises from the idea of the nation-state. Here the nation is defined by political sovereignty. Where there is a sovereign state there is a citizenry; and the citizens of a state constitute a nationality. I am a British national in the sense that legally I am subject to the jurisdiction of the British state and have all the legal privileges of British citizenship.

Complications arise, however. In the typical case and at a level of gross observation, the citizenry of the nation-state is broadly homogeneous in respect of historical, ethnic, linguistic, and religious background. But the conspicuous *lack* of homogeneity within a state can ground a claim for separate statehood. Nobody supposed that the Austro-Hungarian empire embraced a single nation by the criterion of homogeneity. The twelve or so historically, ethnically, linguistically, and religiously defined groups within the empire turned the logic of homogeneity against the Empire itself. Each such group urged its entitlement to separate statehood. Yugoslavia and Czechoslovakia were the main result, with consequences now familiar.

See further Finlayson, 1998; Gellner, 1964: ch. 7; Gellner, 1982 & 1983; Lorberbaum, 1994; Tamir, 1993. In view of the subsequent history of nationalism, Marx's dismissive observation that 'The working men have no country' (PKM 224), may be ascribed to an off-day.

34.2.3 Environmentalism

There is a sense, plainly enough, in which environmentalism yields an ideology. If we cast back to Bernard Williams' characterisation (§26), we find the requisite ideological features. Enviromentalism supports a system of political and social beliefs embodying a set of values or ideals and consequently some (highly general) principles of action, along with theoretical beliefs about human beings, society and the state (again highly general) which confer on those values or ideals their justification. No one acquainted with the growing body of green political theory could fail to recognise its increasing sophistication in all these regards.

Perhaps the main division in environmentalist (or 'green') thinking is between 'shallow' and 'deep' ecologism. Shallow ecologism stresses the importance of environmental issues from a purely human perspective. By contrast, deep ecologism is the view that 'natural things other than humans have value in themselves, value sometimes perhaps exceeding that of or had by humans' (Sylvan, 1985 (1): 2).

While green political theory, 'deep' or 'shallow', is unique in putting environmental considerations at centre-stage, there is virtually no originality in the forms of social and political organisation that it recommends. In nearly all cases, the solution is recognisably socialist, anarchist or liberal.

One of the pioneering tracts of green political thinking was Schumacher's *Small Is Beautiful*, which ends in a plea to socialists to 'recover their vision' (Schumacher, 1975: 260), that of a public enterprise economy serving the public interest and released from the obsessive objectives of capitalist growth.

If you turn to a markedly different approach, that of Alan Carter, you will find that anarchism (or more precisely the anarcho-syndicalism of workers' co-operatives) is to provide the basis of the new, green economy (Alan Carter, 1993: esp. 198-9).

Against Carter we can set environmentalist market theory according to which pollution and the depletion of non-renewable resources are reckoned as 'costs' imposed by specific producers and consumers on others: and costs should be judiciable. On these lines, there is no need for any basic change of economic or political organisation, let alone the abolition of market capitalism; the civil and criminal law have simply to be expanded. See Crocker & Rogers, 1971. This can easily be accommodated by economic liberalism.

The references that Sylvan provides in a hundred and one footnotes enable you to investigate these matters for yourself. You might also usefully consult Alan Carter, 1996; Elliot, 1995; Scherer & Attig, 1983; A. Vincent, 1992: ch. 8. In the classic tradition of political theory, only one major philosopher prior to the twentieth century appears to have given serious attention to environmental issues: namely John Stuart Mill in PPE IV.6: 750-1. On environmentalism and conservatism, see Wenz, 1986. On environmentalism and liberalism, see Sagoff in Elliot, 1995: ch. 10. For environmentalism and socialism, see Hayward, 1990, 1992 & 1994; Dobson, 1994. On environmentalism and feminism, see Plumwood in Elliot, 1995: ch. 9. In addition to the Alan Carter references above, the enviromentalism/anarchism link is explored in Bookchin, 1974.

34.2.4 International relations

Political philosophy has focused, for most of its long history, on the just, the perfect or at least the preferable society. Relations between societies have drawn relatively slight attention. Almost at the start of the tradition neither Plato nor Aristotle was interested in international (or more strictly, inter-*polis*) relations. Plato in fact, both in the *Republic* and in the *Laws*, was distinctly isolationist (cf. K.W. Thompson, 1994: ch. 3-4 for a different emphasis). Four main factors explain the customary neglect.

The first is the assumption that international relations present no significantly different issues, conceptually or normatively, from internal politics. If we believe in the free market domestically, then we should support international free trade. If we believe in democratic public participation, then we should support open diplomacy: and so on. The second, a hangover from the era of the nation-state, is the impression of international politics as peripheral, a matter of means towards more important, domestic ends.

The third factor is the view that 'international ethics' is an oxymoron, a contradiction in terms. The following two points are involved here: (a) the idea that, as a matter of entrenched and virtually irremediable fact, states pursue national interest regardless of the requirements of morality, so that moral appraisal of international relations simply bombinates in a vacuum; and (b) the rather different, less cynical idea that the rational conditions for international morality do not obtain, because morality requires trust and reliable co-operation in ways for which the states-system does not and perhaps cannot provide (cf. B. Barry, 1987: 85-6; Beitz in D. Held, 1991: ch. 9). Both of these viewpoints are known as versions of 'realism'.

Finally, politics and law are closely related; and the influence of the command theory of law (§15.2), which hardly fits the international realm, caused many scholars to think of international law as law only in an analogous or metaphorical sense.

There are, however, clear signs of increased interest in the international dimension of political philosophy. We may quickly mark up some points. The international realm no longer looks marginal in an age of globalisation; and the unco-operative pursuit of national interest is dubiously rational in face of environmental dangers that affect all countries. An old topic, that of the just war, received strongly revived attention during the Gulf War of the early 1990s. The concern for human rights has come into conflict with traditional ideas about non-intervention in the affairs of sovereign states. There is also a growing sense that aid to Third World countries is a matter of justice. So the points run on.

Nor is the historical picture wholly bleak. Past political philosophers have been concerned with international matters, even if this concern has not been central to the tradition. Aquinas speculated on the conditions for a just war (Aquinas, 1965: 159-61; but cf. a rueful Augustine, CG XIX.7: 861-2). Grotius' *De Iure Belli ac Pacis* [*On the Laws of War and Peace*], published in 1625, and Kant's *Idea for a Universal History with a Cosmopolitan Purpose* (1784) and *Perpetual Peace* (1795) are landmarks in the history of international thought. See also Hobbes, L ch. 13: 90; Locke, ST, ch. 16: 384-97; Hegel, PR §§321-60; T.H. Green, 1986: 121-38; Sidgwick, 1891: chs. 15-18; Bosanquet, 1917: ch. 13; Bosanquet, 1923: lix-lxi. On the history of international political theory, see K.W. Thompson, 1994; R.J. Vincent, 1986: ch. 2. For a brief guide to current developments, see Chris Brown's 'International Affairs' in Goodin & Pettit, 1995: ch. 27; C.A.W. Manning, 1962 is an older work which retains a good deal of value, as does Bull, 1977.

34.3 The classic texts

In the opening chapter I explained my reasons for not taking the 'classic texts' route through political philosophy (§9.2). But our discussions have at various points been informed by these texts, by the ideas and arguments which they contain. It is one thing to use the texts cautiously, for limited purposes, and another to let them colour and dominate one's whole approach to the subject.

Now that you have a structured view of political philosophy, you can safely slip into the pool with these ancient killers of the deep. No education in political philosophy is complete, or even properly begun, without acquaintance with:

- Plato's *Republic*
- Hobbes' *Leviathan*
- Hegel's *Philosophy of Right*

Plato and Hegel may safely be read in translation for all purposes of a standard political philosophy course at undergraduate level. Students are often advised to avoid commentaries, usually as a precaution against their reading commentaries instead of the originals. There is also a danger that, taken before one has read the original, a commentary will permanently skew one's later reading of the text. But commentaries are useful aids to study. For many students the classic texts are inert like a Frankenstein monster until galvanised into life by the electric spark of a clear, vigorous commentary. And when you are dealing with a writer as difficult as Hegel, commentary is virtually indispensable.

For the three texts mentioned, the commentaries most useful to a beginner are: (for Plato) Cross & Woozley, 1964 and Annas, 1981; (for Hobbes) Kavka, 1986 and Sorell, 1986; and (for Hegel) Pelczynski, 1971 and 1984.

34.4 Political philosophy and the unity of philosophy

Political philosophy is, as chapter 1 laboured to show, a part of philosophy. One point you will quickly realise about the classic texts is that they nearly all try to integrate politics into a broad philosophical conspectus. Hobbes' *Leviathan*, for instance, contains epistemology, metaphysics, philosophy of mind, philosophy of language, philosophy of religion and ethics, no less than political philosophy. Plato's *Republic* goes one better and includes aesthetics as well. One of the tasks that these texts present to scholars and students alike is the challenging one of working out the logical relations of this wider philosophy to the specific politics. Does Hobbes' epistemology entail certain parts of his political philosophy, or contradict it, or are the two merely consistent?

Aside from working on the classic texts, you can explore these matters in general terms for yourself. J.W.N. Watkins, 1957-58 is a useful short discussion of the relation between political philosophy and empiricist approaches to epistemology; see also Ayer & Naess in Elders, 1974: 27-30. Smellie, 1939, an older and longer work, is still of value, particularly on the relation of politics to metaphysics. This relation is also sharply examined in Unger, 1975, with a response in Ferré, 1978; note also Whyte, 1993: 113. See Parekh, 1968: 174-5, 184-94 on politics, metaphysics, and epistemology. Shearmur, 1990 takes a particular problem in the relation of politics to epistemology in Karl Popper's work. B. Barry, 1965: ch. 2 makes interesting use of J.L. Austin's speech act theory in the philosophy of language. Sidgwick, 1967: Bk I, ch. 2 (already cited in §5.1) is worthwhile on the relation of political philosophy to ethics, as are the articles in Hampshire, 1978.

34.5 Ideology and the unity of theory and practice

Finally you might make a start on the slow, hazardous and painful process of working out your own connected political position, theoretical and practical. Size up the ideologies we have discussed: are you mainly sympathetic to one of them, or do you feel the need to combine (say) socialism and feminism or liberalism and feminism? Using empirical assumptions – social, political, and economic – what policies and programmes in practical politics would best support your ideological principles?

The Cambridge political theorist, Goldsworthy Lowes Dickinson (1862-1932), confessed late in life his earlier belief that he could establish in short order the truth of certain political values and then, without more ado, see how best to translate them into practice. Working out your own commitments in a principled, informed, and realistic way – achieving Rawlsian reflective equilibrium in politics, if we care to use that idea (§5.5) – and deciding on their policy implications: all this is a long cut to which there are no short cuts. The person with whom you are most likely to disagree *en route* is – yourself.

Bibliography

Abbreviations of journal titles

A	*Analysis*
AHR	*American Historical Review*
AJP	*Australasian Journal of Philosophy*
AJPH	*Australian Journal of Politics and History*
APQ	*American Philosophical Quarterly*
APSR	*American Political Science Review*
ASSV	*Aristotelian Society Supplementary Volume*
BJHP	*British Journal for the History of Philosophy*
BJPS	*British Journal of Political Science*
C	*Cogito*
CC	*Capital and Class*
D	*Dialogue*
E	*Ethics*
HPT	*History of Political Thought*
HJ	*Hibbert Journal*
HM	*Historical Materialism*
HT	*History Today*
HTY	*History and Theory*
IMP	*Imprints*
INQ	*Inquiry*
JAP	*Journal of Applied Philosophy*
JHI	*Journal of the History of Ideas*
JHP	*Journal of the History of Philosophy*
JP	*The Journal of Philosophy*
JPI	*Journal of Political Ideologies*
JPP	*Journal of Political Philosophy*
JTP	*Journal of Theoretical Politics*
JVI	*Journal of Value Inquiry*
LRB	*London Review of Books*
LT	*Legal Theory*
MD	*Mind*
MT	*Monist*
NLR	*New Left Review*
NYRB	*New York Review of Books*
P	*Philosophy*
PAS	*Proceedings of the Aristotelian Society*
PBA	*Proceedings of the British Academy*
PE	*Philosophical Exchange*
PEW	*Philosophy East and West*
PHR	*Phronesis*
PHS	*Philosophical Studies*
PN	*Philosophy Now*

POL   *Politics*
PPA   *Philosophy and Public Affairs*
PQ   *Philosophical Quarterly*
PRV   *Philosophical Review*
PS   *Political Studies*
PSC   *Philosophy and Social Criticism*
PSQ   *Political Science Quarterly*
PT   *Political Theory*
R   *Ratio*
RIP   *Revue Internationale de Philosophie*
RM   *Review of Metaphysics*
RP   *Radical Philosophy*
S   *Synthese*
TLS   *The Times Literary Supplement*
U   *Utilitas*

'Original text' in the bibliography below refers to the date of publication (with suitable adjustment to that concept for the Greeks and Romans), not necessarily the date of composition.

Titles listed in the Abbreviations at the beginning of the book (pp. xv-xvi) are not repeated below.

Ackerman, J. (1980) *Social Justice in the Liberal State*, New Haven: Yale University Press.

Acton, H.B. (1972) 'Distributive Justice, the Invisible Hand and the Cunning of Reason', PS, 20.

Adaman, F. & Devine, P. (1997) 'On the Economic Theory of Socialism', NLR, 221.

Adams, I. (1989) *The Logic of Political Belief*, London: Harvester Wheatsheaf.

Adcock, F.E. (1964) *Roman Political Ideas and Practice*, Ann Arbor: University of Michigan Press.

Adlam, D. et al. ed. (1981) *Politics and Power Three: Sexual Politics, Feminism and Socialism*, London: Routledge & Kegan Paul.

Allardyce, G. (1979) 'What Fascism Is Not', AHR, 84.

Allen, B. (1991) 'Government in Foucault', CJP, 21.

Allen, J.W. (1928) 'Sir Robert Filmer', *The Social and Political Ideas of Some Thinkers of the Augustan Age*, ed. F.J.C. Hearnshaw, London: G.G. Harrap.

Allison, L. (1984) *Right Principles*, Oxford: Blackwell.

Altham, J.E.J. (1973) 'Rawls' Difference Principle', P, 48.

Altieri, C. (1989) 'Judgment and Justice under Postmodern Conditions', *Redrawing the Lines*, ed. R.W. Dasenbrock, Minneapolis: University of Minnesota Press.

Althusser, L. (1969) *For Marx*, Harmondsworth: Penguin.

Althusser, L. (1970) *Reading Capital*, London: New Left Books.

Annas, J. (1976) 'Plato's *Republic* and Feminism', P, 51.

Annas, J. (1977) 'Mill and the Subjection of Women', P, 52.

Annas, J. (1981) *An Introduction to Plato's Republic*, Oxford: Oxford University Press.

Apperley, A. (1999) 'Hobbes on Democracy', POL, 19.

Aquinas, St Thomas (1965) *Aquinas: Selected Political Writings*, tr. J.G. Dawson, Oxford: Blackwell. Latin original: *c.* 1250-73.

Arblaster, A. (1987) *Democracy*, Milton Keynes: Open University Press.

Archard, D. (1990a) 'Freedom Not To Be Free', PQ, 40.

Archard, D. (1990b) 'Paternalism Defined', A, 50.

Arendt, H. (1961) *Between Past and Future*, London: Faber & Faber.

Aristotle (1962) *The Politics, Books III & IV*, tr. R. Robinson, Oxford: Oxford University Press.

Aristotle (1981) *The Politics*, tr. T.A. Sinclair, rev. T.J. Saunders, Harmondsworth: Penguin.

Armstrong, T.J. (tr.) (1992) *Michel Foucault Philosopher*, New York: Routledge.

Arneil, B. (1996) 'The Wild Indian's Venison: Locke's Theory of Property and English Colonialism in America', PS, 44.

Arneson, R.J. (1989) 'Equality and Equal Opportunity for Welfare', PHS, 56.

Arneson, R.J. (1991) 'A Defence of Equal Opportunity for Welfare', PHS, 62.

Aron, Raymond. (1965) *Main Currents in Sociological Thought*, 2 vols [Montesquieu, Tocqueville, Comte, Marx, Pareto, Weber, Durkheim], London: Weidenfeld & Nicolson. (Reprinted in Penguin in 1970.)

Arrow, K.J. (1963) *Social Choice and Individual Values*, 2nd ed., New Haven: Yale University Press.

Arthur, C.J. ed. (1996) *Engels Today: A Centenary Appreciation*, London: Macmillan & St Martin's Press.

Ashcraft, R. (1986) *Revolutionary Politics and Locke's Two Treatises of Government*, Princeton NJ: Princeton University Press.

Ashcraft, R. (1987) *Locke's Two Treatises of Government*, London: Unwin Hyman.

Aubenque, P. (1961) 'Sur la notion aristotélicienne d'aporie', *Aristote et les problèmes de méthode*, Louvain: Publications Universitaires.

Auspitz, J.L. (1976) 'Individuality, Civility and Theory: the Philosophical Imagination of Michael Oakeshott', PT, 4.

Austin, J. (1954) *The Province of Jurisprudence Determined*, London: Weidenfeld & Nicolson. Original text: 1832 with subsequent additions.

Austin, J.L. (1961) *Philosophical Papers*, ed. J.O. Urmson & G.J. Warnock, Oxford: Oxford University Press.

Austin, J.L. (1962) *How to Do Things With Words*, ed. J.O. Urmson, Oxford: Oxford University Press.

Averini, S. (1968) *The Social and Political Thought of Karl Marx*, Cambridge: Cambridge Univeristy Press.

Avineri, S & de-Shalit, A. ed. (1992) *Communitarianism and Individualism*, Oxford: Oxford University Press.

Avio, K.L. (1997) 'Constitutional Contract and Discourse Ethics', JTP, 9.

Axford, B et al. (1997) *Politics: An Introduction*, London: Routledge.

Ayers, M.R. (1978) 'Analytical Philosophy and the History of Philosophy', *Philosophy and its Past*, ed. J. Rée et al., Hassocks: Harvester Press.

Bachrach, P. & Baratz, M.S. (1962) 'Two Faces of Power', APSR, 56.

Bachrach, P. & Baratz, M.S. (1970) *Power and Poverty: Theory and Practice*, New York: Oxford University Press.

Bader, V. (1995a) 'Citizenship and Exclusion: Radical Democracy, Community, and Justice. Or What is Wrong with Communitarianism?', PT, 23.

Bader, V. (1995b) 'Reply to Michael Walzer', PT, 23.

Bagehot, W. (1963) *The English Constitution*, ed. R.H.S. Crossman, London: Fontana. Original text: 1867.

Baier, K. (1972) 'The Justification of Governmental Authority', JP, 49.

Bailey, S. (1821) *Essays on the Formation and Publication of Opinions and Other Subjects*, London.

Baker, J. ed. (1995) *Group Rights*, Toronto: University of Toronoto Press.

Baker, J. (1997) 'Studying Equality', I, 2.

Baldwin, T. (1984) 'MacCallum and the Two Concepts of Liberty', R, 26.

Ball, T. (1996) 'Ideology and Consistency: A Dialogical Approach', JPI, 1.

Ball, T., Farr, J. & Hanson, R.L. ed. (1989) *Political Innovation and Conceptual Change*, Cambridge: Cambridge University Press.

Bambrough, R. (1965) 'Aristotle on Justice: A Paradigm of Philosophy, *New Essays on Plato and Aristotle*, ed. R. Bambrough, London: Routledge & Kegan Paul.

Bambrough, R. (1968) 'Universals and Family Resemblances', *Wittgenstein*, ed. G. Pitcher, London: Macmillan.

Barker, C. (1997) 'Some Reflections on Two Books by Ellen Wood', HM, 1.

Barker, E. (1951a) *Essays on Government*, 2nd ed., Oxford: Oxford University Press.

Barker, E. (1951b) *Principles of Social and Political Theory*, Oxford: Oxford University Press.

Barker, E. (1960) *Greek Political Theory: Plato and his Predecessors*, London: Methuen.

Barker, M. (1982) *The New Racism*, London: Junction Books.

Barry, B. (1965) *Political Argument*, London: Routledge.
Barry, B. (1973) *The Liberal Theory of Justice*, Oxford: Oxford University Press.
Barry, B. (1987) 'Can States Be Moral?', *International Ethics in the Nuclear Age*, ed. R.J. Myers, Lanham, MD: University Press of America.
Barry, B. (1995) *Justice as Impartiality*, Oxford: Oxford University Press.
Barry, N. (1981) *An Introduction to Modern Political Theory*, London: Macmillan.
Barry, N. (1997) 'Conservative Thought and the Welfare State', PS, 45.
Barry, N. et al. (1984) *Hayek's 'Serfdom' Revisited*, London: The Institute of Economic Affairs.
Baxter, B. (1982) *Alienation and Authenticity*, London: Tavistock.
Bayles, M.D. (1973) 'Reparations to Wronged Groups', A, 33.
Bayles, M.D. (1984) 'Intuitions in Ethics', D, 23.
Bayles, M.D. (1992) *Hart's Legal Philosophy: An Examination*, Dordrecht: Law and Philosophy Library.
Beal, M.W. (1974) 'Essentialism and Closed Concepts', R, 16.
Bealey, F. (1988) *Democracy in the Contemporary State*, Oxford: Oxford University Press.
Beardsley, M. (1978) 'Intending', *Values and Morals*, ed. A.I. Goldman & J. Kim, Dordrecht, Holland: D. Reidel.
Becker, C.L. (1941) *Modern Democracy*, New Haven: Yale University Press.
Becker, L.C. (1977) *Property Rights: Philosophic Foundations*, Routledge & Kegan Paul.
Bednarowski, W. & Tucker, J.W. (1965) 'Philosophical Argument', ASSV, 39.
Bell, E.F.B. (1908) *The Foundations of Liberty*, London: Methuen.
Beloff, M. ed. (1948) *The Federalist*, Oxford: Blackwell.
Benhabib, S. (1992) *Situating the Self: Gender, Community and Postmodernism in Contemporary Ethics*, New York: Routledge.
Benn, P. (1993) 'Pornography, Degradation and Rhetoric', C, 7.
Benn, S. & Peters, R.S. (1959) *Social Principles and the Democratic State*, London: George Allen & Unwin.
Bentham, J. (1843) *The Constitutional Code, The Works of Jeremy Bentham*, ed. J. Bowring, vol. 9, Edinburgh: William Tait.
Bentham, J. (1967) *Fragment on Government and Principles of Morals and Legislation*, ed. W. Harrison, Oxford: Basil Blackwell. Original texts: FG – 1776 and PML – 1780, rev. 1823.
Bentham, J. (1970) *Of Laws in General*, ed. H.L.A. Hart, London: Athlone Press. Original text: *c.* 1782.
Benton, T. (1981) ' "Objective" Interests and the Sociology of Power', *Sociology*, 15.
Beran, H. (1976) 'Political Obligation and Democracy', AJP, 54.
Beran, H. (1983) 'What is the Basis of Political Authority?', MT, 66.
Berki, R.N. (1975) *Socialism*, London: J.M. Dent & Sons.
Berki, R.N. (1977) *The History of Political Thought*, London: Dent.
Berki, R.N. (1983) *Insight and Vision: The Problem of Communism in Marx's Thought*, London: J.M. Dent.
Berki, R.N. (1988) *The Genesis of Marxism*, London: J.M. Dent.
Berlin, I. (1955) 'Equality', ASSV, 29.
Berlin, I. (1960) *Karl Marx*, London: Oxford University Press.
Berlin, I. (1969) *Four Essays on Liberty*, Oxford: Oxford University Press.
Berlin, I. (1978) 'An Introduction to Philosophy', *Men of Ideas*, ed. B. Magee, Oxford: Oxford University Press.
Berlin, I. (1990) *The Crooked Timber of Humanity*, London: John Murray.
Bernstein, R.J. (1979) *The Restructuring of Social and Political Theory*, London: Methuen.
Bertram, C. (1997) 'Public Reason', IMP, 2.
Bevir, M. (1996a) 'The Individual and Society', PS, 44.
Bevir, M. (1996b) 'Ideology as Distorted Belief ', JPI, 1.
Birch, A.H. (1964) *Representative and Responsible Government*, London: George Allen & Unwin.
Birch, A.H. (1971) *Representation*, London: Macmillan.
Black, A. (1997) 'Communal Democracy and its History', PS, 45.

Black, D. (1971) *The Theory of Committees and Elections*, Cambridge: Cambridge University Press.

Blackburn, R. ed. (1977) *Revolution and Class Struggle*, London: Fontana.

Blanshard, B. (1961) *Reason and Goodness*, London: George Allen & Unwin.

Blaug, R. (1996a) 'New Developments in Discursive Democracy', POL, 16.

Blaug, R. (1996b) 'New Theories of Discursive Democracy', PSC, 22.

Blondel, J. (1966) 'Government', *A Guide to the Social Sciences*, ed. N. Mackenzie, London: Weidenfeld & Nicolson.

Bluestone, N.H. (1987) *Women and the Ideal Society: Plato's Republic and Modern Myths of Gender*, Oxford: Berg Publications.

Bobbio, N. (1987) *The Future of Democracy*, Cambridge: Polity Press.

Bonner, J. (1986) *Politics, Economics and Welfare*, Sussex: Wheatsheaf.

Bookchin, M. (1974) *Post-Scarcity Anarchism*, London: Wildwood House.

Bosanquet, B. (1898) 'Hegel's Theory of the Political Organism', MD, 7.

Bosanquet, B. (1917) *Social and International Ideals*, London: Macmillan.

Bosanquet, B. (1923) *The Philosophical Theory of the State*, 4th ed., London: Macmillan. 1st ed.: 1899; 2nd ed. 1910; 3rd ed. 1920, 4th ed. 1923. The reader may feel envious that I have a copy of Prof. Smellie's annotated 1st ed. A consolation might be that I do not have Prof. Oakeshott's copy of any edition. The master's views remain silent.

Boucher, D. & Kelly, P. ed. (1994) *The Social Contract from Hobbes to Rawls*, London: Routledge.

Bowie, N.E. (1970) 'Equality and Distributive Justice', P, 45.

Bradley, F.H. (1927) *Ethical Studies*, 2nd ed., Oxford: Oxford University Press. Original text: 1876.

Bradley, F.H. (1935) 'The Presuppositions of Critical History', *Collected Essays*, Oxford: Oxford University Press.

Brandist, C. (1996) 'Gramsci, Bakhtin and the Semiotics of Hegemony', NLR, 216.

Brecher, B. (1993) 'Why Patronize Feminists? A reply to Stove on Mill', P, 68.

Breiner, P. (1989) 'Democratic Autonomy, Political Ethics, and Moral Luck', PT, 17.

Brenkert, G. (1991) *Political Freedom*, London: Routledge.

Brierly, J.L. (1949) *The Law of Nations*, Oxford: Oxford University Press.

Britton, K. (1953) *John Stuart Mill*, Penguin: Harmondsworth.

Brown, A. (1986) *Modern Political Philosophy*, Harmondworth: Penguin.

Brownsey, P. (1978) 'Hume and the Social Contract', PQ, 28.

Brunius, T. (1960) *Alexis de Tocqueville: The Sociological Aesthetician*, Uppsala: Almqvist & Wiksell.

Bubeck, D. (1998) Review of Clement (1998), PS, 46.

Buck, P.W. (1975) *How Conservatives Think*, Harmondsworth: Penguin.

Buckley, W.F. (1968) *Up from Liberalism*, New York: Bantam Books.

Bull, H. (1977) *The Anarchical Society*, London: Macmillan.

Burke, E. (1900) *Reflections on the Revolution in France*, ed. F.G. Selby, London: Macmillan. Original text: 1790.

Burke, P. (1986) 'City-States', *States in History*, ed. J.A. Hall, Oxford: Blackwell.

Burnet, J. (1930) *Essays and Addresses*, London: Macmillan.

Burnheim, J. (1985) *Is Democracy Possible?*, Cambridge: Polity Press.

Burns, E.M. (1963) *Ideas in Conflict*, London: Methuen.

Burns, C.D. (1921) *Political Ideals*, London: Oxford University Press.

Butler, E. (1985) *Hayek*, New York: Universe Books.

Butler Clarke, H. (1906) *Modern Spain: 1815-1898*, Cambridge: Cambridge University Press.

Cahm, C. (1989) *Kropotkin and the Rise of Revolutionary Anarchism, 1872-1886*, Cambridge: Cambridge University Press.

Callinicos, A. (1997) 'History, Exploitation and Oppression', IMP, 2.

Campbell, T. (1974) 'Rights without Justice', MD, 83.

Campbell, T. (1981) *Seven Theories of Human Society*, Oxford: Oxford University Press.

Campbell, T. (1988) *Justice*, London: Macmillan.

Caney, S. (1992) 'Thomas Nagel's Defence of Liberal Neutrality', A, 52.

Carling, A. (1997) 'Analytical and Essential Marxism', PS, 45.

Carlyle, T. (1888) 'Democracy', *Past and Present*, London: Chapman & Hall.

Carnoy, M. (1984) *The State and Political Theory*, Princeton: Princeton University Press.

Carr, C. (1983) 'The Problem of Political Authority', MT, 66.

Carr, E.H. (1962) *What is History?*, London: Macmillan.

Carter, Alan (1988) *Property Rights – Philosophic Foundations*, Hemel Hempstead: Harvester Wheatsheaf.

Carter, Alan (1993) 'Creating Co-operative Economy', C, 7.

Carter, Alan (1996) 'The Enviromental Crises and Political Theory', C, 10.

Carter, April (1971) *The Political Theory of Anarchism*, London: Routledge & Kegan Paul.

Carter, April (1973) *Direct Action and Liberal Democracy*, London: Routledge & Kegan Paul.

Carver, T. (1988) 'Ideology', C, 2.

Casey, J. (1978) 'Tradition and Authority', *Conservative Essays*, ed. M. Cowling, London: Cassell.

Cecil, Lord H. (1912) *Conservatism*, London: Williams & Norgate.

Centre for Contemporary Social Studies (1978) *On Ideology*, London: Hutchinson.

Chamberlin, R. (1988) 'On Being Made to Do What is Good for Us', C, 2.

Chapman, J.W. & Pennock, J.R. ed. (1989) *Markets and Justice*, New York & London: University of New York Press.

Charvet, J. (1969) 'The Idea of Equality as a Substantive Principle of Society', PS, 17.

Charvet, J. (1995) *The Idea of an Ethical Community*, Ithaca: Cornell University Press.

Chitty, A. (1993) 'The Early Marx on Needs', RP, 64.

Christiano, T. (1991) 'Difficulties with the Principle of Equal Opportunities for Welfare', PHS, 62.

Christman, J. (1991) 'Self-Ownership, Equality, and the Structure of Property Rights', PT, 19.

Chudnow, A. (1994) 'Natural Rights', PN, 10.

Cicero (1998) *The Republic and the Laws*, tr. N. Rudd, Oxford: Oxford University Prtess. Original texts, 54-52, 52-51 BC.

Clark, L.M.G. (1977) 'Women and John Locke; or, Who Owns the Apples in the Garden of Eden?', CJP, 7.

Clark, S. (1985) 'The Annales Historians', *The Return of Grand Theory in the Social Sciences*, ed. Q. Skinner, Cambridge: Cambridge University Press.

Clarke, E. (1891) *The Clarke Papers*, ed. C.H. Firth, vol. 1, London: Camden Society Publications.

Clement, G. (1996) *Care, Autonomy and Justice: Feminism and the Ethic of Care*, Oxford: Westview.

Coady, M. (1975) 'Considering Equality', P, 50.

Cobban, A. (1964) *Rousseau and the Modern State*, 2nd ed., London: George Allen & Unwin.

Coe, R.D. & Wilber, C.K. (1985) *Capitalism and Democracy: Schumpeter Revisited*, Notre Dame: University of Notre Dame Press.

Cohen, C. (1972) 'Autonomy and Government', JP, 49.

Cohen, G.A. (1978) *Karl Marx's Theory of History: A Defence*, Oxford: Oxford University Press.

Cohen, G.A. (1982) 'Functional Explanation, Consequence Explanation, and Marxism', INQ, 25.

Cohen, G.A. (1984) 'Nozick on Appropriation', NLR, 150.

Cohen, G.A. (1995) *Self-Ownership, Freedom and Equality*, Cambridge: Cambridge University Press.

Cohen, G.A. (1997) 'Commitment without Reverence', IMP, 1.3.

Cohen, M. ed. (1984) *Ronald Dworkin and Contemporary Jurisprudence*, London: Duckworth.

Colby, M. (1995) 'Moral Traditions, MacIntyre and Historicist Practical Reason', PSC.

Cole, G.D.H. (1947) *The Intelligent Man's Guide to the Post-War World*, London: Victor Gollancz.

Coleman, J. (1990) *Against the State: Studies in Sedition and Rebellion*, London: BBC Books.

Coleman, S. (1968) 'Is There Reason in Tradition?', *Politics and Experience*, ed. P. King & B.C. Parekh, Cambridge: Cambridge University Press.

Coleridge, S.T. (1972) *On the Constitution of the Church and State*, ed. J. Barrell, London: J.M. Dent. Original text: 1830, 3rd ed. (posthumous) 1839.

Collingwood, R.G. (1939) *An Autobiography*, Oxford: Oxford University Press.

Collingwood, R.G. (1993) *The Idea of History*, ed. J. van der Dussen, Oxford: Oxford University Press. Original text: ed. T.M. Knox, 1946.

Collini, S., Winch, D. & Burrow, J. (1983) *That Noble Science of Politics*, Cambridge: Cambridge University Press.

Connolly, W.E. (1983) *The Terms of Political Discourse*, 2nd ed., Oxford: Martin Robertson.

Constant, B. (1988) *Political Writings*, tr. & ed. B. Fontana, Cambridge: Cambridge University Press.

Coole, D. (1993a) 'Constructing and Deconstructing Liberty', PS, 41.

Coole, D. (1993b) *Women in Political Theory*, Hemel Hempstead: Harvester.

Cooper, N. (1991) 'The Art of Philosophy', P, 66.

Copleston, F.C. (1955) *Aquinas*, Harmondsworth: Penguin.

Copp, D. (1974) 'Justice and the Difference Principle', CJP, 4.

Covell, C. (1986) *The Redefinition of Conservatism*, London: Macmillan.

Covell, C. (1992) *The Defence of Natural Law*, London: St Martin's Press.

Cowan, J.L. (1972) 'Inverse Discrimination', A, 32.

Cowling, M. (1963a) *Mill and Liberalism*, Cambridge: Cambridge University Press.

Cowling, M. (1963b) *The Nature and Limits of Political Science*, Cambridge: Cambridge University Press.

Cowling, M. ed. (1978) *Conservative Essays*, London: Cassell.

Craib, I. (1988) 'The Personal and Political', RP, 48.

Craig, E. (1986-87) 'The Practical Explication of Knowledge', PAS, 87.

Cranston, M. (1954) *Freedom: A New Analysis*, 2nd ed., London: Longmans.

Cranston, M. (1962) *Human Rights Today*, London: Ampersand

Creppell, I. (1996) 'Locke on Toleration', PT, 24.

Crick, B.R. (1964) *In Defence of Politics*, Harmondsworth: Penguin.

Crick, B.R. (1972) *Political Theory and Practice*, London: Allen Lane.

Crocker, D.A. (1983) *Praxis and Democratic Socialism*, New Jersey: Humanities Press.

Crocker, T.D. & Rogers, A.J. (1971) *Environmental Economics*, Hinsdale, Ill.: Dryden Press.

Cropsey, J. (1977) *Political Philosophy and the Issues of Politics*, Chicago: University of Chicago Press.

Crosland, C.A.R. (1964) *The Future of Socialism*, 2nd ed., London: Jonathan Cape.

Cross, R.C. & Woozley, A.D. (1964) *Plato's Republic*, London: Macmillan.

Culyer, A.J. (1980) *The Political Economy of Social Policy*, Oxford: Martin Robertson.

Cunliffe, J. & Reeve, A. (1996) 'Exploitation: The Original Saint-Simonian Account', CC, 59.

Cunningham, R.L. ed. (1979) *Liberty and the Rule of Law*, Texas: Texas A & M University Press.

Cunliffe, J. & Reeve, A. (1996) 'Exploitation: the Original Saint Simonian Account', CC, 59.

D'Agostino, F. (1996) *Free Public Reason: Making It Up As We Go*, Oxford: Oxford University Press.

Dahl, R.A. (1958) 'Critique of the Ruling Elite Model', APSR, 52.

Dahl, R.A. (1965) 'The Concept of Power', *Human Behavior and International Politics*, ed. J.D. Singer, Chicago: Rand McNally.

Dahl, R.A. (1970) *After the Revolution?*, New Haven: Yale University Press.

Dahl, R.A. (1989) *Democracy and its Critics*, New Haven: Yale University Press.

Dahrendorf, R. (1959) *Class and Class Conflict in Industrial Society*, Stanford: Stanford University Press.

Dancy, J. (1983) 'Ethical Particularism and Morally Relevant Properties', MD, 92.

Dancy, J. (1992) 'Caring about Justice', P, 67.

Daniels, N. ed. (1975) *Reading Rawls*, Oxford: Blackwell.

Daniels, N. (1979) 'Wide Reflective Equilibrium and Theory Acceptance in Ethics', JP, 76.

Daniels, N. (1980) 'Reflective Equilibrium and Archimedian Points', CJP, 10.

Danto, A.C. (1968) *What Philosophy Is*, New York: Harper & Row.

D'Arcy, E. (1961) *Conscience and its Right to Freedom*, London: Sheed & Ward.

Darwall, S.L. (1983) *Impartial Reason*, Cornell: Cornell University Press.
Davis, M. (1983) 'Race as Merit', MD, 92.
Davis, P. (1991) 'Soft Pornography – What's the problem?', PN, 1.
Day, J.P. (1971) 'Locke on Property', *Life, Liberty and Property*, ed. G. Schochet, California: Wadsworth.
Day, J.P. (1977) Review of A. Ryan, J.S. Mill, MD, 136.
Day, P. (1981) 'Compensatory Discrimination', P, 56.
Day, P. (1986) 'Is the Concept of Freedom Essentially Contestable?', P, 61.
Dean, H.E. (1966) *Judicial Review and Democracy*, New York: Random House.
Deane, H.A. (1963) *The Political and Social Ideas of St Augustine*, New York: Columbia University Press.
D'Entrèves, A.P. (1951) *Natural Law*, London: Hutchinson's University Library.
DePaul, M.R. (1987) 'Two Conceptions of Coherence Methods in Ethics', MD, 96.
DePaul, M.R. (1988) 'The Problem of the Criterion and Coherence Methods in Ethics', CJP, 18.
Dent, N.J.H. (1988) *Rousseau*, Oxford: Blackwell.
Derrida, J. (1976) *Of Grammatology*, Baltimore: Johns Hopkins University Press. Original text: 1967.
Deutsch, K.W. (1966) *The Nerves of Government*, New York: Free Press.
Devigne, R. (1994) *Recasting Conservatism*, New Haven & London: Yale University Press.
Devlin, P. (1965) *The Enforcement of Morals*, Oxford: Oxford University Press.
Dews, P. (1987) *Logics of Disintegration*, London: Verso.
Dews, P. (1989) 'The Return of the Subject in late Foucault', RP, 51.
Dews, P. & Osborne, P. (1987) 'The Frankfurt School and the Problem of Critique', RP, 45.
Diamanti, F. (1998) Review of Arthur, 1996, PS, 46.
Dicey, A.V. (1982) *Introduction to the Study of the Law of the Constitution*, Indianapolis: Liberty Press. Original text: 1st ed. 1885, 8th ed. 1915.
Dickinson, G.L. (1905) *A Modern Symposium*, London: George Allen & Unwin.
Dickinson, G.L. (1962) *The Greek View of Life*, London: Methuen. Original text: 1896.
Dilthey, W. (1961) *Meaning in History*, ed. with introduction by H.P. Rickman, London: George Allen & Unwin. German original: mainly 1907-10.
Dobson, A. (1994) 'Ecologism & the Relegitimation of Socialism', RP, 67.
Dommen, E.C. (1964) 'A Paradox Punctured', PS, 12.
Donner, W. (1991) *The Liberal Self: John Stuart Mill's Moral and Political Philosophy*, Ithaca & London: Cornell University Press.
Double, R. (1992) 'Two Types of Autonomy Accounts', CJP, 22.
Dowding, K. (1996) *Power*, Buckingham: Open University Press.
Dowling, R.E. (1959) 'Oakeshott's Theory of Reason, Tradition and Conservatism', AJPH, 5.
Downie, R.S. (1964) *Government Action and Morality*, London: Macmillan.
Downing, D.B. & Bazargan (1991) *Image and Ideology in Modern/ PostModern Discourse*, New York: State University of New York Press.
Downs, A. (1957) *An Economic Theory of Democracy*, New York: Harper & Bros.
Doyle, J. (1998) 'Power and Contentment', POL, 18.
Drucker, H.M. (1972) 'Marx's Concept of Ideology', P, 47.
Dryer, D.P. (1979) *New Essays on John Stuart Mill and Utilitarianism*, ed. W.E. Cooper et al., CJP, Supplementary Volume 5.
Duffield, M. (1984) 'The New Racism and the New Realism', RP, 37.
Duguit, L. (1893) 'La Séparation des Pouvoirs et L'Assemblie Constituante de 1789', *Archives Parliamentaires*, 1st series, 39.
Dunbar, R. (1995) *The Trouble with Science*, London: Faber & Faber.
Dunleavy, P. & O'Leary, B. (1987) *Theories of the State*, London: Macmillan.
Dunn, J. (1984) *The Politics of Socialism*, Cambridge: Cambridge University Press.
Dunn, J. (1990) *Interpreting Political Responsibility*, Princeton NJ: Princeton University Press.
Dupré, J. (1983) 'The Disunity of Science', MD, 92.
Duran, J. (1995) 'The Possibility of a Feminist Epistemology', PSC, 21.
Duverger, M. (1966) *The Idea of Politics*, London: Methuen.

Dworkin, G. (1972) 'Reasons and Authority', JP, 49.
Dworkin, G. (1988) *The Theory and Practice of Autonomy*, Cambridge: Cambridge University Press.
Dworkin, R. ed. (1977) *The Philosophy of Law*, Oxford: Oxford University Press.
Dworkin, R. (1978) *Taking Rights Seriously*, second impression with appendix, London: Duckworth.
Dworkin, R. (1981) 'What is Equality?', Parts 1 & 2, PPA, 10.
Dworkin, R. (1985) *Law's Empire*, London: Collins.
Dworkin, R. (1986) *A Matter of Principle*, Cambridge, Mass.: Harvard University Press.
Dworkin, R. (1990) *A Bill of Rights for Britain*, London: Chatto & Windus.
Dye, T.R. & Zeigler, L.H. (1972) *The Irony of Democracy*, 2nd ed., Belmont, CA: Duxbury Press.
Eder, K. (1993) *The New Politics of Class: Social Movements and Cultural Dynamics in Advanced Societies*, London: Sage.
Edey, M. (1975) 'Inhumanity as a Way of Life', *Ethics in Perspective*, ed. K.J. Struhl & P.R. Struhl, New York: Random House.
Edmundson, W.A. (1995) 'Is Law Coercive?', LT, 1.
Elcock, H. (1976) *Political Behaviour*, London: Methuen.
Elders, F. ed. (1974) *Reflexive Water*, London: Souvenir Press.
Edel, A. (1963) *Method in Ethical Theory*, London: Routledge & Kegan Paul.
Elliot, R. ed. (1995) *Environmental Ethics*, Oxford: Oxford University Press.
Ellis, J.M. (1989) *Against Deconstruction*, Princeton NJ: Princeton University Press.
Elster, J. (1985) *Making Sense of Marx*, Cambridge: Cambridge University Press.
Emmet, D. (1979) *The Moral Prism*, London: Macmillan.
Engelmann, G. (1927) *Political Philosophy from Plato to Jeremy Bentham*, New York: K.F. Geiser.
Engels, F. (1969) *Anti-Dühring*, London: Lawrence & Wishart. German original: 1877-78.
Esquith, S.L. (1988) 'The Original Position as Social Practice', PT, 16.
Etzioni, A. (1996) *The New Golden Rule*, New York: Basic Books.
Eyal, G., Szelényi, I. & Townsley, E. (1997) 'Capitalism without Capitalists', NLR, 222.
Fay, B. (1975) *Social Theory and Political Practice*, London: George Allen & Unwin.
Fehér, F. (1987) *The Frozen Revolution*, Cambridge: Cambridge University Press.
Feinberg, J. ed. (1969) *Moral Concepts*, Oxford: Oxford University Press.
Feinberg, J. (1973) *Social Philosophy*, Englewood Cliffs, NJ: Prentice-Hall.
Fernbach, D. (1981) *The Spiral Path*, London: Gay Men's Press.
Fernbach, D. (1998) 'Biology and Gay Identity', NLR, 228.
Ferré, F. (1978) 'Metaphysical Error: Social Disorder', RM, 31.
Feyerabend, P. (1975a) *Against Method*, London: New Left Books.
Feyerabend, P. (1975b) 'How to Defend Society Against Science', RP, 11.
Field, G.C. (1963) *Political Theory*, London: Methuen.
Figgis, J.N. (1896) *The Theory of the Divine Right of Kings*, Cambridge: Cambridge University Press.
Filmer, Sir R. (1949) *Patriarcha; or, The Natural Powers of the Kings of England, and Other Political Works*, ed. P. Laslett, Oxford: Blackwell. Original text of Patriarcha: *c.* 1636-39.
Findlay, J. (1958) *Hegel*, London: George Allen & Unwin.
Fine, B. (1984) *Democracy and the Rule of Law*, London: Pluto.
Fine, B. et al. (1979) *Capitalism and the Rule of Law*, London: Hutchinson.
Finlayson, A. (1998) 'Ideology, Discourse and Nationalism', JPI 3.
Finley, M.I. (1977) 'Aristotle and Economic Analysis', *Articles on Aristotle: Ethics & Politics*, ed. J. Barnes, M. Schofield & R. Sorabji, London: Duckworth.
Finnis, J.M. (1980) *Natural Law and Natural Rights*, Oxford: Oxford University Press.
Finnis, J.M. (1985) 'A Bill of Rights for Britain? The Moral of Contemporary Jurisprudence', PBA, 71.
Firestone, S. (1970) *The Dialectic of Sex*, St Albans: Paladin.
Fisher, A. (1993) 'Problems in Understanding and Analysing Arguments', C, 7.
Fisher, H.A.L. (1944) *A History of Europe*, London: Edward Arnold & Co. Original text: 1936.

Fitzgerald, D.J. (1976) 'Liberty versus Equality', *Freedom, Proceedings of the American Catholic Philosophical Association*, 50.

Fitzgerald, R. (1980) *Comparing Political Thinkers*, Oxford: Pergamon Press.

Fitzgibbons, A. (1995) *Adam Smith's System of Liberty, Wealth, and Virtue*, Oxford: Oxford University Press.

Flathman, R.E. (1973) *Political Obligation*, London: Croom Helm.

Flathman, R.E. (1980) *The Practice of Political Authority*, Chicago: University of Chicago Press.

Flathman, R.E. (1989) *Toward a Liberalism*, Ithaca: Cornell University Press.

Flew, A.G.N. (1976) 'Three Questions about Justice in the *Treatise*', PQ, 26.

Forbes, I. (1990) *Marx and the New Individual*, London: Unwin Hyman.

Forrest, W.G. (1966) *The Emergence of Greek Democracy*, London: Weidenfeld & Nicolson.

Forsyth, M. et al. (1993) *The Political Classics: Hamilton to Mill*, Oxford: Oxford University Press.

Foucault, M. (1978) *The History of Sexuality*, vol. 1, New York: Pantheon.

Foucault, M. (1980) *Power/Knowledge: Selected Interviews and Other Writings*, New York: Pantheon Books.

Fraenkel, E. (1941) *The Dual State*, London: Oxford University Press.

Franco, P. (1990) *The Political Philosophy of Michael Oakeshott*, New Haven: Yale University Press.

Frankel, B. (1985) 'The Historical Obsolescence of Market Socialism – A Reply to Alec Nove', RP, 39.

Frankel, B. (1997) 'Confronting Neoliberal Regimes: The Post-Marxist Embrace of Populism and Realpolitik', NLR, 226.

Frankel, J. (1970) *National Interest*, London: Macmillan.

Frankena, W.K. (1955) 'Are There Any Natural Rights?', PR, 64.

Frankena, W.K. (1964) 'Natural and Inalienable Rights', PRV, 64.

Franklin, J.H. (1996) 'Allegiance and Jurisdiction in Locke's Doctrine of Tacit Consent', PT, 24.

Fraser, N. (1995) 'From Redistribution to Recognition. Dilemmas of Justice in a "Post-Socialist Age" ', NLR, 212.

Freeden, M. (1991) *Rights*, Minneapolis: University of Minnesota Press.

Freeden, M. (1994) 'Political Concepts and Ideological Morphology', JPP, 2.

Freeden, M. (1997) 'Ideologies and Conceptual History', JPI, 2.

Freedman, J.O. (1978) *Crisis and Legitmacy*, Cambridge: Cambridge University Press.

Freeman, M. (1996) 'Democracy and Dynamite: the People's Right to Self-Determination', PS, 44.

French, P.A. (1972) *Individual and Collective Responsibility*, Cambridge, Mass.: Schenkman Publishing Company.

Frey, R.G. (1977) 'Interests and Animal Rights', PQ, 27.

Frey, R.G. ed. (1985) *Utility and Rights*, Oxford: Blackwell.

Fricker, M. (1991) 'Reason and Emotion', RP, 57.

Friedrich, C.J. (1972) *Tradition and Authority*, London: Pall Mall Press.

Fukuyama, F. (1992) *The End of History and the Last Man*, London: Hamish Hamilton.

Fuller, L. (1969) *The Morality of Law*, New Haven: Yale University Press.

Fuller, S. (1988) *Social Epistemology*, Bloomington & Indianapolis: Indiana University Press.

Fuller, S. (1996) 'The Sokal Hoax', TLS, 20 December.

Gaius (1925) *Institutes of Roman Law*, 4th ed., tr. E. Poste, rev. E.A. Whittuck, London: Oxford University Press. Original text: mid-2nd century AD

Gallie, W.B. (1955-6) 'Essentially Contested Concepts', PAS, 56.

Gallie, W.B. (1964) *Philosophy and the Historical Understanding*, London: Chatto & Windus.

Galston, W.A. (1980) *Justice and the Human Good*, Chicago: University of Chicago Press.

Galston, W.A. (1991) *Liberal Purposes*, Cambridge: Cambridge University Press.

Gane, M. ed. (1986) *Towards a Critique of Foucault*, London: Routledge & Kegan Paul.

Gardiner, P. (1961) *The Nature of Historical Explanation*, Oxford: Oxford University Press.

Gellner, E. (1964) *Thought and Change*, London: Weidenfeld & Nicolson.

Gellner, E. (1982) 'Nationalism and the Two Forms of Cohesion in Complex Societies', PBA, 68.

Gellner, E. (1983) *Nations and Nationalism*, Oxford: Blackwell.

Geras, N. (1983) *Marx and Human Nature: Refutation of a Legend*, London: Verso.

Gert, B. & Culver, C. (1976) 'Paternalistic Behaviour', PPA, 6.

Gert, B. & Duggan, T.J. (1979) 'Free Will as the Ability to Will', N, 13.

Gerth, H. & Wright Mills, C. ed. (1948) *From Max Weber*, New York: Oxford University Press.

Gibson, Q. (1968) 'The Limits of Social Prediction', MT, 52.

Gilbert, M. & Berger, F.R. (1975) 'On an Argument for the Impossibility of Prediction in the Social Sciences', *Studies in Epistemology*, ed. N. Rescher, Oxford: Blackwell.

Gilby, T. (1953) *Between Community and Society*, London: Longmans.

Gilligan, C. (1982) *In a New Voice: Psychological Theory and Women's Development*, Cambridge, Mass.: Harvard University Press.

Gilmour, I. (1978) *Inside Right*, London: Quartet.

Ginsberg, M. (1965) *On Justice in Society*, Harmondsworth: Penguin.

Glotz, G. (1929) *The Greek City*, London: Kegan Paul.

Godwin, W. (1971) *Enquiry Concerning Political Justice*, ed. K.C. Carter, Oxford: Oxford University Press. Original text: 1791.

Goldman, A.H. (1975) 'Reparations to Individuals or Groups?', A, 35.

Goldman, A.H. (1976) 'Affirmative Action', PPA, 5.

Goldman, A.I. & Cox, J.C. (1996) 'Speech, Truth, and the Free Market in Ideas', LT, 2.

Goodin, R.E. (1982) *Political Theory and Public Policy*, Chicago: University of Chicago Press.

Goodin, R.E. & Pettit, P. ed. (1995) *A Companion to Contemporary Political Philosophy*, Oxford: Blackwell.

Goodin, R.E. & Pettit, P. ed. (1997) *Contemporary Political Philosophy*, Oxford: Blackwell.

Goodman, P. (1977) *Drawing the Line*, New York: Free Life Editions.

Goodman, R. (1974) 'Toward Liberation', *Man-Made Futures*, ed. N. Cross et al., London: Hutchinson.

Goodwin, B. (1982) 'The "Authoritarian" Nature of Utopia', RP, 32.

Gordon, C. ed. (1980) *Power/Knowledge: Michel Foucault*, New York: Pantheon Books.

Gordon, J. (1996) 'Liberation Theology as Critical Theory: the Notion of the "Privileged Perspective" ', PSC, 22.

Gorman, J. (1978) 'A Problem in the Justification of Democracy', A, 38.

Gorr, M. (1983) 'Rawls on Natural Inequality', PQ, 33.

Gottfried, P. (1990) Carl Schmitt, London: Claridge Press.

Gould, C. (1980) *Marx's Social Ontology*, Cambridge, Mass.: MIT Press.

Gourevitch, V. (1975) 'Rawls on Justice', RM, 28.

Graham, G. (1986) *Politics in its Place*, Oxford: Oxford University Press.

Graham, G. (1988) *Contemporary Social Philosophy*, Oxford: Blackwell.

Graham, G. (1992) 'Drugs, Freedom and Harm', C, 6.

Graham, G. (1997) *The Shape of the Past*, Oxford: Oxford University Press.

Graham, K. (1986) *The Battle of Democracy*, NJ: Barnes & Noble.

Graham, K. (1986-87) 'Morality and Abstract Individualism', PAS, 87.

Graham, K. (1996) 'Voting and Motivation', A, 56.

Grant, R. (1990) *Oakeshott*, London: Claridge Press.

Gray, A. (1946) *The Socialist Tradition: Moses to Lenin*, London: Longmans.

Gray, J. (1989) *Liberalisms: Essays in Political Philosophy*, London: Routledge.

Gray, J. (1993) *Post-Liberalism*, London: Routledge.

Gray, J. (1995a) *Isaiah Berlin*, London: HarperCollins.

Gray, J. (1995b) *Liberalism*, 2nd ed., Buckingham: Open University Press.

Gray, J. (1996) *Mill on Liberty: A Defence*, 2nd ed., London: Routledge.

Gray, J. & Smith, G.W. (1991) *J.S. Mill: On Liberty in Focus*, London: Routledge.

Gray, J. & Willetts, D. (1997) *Is Conservatism Dead?*, London: Profile.

Grayling, A.C. ed. (1995) *Philosophy*, Oxford: Oxford University Press.

Green, L. (1988) *The Authority of the State*, Oxford: Oxford University Press.

Green, P. (1981) *The Pursuit of Inequality*, New York: Pantheon Books.

Green, T.H. (1986) *Lectures on the Principles of Political Obligation and Other Writings*, ed. P.

Harris & J. Morrow, Cambridge: Cambridge University Press. Original text: 'Principles of Political Obligation' in lecture form, 1879-80.

Greenleaf, W.H. (1964a) *Order, Empiricism and Politics: Two Traditions of English Political Thought 1500-1700*, London: Oxford University Press.

Greenleaf, W.H. (1964b) 'The Divine Right of Kings', *History Today*, 14.

Greenleaf, W.H. (1966) *Oakeshott's Philosophical Politics*, London: Longmans.

Greenleaf, W.H. (1968) 'Idealism, Modern Philosophy and Politics', *Politics and Experience*, ed. P. King & B.C. Parekh, Cambridge: Cambridge University Press.

Greenleaf, W.H. (1983) *The British Political Tradition*, 2, *The Ideological Heritage*, London: Methuen.

Gregor, M. (1996) *I Kant: The Metaphysics of Morals*, Cambridge: Cambridge University Press.

Grey, T.C. (1973) 'The First Virtue', *Stanford Law Review*, 25.

Griffin, R. ed. (1995) *Fascism*, Oxford: Oxford University Press.

Griffin, R. (1993) *The Nature of Fascism*, London: Routledge.

Grimshaw, J. (1982) 'Feminism: History and Morality', RP, 30.

Grimshaw, J. (1989) 'Mary Wollstonecraft and Feminist Thought', RP, 52.

Grimshaw, J. (1996) 'Philosophy, Feminism and Universalism', RP, 76.

Grunebaum, J.O. (1987) *Private Ownership*, London: Routledge & Kegan Paul.

Gunew, S. ed. (1990) *Feminist Knowledge: Critique and Construct*, London: Routledge.

Habermas, J. (1984, 1987) *The Theory of Communicative Action*, 2 vols, Boston, MA: Beacon Press.

Habermas, J. (1993) *Justification and Application*, Cambridge, MA: MIT Press.

Hahn, F. & Hollis, M. ed. (1979) *Philosophy and Economic Theory*, Oxford: Oxford University Press.

Halberg, M. (1989) 'Feminist Epistemology – An Impossible Project?', RP, 53.

Hall, J.C. (1973) *Rousseau: An Introduction to His Political Philosophy*, London: Macmillan.

Hamilton, M.B. (1987) 'The Elements of the Concept of Ideology', PS, 35.

Hamlyn, D.W. (1970) *The Theory of Knowledge*, London: Macmillan.

Hamlyn, D.W. (1984) Review of B. Magee, *The Philosophy of Schopenhauer*, P, 59.

Hammond, M. (1951) *City-state and World-state in Greek and Roman Political Theory until Augustus*, Princeton: Princeton University Press.

Hampsher-Monk, I. (1987) *The Political Philosophy of Edmund Burke*, London: Longmans.

Hampsher-Monk, I. (1992) *A History of Modern Political Thought*, Oxford: Blackwell.

Hampsher-Monk, I. (1996) 'Varieties of Political Thought', BJHP, 4.

Hampshire, S.N. (1978) *Public and Private Morality*, Cambridge: Cambridge University Press.

Hampton, J. (1980) 'Contracts and Choices: Does Rawls Have a Social Contract Theory?', JP, 77.

Hardie, W.F.R. (1980) *Aristotle's Ethical Theory*, 2nd ed., Oxford: Oxford University Press.

Harding, N. (1998) 'Marx, Engels, and the Manifesto: working class, party, and proleteriat', JPI, 3.

Harré, R. & Robinson, D.N. (1995) 'On the Primacy of Duties', P, 70.

Harrington, M. (1993) *Socialism Past and Future*, London: Pluto.

Harris, J.W. (1980) *Legal Philosophies*, London: Butterworths.

Harris, P. ed. (1990) *On Political Obligation*, London: Routledge.

Harrison, J. (1975) 'The Expedient, the Right, and the Just in Mill's Utilitarianism', *New Essays in the History of Philosophy*, ed. T. Penelhum & R.A. Shiner, CJP, Supplementary Volume 1.

Harrison, R. (1970) 'No Paradox in Democracy', PS, 18.

Harsanyi, J.C. (1965) 'Measurement of Social Power, Opportunity Costs, and the Theory of Two-Person Bargaining Games', *Human Behavior and International Politics*, ed. J.D. Singer, Chicago: Rand McNally.

Hart, H.L.A. (1961) *The Concept of Law*, Oxford: Oxford University Press.

Hart, H.L.A. (1963) *Law, Liberty and Morality*, Oxford: Oxford University Press.

Hart, H.L.A. (1967) 'Social Solidarity and the Enforcement of Morals', *University of Chicago Law Review*, 35.

Hart, H.L.A. (1968) *Punishment and Responsibility*, Oxford: Oxford University Press.

Hart, W. (1975) 'How Are We to Read Philosophy?', *Haltwhistle Quarterly*, 3.

Hatzfeld, J. (1962) *Histoire de la Grèce Ancienne*, Paris: Payot.
Havelock, E.A. (1957) *The Liberal Temper in Greek Politics*, London: Jonathan Cape.
Havelock, E.A. (1963) *Preface to Plato*, Cambridge, Mass.: Harvard University Press.
Havelock, E.A. (1978) *The Greek Conception of Justice*, Cambridge, Mass.: Harvard University Press.
Hay, C. (1997) 'Political Theory and the Concept of Power', POL, 17.
Hayek, F.A. (1944) *The Road to Serfdom*, London: Routledge & Kegan Paul.
Hayek, F.A. (1948) *Individualism and Economic Order*, Chicago: University of Chicago Press.
Hayek, F.A. (1960) *The Constitution of Liberty*, London: Routledge & Kegan Paul.
Hayek, F.A. (1978) *New Studies in Philosophy, Politics, Economics and the History of Ideas*, London: Routledge & Kegan Paul.
Hayek, F.A. (1982) *Law, Legislation and Liberty*, London: Routledge & Kegan Paul.
Hayward, T. (1990) 'Ecosocialism – Utopian and Scientific', RP, 56.
Hayward, T. (1992) 'Ecology and Human Emancipation', RP, 62.
Hayward, T. (1994) 'The Meaning of Political Ecology', RP, 66.
Hearnshaw, F.J.C. (1937) 'Austin and State Sovereignty', *Some Great Political Idealists of the Christian Era*, London: G.G. Harrap.
Heath, J. (1995) 'The Problem of Foundationalism in Habermas' Discourse Ethics', PSC, 21.
Heilbroner, R.L. (1970) *Between Capitalism and Socialism*, New York: Vintage Books.
Heinemann, W. et al. (1948-49) 'Autonomous Ethics', HJ, 47.
Held, D. (1989) *Political Theory and the Modern State*, Cambridge: Polity Press.
Held, D. ed. (1991) *Political Theory Today*, Cambridge: Polity Press.
Held, D. & Pollitt, C. (1986) *New Models of Democracy*, London: Open University & Sage.
Held, V. (1970) *The Public Interest and Individual Interests*, New York: Basic Books.
Held, V. (1976) 'Coercion and Coercive Offers', *Coercion*, ed. Pennock & Chapman, Chicago: Aldine Atherton.
Heller, A. & Fehér, F. (1988) *The Postmodern Political Condition*, Cambridge: Polity Press.
Hewitt, G. (1976) *Economics of the Market*, London: Fontana.
Hindess, B. (1987) *Freedom, Equality, and the Market*, London: Tavistock Publications.
Hindess, B. (1996) *Discourses of Power: from Hobbes to Foucault*, Oxford: Blackwell.
Hinsley, F.H. (1966) *Sovereignty*, London: C.A. Watts.
Hirschmann, N.J. (1996) Toward a Feminist Theory of Freedom', PT, 24.
Hirst, P.Q. (1987) 'Carl Schmitt: Enemy or Foe? Carl Schmitt's Decisionism', *Telos*, no. 72.
Hirst, P.Q. (1994) *Associative Democracy*, Cambridge: Polity Press.
Hirst, P.Q. & Khilnani, S., ed. (1996) *Reinventing Democracy*, Oxford: Blackwell.
Hirst, P.Q. & Thompson, G. (1996) *Globalization in Question*, Oxford: Polity Press.
Hobson, P. (1984) 'Another Look at Paternalism', JAP, 1.
Hodges, H.A. (1944) *Wilhelm Dilthey: An Introduction*, London: Kegan Paul, Trench, Trubner.
Hoffman, J. (1997) 'Can We Define Sovereignty?', POL, 17.
Hogg, Q. (1947) *The Case for Conservatism*, Harmondsworth: Penguin.
Hoggart, R. ed. (1989) *Liberty and Legislation*, London: Frank Cass.
Hohfeld, W.N. (1964) *Fundamental Legal Conceptions as Applied in Judicial Reasoning*, ed. W.W. Cook, New Haven: Yale University Press. Original text: 1919.
Hollis, M. (1975) 'Ideological Explanation', *Explanation*, ed. S. Körner, Oxford: Blackwell.
Hollis, M. (1985) *Invitation to Philosophy*, Oxford: Basil Blackwell.
Holloway, J. (1997) 'A Note on Alienation', HM, 1.
Holmes, S. (1982) 'Liberal Uses of Bourbon Legitimism', JHI, 43.
Holmgren, M. (1989) 'The Wide and Narrow of Reflective Equilibrium', CJP, 19.
Honderich, T. (1993) *How Free Are You?*, Oxford: Oxford University Press.
Honig, B. (1993) *Political Theory and the Displacement of Politics*, Ithaca: Cornell University Press.
Honneth, A. (1993) 'Conceptions of Civil Society', RP, 64.
Hornsby, J. (1996) 'Free and Equal Speech', IMP, 1.
Hornsby, J. & Langton, R. (1998) 'Free Speech and Illocution', LS, 4.
Horsburgh, H.J.N. (1958) 'The Relevance of the Utopian', *Ethics*, 67.

Horton, J. (1992) *Political Obligation*, London: Macmillan.

Hsiao, K.C. (1927) *Political Pluralism*, London & New York: Kegan Paul, Trench, Trubner & Co.

Hudson, S.D. (1986) *Human Character and Morality*, London: Routledge & Kegan Paul.

Hume, D. (1975) *Enquiries Concerning the Human Understanding and the Principles of Morals*, ed. L.A. Selby-Bigge, rev. P.H. Nidditch, Oxford: Oxford University Press. Original texts: EHU, 1748; EPM, 1751.

Hume, D. (1978) *A Treatise of Human Nature*, ed. L.A. Selby-Bigge, rev. P.H. Nidditch, Oxford: Oxford University Press. Original text: 1739-40.

Hume, D. (1987) *Essays Moral, Political and Literary*, ed. E.F. Miller, Indianapolis: Liberty Press. Original text: in various editions between 1741 & 1777.

Hunt, I. ed. (1980) *Marxism and Democracy*, London: Lawrence & Wishart.

Hunold, C. & Young, I.M. (1998) 'Justice, Democracy, and Hazardous Siting', PS, 46.

Hunt, I. (1997) 'Engels in His Own Right', RP, 85.

Huntingdon, S.P. (1957) 'Conservatism as an Ideology', APSR, 51.

Hutchinson, J. & Smith, A.D. ed. (1994) *Nationalism*, Oxford: Oxford University Press.

Inge, W.R. (1940) *The Fall of the Idols*, London: Putnam.

Ivison, D. (1997) 'The Secret History of Public Reason: Hobbes to Rawls', HPT, 18.

Jaggar, A.M. ed. (1994) *Living with Contradictions*, Boulder, Colorado: Westview Press.

Janaway, C. (1988) 'History of Philosophy: The Analytical Ideal', ASSV, 62.

Jarrett, B. (1913) *Medieval Socialism*, London: T.C. & E.C. Jack.

Joachim, H.H. (1955) *The Nicomachean Ethics of Aristotle*, ed. D.A. Rees, Oxford: Oxford University Press.

Joad, C.E.M. (1936) *Guide to Philosophy*, London: Victor Gollancz.

Joad, C.E.M. (1938) *Guide to the Philosophy of Morals and Politics*, London: Victor Gollancz.

Johnson, P. (1988) 'Feminism and Images' of Autonomy', RP, 50.

Johnson, P. (1993) 'Feminism and the Enlightenment', RP, 63.

Joll, J. (1979) *The Anarchists*, London: Methuen.

Jones, A.H.M. (1957) *Athenian Democracy*, Oxford: Oxford University Press.

Jones, P. & Sidwell, K. (1997) *The World of Rome*, Cambridge: Cambridge University Press.

Jones, W.T. (1942) *Masters of Political Thought: Machiavelli to Bentham*, London: Harrap.

Jones, W.T. (1987) 'Rousseau's General Will and the Problem of Consent', JHP, 25.

Jordan, B. (1989) *The Common Good*, Oxford: Basil Blackwell.

Joseph, H.W.B. (1931) *Some Problems in Ethics*, Oxford: Oxford University Press.

Joseph, K. & Sumption, J. (1979) *Equality*, London: John Murray.

Jouvenel, B. de (1957) *Sovereignty*, Cambridge: Cambridge University Press.

Jouvenel, B. de (1962) *On Power*, Boston, USA: Beacon Press.

Jowett, B. (1925) 'Introduction' to *The Republic of Plato*, Oxford: Oxford University Press. Original text: 3rd ed. of Jowett's translation of Plato's *Republic*, 1888.

Kaiser, A. (1997) 'Types of Democracy: From Classical to New Institutionalism', JTP, 9.

Kane, J. (1996a) 'Why the Concept of Justice Does Not Presume Equality', PT, 24.

Kane, J. (1996b) 'Basal Inequalities: Reply to Sen', PT, 24.

Kant, I. (1969) *Foundations of the Metaphysics of Morals*, tr. L.W. Beck, New York & London: Macmillan. German original: 1785.

Kant, I. (1973) *Critique of Pure Reason*, tr. N. Kemp Smith, London: Macmillan. German original: 1st ed. 1781, 2nd ed. 1787.

Kaplan, M.B. (1997) 'Liberté, Egalité, Sexualité!: Theorizing Lesbian and Gay Politics', PT, 25.

Kaufmann, F. (1944) *Methodology of the Social Sciences*, Oxford: Oxford University Press.

Kavka, G. (1986) *Hobbesian Moral and Political Theory*, Princeton: Princeton University Press.

Keane, J. ed. (1988) *Civil Society and the State*, London: Verso.

Kedourie, E. (1984) *The Crossman Confessions and Other Essays in Politics, History and Religion*, London: Mansell.

Kernohan, A. (1990) 'Rawls and the Collective Ownership of Natural Abilities', CJP, 20.

Keynes, J.M. (1964) *The General Theory of Employment, Interest and Money*, London: Macmillan. Original text: 1936.

Keyt, D. (1987) 'Three Fundamental Theorems in Aristotle's Politics', *Phronesis*, 32.

Kierkegaard, S. (1962) *The Present Age*, New York: Harper & Row. Danish original: 1846.

Kirk, K.E. (1920) *Some Principles of Moral Theology*, London: Longmans.

Kitching, G. (1988) *Karl Marx and the Philosophy of Praxis*, London: Routledge.

Kline, G.L. (1980) 'The Myth of Marx's Materialism', JP, 77.

Klosko, G (1986) *The Development of Plato's Political Theory*, London: Methuen.

Klosko, G. (1987) 'Presumptive Benefit, Fairness and Political Obligation', PPA, 16.

Knowles, D. (1983) 'Hegel on Property and Personality', PQ, 33.

Kolakowski, L. (1969) *Toward a Marxist Humanism*, New York: Grove Press.

Kolakowski, L. (1978) *Main Currents of Marxism*, 3 vols, Oxford: Oxford University Press.

Kolakowski, L. & Hampshire, S. ed. (1977) *The Socialist Idea*, London: Quartet.

Körner, S. ed. (1975) *Explanation*, Oxford: Blackwell.

Kripke, S. (1972) 'Naming and Necessity', *Semantics of Natural Language*, ed. D. Davidson & G. Harman, Dordrecht: D. Reidel.

Kripke, S. (1980) *Naming and Necessity*, Oxford: Basil Blackwell.

Kropotkin, P. (1902) *Mutual Aid: A Factor in Evolution*, London: William Heinemann.

Kropotkin, P. (1970) *Kropotkin's Revolutionary Pamphlets*, ed. R.N. Baldwin, New York: Dover. Russian original: 1877-1917.

Kukathas, C. (1989) *Hayek and Modern Liberalism*, Oxford: Oxford University Press.

Kultgen, J. (1988) *Ethics and Professionalism*, Philadelphia: University of Pennsylvania Press.

Kurer, O. (1989) 'John Stuart Mill on Government Intervention', HPT, 10.

Kuttner, R. (1984) *The Economic Illusion*, Boston USA: Houghton Mifflin.

Kymlicka, W. (1989) *Liberalism, Community and Culture*, Oxford: Oxford University Press.

Kymlicka, W. (1990) *Contemporary Political Philosophy*, Oxford: Oxford University Press.

Labriola, A. (1908) *Essays on the Materialistic Conception of History*, Chicago: Charles H. Kerr & Co. Original text: 1896.

Lacey, A.R. (1982) *Modern Philosophy*, London: Routledge & Kegan Paul.

Lacey, N. & Frazer, E. (1994) 'Blind Alleys: Communitarianism', POL, 14.

Lacey, N. & Frazer, E. (1996) 'Reply to Lowe', POL, 16.

Lamb, P. (1997) 'Laski on Sovereignty: Removing the Mask from Class Dominance', HPT, 18.

Landesman, B.M. (1983) 'Egalitarianism', CJP, 13.

Langton, R. (1990) 'Whose Right? Ronald Dworkin, Women and Pornographers', PPA, 19.

Laqueur, W. ed. (1979) *Fascism*, Harmondsworth: Penguin.

LaSelva, S.V. (1988) 'Mill on Harm, Paternalism and Good Samaritanism', PS, 36.

Laski, H.J. (1917) *Studies in the Problem of Sovereignty*, New Haven: Yale University Press.

Laski, H.J. (1925) *A Grammar of Politics*, London: George Allen & Unwin.

Laski, H.J. (1933) 'Alexis de Tocqueville and Democracy', *The Social and Political Ideals of Some Representative Thinkers of the Victorian Age*, ed. F.J.C. Hearnshaw, London: George G. Harrap.

Laver, M. (1981) *The Politics of Private Desires*, Harmondsworth: Penguin.

Law, I. (1998) 'The Hierarchical Model of Autonomy', C, 12.

Lawrence, P.K. (1989) *Democracy and the Liberal State*, Aldershot: Dartmouth Publishing Company.

Lee, K. (1985) *A New Basis for Moral Philosophy*, London: Routledge.

Lefebvre, H. (1965) *Métaphilosophie*, Paris: Editions de Minuit.

Leftwich, A. ed. (1984) *What is Politics?*, Oxford: Blackwell.

Lemmon, E.J. (1965) *Beginning Logic*, London: Nelson.

Lessnoff, M. (1974) *The Structure of Social Science*, London: George Allen & Unwin.

Leitch, V. (1979) 'The Book of Deconstructive Criticism', *Studies in the Literary Imagination*, 12.

Lenin, V.I. (1931) *The Paris Commune*, London: Martin Lawrence. Russian original articles & speeches: 1905-19.

Lenin, V.I. (1947) *Materialism and Empirio-Criticism*, London: Lawrence & Wishart. Russian original: 1908.

Lenin, V.I. (1969) *The State and Revolution*, Moscow: Foreign Languages Publishing House. Russian original: written 1917, published 1918.

Lesser, H. (1979) 'Plato's Feminism', P, 54.

Lessnoff, M. (1974) *The Structure of Social Science*, London: George Allen & Unwin.
Levin, M. (1970) 'Rousseau on Independence', PS, 18.
Levin, M. (1981) 'Equality of Opportunity', PQ, 31.
Levin, M. (1982) 'Equality – Right!', PQ, 32.
Levin, M. (1999) 'On a Contradiction in Mill's Argument for Liberty', POL, 19.
Levine, A. (1988) *Arguing for Socialism*, 2nd ed., London: Verso.
Levinson, R.B. (1953) *In Defense of Plato*, Cambridge, Mass.: Harvard University Press.
Levitas, R. ed. (1986) *The Ideology of the New Right*, Oxford: Polity Press.
Levy, D.J. (1993) *The Measure of Man*, St Albans: Claridge Press.
Lewis, E. (1954) *Medieval Political Ideas*, London: Routledge & Kegan Paul.
Lewis, G.C. (1898) *On the Use and Abuse of Some Political Terms*, Oxford: Oxford University Press. Original text: 1832.
Leyden, W. von (1967) 'Aristotle and the Concept of Law', P, 42.
Liddington, J. (1984) 'Oakeshott: Freedom in the Modern European State', *Concepts of Liberty in Political Theory*, ed. J.N. Gray & Z. Pelczynski, London: Athlone Press.
Lilla, M. (1997) 'Germany's Top Anti-Liberal Thinker', NYRB, 15 May.
Limond, D. (1996) 'Anarchist or Antichrist? Bakunin on Fearing and Invoking Anarchy', PN, 16.
Lindsay, A.D. (1923-4) 'Sovereignty', PAS, 24.
Lindsay, A.D. (1943) *The Modern Democratic State*, London: Oxford University Press. (N.B.: the book bears the subtitle 'Volume One' but there is no second volume. Lindsay did not complete the work.)
Lippmann, W. (1937) *The Good Society*, London: George Allen & Unwin.
Lippmann, W. (1955) *The Public Philosophy*, Boston: Little, Brown & Co.
Lively, J. (1962) *The Social and Political Thought of Alexis de Tocqueville*, Oxford: Oxford University Press.
Lively, J. (1965) *The Works of Joseph de Maistre*, London: George Allen & Unwin.
Lloyd, D. (1964) *The Idea of Law*, Harmondsworth: Penguin.
Lloyd Thomas, D.A. (1977) 'Competitive Equality of Opportunity', MD, 86.
Lloyd Thomas, D.A. (1979) 'The Ones in Darkness', P, 54.
Lloyd Thomas, D.A. (1980) 'Kantian and Utilitarian Democracy', CJP, 10.
Lloyd Thomas, D.A. (1988) *In Defence of Liberalism*, Oxford: Blackwell
Lloyd Thomas, D.A. (1995) *Locke on Government*, London: Routledge.
Locke, J. (1975) *An Essay Concerning Human Understanding*, ed. P.H. Nidditch, Oxford: Oxford University Press. Original text: 1690.
Lorberbaum, M. (1994) Review of Tamir, 1993, M, 103.
Lord, A.R. (1921) *The Principles of Politics*, Oxford: Oxford University Press.
Lovibond, S. (1994) 'Feminism and the Crisis of Rationality', NLR, 207.
Lowe, T. (1996) 'Communitarianism as a Blind Alley: A Reply to Lacey and Frazer', POL, 16.
Löwith, K. (1934-35) 'L'Achèvement de la Philosophie Classique par Hegel et sa Dissolution chez Marx et Kierkegaard'. REP, 4.
Luard, E. (1979) *Socialism without the State*, London: Macmillan.
Lucas, J.R. (1965) 'Against Equality', P, 40.
Lucas, J.R. (1973) 'Because You Are A Woman', P, 48.
Lucas, J.R. (1966) *The Principles of Politics*, Oxford: Oxford University Press.
Lucas, J.R. (1972) 'Justice', P, 47.
Lucas, J.R. (1975) 'Equality in Education', *Education, Equality and Society*, ed. B.R. Wilson, London: George Allen & Unwin.
Lucas, J.R. (1976) *Democracy and Participation*, Harmondsworth: Penguin.
Lucas, J.R. (1977) 'Against Equality Again', P, 52.
Lucas, J.R. (1980) *On Justice*, Oxford: Oxford University Press.
Lugg, A. (1977) 'Feyerabend's Rationalism', CJP, 7.
Lukes, S. (1973a) *Individualism*, Oxford: Blackwell.
Lukes, S. (1973b) 'Methodological Individualism Reconsidered', *The Philosophy of Social Science*, ed. A. Ryan, Oxford: Oxford University Press.
Lukes, S. (1976) *Power: A Radical View*, London: Macmillan.

Lukes, S. (1985) *Marxism and Morality*, Oxford: Oxford University Press.
Lukes, S. (1998) 'Berlin's Dilemma', TLS, 27 March.
Lukes, S. ed. (1986) *Power*, Oxford: Blackwell.
Lyons, D. (1975) 'Welcome Threats and Coercive Offers', P, 50.
Lyons, D. (1978) 'Mill's Theory of Justice', *Values and Morals*, ed. A.I. Goldman & J. Kim, London: D. Reidel.
Lyons, D. (1984) *Ethics and the Rule of Law*, Cambridge: Cambridge University Press.
Mabbott, J.D. (1958) *The State and the Citizen*, London: Grey Arrow.
MacAdam, J.I. (1972) 'The Discourse on Inequality and the Social Contract', P, 47.
Macdonald, G. (1985-86) 'Modified Methodological Individualism', PAS, 86.
Macdonald, G. & Pettit, P. (1981) *Semantics and Social Science*, London: Routledge & Kegan Paul.
Macfarlane, L. (1966) 'On Two Concepts of Liberty', PS, 14.
Macfarlane, L. (1970) *Modern Political Theory*, London: Nelson.
MacIntyre, A. (1985) *After Virtue*, 2nd ed., London: Duckworth.
MacIntyre, A. (1988) *Whose Justice? Which Rationality?*, London: Duckworth.
Mackenzie, J.S. (1918) *Outlines of Social Philosophy*, London: George Allen & Unwin.
Mackenzie, W.J.M. (1958) *Free Elections*, London: George Allen & Unwin.
Mackenzie, W.J.M. (1967) *Politics and Social Science*, Hamondsworth: Penguin.
Mackenzie, W.J.M. (1970) *The Study of Political Science Today*, London: Macmillan.
Mackenzie, W.J.M. (1975) *Power, Violence, Decision*, Harmondsworth: Penguin.
Mackenzie, W.J.M. (1979) *Biological Ideas in Politics*, Manchester: Manchester University Press.
MacKinnon, C.A. (1989) *Toward a Feminist Theory of the State*, Cambridge, Mass.: Harvard University Press.
MacKinnon, C.A. (1993) *Only Words*, Cambridge, Mass.: Harvard University Press.
Mackridis, R.C. (1955) *The Study of Comparative Government*, New York: Random House.
Macpherson, C.B. (1962) *The Political Theory of Possessive Individualism*, Oxford: Oxford University Press.
MacRae, D. (1961) *Ideology and Society*, London: Heinemann.
Maine, Sir H. (1976) *Popular Government*, Indianapolis: Liberty Press. Original text: 1885.
Maistre, J. de: *On God and Society*, ed. E. Greifer, Chicago: Henry Regnery. French original: 1808-9.
Maistre, J. de: *The Works of Joseph de Maistre*, ed. J. Lively, London: George Allen & Unwin.
Maitland, F.W. (1911a) 'Equality', *Collected Papers*, ed. H.A.L. Fisher, Cambridge: Cambridge University Press.
Maitland, F.W. (1911b) 'Liberty', *Collected Papers*, ed. H.A.L. Fisher, Cambridge: Cambridge University Press.
Makkreel, R.A. (1975) *Dilthey, Philosopher of the Human Studies*, Princeton NJ: Princeton University Press.
Mann, M. (1988) *States, War and Capitalism*, Oxford: Basil Blackwell.
Manning, C.A.W. (1962) *The Nature of International Society*, London: G. Bell & Sons.
Manning, D.J. (1976) *Liberalism*, London: J.M. Dent.
Manning, D.J. ed. (1980) *The Form of Ideology*, London: George Allen & Unwin.
Mansbridge, J. (1983) *Beyond Adversary Democracy*, Chicago: University of Chicago Press.
Manuel, F.E. (1973) *Utopias and Utopian Thought*, London: Souvenir Press.
Margalit, E. & A. ed. (1991) *Isaiah Berlin: A Celebration*, London: Hogarth Press.
Maritain, J. (1947) *An Introduction to Philosophy*, tr. I.I. Watkin, London: Sheed & Ward.
Maritain, J. (1966) *The Person and the Common Good*, Notre Dame: University of Notre Dame Press.
Markovic, M. (1984) 'The Language of Ideology', S, 59.
Marshall, P. (1992) *Demanding the Impossible: A History of Anarchism*, London: HarperCollins.
Martin, M. & McIntyre, L.C. ed. (1994) *Readings in the Philosophy of Social Science*, Cambridge, Mass.: MIT.
Martin, R. (1974) 'Wolff's Defence of Philosophical Anarchism', PQ, 24.
Martin, R. (1977) *Historical Explanation*, Ithaca & London: Cornell University Press.

Martin, R. (1986) 'T.H. Green on Natural Rights in Hobbes, Spinoza, and Locke', *The Philosophy of T.H. Green*, ed. A. Vincent, Aldershot: Gower Press.
Martin, R. (1993) *A System of Rights*, Oxford: Oxford University Press.
Martin, R. (1995) 'Hart's Legal Philosophy', U, 7.
Marx, K. (1975) *The Poverty of Philosophy*, Moscow: Progress Publishers. Original text: 1847.
Marx, K. (1976) *Capital*, I, tr. B. Fowkes, Harmondsworth: Penguin. German original: 1867.
Marx, K. (1977) *Economic and Philosophic Manuscripts of 1844*, Moscow: Progress Publishers.
Marx, K. (1979) *The Class Struggles in France*, Moscow: Progress Publishers. Original text: 1850.
Marx, K. & Engels, F. (1950) *Selected Works*, Vol. II, London: Lawrence & Wishart.
Marx, K. & Engels, F. (1942) *Marx-Engels: Selected Correspondence*, New York: International.
Marx, K. & Engels, F. (1965) *The German Ideology*, London: Lawrence & Wishart. Original text: 1845-6.
Mason, A. (1990) 'Politics and the State', PS, 38.
Masters, R.D. (1989) *The Nature of Politics*, New Haven & London: Yale University Press.
Matthews, R.C.O. (1981) 'Morality, Competition and Efficiency', *Manchester School of Economic and Social Studies*, No. 4.
May, J.D. (1978) 'Defining Democracy: A Bid for Coherence and Consensus', PS, 26.
Mayer, J.P. (1977) 'Reflections on Equality', *The Socialist Idea*, ed. L. Kolakowski & S. Hampshire, London: Quartet Books.
Mayo, B. (1965) 'Human Rights', ASSV, 39.
Mayo, H.B. (1960) *An Introduction to Democratic Theory*, New York: Oxford University Press.
McCabe, M.M. (1998) 'What Kind of Equality Do We Want?', TLS, 20 March.
McCallum, R.B. (1946) 'Introduction', *On Liberty and Representative Government* (J.S. Mill), Oxford: Blackwell.
McCloskey, H.J. (1958) 'The State as an Organism, as a Person, and as an End in Itself', PRV, 67.
McCloskey, H.J. (1971) *John Stuart Mill: A Critical Study*, London: Macmillan.
McCoubrey, H. (1987) *The Development of Naturalist Legal Theory*, London: Croom Helm.
McKerlie, D. (1984) 'Egalitarianism', D, 23.
McLennan, G. (1989) *Marxism, Pluralism and Beyond*, Oxford: Polity Press.
McMahon, C. (1989) 'The Better Endowed and the Difference Principle', A, 49.
McPherson, C.B. (1962) *The Political Theory of Possessive Individualism*, Oxford: Oxford University Press.
McPherson, T.H. (1967) *Political Obligation*, London: Routledge & Kegan Paul.
McPherson, T.H. (1970) *Social Philosophy*, London: Van Nostrand Reinhold Co.
McTaggart, J.M.E. (1918) *Studies in Hegelian Cosmology*, Cambridge: Cambridge University Press. Ist ed.: 1901.
Mellor, M. (1996) 'The Politics of Women and Nature: Affinity, Contingency or Material Relation?', JPI, 1.
Mendus, S. (1986-87) 'Liberty and Autonomy', PAS, 87.
Mendus, S. (1992) 'Strangers and Brothers: Liberalism, Socialism and the Concept of Autonomy', *Liberalism, Citizenship and Autonomy*, ed. D. Milligan & W. Watts-Miller, Aldershott: Avebury.
Mepham, J. (1972) 'The Concept of Ideology in *Capital*', RP, 2.
Mepham, J. & Ruben, D.-H. (1981) *Issues in Marxist Philosophy*, Brighton: Harvester.
Merquior, J.G. (1985) *Foucault*, London: Fontana.
Mészaros, I. (1986) 'Marx's "Social Revolution" and the Division of Labour', RP, 44.
Miliband, R. (1973) *The State in Capitalist Society*, London: Quartet.
Mill, J.S. (1950) *Mill on Bentham and Coleridge*, London: Chatto & Windus.
Mill, J.S. (1958) *Considerations on Representative Government*, ed. C.V. Shields, Indianapolis & New York: Library of Liberal Arts. Original text: 1861.
Mill, J.S. (1971) *Essential Works of John Stuart Mill*, ed. M. Lerner, NY: Bantam Books.
Mill, J.S. (1987a) *Principles of Political Economy*, ed. Sir William Ashley, Fairfield, NJ: Augustus M. Kelley. Original text: 1st ed. 1848; 7th ed. 1871.

Mill, J.S. (1987b) *The Logic of the Moral Sciences*, Book VI of Mill, 1970, with introduction by A.J. Ayer.
Mill, J.S. (1989) *On Liberty and Other Writings*, ed. S. Collini, Cambridge: Cambridge University Press. Original text of *On Liberty*: 1859.
Mill, J.S. (1991) *On Liberty and Other Essays*, ed. J. Gray, Oxford: Oxford University Press.
Miller, D. (1976) *Social Justice*, Oxford: Oxford University Press.
Miller, D. (1977) 'Socialism and the Market', PT, 5.
Miller, D. (1980) 'Justice and Property', R, 22.
Miller, D. (1981) *Philosophy and Ideology in Hume's Political Thought*, Oxford: Oxford University Press.
Miller, D. (1984) *Anarchism*, London: Dent.
Miller, D. (1989) *Market, State and Community*, Oxford: Oxford University Press.
Miller, D. (1996) 'My Body is My Own', LRB, 31.
Millett, K. (1969) *Sexual Politics*, London: Abacus.
Mills, C. Wright (1963) *The Marxists*, Harmondsworth: Penguin.
Milne, A.J. M. (1997) Review of Charvet, 1995, U, 9.
Milo, R. (1995) 'Contractarian Constructivism', JP, 92.
Minogue, K. (1959) 'Power in Politics', PS, 7.
Minogue, K. (1964) Review of Cowling, 1963b, P, 39.
Minogue, K. (1972) 'Epiphenomenalism in Politics: The Quest for Political Reality', PS, 20.
Minogue, K.R. (1981) 'Method in Intellectual History', P, 56.
Mitchell, D. (1970) *Law, Morality, and Religion*, Oxford: Oxford University Press.
More, T. (1965) *Utopia*, tr. P. Turner, Harmondsworth: Penguin.
More, T. (1989) *Utopia*, tr. G.M. Logan & R.M. Adams, Cambridge: Cambridge University Press.
Morrall, J.B. (1977) *Aristotle*, London: George Allen & Unwin.
Morton, A.L. (1969) *The Life and Ideas of Robert Owen*, New York: International Publishers.
Mosse, G. (1970) *The Crisis of German Ideology*, London: Weidenfeld & Nicolson.
Mount, F. ed. (1992) *Communism*, Harvill [HarperCollins]: London.
Mueller-Vollmer, K. ed. (1986) *The Hermeneutics Reader*, Oxford: Blackwell.
Mulgan, R.G. (1977) *Aristotle's Political Theory*, Oxford: Oxford University Press.
Mulhall, S. & Swift, A. (1992) *Liberals and Communitarians*, Oxford: Blackwell.
Murdoch, I. (1992) *Metaphysics as a Guide to Morals*, London: Chatto & Windus.
Myres, J.L. (1927) *The Political Ideas of the Greeks*, New York: Abingdon Press.
Nagel, T. (1973) 'Equal Treatment and Compensatory Discrimination', PPA, 2.
Nagel, T. (1979) *Mortal Questions*, Cambridge: Cambridge University Press.
Nathan, N.M.L. (1993) 'Democracy', PAS, 93.
Neal, P. (1995) 'Dworkin on the Foundations of Liberal Equality', LT, 1.
Neocleous, M. (1996) 'Friend or Enemy? Reading Schmitt Politically', RP, 79.
Neocleous, M. (1997) *Fascism*, Milton Keynes: Open University Press.
Nesbet, R. (1981) *Twilight of Authority*, New York: Oxford University Press.
Newey, G. (1997) 'Metaphysics Postponed: Liberalism, Pluralism, and Neutrality', PS, 45.
Newfield, J.G.H. (1965-66) 'Equality in Society', PAS, 66.
Newman, J. (1954) *Foundations of Justice*, Cork: Cork University Press.
Nicholls, D. (1994) *The Pluralist State*, 2nd ed., London: Macmillan.
Nichols, M.P. (1992) *Citizens and Statesmen: A Study of Aristotle's Politics*, Savage, MD: Rowman & Littlefield.
Nicholson, P. (1973) 'The Relationship Between Political Theory and Political Practice', PS, 21.
Nicholson, P. (1990) *The Political Philosophy of the British Idealists*, Cambridge: Cambridge University Press.
Nickel, J.W. (1972) 'Discrimination and Morally Relevant Characteristics', A, 32.
Nickel, J.W. (1974a) 'Classification by Race in Compensatory Programs', E, 84.
Nickel, J.W. (1974b) 'Should Reparations be to Individuals or to Groups?', A, 34.
Nielsen, K. (1983) 'A Marxist Conception of Ideology', *Ideology, Philosophy and Politics*, ed. A. Parel, Ontario: Wilfred Laurier University Press.

Nielsen, K. (1991) 'Can there be Justified Philosophical Beliefs?', *Iyyun: The Jerusalem Philosophical Quarterly*, 40.

Nielsen, K. & Shiner, R.A. ed. (1977) *New Essays on Contract Theory*, CJP, Supp. Vol. 3.

Nietzsche, F. (1961) *Thus Spake Zarathustra*, tr. R.J. Hollingdale, Harmondsworth: Penguin. German original: 1883-85.

Nisbet, R. (1981) *Twilight of Authority*, New York: Oxford University Press.

Noone, J.B. (1981) *Rousseau's Social Contract*, London: George Prior Publishers.

Norman, R. (1985) 'The Politics of Equality', Review of Walzer, 1983, RP, 39.

Norman, R. (1986) 'Civil Disobedience and Nuclear Protest: A Reply to Dworkin', RP, 44.

Norman, R. (1996) 'From the Inside Out', RP, 76.

Norman, W. (1998) ' "Inevitable and Unacceptable?" Methodological Rawlsianism in Anglo-American Political Philosophy', PS, 46.

Norris, C. (1985) *The Contest of Faculties: Philosophy and Theory after Deconstruction*, London: Methuen.

Norris, C. (1987) *Derrida*, London: Fontana.

Norris, J. (1993) 'Lord Devlin and the Enforcement of Morals', C, 7.

Norton, D.L. (1987) 'Tradition and Autonomous Individuality', JVI, 21.

Nove, A. (1985) 'A Reply to Boris Frankel's Reply', RP, 39.

Nozick, R. (1977) 'On Austrian Methodology', S, 36.

Nozick, R. (1981) *Philosophical Explanations*, Oxford: Oxford University Press.

Nunn, W.A. (1974) 'Reverse Discrimination', A, 34.

Nuyen, A.T. (1993) 'The Unbearable Slyness of Deconstruction', P, 68.

O'Brien, D. (1994) 'Friedrich August von Hayek 1899-1992', PBA, 84.

O'Hear, A. (1985) *What Philosophy Is*, Atlantic Highlands, NJ: Humanities Press.

O'Neill, O. (1988-9) 'Moral Constructivisms', PAS, 89.

O'Neill, O. (1989) *Constructions of Reason*, Cambridge: Cambridge University Press.

O'Sullivan, N.K. (1976) *Conservatism*, New York: St Martin's Press.

O'Sullivan, N.K. (1983) *Fascism*, London: J.M. Dent.

O'Sullivan, N.K. (1992) *Santayana*, St Albans: The Claridge Press.

O'Sullivan, N.K. (1997) 'Difference and the Concept of the Political in Contemporary Political Philosophy', PS, 45.

O'Sullivan, N.K. (1998) 'The Tragic Vision in the Political Philosophy of Nikolai Berdyaev (1874-1948)', HPT, 19.

Oakeshott, M.J. (1933) *Experience and its Modes*, Cambridge: Cambridge University Press.

Oakeshott, M.J. (1936) 'History and the Social Sciences', *The Social Sciences*, Institute of Sociology, London: Le Play House Press.

Oakeshott, M.J. (1939) *The Social and Political Doctrines of Contemporary Europe*, Cambridge: Cambridge University Press.

Oakeshott, M.J. (1965) 'Rationalism in Politics: A Reply to Professor Raphael', PS, 13.

Oakeshott, M.J. (1975a) *On Human Conduct*, Oxford: Oxford University Press.

Oakeshott, M.J. (1975b) 'The Vocabulary of a Modern European State', PS, 23.

Oakeshott, M.J. (1976) 'On Misunderstanding Human Conduct: A Reply to My Critics', PT, 4.

Oakeshott, M.J. (1983) *On History*, Oxford: Blackwell.

Oakeshott, M.J. (1991) *Rationalism in Politics and Other Essays*, 2nd ed., T. Fuller, ed., Indianapolis: Liberty Press. (There is no revision of viewpoint between Fuller's edition and the original edition of 1962. Everything in the 1st edition is reprinted without amendment in the second. But Fuller usefully includes some extra items.)

Oakeshott, M.J. (1993) *Religion, Politics and the Moral Life*, ed. T. Fuller, New Haven & London: Yale University Press.

Oakeshott, M.J. (1996) *The Politics of Faith and the Politics of Scepticism*, New Haven: Yale University Press.

Œglart, B. (1970) *Idéologues et idéologies de la nouvelle gauche*, Paris: Union Générale d'Editions.

Okin, S. (1980) *Women in Western Political Thought*, London: Virago.

Okin, S.M. (1989) *Justice, Gender and the Family*, New York: Basic Books.

Olivecrona, K. (1974a) 'Locke on the Origin of Property', JHI, 35.

Olivecrona, K. (1974b) 'Locke's Theory of Appropriation', PQ, 24.

Oliver, K. (1988) 'Nietzsche's Woman', RP, 48.

Ollman, B. (1971) *Alienation: Marx's Conception of Man in Capitalist Society*, Cambridge: Cambridge University Press.

Oppenheim, F. (1981) *Political Concepts*, Oxford: Blackwell.

Orwell, G. (1949) *Nineteen Eighty-Four*, London: Secker & Warburg.

Orwell, G. (1938) *Homage to Catalonia*, London: Secker & Warburg.

Overend, T. (1983) *Social Idealism and the Problem of Objectivity*, St Lucia, Queensland: University of Queensland Press.

Palma. A.B. (1986) 'Intellectual Robotry', P, 61.

Palma, A.B. (1991) 'Philosophizing', P, 66.

Pangle, T. (1988) *The Laws of Plato*, Chicago: University of Chicago Press.

Pangle, T. (1989) *Montesquieu's Philosophy of Liberalism: A Commentary on The Spirit of the Laws*, Chicago & London: University of Chicago Press.

Parekh, B.C. (1968) 'The Nature of Political Philosophy', *Politics and Experience*, ed. P. King & B.C. Parekh, Cambridge: Cambridge University Press.

Parekh, B. ed. (1975) *The Concept of Socialism*, London: Croom Helm.

Parekh, B. & Berki, R.N. (1973) 'The History of Political Ideas', JHI, 34.

Parel, A. ed. (1983) *Ideology, Philosophy and Politics*, Calgary: Wilfred Laurier University Press.

Parent, W.A. (1974) 'Some Recent Work on the Concept of Liberty', APQ, 11.

Parker, M. (1996) 'Communitarianism and its Problems', C, 10.

Parker, N. (1982) 'What's So Right About Adam Smith?', RP, 30.

Parry, G. (1969) *Elites and Society*, London: George Allen & Unwin.

Parry, G. (1982) 'Tradition, Community and Self-Determination', BJPS, 12.

Parsons, S. (1987) 'Feminism and the Logic of Morality', RP, 47.

Partridge, P.H. (1963) 'Some Notes on the Concept of Power', PS, 11.

Pasquino, P. (1998) 'Locke on King's Prerogative', PT, 26.

Passmore, J. (1970) *Philosophical Reasoning*, 2nd ed., London: Duckworth.

Pateman, C. (1970) *Participation and Democratic Theory*, Cambridge: Cambridge University Press.

Pateman, T. (1988) 'Majoritarianism: An Argument from Rousseau and Condorcet', C, 2.

Patten, A. (1995) 'Hegel's Justification of Private Property', HPT, 16.

Paul, E.F. et al. (1995) *Contemporary Political and Social Philosophy*, Cambridge: Cambridge University Press.

Paul, J. ed. (1982) *Reading Nozick*, Oxford: Blackwell.

Paul, J. (1983) 'Substantive Social Contracts', MT, 66.

Peck, W.G. (1925) *The Divine Society: Christian Dogma and Social Redemption*, London: SCM.

Pelczynski, Z.A. ed. (1971) *Hegel's Political Philosophy*, Cambridge: Cambridge University Press.

Pelczynski, Z.A. ed. (1984) *The State and Civil Society*, Cambridge: Cambridge University Press.

Pennock, J.R. (1965) 'Hobbes' Confusing "Clarity" – the Case of "Liberty" ', *Hobbes Studies*, ed. K. Thomas, Oxford: Blackwell.

Pennock, J.R. (1979) *Democratic Political Theory*, Princeton: Princeton University Press.

Pennock, J.R. & Chapman, J.W. (1981) *Human Rights: Nomos*, 23, New York: New York University Press.

Perelman, C. (1963) *The Idea of Justice and the Problem of Argument*, London: Routledge & Kegan Paul.

Perlin, T.M. ed. (1979) *Contemporary Anarchism*, New Brunswick: Transaction Books.

Peters, R.S. (1956) *Hobbes*, Harmondsworth: Penguin.

Peters, R.S. (1966) *Ethics and Education*, London: George Allen & Unwin.

Peterson, R.T. (1988) 'The Original Position as Social Practice', PT, 16.

Pettit, P. (1980) *Judging Justice: An Introduction to Contemporary Political Philosophy*, London: Routledge & Kegan Paul.

Pettit, P. (1985-86) 'Social Holism and Moral Theory', PAS, 86.

Philp, M. (1986) *Godwin's Political Justice*, London: Duckworth.

Phillips, A. (1992) 'Must Feminists Give Up On Liberal Democracy?', PS, 40.

Pimlott, B. ed. (1984) *Fabian Essays in Socialist Thought*, London: Heinemann.

Pitkin, H. (1965) 'Obligation and Consent, I', APSR, 59.

Pitkin, H. (1967) *The Concept of Representation*, Berkeley & Los Angeles: University of California Press.

Pitkin, H. (1976) 'Inhuman Conduct and Unpolitical Theory', PT, 4.

Plamenatz, J.P. (1954) *German Marxism and Russian Communism*, London: Longmans.

Plamenatz, J.P. (1963) *Man and Society*, 2 vols, London: Longmans.

Plamenatz, J.P. (1968) *Consent, Freedom and Political Obligation*, 2nd ed., Oxford: Oxford University Press.

Plamenatz, J.P. (1970) *Ideology*, London: Macmillan.

Plamenatz, J.P. (1972) 'On le Forcera "Être Libre" [One Forces him to be Free]', *Hobbes and Rousseau*, ed. M. Cranston & R.S. Peters, New York: Doubleday Anchor. (Text in English.)

Plamenatz, J.P. (1973) *Democracy and Illusion*, London: Longmans.

Plamenatz, J.P. (1975) *Karl Marx's Philosophy of Man*, Oxford: Oxford University Press.

Plant, R. (1981) 'Democratic Socialism and Equality', *The Socialist Agenda*, ed. D. Lipsey & D. Leonard, London: Jonathan Cape.

Plant, R. (1991) *Modern Political Thought*, Oxford: Blackwell.

Plant, R. et al. (1980) *Political Philosophy and Social Welfare*, London: Routledge & Kegan Paul.

Plato (1956) *Protagoras*, ed. G. Vlastos, Indianapolis: Bobbs-Merrill.

Plato (1960) *Crito*, tr., H.N. Fowler, London: Heinemann [Loeb Library]. Greek original: *c.* 400 BC.

Plato (1961) *The Statesman*, tr. J.B. Kemp, London: Routledge & Kegan Paul. Greek original: *c.* 360 BC.

Plato (1970) *The Laws*, tr. T.J. Saunders, Harmondworth: Penguin. Greek original: *c.* 354-347 BC.

Plumwood, V. (1989) 'Do We Need a Sex/ Gender Distinction?', RP, 51.

Pocock, J.G.A. (1971) *Politics, Language and Time*, New York: Atheneum.

Pocock, J.G.A. ed. (1993) *The Varieties of British Political Thought, 1500-1800*, Cambridge: Cambridge University Press.

Popper, K.R. (1945) *The Open Society and its Enemies*, London: Routledge & Sons.

Popper, K.R. (1957), *The Poverty of Historicism*, London: Routledge & Kegan Paul.

Popper, K.R. (1963) 'Towards a Rational Theory of Tradition', *Conjectures and Refutations*, London: Routledge & Kegan Paul.

Poulantzas, N. (1978) *Political Power and Social Classes*, London: Verso.

Powell, J.E. (1965) *A Nation Not Afraid*, ed. J. Wood, London: B.T. Batsford.

Proudhon, P.-J. (1994) *What is Property?*, tr. & ed. D.R. Kelley & B.G. Smith, Cambridge: Cambridge University Press. French original: 1840.

Putnam, H. (1995a) 'Are Moral and Legal Values Made or Discovered?', LT, 1.

Putnam, H. (1995b) 'Replies to Brian Leiter and Jules Coleman', LT, 1.

Putnam, R. (1976) 'Rights of Persons and the Liberal Tradition', *Social Ends and Political Means*, ed. T. Honderich, London: Routledge & Kegan Paul.

Quinton, A.M. ed. (1967) *Political Philosophy*, Oxford: Oxford University Press.

Quinton, A.M. (1975-76) 'Social Objects', PAS, 76.

Raphael, D.D. (1950-51) 'Justice and Liberty', PAS, 51.

Raphael, D.D. (1964) 'Conservative and Prosthetic Justice', PS, 12.

Raphael, D.D. (1965) 'Human Rights', ASSV, 39.

Raphael, D.D. (1970) *Problems of Political Philosophy*, London: Macmillan.

Raz, J. (1986) *The Morality of Freedom*, Oxford: Oxford University Press.

Raz, J. (1990) *Authority*, Oxford: Blackwell.

Rawls, J. (1958) 'Justice as Fairness', PR, 57.

Rawls, J. (1963a) 'Constitutional Liberty and the Concept of Justice', *Nomos VI: Justice*, ed. C.J. Friedrich & J. Chapman, New York: Atherton Press.

Rawls, J. (1963b) 'The Sense of Justice', PR, 62.

Rawls, J. (1967) 'Distributive Justice', PPS 3.

Rawls, J. (1968) 'Distributive Justice: Some Addenda', *Natural Law Forum*, 13.
Rawls, J. (1969) 'The Justification of Civil Disobedience', *Civil Disobedience*, ed. H.A. Bedau, New York: Pegasus.
Rawls, J. (1974-75) 'The Independence of Moral Theory', *Proceedings and Addresses of the American Philosophical Association*.
Rawls, J. (1987) 'The Idea of an Overlapping Consensus', *Oxford Journal of Legal Studies*, 7.
Rawls, J. (1992) 'Justice as Fairness: Political not Metaphysical', *The Self and the Political Order*, ed. T.B. Strong, Oxford: Blackwell.
Rawls, J. (1993) *Political Liberalism*, New York: Columbia University Press.
Rawls, J. (1999) *Collected Papers*, Cambridge, Mass: Harvard University Press.
Raz, J. (1986) *The Morality of Freedom*, Oxford: Oxford University Press.
Raz, J. (1994) *Ethics in the Public Domain*, Oxford: Oxford University Press.
Réaume, D. (1996) 'What's Distinctive About Feminist Analysis of Law?', LT, 2.
Rees, J.C. (1971) *Equality*, London: Macmillan.
Rees, J.C. (1985) *John Stuart Mill's On Liberty*, Oxford: Oxford University Press.
Reeve, A. ed. (1987) *Modern Theories of Exploitation*, London: Sage Publications.
Regan, T. (1977) 'Frey on Interests and Animal Rights', PQ, 27.
Reid, L.A. (1962) *Philosophy and Education*, London: Heinemann.
Renan, E. (1939) 'What is a Nation?', *Modern Political Doctrines*, ed. A.E. Zimmern, London: Oxford University Press. French original: 1882.
Richards, J.R. (1982) *The Sceptical Feminist*, Harmondsworth: Penguin.
Richards, J.R. (1995) 'Why Feminist Epistemology Isn't (And the Implications for Feminist Jurisprudence)', LT, 1.
Rickman, H.P. (1979) *Wilhelm Dilthey: Pioneer of the Human Studies*, London: Paul Elek.
Riley, J. (1996) 'J.S. Mill's Liberal Utilitarian Assessment of Capitalism Versus Socialism', U, 8.
Ritchie, D.G. (1952) *Natural Rights*, London: George Allen & Unwin. Original text: 1894.
Robbins, L. (1984) *An Essay on the Nature and Significance of Economic Science*, 3rd ed., New York: New York University Press. 1st ed.: 1932.
Roberts, J. (1989) 'Political Animals in the Nicomachean Ethics', *Phronesis*, 34.
Roberts, M. (1996) *Analytical Marxism: A Critique*, London: Verso.
Rocco, C. (1995) 'The Politics of Critical Theory', PSC, 21.
Rodewald, C. (1974) *Democracy: Ideas and Realities*, London: Dent.
Roemer, J. (1988) *Free to Lose*, London: Radius [Century Hutchinson].
Rorty, R. et al. (1984) *Philosophy in History*, Cambridge: Cambridge University Press.
Rorty, R. (1988) 'The Priority of Democracy to Philosophy', *The Virginia Statute for Religious Freedom*, ed. M.D. Peterson & R.C. Vaughan, Cambridge: Cambridge University Press.
Rorty, R. (1991) 'Feminism and Pragmatism', RP, 59.
Rosen, F. (1975) 'The Political Context of Aristotle's Principles of Justice', PHR, 20.
Rosen, F. (1996) 'Editing Bentham', P, 16.
Rosen, M. (1996) 'The Problem of Ideology', ASSV, 70.
Rosenblum, N.L. ed. (1991) *Liberalism and the Moral Life*, Cambridge, Mass.: Harvard University Press.
Ross, W.D. (1930) *The Right and the Good*, Oxford: Oxford University Press.
Ross, W.D. (1949) *Aristotle*, 5th ed., London: Methuen.
Rousseau, J.-J. (1953) *Political Writings*, tr. & ed. F.M. Watkins, London: Nelson. French original of *Considerations on the Government of Poland*: 1772. French original of *Constitutional Project for Corsica*: 1765.
Rowe, C. (1992) 'Parasite or Fantasist? The Role of the Literary Commentator', C, 6.
Ruben, D.-H. (1977) *Marx and Materialism*, Sussex: Harvester Press.
Runciman, W.G. & Sen, A. (1965) 'Games, Justice, and the General Will', MD, 74.
Ruse, M. (1995) 'Gay Rights & Affirmative Action: A reply to Sartorelli', A, 55.
Russell, B.A.W. (1938) *Power: A New Social Analysis*, London: George Allen & Unwin. (Ch. 3 reprinted in S. Lukes, 1986: 19-27.)
Ryan, A. (1970) *The Philosophy of the Social Sciences*, London: Macmillan.
Ryan, A. ed. (1973) *The Philosophy of the Social Sciences*, Oxford: Oxford University Press.

Ryan, A. (1975) *J.S. Mill*, London: Routledge & Kegan Paul.

Ryan, A. (1984a) 'Changing Fashions in the Social Sciences', *History Today*, 34.

Ryan, A. (1984b) *Property and Political Theory*, Oxford: Blackwell.

Ryan, C.C. (1980) 'The Normative Concept of Coercion', MD, 89.

Sabine, G.H. (1951) *A History of Political Theory*, New York: Henry Holt.

Safire, W. (1972) *The New Language of Politics*, New York: Collier Books.

Safranski, R. (1998) *Martin Heidegger: Between Good and Evil*, Cambridge, Mass.: Harvard University Press.

Salisbury, R., 3rd Marquis (1871) 'The Commune and the Internationale', *Quarterly Review*, 131, October.

Samuelson, P.A. (1947) *Foundations of Economic Analysis*, Cambridge, Mass.: Harvard University Press.

Sandel, M. (1982) *Liberalism and the Limits of Justice*, Cambridge: Cambridge University Press.

Sankey, H. (1994) 'Relativism and Epistemological Anarchism', C, 8.

Sarkar, H. (1982) 'The Lockean Proviso', CJP, 12.

Sartorelli, J. (1994) 'Ruse on Gay Rights and Affirmative Action', A, 54.

Sartori, G. (1965) *Democratic Theory*, New York: Praeger.

Scherer, D. & Attig, T. ed. (1983) *Ethics and the Environment*, Englewood Cliffs, NJ: Prentice-Hall.

Scheuerman, W.E. (1997) 'The Rule of Law at Century's End', PT, 25.

Schlossenberger, E. (1989) 'Civil Disobedience', A, 49.

Schmitt, C. (1976) *The Concept of the Political*, tr. G. Schwab, New Brunswick: Rutgers University Press. German original: 1927.

Schopenahuer, A. (1951) *Essays from the Parerga and Paralipomena*, tr. T.B. Saunders, London: George Allen & Unwin. German original: 1851. (The title means roughly 'marginalia and omissions'.)

Scott, J. (1997) 'French Feminists Go for Equal Shares', NLR, 227.

Schumacher, E.F. (1975) *Small Is Beautiful*, New York: Harper & Row.

Schumpeter, J. (1947) *Capitalism, Socialism, and Democracy*, London: George Allen & Unwin.

Schwarzmantel, J. (1987) *Structures of Power*, Sussex: Wheatsheaf Books.

Scruton, R. (1982) *Kant*, Oxford: Oxford University Press.

Scruton, R. (1983) *A Dictionary of Political Thought*, London: Pan.

Scruton, R. (1984) *The Meaning of Conservatism*, 2nd ed., Harmondsworth: Penguin.

Scruton, R. ed. (1991) *Conservative Texts*, London: Macmillan.

Segal, L. (1990) *Slow Motion: Changing Masculinities, Changing Men*, London: Virago.

Sen, A.K. (1970) *Collective Choice and Social Welfare*, San Francisco: Holden-Day.

Sen, A.K. (1996) 'On the Status of Equality', PT, 24.

Sennett, R. (1997) 'Drowning in Syrup: The Dangers of Seeking Catharsis in Shared Values', TLS, 7 February.

Shalom, S.R. ed. (1983) *Socialist Visions*, London: Pluto.

Shapiro, D. (1982) 'Does Ronald Dworkin Take Rights Seriously?', CJP, 12.

Shapiro, I. (1996) 'Elements of Democratic Justice', PT, 24.

Sharma, A. (1979) 'All Religions are – Equal? One? True? Same?: A Critical Examination of Some Formulations of the Neo-Hindu Position', PEW, 29.

Shaw, M. (1975) *Marxism and Social Science*, London: Pluto Press.

Shearmur, J. (1990) 'Epistemological Limits of the State: Reflections on Popper's Open Society', PS, 38.

Sher, G. (1974) 'Justifying Reverse Discrimination in Employment', PPA, 3.

Sherwin, E. (1995) 'How Liberal is Liberal Equality?', LT, 1.

Shiner, R.A. (1973) 'Individuals, Groups and Inverse Discrimination', A, 33.

Shklar, J.N. (1966) 'Rousseau's Two Models: Sparta and the Age of Gold', PSQ, 81.

Shklar, J.N. (1972) 'Rousseau's Images of Authority', *Hobbes and Rousseau*, ed. M. Cranston & R.S. Peters, New York: Doubleday Anchor.

Sidgwick, H. (1891) *The Elements of Politics*, London: Macmillan.

Sidgwick, H. (1967) *The Methods of Ethics*, 7th ed., London: Macmillan. Original text: 1st ed., 1874; 7th ed., 1907.

Sigmund, P.E. (1971) *Natural Law in Political Thought*, Cambridge, Mass.: Winthrop Publishers.

Silvestri, P. (1973) 'The Justification of Inverse Discrimination', A, 34.

Simhony, A. (1991) 'On Forcing Individuals to be Free: T.H. Green's Liberal Theory of Politive Freedom', PS, 39.

Simhony, A. (1993) 'Beyond Negative and Positive Freedom', PT, 21.

Simmons, A.J. (1979) *Moral Principles and Political Obligations*, Princeton: Princeton University Press.

Simmons, A.J. (1996) 'Philosophical Anarchism', *For & Against the State*, ed. J. Narveson et al., Maryland: Rowman & Littlefield.

Simon, R. (1974) 'Preferential Hiring: A Reply to Judith Jarvis Thomson', PPA, 3.

Sinclair, T.A. (1951) *A History of Greek Political Thought*, London: Routledge.

Singer, P. (1973) *Democracy and Disobedience*, Oxford: Oxford University Press.

Singer, P. (1983) *Hegel*, Oxford: Oxford University Press.

Singh, R. (1967) *Reason, Revolution and Political Theory*, New Delhi: People's Publishing House.

Skillen, A. (1972) 'The Statist Conception of Politics', RP, 2.

Skillen, A. (1977) *Ruling Illusions*, Hassocks: Harvester.

Skillen, A. (1985) 'Politics Re-entered: the State in its Place', RP, 41.

Skillen, A. (1992) 'Reply to Rorty on Pragmatism and Feminism', RP, 62.

Skinner, Q. (1969) 'Meanings and Understanding in the History of Ideas', HTY, 8.

Skinner, Q. (1979) *The Foundations of Modern Political Thought*, 2 vols, Cambridge: Cambridge University Press.

Skinner, Q. (1984) 'The Idea of Negative Liberty: Philosophical and Historical Perspectives', *Philosophy in History*, ed. R. Rorty.

Skinner, Q. (1989) 'The State', *Political Innovation and Conceptual Change*, ed. T. Ball, J. Farr & R.L. Hanson, Cambridge: Cambridge University Press. (Reprinted in Goodin & Pettit, 1997.)

Sklar, L. (1975) 'Methodological Conservatism', PR, 84.

Smellie, K.B. (1939) *Reason in Politics*, London: Duckworth.

Smith, A. (1961) *An Inquiry into the Nature and Causes of the Wealth of Nations*, I & II, London: Methuen. Original text: 1776.

Smith, J.A. (1911) 'Introduction' to *The Nicomachean Ethics of Aristotle*, tr. D.P. Chase, London: J.M. Dent.

Soper, K. (1990) *Troubled Pleasures*, London: Verso.

Sorel, G. (1950) *Reflections on Violence*, tr. T.E. Hulme & J. Roth, Glencoe, Ill.: Free Press. Original text: 1907.

Sorell, T. (1986) *Hobbes*, London: Routledge & Kegan Paul.

Spencer, H. (1969) *The Man versus the State, With Four Essays on Politics and Society*, ed. D. MacRae, Harmondsworth: Penguin. Original texts: 1884, 1892.

Spitz, D. (1964) *Essays in the Liberal Idea of Freedom*, Tucson: University of Arizona Press.

Spitz, D. (1976) 'A Rationalist *Malgré Lui*', PT, 4.

Stace, W.T. (1955) *Hegel*, New York: Dover.

Stalley, R.E. (1983) *An Introduction to Plato's Laws*, Oxford: Blackwell.

Stankiewicz, W.J. (1976) *Aspects of Political Theory*, London: Collier Macmillan.

Steiner, H. (1977) Critical Notice of Nozick, *Anarchy, State and Utopia*, MD, 86.

Stephen, J.F. (1873) *Liberty, Equality, Fraternity*, London: Smith, Elder.

Stoller, R. (1968) *Sex and Gender*, New York: Science House.

Stone, L. (1981) *The Past and the Present*, London: Routledge.

Stove, D. (1993) 'The Subjection of John Stuart Mill', P, 68.

Stratton-Lake, P. (1997) Review of Charvet, *The Idea of an Ethical Community*, MD, 106.

Strauss, L. (1936) *The Political Philosophy of Hobbes*, Oxford: Oxford University Press.

Strauss, L. (1953) *Natural Right and History*, Chicago: University of Chicago Press.

Strauss, L. (1959) *What is Political Philosophy?*, Chicago: University of Chicago Press.

Strauss, L. (1964) *The City and Man*, Chicago: Rand McNally.

Suchting, W. (1982) 'On Materialism', RP, 31.

Summers, R.S. ed. (1968) *Essays in Legal Philosophy*, Berkeley: University of California Press.

Susser, B. (1988) *The Grammar of Modern Ideology*, London: Routledge.

Susser, B. (1996) 'The Domains of Ideological Discourse', JPI, 1.

Swanson, S.G. (1997) 'The Medieval Foundations of John Locke's Theory of Natural Rights: Rights of Subsistence and the Principle of Extreme Necessity', HPT, 18.

Swanton, C. (1979) 'The Concept of Overall Freedom', AJP, 57.

Swanton, C. (1981) 'Is the Difference Principle a Principle of Justice?', MD, 90.

Sweet, W. (1996) 'F.H. Bradley and Bernard Bosanquet', *Philosophy After Bradley*, ed. J. Bradley, Bristol: Thoemmes Press.

Sweet, W. (1997) *The Social Ontology of Rights in the Political Thought of Bernard Bosanquet*, Lanham: MD: University Press of America.

Sylvan, R. (1985) 'A Critique of Deep Ecology', (1) RP, 40. (2) RP, 41.

Sypnowich, C. (1990) *The Concept of Socialist Law*, Oxford: Oxford University Press.

Tamir, Y. (1993) *Liberal Nationalism*, Princeton NJ: Princeton University Press.

Tännsjö, T. (1990) *Conservatism For Our Time*, London: Routledge.

Tate, J.W. (1997) 'Dead or Alive? Reflective versus Unreflective Traditions', PSC, 23.

Tawney, R.H. (1964) *The Radical Tradition*, ed. R. Hinden, Penguin: Harmondsworth.

Taylor, A.E. (1965) 'The Ethical Doctrine of Hobbes', *Hobbes Studies*, ed. K. Thomas, Oxford: Blackwell. Original text: 1938.

Taylor, A.J.P. (1976) *Essays in English History*, Harmondsworth: Penguin.

Taylor, P.W. (1973) 'Reverse Discrimination and Compensatory Justice', A, 33.

Teichman, J. (1993) 'Deconstruction and Aerodynamics', P, 68.

Thomas, G. (1993) *An Introduction to Ethics*, London: Duckworth.

Thomas, R. (1997) 'Enigmatic Writings: Karl Marx's The Civil War in France and the Paris Commune of 1871', HPT, 18.

Thompson, D.F. (1987) *Political Ethics and Public Office*, Cambridge, Mass.: Harvard University Press.

Thompson, E.P. (1978) *The Poverty of Theory*, New York: Monthly Review.

Thompson, J. (1983) 'Women and the High Priests of Reason', RP, 34.

Thompson, K.W. (1994) *Fathers of International Thought*, Baton Rouge: Louisiana State University Press.

Thomson, A. (1993) 'Page three – to ban or not to ban', C, 7.

Thomson, G. (1987) *Needs*, London: Routledge.

Thomson, J.J. (1973) 'Preferential Hiring', PPA, 2.

Thoreau, H.D. (1960) *Walden and Civil Disobedience*, New York: Signet Classics.

Thucydides (1954) *The Peloponnesian War*, tr. R. Warner, Harmondsworth: Penguin. Greek original: *c.* 400-420 BC.

Tiles, J. (1984) 'On a New Methodological Individualism', R, 26.

Todd, N. (1986) *Roses and Revolutionists*, London: People's Publications.

Trevor-Roper, H.R. (1962) 'E.H. Carr's Success Story', *Encounter*, 18.

Tuck, R. (1979) *Natural Rights Theories: Their Origin and Development*, Cambridge: Cambridge University Press.

Tuck, R. (1981) Review of Finnis, 1980, PQ, 31.

Twining, W. ed. (1991) *Issues of Self-Determination*, Aberdeen: Aberdeen University Press.

Unger, R.M. (1975) *Knowledge and Politics*, New York: Free Press.

Vaisey, J. ed. (1975) *Whatever Happened to Equality?*, London: British Broadcasting Corporation.

Vendler, Z. (1967) *Linguistics in Philosophy*, Ithaca: Cornell University Press.

Verges, F.G. (1992) 'The Unbearable Lightness of Deconstruction', P, 67.

Vernon, R. (1998) 'Liberals, Democrats and the Agenda of Politics', PS, 46.

Vetlesen, A.J. (1995) 'Hannah Arendt, Habermas and the Republican Tradition', PSC, 21.

Vierek, P. (1962) *Conservatism Revisited*, New York: Free Press.

Vincent, A. (1987) *Theories of the State*, Oxford: Blackwell.

Vincent, A. (1992) *Modern Political Ideologies*, Oxford: Blackwell.

Vincent, R.J. (1986) *Human Rights and International Relations*, Cambridge: Cambridge University Press.

Vlastos, G. (1962) 'Justice and Equality', *Social Philosophy*, ed. R.B. Brandt, Englewood Cliffs, NJ: Prentice-Hall.

Voegelin, E. (1952) *The New Science of Politics*, Chicago: University of Chicago Press.

Waismann, F. (1956) 'How I See Philosophy', *Contemporary British Philosophy*, 3rd Series, ed. H.D. Lewis, London: George Allen & Unwin.

Waldron, J. (1979) 'Enough and as Good Left for Others', PQ, 29.

Waldron, J. (1983) 'Two Worries about Mixing One's Labour', PQ, 33.

Waldron, J. ed. (1984) *Theories of Rights*, Oxford: Oxford University Press.

Waldron, J. (1988) *Nonsense Upon Stilts: Bentham, Burke and Marx on the Rights of Man*, London: Methuen.

Waldron, J. (1990) *The Law*, London: Routledge.

Waldron, J. (1995) 'The Wisdom of the Multitude: Some Reflections on Book 3, Chapter 11 of Aristotle's *Politics*', PT, 23.

Waldron, J. (1998) 'Participation: The Right of Rights', PAS, 98.

Wallace, W. (1898) *Lectures and Essays on Natural Theology and Ethics*, ed. E. Caird, Oxford: Oxford University Press.

Waller, B.N. (1989) 'Uneven Starts and Just Deserts', A, 49.

Walliman, I. (1981) *Estrangement: Marx's Conception of Human Nature and the Division of Labour*, Westport, Conn.: Greenwood Press.

Walsh, W.H. (1967) *An Introduction to the Philosophy of History*, 3rd ed., London: Hutchinson.

Walzer, M. ed. (1974) *Regicide and Revolution: Speeches at the Trial of Louis XVI*, Cambridge: Cambridge University Press.

Walzer, M. (1983) *Spheres of Justice: A Defence of Pluralism and Equality*, Oxford: Martin Robertson.

Walzer, M. (1995) 'Response to Veit Bader', PT, 23.

Waluchow, W.J. (1989) Critical Notice of Raz, *The Morality of Freedom*, CJP, 19.

Ward, A. (1973) 'The Idea of Equality Reconsidered', P, 48.

Warrender, H. (1957) *The Political Philosophy of Hobbes*, Oxford: Oxford University Press.

Watkins, F.M. (1964) *The Age of Ideology: Political Thought, 1750 to the Present*, Englewood Cliffs, NJ: Prentice-Hall.

Watkins, J.W.N. (1957-58) 'Epistemology and Politics', PAS, 58.

Watkins, J.W.N. (1952) 'Political Tradition and Political Theory: an Examination of Professor Oakeshott's Political Theory', PQ, 2.

Watkins, J.W.N. (1973) *Hobbes's System of Ideas*, 2nd ed., London: Hutchinson.

Watt, J. (1988) 'John Rawls and Human Welfare', RP, 49.

Watts Miller, W. (1993) 'Iconocide: the Case of the Trial and Execution of Louis XVI', C, 7.

Weatherford, R.C. (1983) 'Defining the Least Advantaged', PQ, 33.

Weber, E. (1964) *Varieties of Fascism*, Princeton NJ: Princeton University Press.

Weber, M. (1959) *The Methodology of the Social Sciences*, New York: Free Press.

Weber, M. (1964) *The Theory of Social and Economic Organisation*, New York: Free Press.

Weldon, T.D. (1953) *The Vocabulary of Politics*, Harmondsworth: Penguin.

Weldon, T.D. (1962) *States and Morals*, London: Murray.

Wenz, P.S. (1986) 'Conservatism and Conservation', P, 61.

Wertheimer, A. (1996) 'Consent and Sexual Relations', LT, 2.

West, R.J. ed. (1994) *Human Rights of Women: National and International Perspectives*, Philadelphia: University of Pennsylvania Press.

Wheare, K.C. (1963) *Federal Government*, Oxford: Oxford University Press.

White, R.J. (1950) *The Conservative Tradition*, London: Nicholas Kaye.

White, S. (1996) 'Needs, Labour and Marx's Conception of Justice', PS, 44.

Whyte, J.T. (1993) 'Relativism is Absolutely False', C, 7.

Wiggins, D. (1987) *Needs, Values, Truth*, Oxford: Blackwell.

Wilkerson, T.E. (1993) 'Species, Essences and the Names of Natural Kinds', PQ, 43.

Williams, B. (1967) 'Democracy and Ideology', *Democracy: The Contemporary Theories*, ed. M. Rejai, New York: Atherton Press.

Williams, M.S. (1995) 'Justice Towards Groups: Political not Juridical', PT, 23.

Williamson, P.J. ed. (1989) *Corporatism in Perspective*, London: Sage.

Wilson, C. (1992) 'Reply to Rorty on Pragmatism and Feminism', RP, 62.

Wilson, E. (1940) *To the Finland Station*, New York: Doubleday.

Wilson, P. (1982) 'Ryan on Coercion', MD, 91.

Wilson, T. & Skinner, A.S. ed. (1976) *The Market and the State*, Oxford: Oxford University Press.

Winch, P. (1958) *The Idea of a Social Science*, London: Routledge & Kegan Paul.

Winfrey, J.C. (1981) 'Charity vs. Justice: Locke on Property', JHI, 42.

Winny, J. ed. (1957) *The Frame of Order*, London: George Allen & Unwin.

Wittgenstein, L. (1953) *Philosophical Investigations*, 2nd ed., Oxford: Blackwell. (Minor changes were made to the text by Wittgenstein's editors for the 2nd ed., 1958: either edition will serve most purposes.)

Wokler, R. (1995) *Rousseau*, Oxford: Oxford University Press.

Wolf-Phillips, L.A. (1964) 'Metapolitics: Reflections on a Methodological Revolution', PS, 12.

Wolff, J. (1991) *Robert Nozick: Property, Justice and the Minimal State*, Cambridge: Polity Press.

Wolff, J. (1992) 'Playthings of Alien Forces: Karl Marx and the Rejection of the Market Economy', C, 6.

Wolff, J. (1994) 'Democratic Voting and the Mixed-Motivation Problem', A, 54.

Wolff, J. (1996a) 'Anarchism and Scepticism', *For and Against the State*, ed. J.T. Sanders & J. Narveson, Lanham, MD: Rowman & Littlefield Publications.

Wolff, J. (1996b) *An Introduction to Political Philosophy*, Oxford: Oxford University Press.

Wolff, J. (1996c) 'The Problem of Ideology', ASSV, 70.

Wolff, J. (1998) 'Mill, Indecency and the Liberty Principle', U, 10.

Wolff, R.P. (1976) *In Defence of Anarchism*, New York: Harper Colophon.

Wolff, R.P. (1977) *Understanding Rawls: A Reconstruction and Critique of A Theory of Justice*, Princeton: Princeton University Press.

Wolin, R. (1992) 'Carl Schmitt', PT, 20.

Wolin, S. (1976) 'The Politics of Self-Disclosure', PT, 4.

Wolin, S. (1996) 'The Liberal/ Democratic Divide: On Rawls' *Political Liberalism*', PT, 24.

Wollheim, R. (1955) 'Equality', ASSV, 29.

Wollheim, R. (1959) 'Crime, Sin and Mr Justice Devlin', *Encounter*, 74.

Wollstonecraft, M. (1975) *A Vindication of the Rights of Women*, Harmondsworth: Penguin. Original text: 1792.

Wood, E.M. (1988) *Peasant-Citizen and Slave. The Development of Athenian Democracy*, London: Verso.

Wood, E.M. (1991) *The Pristine Culture of Capitalism*, London: Verso.

Wood, E.M. (1995) *Democracy Against Capitalism*, Cambridge: Cambridge University Press.

Woodcock, G. (1962) *Anarchism*, Harmondsworth: Penguin.

Wright, A. (1996) *Socialisms*, 2nd ed., Oxford: Oxford University Press.

Young, I.M. (1990) *Justice and the Politics of Difference*, Princeton: Princeton University Press.

Young, I.M. (1997) 'Identity versus Social Justice?', NLR, 222.

Young, R. (1980) 'Autonomy and Socialization', MD, 89.

Young, R. (1986) 'Egalitarianism', *Law, Rights and the Welfare State*, ed. C. Sampford & D.J. Galligan, Beckenham: Croom Helm.

Young, R. (1989) 'Autonomy and Egalitarianism', PS, 36.

Zarka, Y.C. (1999) 'The Invention of the Subject of the Law', BJHP, 7.

Zimmern, A.E. (1915) *The Greek Commonwealth*, 2nd ed., Oxford: Oxford University Press.

Zuckert, M.P. (1994) *Natural Rights and the New Republicanism*, Princeton NJ: Princeton University Press.

Index

Biographical dates are not included for contemporary names.